Archiving SAP® Data—Practical Guide

SAP PRESS is a joint initiative of SAP and Rheinwerk Publishing. The know-how offered by SAP specialists combined with the expertise of Rheinwerk Publishing offers the reader expert books in the field. SAP PRESS features first-hand information and expert advice, and provides useful skills for professional decision-making.

SAP PRESS offers a variety of books on technical and business-related topics for the SAP user. For further information, please visit our website: *www.sap-press.com*.

Sebastian Schreckenbach
SAP Administration—Practical Guide (2nd edition)
2015, 912 pages, hardcover
ISBN 978-1-4932-1024-4

Brague, Dichmann, Keller, Kuppe, On
Enterprise Information Management with SAP (2nd edition)
2014, 605 pages, hardcover
ISBN 978-1-4932-1045-9

Mark Mergaerts, Bert Vanstechelman
Upgrading SAP: The Comprehensive Guide
2015, 572 pages, hardcover
ISBN 978-1-4932-1015-2

Thomas Schneider
SAP Performance Optimization Guide:
Analyzing and Tuning SAP Systems (7th edition)
2013, 837 pages, hardcover
ISBN 978-1-59229-874-7

Ahmet Türk

Archiving SAP® Data—Practical Guide

Bonn • Boston

Editor Sarah Frazier
Acquisitions Editor Kelly Grace Weaver
German Edition Editor Janina Schweitzer
Translation Lemoine International, Inc., Salt Lake City, UT
Copyeditor Melissa Brown Levine
Cover Design Nadine Kohl, Graham Geary
Photo Credit Shutterstock.com: 39441130/© spiber.de; 203752897/© Pressmaster;
  144698098/© kubais
Layout Design Vera Brauner
Production Graham Geary
Typesetting III-satz, Husby (Germany)
Printed and bound in the United States of America, on paper from sustainable sources

ISBN 978-1-4932-1278-1
© 2015 by Rheinwerk Publishing, Inc., Boston (MA)
1st edition 2015
1st German edition published 2015 by Rheinwerk Verlag, Bonn, Germany

Library of Congress Cataloging-in-Publication Data:
Türk, Ahmet, author.
[Praxishandbuch SAP--Datenarchivierung. English]
Archiving SAP data : practical guide / Ahmet Türk. -- 1st edition.
pages cm
Translation of: Praxishandbuch SAP--Datenarchivierung.
Includes index.
ISBN 978-1-4932-1278-1 (print : alk. paper) -- ISBN 1-4932-1278-8 (print : alk. paper) -- ISBN 978-1-4932-1279-8 (ebook)
-- ISBN 978-1-4932-1280-4 (print and ebook : alk. paper)
1. Electronic data processing--Backup processing alternatives. I. Title.
QA76.9.B32T8713 2015
005.7--dc23
2015025921

Contents at a Glance

Dear Reader,

There's some wisdom behind the phrase "a clean home is a happy home." The functionality of a home excels within the boundaries of a well-organized space. Similarly, archiving within an SAP system works to organize and optimize system performance while holding onto still vital documentation.

Led by author and data archiving expert, Ahmet Türk, this book functions as a single source for all of your SAP archiving needs. Sharing his experience from numerous customer projects, Ahmet provides insight into both a classical SAP data archiving approach as well as premium options such as SAP Information Lifecycle Management. In this practical guide, you'll begin by looking at the basic legal and technical processes, then discover options for storing and accessing your archived data. I guarantee that with this book you'll get the know-how you need to plan and implement your next SAP data archiving strategy.

What did you think about *Archiving SAP Data—Practical Guide*? Your comments and suggestions are the most useful tools to help us make our books the best they can be. Please feel free to contact me and share any praise or criticism you may have.

Thank you for purchasing a book from SAP PRESS!

Sarah Frazier
Editor, SAP PRESS

Rheinwerk Publishing
Boston, MA

sarahf@rheinwerk-publishing.com
www.sap-press.com

Contents

PART II Implementing Data Archiving Projects

Introduction

You have certainly heard the terms *data* and *archiving* in various contexts. In this book, we combine these two terms to deliver a focused topic. But let's first take a look at the two words separately. What is data? And what is archiving? If you get the meaning of these two terms, you will better understand the whole concept of data archiving.

Data consists of various characters (e.g., numbers, letters, or special characters). If we bring together different data in one context, we refer to this as *information*. Table 1 provides an example of the relationships between characters, data, information, knowledge, and decisions.

What is data?

Level	Description	Example
1	Characters	8, 6, °, c, h, i, c, a, g, o
2	Data	86°, Chicago
3	Information	Temperature of 86 degrees in Chicago
4	Knowledge	It is quite warm and sunny in Chicago
5	Decision	I will go to the beach

Table 1 Example of the Relationships between Data and Information

The first level contains the characters 8, 6, °, c, h, i, c, a, g, and o. If we organize these characters in a table, we can group the characters into two columns:

Example: temperature

- The column Temperature in which we can enter the value "86°"
- The column Location in which we can enter the value "Chicago"

These values are our data from which we cannot draw any conclusions if we look at it separately. Eighty-six degrees alone tells us nothing. It could be the water temperature or even an uphill slope. Only if we combine value and column can we derive that it must be a temperature. If we bring together the two values, 86° and Chicago, at the third level, we can even talk of information. The information derived from this data is that the temperature in Chicago is 86°. At the fourth level, we can determine that it is quite warm in Chicago—if the temperature of 86° was measured in Fahrenheit. So with this information, we gain new *knowledge* about the temperature in Chicago and can even guess the season.

The last level is an optional decision. If we have processed the information and the knowledge based on it, we can decide what to do with it. We could, for example, go to the beach, take a swim, and enjoy the sun.

There are numerous other examples, in particular for data that is generated in business processes in enterprises on a daily basis, upon which we can make completely different decisions.

Intangible capital Consequently, the data of enterprises is considered a business resource that we can also define as an *intangible asset*. Of course, the value and benefit of the data varies from industry and category. For enterprises that specialize in weather forecasts, for example, the data on temperature and location is a business requirement.

Valuable data In the last several years, data has increasingly gained importance. We collect and store it in various ways using different methods. You've probably already been asked at a checkout counter if you own a Plenti card. If you use this card, you sell the data of your buying behavior to the participating enterprises by earning points for rewards. These enterprises then use this data to make business-related decisions (level 5 of our model) and thus to optimize their business model and adapt it to customers' requirements.

We also transfer data without always being aware of it, for example, by using apps on our smartphones. How long and at which location we use an app is critical data for enterprises. So as you can see, data has never been more valuable. The trend is that enterprises store all available data across various IT systems in order to process it and draw conclusions (*big data*). Consequently, data protection and security play an increasingly important role as well.

Data in the SAP system SAP systems also constantly generate new data. Here, we differentiate between *master* and *transaction data*. Master data is data that is created once and individually and rarely changes, for example, personnel numbers. If employees are employed at an enterprise, their data, such as first name, last name, and date of birth, is specified. The date of birth will certainly not change, but the last name could change after a marriage, for example. So the master data of employees may change slightly.

If employees receive their wages or enter travel expenses for their business trips into the SAP system, transaction data is generated. So transaction data is data that is generated on a regular basis and usually depends on master data. Master data's other special characteristics include having a much smaller quantity than that of transaction data and being kept in the SAP system for a very long time.

In an old presentation of SAP SE regarding data archiving, we came across the following quote:

What is archiving?

> *Archivists have literally lost control over the definition of archive.*

Indeed, it is not very easy to define archiving clearly. Let me try it: archiving simply means storage; we keep something for a defined period of time. There are different reasons for archiving and different types of it. We certainly keep private photos in a photo album at home or store them on electronic data carriers. Over time, we discard some of the photos but special pictures we keep a lifetime.

State institutions also have archiving departments that store critical documents, such as historical agreements, on paper and in digitized form as files for a very long time. Enterprises, instead, keep business documents for a defined period, according to legal requirements. In the United States, a balance sheet must be archived in paper form until the close of all tax audits for the year the record was created. Many enterprises keep their first balance sheets for even longer for symbolic reasons.

Documents can be archived for private, legal, or business reasons. The examples mentioned have one thing in common: over the entire archiving or storage period, it is ensured that the documents to be archived (emails, photos, files, documents, data, etc.) are safely stored and can be accessed physically or electronically if required.

Reasons

Archiving in Various Areas

[◉]

Today, archiving is used in various areas. Important areas include the following:

► Archiving of emails
► Archiving of data
► Archiving of documents

This book mainly focuses on the archiving of data.

What is data archiving? When we speak of *data archiving*, we refer to the archiving or storage of data. The important information here is where the data that we want to archive is located. In a way that is similar to how we safely store our money in a bank, we store our data in a database. In a very simplified model, our money is either in a bank or in our wallets. And our data can be stored either in a database or in an archive. A database manages the data in respective tables; these are comparable with the wallet. And storing archive files corresponds to storing money in a safe at the bank.

So data archiving enables us to archive our data from the respective tables in a database after a defined period of time (residence time). But how do you archive your data from an SAP system? Which options are available? How can you ensure that all relevant data from the tables is archived, for example, if you want to archive an invoice (billing document)? This sounds simple, but usually involves a great deal of effort and costs.

Data archiving with SAP You can master these challenges with SAP data archiving. Even though data archiving is a default function in every SAP system, you must still set it up and manage it. Before starting the actual data archiving process, you need to consider several critical aspects. This book illustrates every step of the data archiving process in the SAP system. In this guide, we will refer to various examples from our nearly ten years of professional experience as an archiving specialist.

Structure of the book **Chapter 1**, Basic Principles and Legal Frameworks of SAP Data Archiving, describes the most critical terms in the context of data archiving and presents the tools that are used most frequently. Additionally, it illustrates the environment of data archiving, for instance, legal framework conditions as well as involved parties and institutions and their tasks. Furthermore, this chapter outlines the technical environment by describing the interfaces that are relevant for data archiving in the SAP system landscape, for example, system landscapes from multiple SAP systems.

Chapter 2, Storage Options for Archived Data, describes the usage of the ArchiveLink interface, which involves a service that is integrated with SAP NetWeaver Application Server AS ABAP for linking archived documents with the application documents that are entered in the SAP system for this purpose. We also introduce the WebDAV interface, which assumes these functions for SAP Information Lifecycle Management (SAP ILM). To be able to use these tools, you will require a storage system for which different options are available. The tools are presented individually and are discussed with regard to costs and specific requirements in various scenarios. Additionally, this chapter provides a decision matrix that will help you to select a storage system.

Chapter 3, Options for Accessing Archived Data, describes the various options for accessing archived data using examples. We also detail the pros and cons of the individual solutions here. Because some transactions do not access the archive at all or only in parts we present some alternatives, such as Transaction VA03. We also provide an overview of supplementing add-ons whose focus is to compensate specific weaknesses.

Chapter 4, Developing a Data Archiving Strategy, discusses the time and concept of an archiving project. It outlines how and if fast success can be achieved and the best way to proceed to avoid performance losses. The concept of a data archiving strategy is described in detail. For example, we introduce a best practices model for documentation, which many enterprises use as a basis.

Chapter 5, Planning Archiving Projects, and **Chapter 6**, Implementing Archiving Projects, discuss the planning and implementation of archiving projects based on three sample enterprises from three different industries. For this reason, Chapter 5 first details the specifics of the respective industries with regard to data archiving requirements. Typical archiving objects from the sample industries are used, which could be relevant for you when implementing your own archiving projects. Finally, we provide tips for effective management and preparation of archiving projects.

Based on the sample enterprises presented in Chapter 5, Chapter 6 further describes the archiving procedure. You get concrete instructions on how to process the selected archiving objects for archiving. You can transfer these instructions to your own projects. In this context, we illustrate how you can implement the customizing of archiving objects and possible troubleshooting in case of performance or access problems after archiving.

Chapter 7, Managing Archiving Systems, describes the important tasks of administration in the context of data archiving. A periodic system analysis forms the basis of data archiving. Communication with parties and institutions involved is of high significance for the success of archiving projects. This chapter additionally contains our recommendations for operating, monitoring, and documenting an archiving system.

Chapter 8, SAP Information Lifecycle Management, presents the SAP ILM solution and its components. It describes the tool's range of functions and outlines how to proceed in data archiving using SAP ILM. Useful additional functions such as retention management and the shutdown of unused systems are discussed using real-life examples, including a discussion on the administration of storage rules.

Chapter 9, Future of SAP Data Archiving, evaluates important developments and technologies—for instance, SAP HANA and SAP ILM—that will influence the future of data archiving. We provide an assessment and an outlook.

Working with this book

The highlighted boxes in this book contain information that is useful to know, but it is outside the context of the topic we are discussing. To enable you to categorize this information, we marked the boxes with the following icons:

[+] Here you'll find useful information as well as special *tips and tricks* that can make your work easier.

[»] Boxes marked with the arrow icon call out information about *advanced topics* or things you should keep in mind.

[Ex] *Examples* with this icon refer to sample usage scenarios from real life.

[◉] Text passages highlighted with this icon summarize thematic relationships *at a glance*.

Acknowledgments

This book is not only the result of my nearly ten years of professional experience in the area of data archiving, but also the product of obtaining knowledge from numerous colleagues who helped me deepen my knowledge and thus indirectly contributed to the success of this book.

Without mentioning every single person specifically, I want to thank all of my colleagues for the great collaboration.

A special thank you goes to my family and friends for doing without my presence on many occasions while I wrote this book.

I would also like to thank Janina Schweitzer for making this book possible in the first place, Robert Wassermann for providing new screenshots, and Erkan Aksoy for creating the figures for the SAP Information Lifecycle Management solution.

I hope you enjoy reading this book.

Ludwigsburg (Germany), August 2015
Ahmet Türk

PART I
Basic Principles

In this chapter, you will learn about the legal framework condi-
tions associated with data archiving. We will also introduce you
to the parties and institutions involved, along with their specific
tasks. Finally, we will introduce you to some key terms and
essential tools in SAP data archiving.

1 Basic Principles and Legal Frameworks of SAP Data Archiving

You should not dive headfirst into an SAP data archiving project without first knowing the basic principles and legal framework conditions associated with archiving SAP system data. Even though the potential sources of error in these types of projects are not immediately apparent, the impact of such errors is considerable. Frequently, for example, legal specifications are unknowingly violated or the requirements of those user departments that generate the data to be archived are not fully taken into consideration.

> **Potential Mistakes in Archiving Projects** [Ex]
>
> The IT department within an enterprise decides to archive data from Financial Accounting after a period of twelve months and therefore commences an archiving project in accordance with these specifications. However, the data extracts required for the tax auditors were not created beforehand. During the tax audit, the company is threatened with fines because the tax auditor insists on using data extracts to conduct the tax audit in electronic form.
>
> Furthermore, the enterprise has not analyzed any of the transactions and reports that it created and enhanced in custom developments in order to determine if their functionality is impaired by data archiving. After the data archiving process, employees who work with these transactions ascertain that they no longer work as expected.
>
> To make matters worse, the enterprise has not stored the archived data securely. An IT employee with extensive authorization has inadvertently deleted individual archive files. Furthermore, the enterprise has not fully eval-

> uated and tested the various options for accessing the archive in conjunction with the users. Consequently, the users complain that they are unable to access archived data.

As you can see, a number of things can go wrong in a data archiving project. To ensure that you do not find yourself in a similar situation as our sample enterprise, we will now introduce you to the most important framework conditions and specifications of SAP data archiving before taking a detailed look, in subsequent chapters, at the individual steps that need to be performed. We can already say with confidence that the following statement is the most important prerequisite for successful data archiving: a one-sided consideration solely from the perspective of the IT department will not satisfy the legal and functional requirements of an enterprise. In other words, SAP data archiving is not a task that can be undertaken by the IT department alone.

In the sections that follow, we will kick-start this topic by examining the main driving forces and technological foundations for SAP data archiving. We will then take a step back from the IT perspective and turn our attention to the *big picture* in terms of SAP data archiving. To this end, we will provide a table that outlines the most important legal regulations concerning data archiving both in the United States and internationally. Lastly, you will learn about the tools used to conduct an electronic tax audit, the interfaces frequently used in an IT landscape, and the parties and organizations involved in SAP data archiving projects.

1.1　Safeguarding Performance of SAP Systems

SAP data archiving is not only used to free up memory space in the database, but also to safeguard the stable performance of your SAP systems. SAP system performance is very often associated with the processing time. The faster the transactions and reports deliver their results, the better the performance of your SAP system.

Effects on performance
But what exactly happens in an SAP system when you call a transaction? In other words, which factors affect performance? The first thing to

know here is that an SAP system stores its data in various tables within a database. For example, the header data and item data associated with deliveries is stored in the tables LIKP (Deliveries Header Data) and LIPS (Deliveries Item Data). The relevant users regularly call Transaction VL03N (Display Outbound Delivery) or Transaction VL33N (Display Inbound Delivery) to access this data. When these inbound and outbound deliveries are maintained, they automatically generate new data records in both tables. Consequently, the tables grow continuously.

Therefore, the larger the table, the longer it takes to access the data stored there because, in comprehensive tables, it is necessary to select and process a larger number of data records. Such tables also require more memory space in the database. Therefore, to increase performance again, you must check the growth of the tables. From both a legal and business perspective, it is not possible to prevent data records from being generated (in our example, data records for the individual deliveries) or to delete these directly from the tables. For example, users must be able to access the data in order to create a delivery note for each delivery. This delivery note must also be retained, as required by law.

Large tables—long access times

To keep the size of the tables as small as possible, the only option is to use SAP data archiving to archive (and therefore remove from the tables) those deliveries that have been completed and are rarely accessed.

Checking growth in tables

Therefore, to safeguard SAP system performance, you should remove and archive data records from the database at regular intervals. Then once the statutory retention periods have elapsed (see Section 1.2.5), these data records can be permanently destroyed.

Consider your data as a living being with its own lifecycle. Delivery data may have a different lifecycle than Financial (FI) documents. In order to make well-informed decisions in their daily work, SAP system users must use the original documents (that is, the delivery note and the invoice) for both data types. In each case, you must consider the individual retention period for your data.

Choosing the right data lifecycle

To borrow from the well-known saying "All roads lead to Rome," the search for better performance will, sooner or later, always lead you to SAP data archiving. It is only a matter of time before the tables in your SAP system will grow to a size that will cause you performance problems. By then you will gradually have to part with the old data in your SAP system and give some thought to the lifecycle of the various information objects.

[»] **Information Object or Data Object**

In an SAP system, information or data is managed in different tables in the form of individual data records. Therefore, in the case of a delivery, for example, the system generates data records in the tables LIKP and LIPS. These related data records for a delivery form an *information object* or *data object*.

In printed form, the information concerning a delivery is compiled in a document. In tabular form, it is compiled in an information object. If you want to archive this delivery, you must archive and delete the entire information object from the corresponding tables.

In different countries, the lifecycle of an information object can have very different attributes, depending on the respective legal framework conditions. We use the term *Information Lifecycle Management* (ILM) only when the entire cycle (that is, from generating data through to destroying data) is taken into consideration and is a closed loop.

1.2 Information Lifecycle Management

Retaining data beyond the retention periods

The statutory obligations to retain data predefine the lifecycle of an information object in your SAP system. However, you can also retain an information object beyond the statutory retention period if there is an internal requirement to do so. This is the case, for example, if an enterprise wants to protect itself against possible legal disputes in the future or other events for which evidence may be required. However, one prerequisite for such an extension of the retention time is that there is no legal *obligation to delete the data*. Legal proceedings or other special circumstances may therefore deem it necessary to not yet destroy data after the lifecycles defined by law have elapsed. In such scenarios, it is advisable to prevent destruction of such data by means of a *deletion lock*.

Harmonizing all requirements

The purpose of ILM is to control the information lifecycle to optimum effect. To this end, it is necessary to harmonize the technical, legal, and functional requirements. Here data archiving is the cornerstone of the various measures that need to be taken.

Information passes through various phases during its lifecycle. In each phase, corresponding measures must be taken in relation to the relevant requirements. The individual phases of an information lifecycle are shown in Figure 1.1. We will discuss each of these phases in detail in the sections that follow.

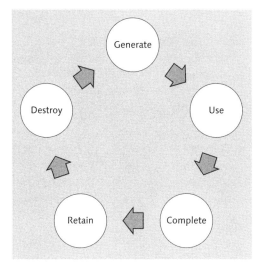

Figure 1.1 Phases in the Information Lifecycle

1.2.1 Generating Data

The business transactions in your enterprise are documented in your SAP system. Consequently, several data records are created in different tables. In order to influence system performance, even at this early stage, and not to consume the data store unnecessarily, you can ask yourself if the data needs to be generated at all or, from a business perspective, if this data is necessary for your enterprise. If this is not the case, the following options are available to you:

▸ You can configure technical settings to prevent these data records from being generated.

▸ Alternatively, you can also delete this data immediately after it has been generated (because you do not need it and do not have to retain it).

▸ A third option would be to summarize the data generated (if the summarized information is sufficient for your needs).

[Ex] **Data Summarization**

An example of such information summarization is cost center summarization in Controlling. Here, the line items from the table COEP are summarized in totals tables so that reports can access the more compact totals tables instead of accessing the single tables and therefore can be executed more quickly in this way.

Taking measures early on to ensure that the database does not grow unnecessarily (and generate unused data records) satisfies an important technical requirement for SAP data archiving.

[Ex] **Information Structures**

In many of the SAP systems that we accessed while working on our customer projects, we noticed that certain tables are not used, but nevertheless continuously filled with data. Typical examples include information structures in the Sales & Distribution component, which can be used for analyses. Concealed behind such an information structure is a table that is updated with information from deliveries, billing documents, and/or orders in accordance with self-defined rules and conditions. Some of these information structures are already activated in the standard SAP system in its delivery state. Frequently, when implementing an SAP system, no consideration is given to deactivating unused information structures in Customizing.

In customer developments, many programmers are also prone to generating more data than necessary. Therefore, clarify if you can dispense with this data, especially in the case of tables with large volumes of data.

1.2.2 Using Data

Almost on a daily basis, SAP system users work with different transactions and reports in order to access the data contained in the system. They tend to access the latest data or recently generated data much more frequently than data that was generated during the last few years. In the data usage phase, you check how often generated data is used in transactions and reports. Depending on the usage intensity, you can ascertain how long this data needs to be available in the database or in an archive.

Usage intensity determines the residence time
Generally, the following applies: the more frequent the usage, the longer this data should be stored in the database. This is referred to as the *residence time*. The residence time specifies the minimum length of time

for which data records must be available in the database before they can even be archived.

1.2.3 Completing Data Records

A data record can obtain various statuses within an SAP system. For the data record completion phase, you define the rules and conditions under which your data records will be deemed to be *completed*. Alternatively, these are predefined in the system. Before you assign this status, you manually check or the system automatically checks (depending on the business process) if these criteria have been fulfilled. SAP data archiving can only archive data records for completed business transactions. Any process weak points that result in an incomplete status should be identified and resolved before the status *completed* is assigned. This ensures that your data records do not languish in the status *open* or *in process* forever. In many projects, it is precisely this step that prevents data from being archived.

Increasing the quality of data archiving

Status of a Delivery? [Ex]

The status of a data record in an SAP system is controlled very differently, depending on which type of data record it concerns. In the case of a delivery, for example, separate statuses are output for the individual items within a delivery and for all related processes (for example, the status of the billing documents, the goods movements (goods receipt/goods issue), or transportation planning).

Here the status can adopt the following values:

▶ Not relevant: blank

▶ Not yet processed: A

▶ Partially processed: B

▶ Completely processed: C

During data archiving, the write program for creating archive files checks, among other things, if the status of the billing documents and the status of transportation planning have obtained the value C (completely processed). For billing documents, this is the case if they have been forwarded to Financial Accounting. In the case of transportation-relevant deliveries, transportation must have been fully processed and the related shipment document archived using the archiving object SD_VTTK (SD Transport).

> However, an exception is possible for deliveries without a shipment document: in the case of non-transportation-relevant deliveries, the transportation planning check can, if required, also be deactivated in the write program so that these deliveries can be archived once all other criteria have been fulfilled.
>
> If a delivery in this area cannot show that it has the necessary status for the archivability criteria of the write program, data archiving is prevented. In accordance with the SAP system logic, the business process is not fully completed in this case.

1.2.4 Retaining Data

Adjusting retention to the lifecycle

For the data retention phase, you define how long you will retain the various information objects. The statutory retention periods, supplemented by an enterprise's own internal requirements, form the basis for this decision. The lifecycle of information objects always comprises the residence time in the database and the retention time in the archive. If a lifecycle spans ten years and the residence time is two years, the retention period in the archive is at least eight years.

1.2.5 Destroying Data

Completing the lifecycle

Your data has now reached the end of its lifecycle. The last phase involves destroying this data. The processes and responsibilities in the information lifecycle must be clearly defined so that this last step can actually be performed. In practice, many enterprises are prone to retaining data beyond the lifecycle duration defined originally. If data is not destroyed, the ILM cycle is not complete. In particular, it is necessary to adhere to statutory obligations to delete data. If such obligations to delete data exist for your information objects, you cannot and must not retain this data beyond the defined lifecycle duration.

Automatic deletion of data

Classic SAP data archiving does not provide a function to facilitate the automatic destruction of data by the relevant programs in the SAP system. However, the archive systems used generally have a program that automatically identifies and deletes stored data after the defined retention period has elapsed. If, however, the data was stored in a file system, all you can do is manually identify such data by means of the physical file names and then delete the relevant files from the directories.

In this last phase of the information lifecycle, always remember to take any deletion locks into consideration. Such deletion locks may result from a legal case that now requires data to be stored for a longer period of time than defined originally. Classic SAP data archiving does not provide an automatic function for this either. In other words, you cannot select the individual data records and archive files and mark them for deletion. Here the only option is to develop your own solution.

Taking deletion locks into consideration

One possible solution to the manual deletion lock could be, for example, as follows:

Developing manual deletion locks

1. **Determine all data records.**
   Determine all data records that belong to the relevant business transaction. To do this, you can display the document flow in the display transactions. To check if archived data records already exist for the business transaction, you can use Transaction ALO1 to call the *Document Relationship Browser* (DRB). The DRB is able to search both the database and the archive for documents.

   If all of the data records are located in the database and if, in the short term, there are no plans to archive these data records, no further activities are required. If, however, data records have been archived, you need to determine the archive files and prevent these archive files from being deleted.

2. **Determine all archive files.**
   Determine all archive files associated with the data records that have already been archived. To do this, use Transaction AS_AFB to call the *Archive File Browser*. Here you can search the archive files according to document number.

3. **Do not delete archive files that have been determined.**
   In the case of archive files that have already been determined, do not delete them from the file system or archive system. If a program for automatically deleting the files is scheduled in the archive system, you must deactivate it. The archive files that have been assigned a deletion lock are then backed up or removed from the deletion worklist, and the remaining archive files are deleted manually.

In practice, deletion locks are rarely applied to archive files, because they are time-consuming to implement. Furthermore, there are rarely legal cases that require archive files to be retained beyond the statutory retention period. If, however, you are faced with this requirement at any time, you can proceed as outlined here. The procedure described in this section is just one possible option that you can use without any programming effort. It is also conceivable for a developer to develop and implement a custom search program in which you need to enter only the relevant document number to enable the program to automatically read the document flow and then determine the archive files. However, you must also back up the archive files at this point. For this reason, we advise you to document the "manual deletion lock" solution that we described earlier and use it, if required.

[»]

Classic SAP Data Archiving in ILM

In the first three phases (*generate data*, *use data*, and *complete data records*), you use the existing transactions and reports in an SAP system. Here there are no differences between classic SAP data archiving and SAP ILM. In the last two phases (*retain data* and *destroy data*), however, classic SAP data archiving does not have any tools for managing the lifecycle of your data (as provided for in ILM) on an IT basis. Therefore, for these phases, you need to resort to other tools or schedule some manual activities. In particular, when compared with SAP ILM, classic SAP data archiving has the following weak points:

▸ **Manual control of the lifecycle**
In the SAP system, it is not apparent when archive files can be deleted. You must either control and document this manually, or you must use an archive system that provides the relevant function.

▸ **Manual destruction of data**
In the SAP system, there is no transaction or report to automatically delete archive files after the retention period has elapsed. You must either select and delete the relevant archive files manually or you must use an archive system that provides the relevant function.

▸ **Necessary to develop a custom solution for setting deletion locks**
In the SAP system, you cannot automatically determine the archive files for an information object or data object and protect them by setting a deletion lock. Therefore, it is necessary to develop a custom solution. We have already described one such possible solution in Section 1.2.5.

SAP Information Lifecycle Management

Thanks to SAP Information Lifecycle Management (SAP ILM), new functions that eliminate these weak points, among other things, are now available to you. They will be described in detail in Chapter 8.

1.3 Archive Development Kit

The *Archive Development Kit* (ADK) is the technical basis for SAP data archiving—the cornerstone of ILM. In this chapter, we will lay the foundation for the remaining chapters by using a comparison in an attempt to convey the tasks performed by the ADK. We will not discuss the technical details here. For us, it is important that you are simply aware of the ADK and have some understanding of how it works.

Imagine that you are a chef who wants to prepare a selection of nutritious and tasty dishes. In addition to fresh ingredients, you also require some kitchen appliances and utensils (for example, a whisk, pot, or oven). The nearest grocery store has everything that you could possibly imagine. You are therefore able to prepare any dish you desire. Of course, this environment is paradise on earth for a chef.

Comparison: chef, ingredients, and tools

For SAP data archiving, the ADK provides similar benefits for archiving experts. Here you, like the chef, can avail all of the "ingredients, appliances, and utensils" that you need for SAP data archiving.

We will use FI documents as an example. In the context of SAP data archiving, they are known as `FI_DOCUMNT`. They are also referred to as the *archiving object* `FI_DOCUMNT`. More than 500 different archiving objects are available to you for different information objects in your SAP system.

The archiving object is our dish

In our culinary comparison, the archiving object `FI_DOCUMNT` represents one particular dish. Here the archiving objects are comparable with ready-to-serve meals. The associated tables and reports (write program, delete program, and so on) are assigned to the archiving object, are known to the chef, and can, in most cases, be used directly. Sometimes, however, it is necessary to first maintain entries such as the residence time in Customizing before the archiving object can be used.

The ADK is a development and runtime environment. Since the ADK is a development environment, you can, if necessary, develop a custom archiving object for your customer-defined tables. In this case, the tables

Development and runtime environment

would be the ingredients from our culinary comparison and the new archiving object would be your new dish. Similarly, you can enhance existing archiving objects (that is, conjure up new creations from existing dishes).

However, the ADK is also a runtime environment. Comparable with a cooker, the ADK unites all key features of a runtime environment in one place. If, for example, you use the write program assigned to the archiving object to create a new archive file, or if you want to use a corresponding transaction to display archived data, the system automatically calls various ADK function modules in the background.

1.4 Transactions and Processes

To enable the use of various ADK functions, a wide range of transactions are available to you. A key SAP data archiving process is concealed behind each transaction. In order to give you a quick overview of the most important functions, we will now take a look at the most important transactions and processes.

1.4.1 Transaction DB02: Determining the Database Size and Table Size

Obtaining an overview of the database

Using Transaction DB02 (Database Analysis) to determine the database size will give you a very good introduction to planning SAP data archiving. Transaction DB02 is integrated into Transaction DBACOCKPIT (DBA Cockpit) for database management. You can call it directly in Transaction DB02 or via Transaction DBACOCKPIT. In Transaction DB02, you can also display the largest tables and indexes in your SAP system. The display in the transaction is independent of the database system used. In our example, this concerns an Oracle database (DB SYSTEM: ORA).

Analyzing memory space

Call Transaction DB02. The SPACE OVERVIEW screen shown in Figure 1.2 provides an overview of the database. Here the DATABASE area of the screen contains information about the size of the database (SIZE) and the amount of free memory space still available (FREE SPACE). The smaller the amount of free memory space available, the greater the need to perform data archiving. Compressing the tables and increasing the memory are short-term options for controlling the growth of the database. However, they are not valid alternatives to SAP data archiving.

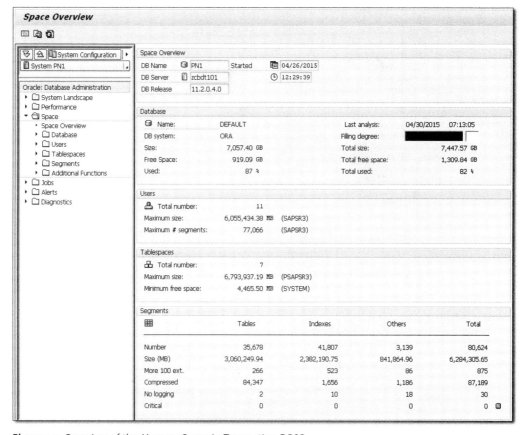

Figure 1.2 Overview of the Memory Space in Transaction DB02

Now choose the menu path SEGMENTS • OVERVIEW in the navigation column on the left-hand side of the screen to navigate to the segment overview. Then select the TOP SIZES tab (see Figure 1.3).

Identifying large tables

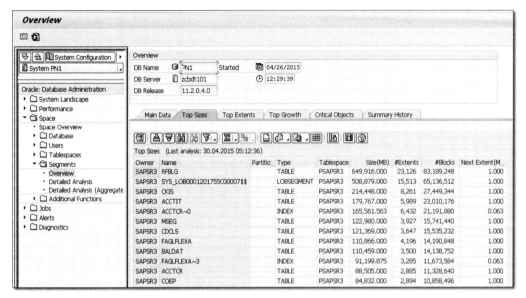

Figure 1.3 Overview of the Largest Tables

Here you can display the tables that occupy the most memory space. The NAME and SIZE(MB) columns are particularly important here. They provide a good indication of which archiving objects are suitable for data archiving. Note when the last analysis of the table sizes was performed. This is shown in the LAST ANALYSIS field in Figure 1.2. If data has already been archived, but the corresponding tables have not been reorganized yet, the information about the size of the table is not up-to-date. On the TOP GROWTH tab, you can also determine the fastest growing table.

[◉] **Goals within Transaction DB02**

In summary, you can use Transaction DB02 to prepare for your data archiving project as follows:

- Obtain an overview of the size of the database.
- Determine the amount of free memory space available.
- Identify the largest tables and indexes.
- Analyze the growth of the database.

Transaction DB02 also contains other functions for analyzing the database. However, we will not discuss them in further detail here. We have taken a look at only those sections that are of primary importance for data archiving.

1.4.2 Transaction DB15: Determining Archiving Objects

On the basis of the large tables that you have identified, you can now use Transaction DB15 (Tables and Archiving Objects) to determine the associated archiving objects. As an example, we will select the largest table in our sample database, table RFBLG (Cluster for Accounting Document), and enter its name in the OBJECTS FOR TABLE field (see Figure 1.4). Then choose SHOW TABLES. The archiving object FI_DOCUMNT is displayed. In other words, you use the archiving object FI_DOCUMNT to archive this table.

Determining tables and archiving objects

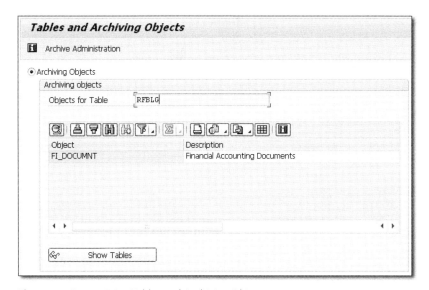

Figure 1.4 Determining Tables and Archiving Objects

Several archiving objects may exist for one table. Test the same operation with the table CKIS (Items for Unit Costings). A wide range of archiving objects is displayed. This is because this controlling table is heavily integrated with other modules within the SAP system. From the list of objects proposed, you must select precisely those archiving objects that are most suitable for archiving. If, for example, you use a sales order to cost an order BOM and therefore generate a large number

Table with several archiving objects

of data records in the table CKIS, the archiving object SD_VBAK (Sales Documents) would be the ideal choice here, because with this archiving object, you would archive not only the sales documents but also the costing data.

Displaying tables for the object

Alternatively, you can call Transaction DB15 and enter the archiving object in the TABLES IN OBJECT field in order to display the related tables (see Figure 1.5). The standard system displays all of the tables from which data records can be deleted after data archiving (TABLES WITH DELETION). You can also select the ALL TABLES display variant so that you can also view those tables from which information is written to the archive file but no data records are deleted. You can then use the ONLINE SPACE and SPACE STATISTICS buttons to display further details. You use the ONLINE SPACE button to view the information provided by the database (Oracle, in our example). If you choose SPACE STATISTICS, the SAP system provides details such as the size of the table, the size of the index, and the number of data records for the table selected.

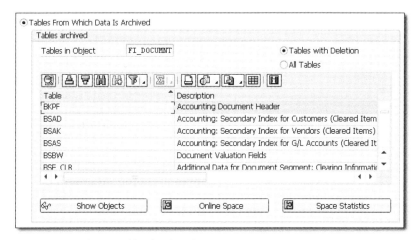

Figure 1.5 Displaying Tables for the Object

[◉]   **Goals within Transaction DB15**

In summary, you can perform the following steps in Transaction DB15:

► Determine the archiving objects for the large tables.
► Display all tables for an archiving object.
► Display further details about the memory space for the tables.

1.4.3   Transaction TAANA: Performing Table Analyses

You can use Transaction TAANA (Table Analysis: Administration) to analyze tables according to certain fields. This function is very suitable for analyzing the main tables (header tables or item tables) of an archiving object in detail. These tables contain key information such as the number of data records by organizational unit or document type, which are two sort options available to you. You can use the information that you obtain in Transaction TAANA specifically to clarify important questions that will later arise in workshops with user department employees and to make decisions more quickly. You can also use these analyses to plan data archiving better because you roughly know the percentage of data in certain organizational units and document types in relation to the total data volume. Therefore, the following questions are important in the context of data archiving: Which sales organizations in Sales and Distribution have generated the most data records and which document types were used for this purpose? These are typical questions that you can very quickly answer in the course of your analysis.

Table analysis delivers detailed information

As an example, we will analyze the table `LIKP`:

1. First call Transaction TAANA.

2. Then choose Execute ⊕ to start the analysis (see Figure 1.6).

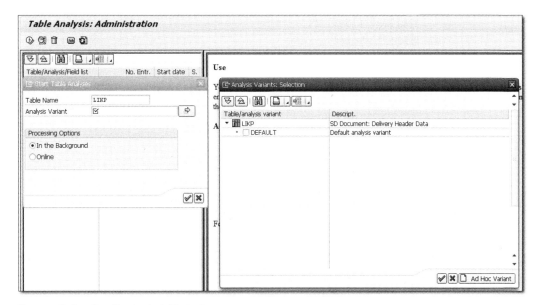

Figure 1.6 Creating the Analysis Variant

3. In the TABLE NAME field, enter LIKP and then choose the yellow arrow ⇨ to select an analysis variant.

4. In the PROCESSING OPTIONS area, the IN THE BACKGROUND and ONLINE options are available for selection. For large tables and long runtimes, we always recommend that you activate the default setting IN THE BACKGROUND.

5. The system displays the ANALYSIS VARIANTS: SELECTION dialog box in which you can choose between the DEFAULT analysis variant and an AD HOC VARIANT. The latter variant is most suitable for performing an analysis according to your own criteria. It is also possible to start both variants simultaneously. With the DEFAULT variant, only the number of entries for this table is determined in the client.

   For many tables (for example, table LIPS), the STANDARD variant with preselected fields is also available. You can use Transaction TAANA_AV (Table Analysis—Analysis Variants) to see those tables for which STANDARD variants already exist.

6. Choose AD HOC VARIANT to perform an analysis according to your own criteria. In particular, you want to know which sales organizations (field VKORG) and which delivery types (field LFART) in table LIKP occur as data records and how often this happens.

7. In the dialog box for creating the ad hoc variant, all of the fields in table LIKP are listed in the OPTIONAL FIELDS area (see Figure 1.7). You can select these fields and then use the arrow buttons to transfer them to the ANALYSIS VARIANT FIELDS area on the left-hand side of the screen.

   Make sure that you do not select an unnecessarily large number of fields. Fields containing information about the date and time are not very suitable for the analysis, because the granularity is too high. In other words, the information contained in these fields is too detailed. During analysis, the goal is to group the data records (from the table to be analyzed) according to fields that make sense in this context. If each data record now has another time and another date, it is not possible to group by the DATE and TIME fields. Fields that contain information about a period or a fiscal year are more meaningful because you can group data records by period or fiscal year here.

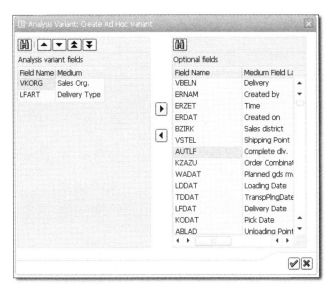

Figure 1.7 Selecting Fields for the Table Analysis

Virtual Fields in Transaction TAANA_VF [«]

Before you analyze a table, you can also include other fields from other tables in the OPTIONAL FIELDS area (in the form of virtual fields). In Transaction TAANA_VF (Table Analysis—Virtual Fields), you see all the fields already created for the table selected. If necessary, you can define new virtual fields here.

To analyze table LIPS, you can also include, for example, the virtual field OVERALL STATUS OF THE DELIVERY (GBSTK) in the analysis. This will enable you to find out how many deliveries are fully processed and therefore have the overall status C. Such deliveries can be archived.

---

8. Confirm your selection with the green check mark ☑, and start the analysis in the background. You then obtain the number of data records from table LIKP, sorted according to your analysis fields (see Figure 1.8), as the result.

For table LIKP, you can perform several analyses with different ad hoc variants. However, always remember to delete analysis variants that you no longer require. To do this, select the analysis variant and choose the trash icon 🗑.

Deleting analysis variants

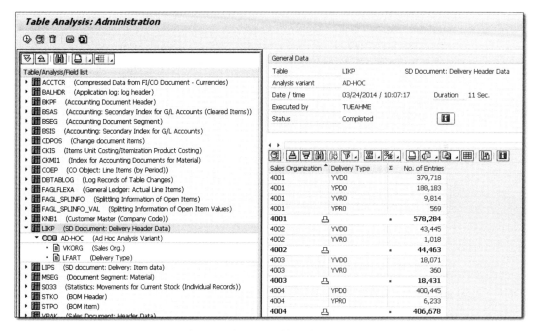

Figure 1.8 Analysis Result Grouped by Sales Organization

Grouping data   Once you have created the table analysis variant, you can use the TOTAL ⊠. or SUBTOTAL ⊠. buttons to format them in a user-friendly manner. In the first column (SALES ORGANIZATION) in Figure 1.8, we have created a subtotal, for example. You therefore immediately see that, for sales organization 4001, a total of 578,284 deliveries exist across all delivery types. You will also immediately notice the delivery type YVD0 in our analysis. With a total of 379,718 data records, the system has generated the most entries for this delivery type.

This analysis is a good data basis for hosting user department workshops in which you discuss which data records can be archived and when. On this basis, you can, for example, specify whether the same residence time is to be used for all delivery types or exceptions need to be taken into consideration.

Goals within Transaction TAANA

You should use Transaction TAANA to obtain information in preparation for an archiving project. To this end, you can use the following functions:

▸ Use the DEFAULT variant to analyze tables.

▸ Use the STANDARD variant to analyze tables.

▸ Use Transaction TAANA_AV to define STANDARD variants.

▸ Analyze tables with the ad hoc variant according to your own criteria.

▸ Use Transaction TAANA_VF to define virtual fields.

▸ Use the total and subtotal functions.

▸ Obtain information for workshops and data archiving.

1.4.4   Transaction SARA: Managing Data Archiving

The most important transaction in the context of SAP data archiving is Transaction SARA (Archive Administration: Initial Screen). It is the main entry point for managing individual data archiving objects.

Managing archiving objects

Immediately after you call Transaction SARA, you can enter an ARCHIVING OBJECT. The system then displays all possible ACTIONS associated with this archiving object.

1. As an example, we will select the archiving object RV_LIKP for the deliveries in our sample table LIKP from the previous section (see Figure 1.9).

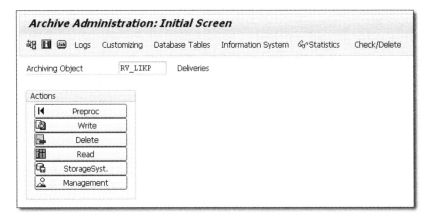

Figure 1.9 Archiving Object RV_LIKP in Transaction SARA

2. As soon as you enter RV_LIKP in the Archiving Object field and press Enter, six buttons are displayed in the Actions area. A specific action is concealed behind each of these buttons. Other actions (for example, Postproc instead of Preproc) may be displayed for other archiving objects.

Actions in Transaction SARA

In the sections that follow, we will describe all of the actions and processes available within Transaction SARA for the various archiving objects.

Preproc

You can use the Preproc action (preprocessing) to schedule a job in preparation for SAP data archiving. Depending on the archiving object, this job may perform an archivability check or it may set a deletion flag or deletion indicator.

Write

Ensuring that you use the right selection criteria

The Write action is available for all archiving objects. First, the write program defined for the archiving object creates the archive files. For the write program (report S3LIKPWRS), you require a *selection variant* to select the data to be archived. The selection variant is extremely important here. The selection screen for the report determines the relevant archiving criteria. Its layout varies for each archiving object. It is very important to create the selection variant without error. Otherwise, the write program will produce unwanted results. For test purposes, you can also start this write process in test mode.

Write phase

During the write phase, the data records are selected and checked against the criteria in SAP data archiving and the settings made in Customizing. Only archivable data records are written to archive files. In the case of archiving object RV_LIKP, the selection screen looks as shown in Figure 1.10.

In the Delivery Category field, you can select whether you want to archive Outbound Deliveries and Returns, Inbound Deliveries, or ROUGH GOODS RECEIPTS for this object. You can also provide further information (for example, the DELIVERY TYPE or the SALES ORGANIZATION) here in order to restrict your selection on an individual basis.

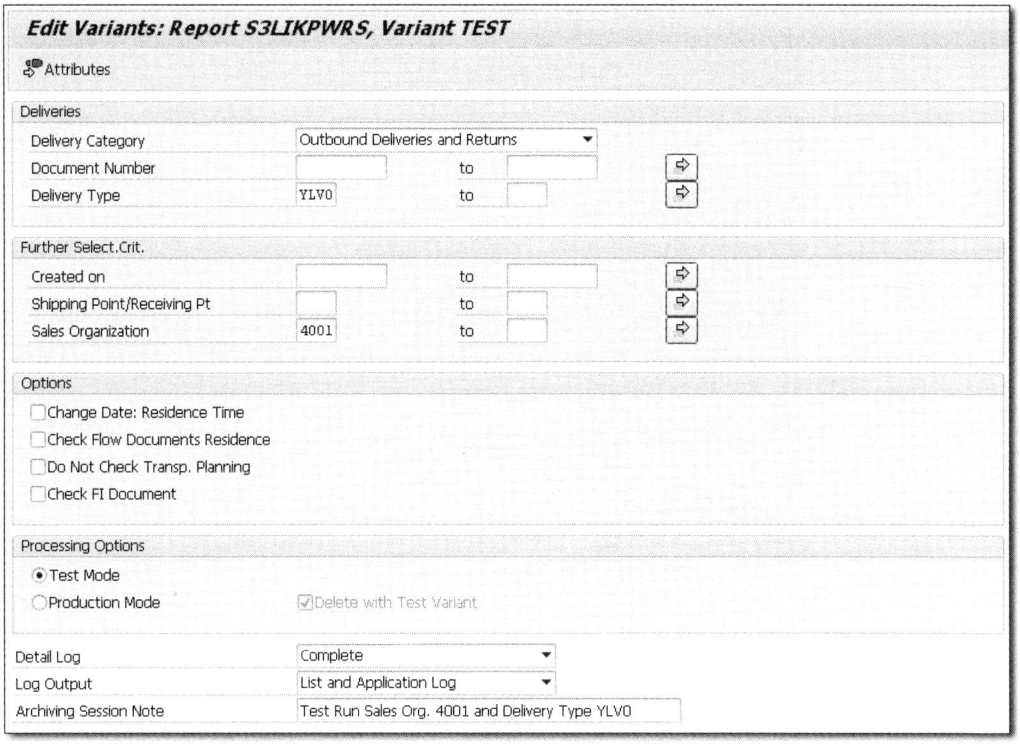

Figure 1.10 Selection Screen for the Write Job for the Archiving Object RV_LIKP

Delete

The DELETE step is another mandatory action. The archive files previously created in the write program are deleted here. To do this, you maintain the relevant settings in Transaction SARA.

Deleting archive files

1. First, choose CUSTOMIZING (see Figure 1.9).

2. In the next dialog box, select TECHNICAL SETTINGS in the ARCHIVING OBJECT-SPECIFIC CUSTOMIZING area (see Figure 1.11).

Figure 1.11 Customizing in Transaction SARA

3. This opens the menu shown in Figure 1.12.

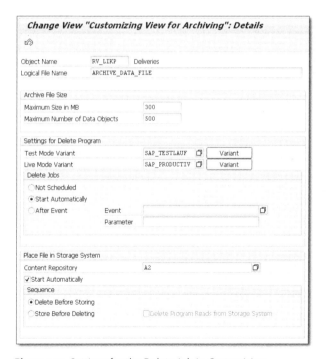

Figure 1.12 Settings for the Delete Job in Customizing

4. Here you can choose between the following three options for the delete job:

   ▸ NOT SCHEDULED

   ▸ START AUTOMATICALLY

   ▸ AFTER EVENT

In practice, the first two options are generally used. For manual administration, select the NOT SCHEDULED option. With this option, you must remember to start the delete job independently at a suitable time. If you want to start the delete jobs immediately after the write phase, select START AUTOMATICALLY. The AFTER EVENT option starts the delete job automatically, if a specific event has occurred. If you want to run the delete jobs over the weekend, for example, but you need to run a particularly important program before you can start other programs, you can link the start of the delete job to the other program. As soon as this program issues the event stating that the program has ended, the delete job then starts automatically.

Delete options

Delete or Destroy?

Once you have completed the delete jobs, the data is deleted from the database and, from now on, is available in the form of archive files only. Do not confuse deleting data from the database with destroying archive files from storage, which does not occur until the end of the retention period in order to fully complete the lifecycle.

[«]

Postproc

The POSTPROC action (postprocessing) is available for specific archiving objects. At this point, we wish to give particular mention to the SAP data archiving object FI_DOCUMNT. You can use Postproc to delete the *secondary indexes* from the relevant tables, if required. This will then create additional memory space.

Deleting secondary indexes

Keep in mind, however, that many accesses occur via the secondary index tables. If you delete these, you need to access the archive files more frequently and maintain the technical settings first. We recommend that you coordinate this action with the relevant user department in detail or that you retain the secondary indexes in the SAP system for a longer period than the original data records.

Read

Programs that enable you to display archived data are concealed behind the Read action. For more information, see Chapter 3.

StorageSyst.

Storage in the content repository

You can use the Storage Syst. action to store the archive files in the Content Repository defined in Customizing (see Figure 1.12). If required, you can retrieve the archive files and make them available in the file system again. A *content repository* may refer to an external archive server or it can be located within the SAP system.

You can use Transaction OAC0 (Display Content Repositories) to view the content repositories available and to redefine them, if necessary. In practice, several content repositories are generally created with different retention times and information objects.

Storage options

Under Place File in Storage System, the following options are available to you:

▶ Delete Before Storing

▶ Store Before Deleting

▶ Store Before Deleting and Delete Program Reads From Storage System

Similar to the delete job, you can also automate the process of storing archive files here. To do this, you simply need to select the Start Automatically checkbox. It is best to select this option in accordance with the significance of the information that you want to archive. The reason for archiving these files also plays an important role here. If you want to use data archiving to remove data from the SAP system only, without retaining it, the first option is most suitable because, in this case, it is not necessary to store this data in a storage system.

The second option (Store Before Deleting) ensures that the archive files are first stored before the deletion phase. It is therefore more secure than the first option. A prerequisite for this is that a corresponding content repository must exist. Since you have created archive files that are still located in the file system and you then use the delete job to immediately delete the data from the database, the data is irrevocably lost if someone inadvertently deletes the archive files from the file system before they are placed in storage.

The third option is the most secure variant. One disadvantage, however, is that the runtime is considerably longer for this option than the other two options. In contrast to the second option, the system performs another poststorage check during the deletion phase to determine if the stored archive files can also be read. If the stored archive files cannot be read, the data is not deleted and it is necessary to create new readable archive files and store them again.

Management

You can use the MANAGEMENT action to obtain an overview of all archiving sessions. The menu displayed after you choose this button (see Figure 1.13) contains, in particular, all incorrect (run number 10), incomplete (run number 11), and complete archiving sessions (run numbers 1 and 12).

Overview of archiving sessions

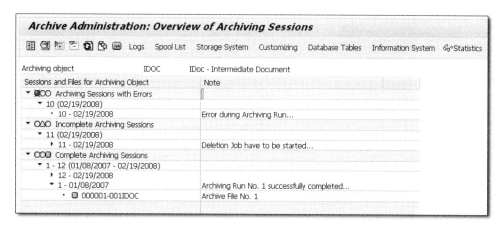

Figure 1.13 Overview of Archiving Sessions in the Management Area

Each time you start the WRITE action, a new archiving session is created. These sessions are numbered consecutively. At least one archive file is generated for each session. On the detail screen for this archive file, you can enter your own NOTE and obtain other important information, such as the size of the archive file, the file name, and the path. You can also mark incorrect archiving sessions as invalid sessions. To do

this, select the relevant session and choose the DETAIL SCREEN button
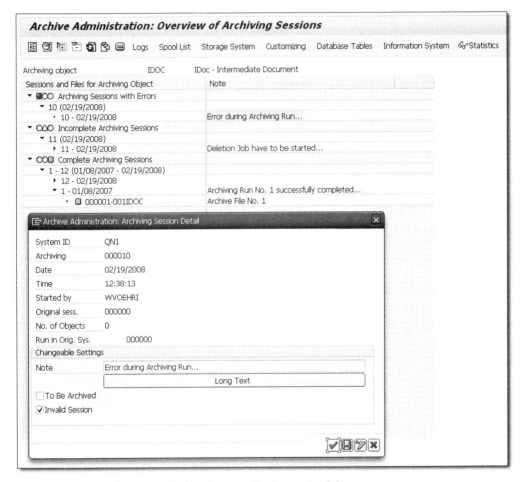 (see Figure 1.14).

Figure 1.14 Marking Incorrect Sessions as Invalid

In the NOTE field, you can enter a note, for example, as to why an error
occurred during the session. You can also select if this concerns an
invalid session.

Archiving archive
administration data
In order to be able to use the archiving object BC_ARCHIVE (Archiving of
Archive Administration Data) to archive the archive administration data
of already destroyed archive files, first select TO BE ARCHIVED to select

the relevant archiving sessions. By doing so, you ensure that in the long term the OVERVIEW OF ARCHIVING SESSIONS does not contain information about archive files that no longer exist.

Reload, Interrupt, and Continue

The RELOAD, INTERRUPT, and CONTINUE actions are used in very exceptional cases only. These actions are not provided as buttons in Transaction SARA. Instead, you can call these functions under the menu path GOTO • RELOAD, INTERRUPT or CONTINUE.

In general, it should not be necessary to reload archived data. This should be considered only if, shortly after data archiving, you notice that incorrect data was archived. In most cases, however, it is not possible to fully reload all of the data into the relevant tables because the reload programs available were designed for emergency use only and therefore focus only on the most important tables. In any event, we recommend that you consult with SAP experts before you reload data so that this action does not result in data inconsistencies in your SAP system.

Reloading data

If necessary, you can use the INTERRUPT and CONTINUE actions to stop and then restart data archiving. In particular, this makes sense if data archiving takes a very long time and you want to schedule a break during the day (that is, in phases in which you do not want system performance to be impaired by the archiving session) or if, in the meantime, you need to increase the memory space in the file system or archive system. In Transaction AOBJ, you can check if an interruption is possible for the archiving object used.

Stopping the archiving process

Additional Functions in the Application Bar in Transaction SARA

In addition to the actions described earlier, additional functions are available to you in the application bar in Transaction SARA. We will describe these functions in the following sections.

Network Graphic

You can use the NETWORK GRAPHIC to display, in a graphic, possible dependencies between the individual archiving objects. To call the network graphic, choose 🔲 after you enter an archiving object (for example, RV_LIKP) in the ARCHIVING OBJECT field in Transaction SARA. The dependencies shown in the network graphic are determined in the checks performed during the WRITE action. For example, you should not archive the deliveries (RV_LIKP) before you have archived the material documents (MM_MATBEL) for the relevant deliveries.

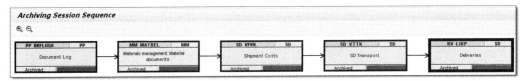

Figure 1.15 Archiving Session Sequence

Archiving session sequence

The network graphic in Figure 1.15 contains possible archiving objects whose archiving sessions should be started before the archiving object RV_LIKP. In particular, the material documents, the shipment costs, and the SD transports, along with their archiving objects, should be considered for archiving in order to significantly improve the chances of successfully archiving the deliveries. If you do not observe the sequence and instead start to archive the deliveries immediately, you will most likely not be able to archive a great deal of data, because the archivability criteria of SAP data archiving will have been violated. The spool file for the write program for the archiving object RV_LIKP will show that no data was archived or only a very low volume of data could be archived. For some archiving objects, the reasons as to why it was not possible to archive the data are specified in the spool file. However, this is not the case for every archiving object.

Documentation

Reference material

The information available under DOCUMENTATION provides very good support when archiving data. Here a detailed description is available for each SAP data archiving object. If you encounter an archiving object for the first time, you should always read the description provided for this object. However, the documentation is also a very good source of reference for those archiving objects that you already know.

Job Overview

Analyzing terminated jobs

The JOB OVERVIEW contains all of the jobs generated for the data archiving object selected. The job overview is the optimum environment for planning, monitoring, and calculating archiving runtimes. In the case of terminated jobs, it is particularly necessary to analyze the cause so that appropriate measures can be taken to ensure that archiving is fully executed without error.

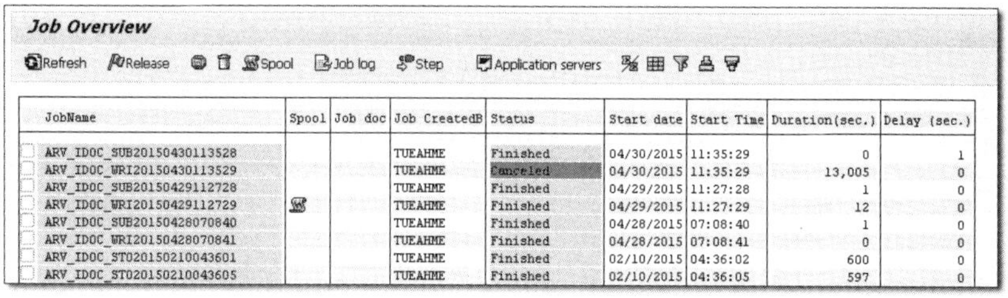

JobName	Spool	Job doc	Job CreatedB	Status	Start date	Start Time	Duration(sec.)	Delay (sec.)
ARV_IDOC_SUB20150430113528			TUEAHME	Finished	04/30/2015	11:35:29	0	1
ARV_IDOC_WRI20150430113529			TUEAHME	Canceled	04/30/2015	11:35:29	13,005	0
ARV_IDOC_SUB20150429112728			TUEAHME	Finished	04/29/2015	11:27:28	1	0
ARV_IDOC_WRI20150429112729			TUEAHME	Finished	04/29/2015	11:27:29	12	0
ARV_IDOC_SUB20150428070840			TUEAHME	Finished	04/28/2015	07:08:40	1	0
ARV_IDOC_WRI20150428070841			TUEAHME	Finished	04/28/2015	07:08:41	0	0
ARV_IDOC_ST020150210043601			TUEAHME	Finished	02/10/2015	04:36:02	600	0
ARV_IDOC_ST020150210043605			TUEAHME	Finished	02/10/2015	04:36:05	597	0

Figure 1.16 Job Overview

Figure 1.16 shows the job overview for the archiving object `IDOC` in which a terminated job is also listed. If you want to analyze the reason for the termination, you can select the terminated job and choose Job Log to access the overview shown in Figure 1.17.

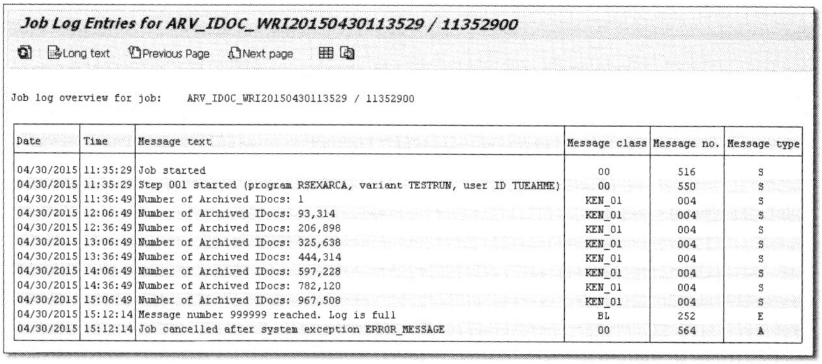

Date	Time	Message text	Message class	Message no.	Message type
04/30/2015	11:35:29	Job started	00	516	S
04/30/2015	11:35:29	Step 001 started (program RSEXARCA, variant TESTRUN, user ID TUEAHME)	00	550	S
04/30/2015	11:36:49	Number of Archived IDocs: 1	KEN_01	004	S
04/30/2015	12:06:49	Number of Archived IDocs: 93,314	KEN_01	004	S
04/30/2015	12:36:49	Number of Archived IDocs: 206,898	KEN_01	004	S
04/30/2015	13:06:49	Number of Archived IDocs: 325,638	KEN_01	004	S
04/30/2015	13:36:49	Number of Archived IDocs: 444,314	KEN_01	004	S
04/30/2015	14:06:49	Number of Archived IDocs: 597,228	KEN_01	004	S
04/30/2015	14:36:49	Number of Archived IDocs: 782,120	KEN_01	004	S
04/30/2015	15:06:49	Number of Archived IDocs: 967,508	KEN_01	004	S
04/30/2015	15:12:14	Message number 999999 reached. Log is full	BL	252	E
04/30/2015	15:12:14	Job cancelled after system exception ERROR_MESSAGE	00	564	A

Figure 1.17 Job Log and Cause of Error

In the second to last row in the Message text column, you see that there were too many IDocs to be archived at once and, at the same time, a detailed log has been selected in the selection variant. However, the write program is designed to create a maximum of 999,999 logs only. If this number is exceeded, the write program terminates. To bypass the problem, you can choose not to create a detailed log or you can restrict the selection variant.

The archiving session is then listed correctly in the MANAGEMENT area in Transaction SARA (see Figure 1.13).

Logs

You can create LOGS within the selection variant. In the case of LOG OUTPUT, you can choose between the following options in the selection variant (see Figure 1.10):

▶ LIST

▶ APPLICATION LOG

▶ LIST AND APPLICATION LOG

You can also specify how detailed you want the log to be. In the DETAIL LOG area, the following options are available for selection:

▶ NO DETAIL LOG

▶ WITHOUT SUCCESS MESSAGE

▶ COMPLETE

We recommend that you select the LIST and APPLICATION LOG options in the LOG OUTPUT selection field and the COMPLETE option in the DETAIL LOG selection field. This combination will provide you with a complete spool file as well as a brief message text in the job log every thirty minutes informing you about the progress of the archiving process. If this information is too detailed for you, you can select another combination.

The *spool lists* are particularly important here because they contain key information about the archiving session. We recommend that you also store these spool lists in the archive as a print list, because the spool lists are generally not saved in the SAP system for too long.

Customizing

Settings for archiving objects

Important properties of the SAP data archiving object are maintained in CUSTOMIZING. Here four areas are available to you:

▶ CROSS-ARCHIVING OBJECT CUSTOMIZING

▶ ARCHIVING OBJECT-SPECIFIC CUSTOMIZING

▶ BASIS CUSTOMIZING

▶ APPLICATION-SPECIFIC CUSTOMIZING

Basis Customizing in Transaction FILE will be described in detail in Section 1.4.5. Application-specific Customizing is not available for all SAP data archiving objects. In general, the residence time is maintained here. In archiving object-specific Customizing, you maintain, among other things, the logical file name, the size of the archive file, and settings for deleting the archive data as described in the section that discusses the DELETE action. Here you also specify the sequence in which archive files are to be stored. In this area, the *archive routing* function also enables you to store the archive files in different areas according to certain rules and conditions. In the case of cross-archiving object Customizing, you do not have to maintain any additional Customizing settings.

Database Tables

You can use the DATABASE TABLES menu option to navigate directly to Transaction DB15 and display the database tables for an archiving object (see also Section 1.4.2).

Navigating to the analysis transaction

Information System

You can use the INFORMATION SYSTEM menu option to navigate directly to Transaction SARI to manage the Archive Information System. For more information, see Chapter 3, Section 3.3.

Statistics

The STATISTICS display various pieces of information about an archiving session and the data archiving objects. Of particular interest is the information about the deleted data volume and the newly generated archive files.

Figure 1.18 shows the statistics relating to the archiving object IDOC. To call this, choose STATISTICS in Transaction SARA. When calculating archiving success, it is important to select only those archiving sessions that have been assigned the status COMPLETE ⬤⬤◻. RUN NUMBER 11 has, for example, the status INCOMPLETE ⬤◪◯. Here only the archive file was created. The delete job, however, was not started. For this reason, the value 0,000 is also displayed in the DB SPACE (DELETE) column. You can obtain the DB SPACE (DELETE) key figure from the memory space acquired by data archiving for completed archiving sessions.

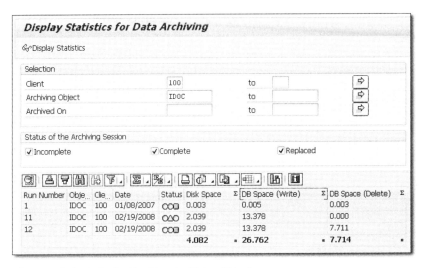

Figure 1.18 Statistics for the IDoc Archiving Object

Depending on the SAP data archiving object, the archive files are compressed to varying degrees. One rule of thumb is that, on average,
approximately 80% of memory space is released after an archive file has
been compressed. Let's take RUN NUMBER 12 (Complete) as an example.
Here 7,711 megabytes (MB) of data was deleted from the database.
However, 13,378 MB of data was needed to create the archive file. After
compression, the size of the archive file is only 2,039 MB. We have
therefore acquired 74% memory space if we compare the deleted data
volume against the newly generated archive file (2,039/7,711). If you
consider the fact that it is more favorable to have additional memory
space in the archive system than in the database, the benefit of SAP data
archiving in terms of memory space becomes even more apparent.

Check/Delete

You can use the CHECK/DELETE function to check the data of several
archiving objects simultaneously to see if they can be archived and then
delete them from the database. Even though this function provides support for large data volumes, it is rarely used in practice.

Goals within Transaction SARA

You can use the earlier noted functions in Transaction SARA to achieve the following goals:

▸ Perform Customizing for the archiving object.

▸ View the network graphic for the archiving session sequence.

▸ Execute various actions (for example, write or delete).

▸ Display the job overview.

▸ Display archiving sessions in the management action.

▸ Display logs for the archiving sessions.

▸ Display statistics for the archiving sessions.

▸ Interrupt and continue the write job, if necessary.

▸ Navigate to other transactions (for example, Transaction DB15 or Transaction SARI).

1.4.5 Transaction FILE: Defining Path Names and File Names

One important task during SAP data archiving is to define suitable path names and file names for the archive files. Descriptive file names with a logical structure will enable you to identify archive files more quickly. You can also store the archive files in different directories if you have created the relevant path names for them. You can define the path names and file names on a client-specific basis in Transaction SF01 and on a cross-client basis in Transaction FILE. Since the cross-client variant is the standard procedure, we will now take a closer look at this variant in Transaction FILE.

Cross-client file names

When defining names, a distinction is made between logical and physical path names and file names. In the file system, the archive files created are always stored under a *physical* path name and file name. These physical path names and file names are derived from the *logical* path name and file name. All areas can be defined on an individual basis. In a standard SAP system, settings for the archiving objects are already defined in Basis Customizing (see Figure 1.19). Procced with the following steps:

Logical and physical names

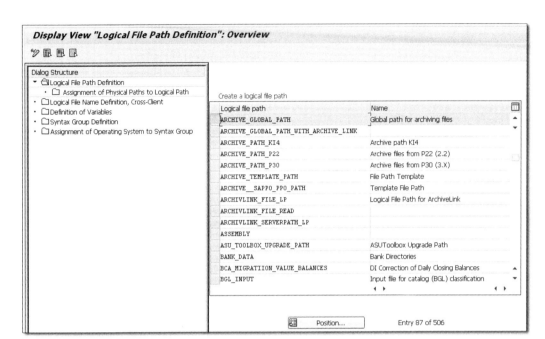

Figure 1.19 Defining Logical File Paths

1. The first step is to define a logical file path. In the standard SAP system, the logical path *ARCHIVE_GLOBAL_PATH* for archiving is already available as a default setting. You can use this logical path or create a new entry.

2. In the second step, this logical path is assigned to a physical path (see Figure 1.20).

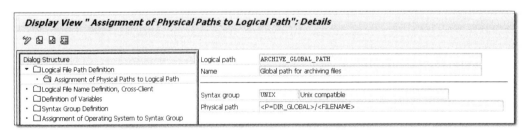

Figure 1.20 Assigning the Logical Path to the Physical Path

Significance of Physical and Logical File Paths   **[Ex]**

When you assign the physical file path to the logical file path, you need to specify a syntax group. The syntax group represents identical operating systems that use the same syntax for the file names and paths. If your SAP system is running on a Unix-compatible operating system (for example, SunOS or Linux), it is assigned to the syntax group Unix. In our example, the physical path *<P=DIR_GLOBAL>/<FILENAME>* for Unix-compatible operating systems (SYNTAX GROUP: UNIX) has the following significance:

- *<P=DIR_GLOBAL>* is the temporary storage area in the file system. The archive files are written to this directory.
- *<FILENAME>* is a reserved word or a mandatory placeholder for the physical file name. This must always appear at the end of the physical path.

Other reserved words are available for use within the physical path and file name. Examples of frequently used file names are provided in Table 1.1. You can use these words to define individual path names and file names.

Reserved Word	Substitution Value at Runtime with System Fields (SY-*) from the Structure SYST (ABAP System Fields)
<SYSID>	Name of the SAP ERP application according to the field SY-SYSID
<CLIENT>	Client according to the field SY-MANDT
<DATE>	Date according to the field SY-DATUM
<TIME>	Time according to the field SY-UZEIT
<YEAR>	Year according to the field SY-DATUM, four-digit
<MONTH>	Month according to the field SY-DATUM
<PARAM_1>	External parameter 1 Two-character application ID (for example, FI, SD, CO, and BC)
<PARAM_2>	External parameter 2 One-digit alphanumeric character (for example, 0 – 9 and A – Z)
<PARAM_3>	External parameter 3 Name of the archiving object (for example, RV_LIKP)

Table 1.1 Reserved Words for File Names within an Archiving Path

3. In the third step, we define the logical file name. When defining the logical path name `ARCHIVE_DATA_FILE`, the logical file name from the LOGICAL FILE field, the physical file name from the PHYSICAL FILE field, and the logical file path from the LOGICAL PATH field are linked together (see Figure 1.21). Here you can also define the physical file name in the PHYSICAL FILE field. You can use the logical path *ARCHIVE_GLOBAL_PATH* to determine the physical path *<P=DIR_GLOBAL>/<FILENAME>*, which we specified in the second step.

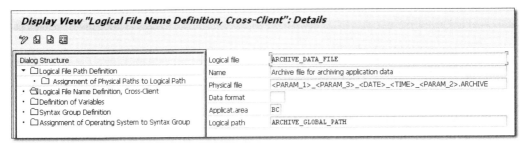

Figure 1.21 Cross-Client Definition of the Logical File Name

4. In the last step, you enter the logical file name `ARCHIVE_DATA_FILE` in the archiving object-specific Customizing, specifically in the LOGICAL FILE NAME field in the TECHNICAL SETTINGS area (see Figure 1.22).

Figure 1.22 Assigning the Logical File Name for the Archiving Object RV_LIKP

Customizing of the path names and file names is now complete for the archiving object. In our example, we obtain the logical and physical path names and file names from Table 1.2.

Field	Name
LOGICAL PATH	*ARCHIVE_GLOBAL_PATH*
PHYSICAL PATH	*<P=DIR_GLOBAL>/<FILENAME>*
LOGICAL NAME	*ARCHIVE_DATA_FILE*
PHYSICAL NAME	*<PARAM_1>_<PARAM_3>_*
	<DATE>_<TIME>_<PARAM_2>.ARCHIVE

Table 1.2 Overview of How Path Names and File Names Are Linked Together

If we were to now generate an archive file with the archiving object RV_ LIKP, its name would be (in accordance with the physical file name *<PARAM_1>_<PARAM_3>_<DATE>_<TIME>_<PARAM_2>.ARCHIVE* used in our example):

Physical file name

SD_RV_LIKP_20140101_142032_0.ARCHIVE

From the information that was provided instead of the reserved words *<DATE>* and *<TIME>*, you can see that this archive file was created on January 01, 2014 at 14:20:32. The physical file name must be chosen in such a way that it can be assigned once only. Two identical file names will cause a termination during the WRITE action.

Define Meaningful Physical File Names [+]

The physical file name in our example does not provide any information about the pre-archiving residence time. Furthermore, you cannot ascertain for how long this archive file is to be retained. We only know when this archive file was created. A slight modification can enable you to add the residence time and retention period to the physical file name. If you add the ending *.6M_144M_ARCHIVE*, you can deduct from this that the residence time is to be six months and the retention period is to be 144 months.

Defining Path Names and File Names

The following is a brief summary of the individual steps associated with defining path names and file names:

- Define the logical path name.
- Assign the logical path name to the physical path name.
- Define the logical file name and physical file name.
- Transfer the logical file name to archiving object-specific Customizing.

Digression: Archive Routing

In Customizing for the data archiving object, you can enter only one content repository and one logical file name. Therefore, all archive files for this archiving object are stored in the same area and the physical file name of each archive file has a very similar structure.

Greater flexibility with archive routing

Archive routing enables you to use rules and conditions to automatically store the archive files in different areas. You can also define different logical file names in Customizing for archive routing. You can store the archive files separately (for example, according to fiscal year or SAP organizational unit).

Two entry options are available to you here:

▸ Content repository for storage in the archive (CONTENT REP. field, see Figure 1.23)

▸ Logical file name for storage in the file system (LOG. FILE NAME field)

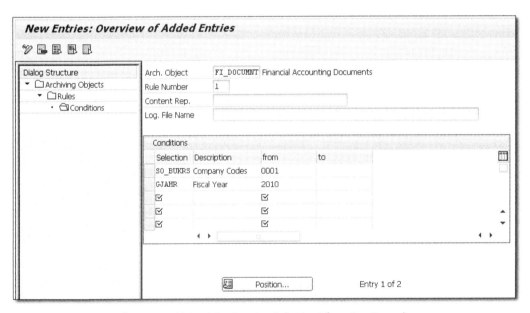

Figure 1.23 Maintaining Routing Rule No. 1 from Our Example

The content repository is maintained only if an archive is available for storage. Maintenance can also occur retroactively. However, it is absolutely imperative that you maintain the logical file name. If this is not explicitly defined in Customizing for archive routing, the entry will be taken from Customizing for the data archiving object.

The example in Table 1.3 shows you different options for creating rules and conditions.

Maintaining rules and conditions

Rule No.	Condition 1/ Company Code	Condition 2/ Fiscal Year	Content Repository	Logical File Name
1	0001	2010		ARCHIVE_ DATA_FILE
2	1000		D1	
3	4001		A2	Z_ARCHIVE_ DATA_FILE_1

Table 1.3 Rule and Conditions for Archive Routing

To create routing rules, first enter the data archiving object in the ARCH. OBJECT field. Then enter the RULE NUMBER and assign the corresponding content repository in the CONTENT REP. field and the logical file name in the LOG. FILE NAME field for this rule (optional). The last step is to maintain the CONDITIONS, as shown in Figure 1.23. Here we created rule no. 1 in such a way that the logical file name from Customizing (ARCHIVE_ DATA_FILE) is to be used for the FI documents from company code 0001 and fiscal year 2010. If you want the archive files to be stored in content repository D1 (rule number 2), you must enter the condition "Company Code 1000" in a second rule.

At the same time, you must also select the selection variant for the WRITE action in such a way that the storage area is unique and corresponds to exactly one maintained rule. If this is not the case, the write job will terminate. If you create the selection variant for rule no. 1, you must enter only company code 0001 and fiscal year 2010 in this selection. For rule no. 2 to take effect, you must enter only company code 1000.

Reconciling the selection variant with the rule

[◉]
Goals within Transaction FILE

In Transaction FILE, you can use the following functions:

▶ Define logical path names and file names.

▶ Define physical path names and file names.

▶ Use reserved words and custom definitions.

▶ Use the archive routing options.

1.5 Legal Regulations

Observing different sources

Enterprises must observe the statutory requirements associated with data retention in the countries in which they are active. The obligation to retain data may result from specifications contained in different sources. *The Internal Revenue Code* (IRC) has different requirements than the *Uniform Commercial Code* (UCC). In addition to the applicable laws, guidelines from the relevant tax authorities are also extremely important. In the following section we will provide you with extracts from the most important laws and guidelines in relation to data archiving. This list is not intended to be exhaustive and must be checked by each enterprise (while drawing on the knowledge of both internal and external experts) in terms of timeliness and relevance.

Consulting with internal and external experts

In order to completely satisfy the various legal regulations (in particular, commercial law and taxation law), we recommend that you also consult with a local tax auditor or tax consultant as well as an official from the tax office. The legal, finance, or tax departments within your enterprise can also support you in answering any questions you may have. In addition to the legal regulations, it is also important to consider or update internal guidelines. In the following sections, we will take a closer look at those United States laws that affect data archiving. In this context, we will briefly explain some key features of international projects in countries that have different laws in relation to data archiving.

Key questions

You should use the relevant laws and guidelines as a basis for answering the following key issues:

▶ Retention location

▶ Retention time

- Data access

- Transfer to data medium

- Technology and archive media

It is also necessary to clarify where data is permitted to be retained and for how long. Your chosen technology and archive media must facilitate, beyond the entire retention time, the necessary access to the archive and, where required, the transfer of data to a data medium.

1.5.1   Data Archiving Laws for the United States

The data in an SAP system is extremely important for various external recipients. In the case of external auditors and tax auditors, the most important laws and regulations on data retention are contained in the *Internal Revenue Code* (Title 26 IRC) and the *Code of Federal Regulations* (Title 26 CFR). Extracts of the relevant sections are provided in Table 1.4.

External audits and tax audits

Source	Extract	Requirement
26 US Code § 6001	Every person liable for any tax imposed by the Code, or for the collection thereof, must keep such records, render such statements, make such returns, and comply with such rules and regulations as the Secretary may from time to time prescribe. Whenever necessary, the Secretary may require any person, by notice served upon that person or by regulations, to make such returns, render such statements, or keep such records, as the Secretary deems sufficient to show whether or not that person is liable for tax. [...]	Retention of Records

Table 1.4 Extracts of the Relevant Specifications

Source	Extract	Requirement
26 CFR 1.6001-1(a)	[...] Any person subject to tax under subtitle A of the Code (including a qualified State individual income tax which is treated pursuant to section 6361(a) as if it were imposed by chapter 1 of subtitle A), or any person required to file a return of information with respect to income, shall keep such permanent books of account or records, including inventories, as are sufficient to establish the amount of gross income, deductions, credits, or other matters required to be shown by such person in any return of such tax or information.	Retention Scope
26 CFR 1.6001-1(e)	[...]The books or records required by this section shall be kept at all times available for inspection by authorized internal revenue officers or employees, and shall be retained so long as the contents thereof may become material in the administration of any internal revenue law.	Retention Time

Table 1.4 Extracts of the Relevant Specifications (Cont.)

Archiving and extraction quality

Furthermore, the *Revenue Procedure 97-22* (Rev. Proc. 97-22) and the *Revenue Procedure 98-25* (Rev. Proc. 98-25) issued by the Internal Revenue Service (IRS) are extremely important for archiving and extraction quality (see Table 1.5).

Source	Extract	Requirement
Rev. Proc. 98-25 Section 5.01	The taxpayer must retain machine-sensible records so long as their contents may become material to the administration of the internal revenue laws under § 1.6001-1(e). At a minimum, this materiality continues until the expiration of the period of limitation for assessment, including extensions, for each tax year. In certain situations, records should be kept for a longer period of time.	Retention Time
Rev. Proc. 98-25 Section 11.01	The provisions of this revenue procedure do not relieve taxpayers of their responsibility to retain hardcopy records that are created or received in the ordinary course of business as required by existing law and regulations. Hardcopy records may be retained in microfiche or microfilm format in conformity with Rev. Proc. 81-46, 1981-2 C.B. 621. Hardcopy records may also be retained in an electronic storage system in conformity with Rev. Proc. 97-22. These records are not a substitute for the machine-sensible records required to be retained by this revenue procedure.	Archive Medium
Rev. Proc. 97-22 Section 3.01	This revenue procedure applies to taxpayers who maintain books and records using an "electronic storage system." An electronic storage system is a system to prepare, record, transfer, index, store, preserve, retrieve, and reproduce books and records by either [...]	Electronic Storage System

Table 1.5 Extracts of the Relevant Specifications

Source	Extract	Requirement
Rev. Proc. 97-22 Section 6.01	A taxpayer's electronic storage system that meets the requirements of this revenue procedure will be treated as being in compliance with the recordkeeping requirements of § 6001 and the regulations thereunder.[...]	Compliance
Rev. Proc. 97-22 Section 4.02	The implementation of records management practices is a business decision that is solely within the discretion of the taxpayer. Records management practices may include the labeling of electronically stored books and records, providing a secure storage environment, creating back-up copies, selecting an off-site storage location, retaining hardcopies of books or records that are illegible or that cannot be accurately or completely transferred to an electronic storage system, and testing to confirm records integrity.	Data Security

Table 1.5 Extracts of the Relevant Specifications (Cont.)

At this point, we do not wish to cite any further laws, guidelines, or statements relating to the United States. The excerpts shown in Table 1.3 contain the most important information about data archiving and extraction and are intended to provide you with a good overview of this topic as well as a basic introduction so that you do not regard SAP data archiving solely as a technical task. Only when you have built your project on a legally stable foundation can you start data archiving with a clear conscience.

1.5.2 International Data Archiving Laws

Observing international laws

An SAP system can be used productively in the Unites States for both American and foreign companies. Foreign companies may also use their own SAP systems on-site. Irrespective of which scenario you choose, it is also necessary to know the international legal regulations in relation to data archiving.

In particular, you should be aware of major deviations between the data archiving laws in individual countries so that you can prepare accordingly. In order to retain a compact overview here, Table 1.6 will focus solely on the requirements associated with the *retention location, retention time*, and *transfer to data medium* for China, Belgium, France, Switzerland, and Germany in comparison with the United States:

Country	Retention Location	Retention Time	Transfer to Data Medium
United States	Domestic	10 years	Yes
China	Domestic	10 years	No
Belgium	Domestic	7 years	Yes
France	Domestic	6 years	Yes
Switzerland	Domestic	10 years	No
Germany	Domestic	10 years	Yes

Table 1.6 Overview of the Requirements in Five Different Countries

In the course of our international SAP data archiving projects, we have consulted with various in-house and external parties in relation to the statutory requirements in the respective countries. Depending on the size of the international subsidiary, the chief financial officer (CFO) or the head of the tax, finance, or legal departments answered our questions. External parties from auditing companies and tax consultancy firms provided additional information. Interestingly, we frequently obtained different answers with regard to the relevant requirements. It was very tedious and time-consuming to determine specifically those requirements that were applicable in each country. The general consensus obtained from the various answers is listed in Table 1.6. This overview is nonbinding. Furthermore, the individual requirements may be subject to change at any time.

Some requirements are difficult to determine

In the sections that follow, we will provide recommendations in relation to fulfilling and reaching agreement on the relevant requirements in an international context.

Retention Location

Flexibility in relation to the retention location

In accordance with US law, documentation that is subject to a retention obligation as defined by 26 US Code § 6001 should be retained in the United States. However, the tax office may, upon submission of a written request and once all conditions have been observed, allow this data to also be retained abroad. Foreign legislation also contains similar formulations. If an American corporate group uses a central SAP system in the United States but various international subsidiaries also keep their electronic accounts in this SAP system, the tax department will generally submit the relevant relief requests for the international subsidiaries to the local tax offices so that this data is also permitted to be retained in the US.

Technical requirements

In addition to the statutory requirements, the retention location must also satisfy some technical requirements. It is therefore imperative that you ask yourself the following questions:

- Does the software provider allow its software to be installed in a particular country?
- Does it make sense to define only one central retention location?
- Are the access times from the various countries acceptable?

Therefore, the retention location plays a very important role within an SAP data archiving project.

Retention Time

Adhering to legal specifications

The various pieces of legislation specify different retention periods for different information objects. Internationally, these retention periods generally vary between six and ten years. Thanks to technological advances and an increase in electronically supported tax audits, the argument for reducing the retention period repeatedly comes up for discussion.

From experience, we know that enterprises tend to err on the side of caution and have a longer retention period than legally required. Generally speaking, the following is a good rule of thumb: do not extend the retention period unnecessarily. Under no circumstances should this result in a conflict with the statutory obligation to delete data. Here we recommend the following: Adhere to the statutory retention periods at all times. You should not choose a retention time that is too short or overly long. When you use content repositories, you can specify a different retention period for each country and therefore retain the data in separate content repositories (for example, for a period of six years for France and for a period of ten years for Switzerland).

Transfer to Data Medium

Enterprises in the United States very often use media data in the context of electronic tax audits. The relevant tools will be introduced in Section 1.6. Other countries have also incorporated the concept of an electronic tax audit into their respective legal regulations. Even in countries where data archiving is to be introduced in the near future and, as yet, there are no legal obligations to transfer data to a data medium, we recommend that you inform the relevant parties in the user department and tax department ahead of time about the possibility of using audit software to perform electronic tax audits, along with the possibility of data extraction.

Electronic tax audit

Legal Regulations

If you want to build your SAP data archiving project on a stable foundation, the first step is to determine the legal regulations. In summary, we can state that the laws in most countries correspond, more or less, to the laws in the United States. In this section, we took a look at only five countries. However, they do not differ significantly from other countries around the world. Furthermore, the authorities are no longer so strict in terms of where the retention location should be.

There will always be slight variances between the legally prescribed retention periods for individual countries. Here it is important to adhere to those periods prescribed for the individual countries.

Nowadays, transferring data to a data medium has almost become standard practice. It is anticipated that countries that have not yet stated this in law will do so in the near future. Therefore, thinking ahead to the future, your colleagues in the relevant countries should be informed about this topic. Furthermore, local information should be obtained and evaluated.

1.6   Tools for Electronic Tax Audits

During tax audits, external auditors and tax auditors use IT-based tools to analyze the quality of the tax-relevant data in an SAP system on the basis of statistical methods. Such analyses are to provide the basis for making statements in relation to data accuracy.

Analyzing data accuracy

First, however, it is necessary to use an IT tool to extract the tax-relevant data from the SAP system and provide it in the format required by the auditor. For such extractions, we will describe the *Data Retention Tool* (DART), which is available in every SAP system as standard (that is, at no extra cost). Alternatively, other tools are available (subject to a fee). In addition to the data in the database, such tools can also include archived data in the extraction process. Since DART can read from the database only, data extraction must precede data archiving. To facilitate an analysis of the data from the DART extract, we will briefly introduce you to the products of two leading audit software providers, namely, ACL and CaseWare. Even if you do not require the ACL and IDEA products directly for data archiving, you should nevertheless learn about them in the context of data archiving.

1.6.1   Extraction Using the Data Retention Tool (DART)

Standard SAP extractor

DART is used to extract tax-relevant data from the SAP system. Originally, it was developed for the requirements of the US tax authorities. In recent years, other countries have also amended their laws and introduced new guidelines for electronic tax audits. Since then, DART is also used in these countries.

Data catalogs

The SAP user groups *Americas SAP Users Group* (ASUG) and the *German-Speaking SAP User Group* (DSAG) have made some proposals for the United States (US data volume) and Germany (DE data volume). As a result, country data catalogs now contain corresponding data segments, which can be used in the respective countries. Ultimately, concealed behind these data segments are specific tables from the SAP system that are important for the tax audit and that the tax auditor can analyze using IDEA or ACL, for example. It is also possible to combine these two data catalogs in order to obtain a compilation of the relevant data segments for all data volumes. Notably, this option is applied if you want to extract the maximum scope of data. For more information about these data catalogs, see the "Configuration" section.

Defining tax-relevant data

The first key question when using DART is: Which data in the SAP system is tax-relevant data? Since the data is stored in tables, the question should really be: Which tables in the SAP system are tax-relevant tables?

To answer this question, we will first use Transaction FTW0 to access the DART area menu directly (see Figure 1.24).

Figure 1.24 Transaction FTW0 (DART Area Menu)

The area menu for Transaction FTW0 is divided into the following four areas:

▶ UTILITIES

▶ INFORMATION SYSTEM

▶ EXTRAS

▶ CONFIGURATION

In the following sections, we will describe the most important settings and functions from these four areas.

Utilities

The most important transaction in the UTILITIES area is Transaction FTW1A (Extract Data). You can use this transaction to extract the data segments defined in the CONFIGURATION area (see Figure 1.25).

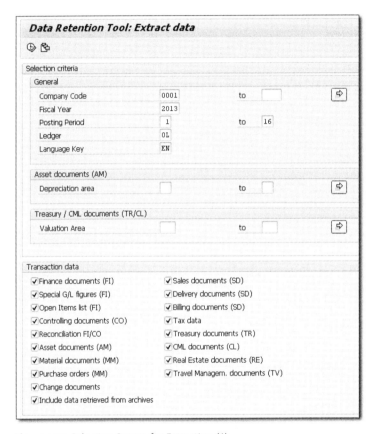

Figure 1.25 Selection Screen for Extraction (1)

Here it is important that you always extract data for one company code only and for one fiscal year only. To start the data extraction process, we require a suitable file name, a storage directory, and a meaningful description (see Figure 1.26). The following file name format has proven itself in real life:

<company code>_<fiscal year>_<from period>_<to period>

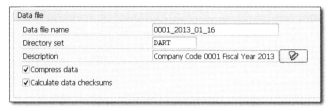

Figure 1.26 Selection Screen for Extraction (2)

If the file name has this structure, you can quickly identify the company code and fiscal year from which the data contained in an extract originates.

The other transactions in the UTILITIES area (for splitting or rejoining data segments, for example) are very rarely used in real life. If, however, you have created a DART extract for test purposes, for example, and you now want to delete this again, you can do so using Transaction FTWK (Delete Data Extracts).

Information System

Within the information system, you can use Transaction FTWF (Data Extract Browser) to display all existing data extracts. You can search the extract contents for data records. You can also delete the extract, export it into an archive, or reimport it from the archive into the file system (see Figure 1.27).

Data extract browser

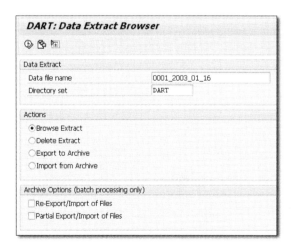

Figure 1.27 Transaction FTWF (Data Extract Browser)

75

Data extract views   Ultimately, you use Transaction FTWH (Data Extract Views) to create the exact subset of data required by the tax auditor. Standard data views are available to you here (see Figure 1.28). However, we recommend that you use Transaction FTWY (View Definition) to create your own data views in accordance with the requirements of the tax auditor.

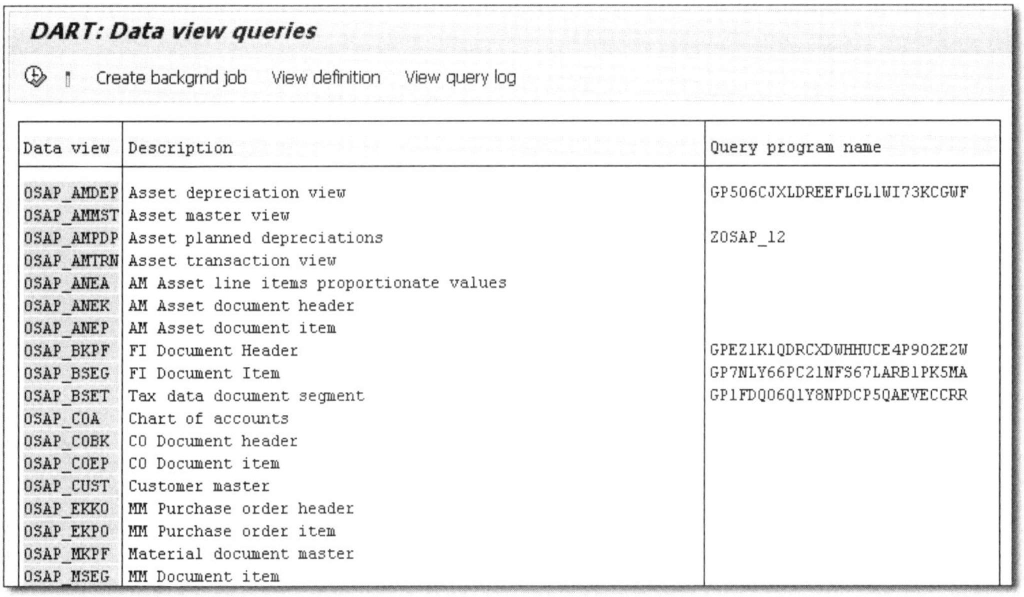

DART: Data view queries

⊕ ▯ Create backgrnd job   View definition   View query log

Data view	Description	Query program name
OSAP_AMDEP	Asset depreciation view	GP506CJXLDREEFLGL1WI73KCGWF
OSAP_AMMST	Asset master view	
OSAP_AMPDP	Asset planned depreciations	ZOSAP_12
OSAP_AMTRN	Asset transaction view	
OSAP_ANEA	AM Asset line items proportionate values	
OSAP_ANEK	AM Asset document header	
OSAP_ANEP	AM Asset document item	
OSAP_BKPF	FI Document Header	GPEZ1K1QDRCXDWHHUCE4P902E2W
OSAP_BSEG	FI Document Item	GP7NLY66PC21NFS67LARB1PK5MA
OSAP_BSET	Tax data document segment	GP1FDQ06Q1Y8NPDCP5QAEVECCRR
OSAP_COA	Chart of accounts	
OSAP_COBK	CO Document header	
OSAP_COEP	CO Document item	
OSAP_CUST	Customer master	
OSAP_EKKO	MM Purchase order header	
OSAP_EKPO	MM Purchase order item	
OSAP_MKPF	Material document master	
OSAP_MSEG	MM Document item	

Figure 1.28 Transaction FTWH (Data View Queries)

Creating a view file   To create a view file, proceed as follows:

1. Select an existing DATA VIEW (for example, OSAP_BKPF) and then choose EXECUTE ⊕.

2. On the selection screen shown in Figure 1.29, first select a SOURCE EXTRACT. Then use the existing selection criteria to narrow down the selection if, for example, you want to consider it for a specific POSTING PERIOD only.

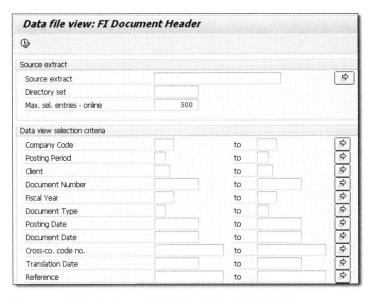

Figure 1.29 Selection Screen for the Data View 0SAP_BKPF

3. It is particularly important to export the data views to a file in SAP AUDIT FORMAT. To do this, first select EXPORT TO FILE and assign a suitable name to the data file (see Figure 1.30). For the most part, the tax auditors specify how the view files should be named.

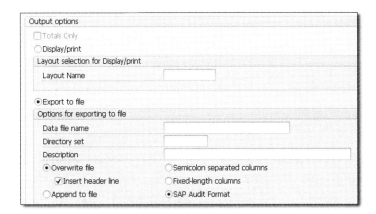

Figure 1.30 Creating a View File in SAP Audit Format

4. Then select the relevant DIRECTORY SET for storing the view file and enter text in the DESCRIPTION field. Make sure to select the SAP AUDIT FORMAT option. Tax auditors generally request the view files in this format.

Segment catalog and field catalog

The segment catalog and the field catalog display (depending on the country code for the company code) the segments and fields that are taken into consideration during data extraction. DART uses the ASSOCIATED DATA DETECTOR (Transaction FTWAD) to determine, on the basis of table TXW_C_RELA (Relations of Tables and Domains), additional segments (that is, those associated with the segments selected) for which you can also create a view file in a single step.

Extras

Various log functions and audit functions are available to you in the EXTRAS area. Two transactions are particularly important here. We will therefore introduce you to them in the following section.

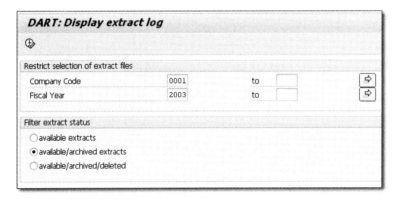

Figure 1.31 Transaction FTWL (Display Extract Log)

Extract log

You can use Transaction FTWL (Display Extract Log) to display all archived and deleted data extracts available (see Figure 1.31). In this way, you can quickly check the company codes and fiscal years for which a DART extract has already been created. If the requisite DART extracts for a company code are missing, you can rectify this promptly. It is also important to check if the DART extracts have been stored and backed up in an archive, because if the DART extracts are located in the file system only, they may be inadvertently deleted. Even though you can no longer access deleted data extracts (which were created for test purposes or are incorrect), you can see when this data extract was deleted from the SAP system and by whom (see Figure 1.32).

Figure 1.32 Transaction FTWN (Display View Log)

In Transaction FTWN (Display View Log), you see all of the view files that you have created. You can choose EXPORT TO LOCAL FILE to export the view file as a file for auditing purposes.

> View log

FI control totals and data checksums are created during data extraction. At any time, however, you can also use Transactions FTWE (Verify FI Control Totals), FTWE1 (Verify FI Control Totals), and FTWD (Verify Data Checksums) to retroactively check a data extract for accuracy.

> Checking the DART extract

Configuration

In the CONFIGURATION area, we wish to draw your attention to Transaction FTWP (Data Extracts) for configuring the extraction scope and Transaction FTWSCC (Settings for Company Codes) for creating the data catalog.

You use Transaction FTWP to make important settings in relation to data extraction. Here you determine which data can be extracted (for example, transaction data, master data, or other data) and where these data extracts are to be stored (see Figure 1.33). On the DATA EXTRACTION tab, you can choose between the lower-level TRANSACTION DATA or MASTER DATA tabs. Figure 1.33 shows the TRANSACTION DATA tab. Here you see, in the TRANSACTION DATA area, that all types of data are selected and therefore are to be included in the extraction scope. For example, selecting FINANCE DOCUMENTS (FI) ensures that all data from the tables BKPF and BSEG, which are

> Extracting the maximum scope

required for FI documents, are extracted. Selecting DELIVERY DOCUMENTS (SD), on the other hand, ensures that data from tables `LIKP` and `LIPS` is extracted.

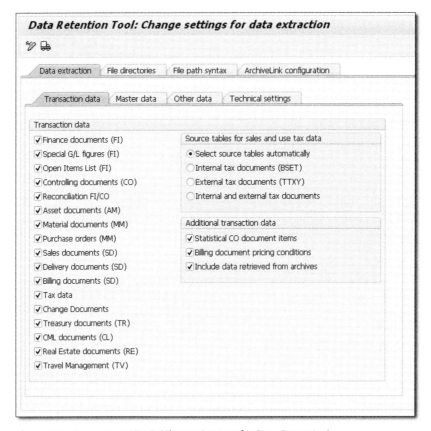

Figure 1.33 Transaction FTWP (Change Settings for Data Extraction)

We recommend that you always extract the maximum scope of data from your SAP system so that your DART extract actually contains all of the data relevant for taxation purposes. In Section 1.7, we will introduce you to various SAP landscapes. In the cases of distributed SAP landscapes, always remember to extract data from all SAP systems so that the DART extract is complete for a company.

Specifying the right data volume

It is best to use Transaction FTWSCC if the country code for the company codes (independent companies in the SAP system) is not US

(United States) or DE (Germany). For companies headquartered in the United States (that is, company codes with the country code US), the US DATA VOLUME data catalog is used in the standard system. For all other company codes except for Germany, the US DATA VOLUME catalog is also used in the standard system. For company codes with country code DE, the DE DATA VOLUME catalog is used. These catalogs were created by the respective SAP user groups, namely DSAG and ASUG. Additional data catalogs for other countries do not exist in the SAP system, nor are they required because the existing data catalogs generally suffice or can be supplemented with minor enhancements to the segments, namely additional fields. You can also use a Customizing entry to determine which data catalog is to be used (see Figure 1.34).

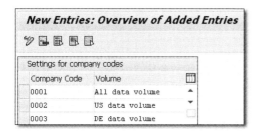

Figure 1.34 Transaction FTWSCC (Settings for Company Codes)

In the VOLUME column, you can also select ALL DATA VOLUME as the data volume for a COMPANY CODE (for example, 0001). In this way, you ensure that your extract contains both the segments defined by the DSAG and the segments defined by the ASUG.

We will not discuss other possible configuration steps (for example, enhancing segments) in detail here because the purpose of this section is to provide an overview of DART. Based on our experience, we can merely advise the following: Check all of the tables in your SAP system that DART will include in an extraction. If any customer-defined fields are assigned to one or more of these tables (for example, table BKPF), you should also add the corresponding customer-defined field (for example, from table BKPF) to the corresponding DART segment (for example, TXW_FI_HD for the FI document header) if there is a possibility that this customer-defined field may be important at a later stage for the electronic tax audit.

Enhancing the data segments

[+] **Always Create the DART Extract before Data Archiving**

You should be aware that DART can only extract data from the database. As soon as data has been archived and deleted, you can no longer generate DART extracts for such data, because DART provides the option to reload data from the archive for a very few information objects only. Therefore, you must always create the DART extract before SAP data archiving and then store the DART extract securely.

[+] **DART in the Context of SAP Data Archiving**

In the context of SAP data archiving, DART extracts are mandatory in the United States. In other countries, you are also increasingly confronted with DART. In summary, you can achieve the following goals with DART:

▶ DART extracts tax-relevant data from tax-relevant tables in accordance with a data catalog.

▶ DART can extract data from the database only (in other words, not from the archive files). Consequently, you must extract the relevant data first and then continue to archive the data in the corresponding tables.

▶ Tax auditors want to see only a subset of the data from the DART extracts. You must therefore define the relevant view queries and then make this information available in SAP Audit format.

1.6.2 Audit Software from IDEA and ACL

In the context of electronic data audits, two audit software products—namely, ACL and IDEA—have made a major impact on the market. Even though these products have no direct link with SAP data archiving, it is ultimately these tools that are used to check the DART extracts from the SAP system for accuracy in the context of tax audits. Next we will briefly introduce you to both products so that you will have some knowledge of the concept behind IDEA and ACL when you hold discussions with the tax department.

Audit software for financial management

IDEA

IDEA was originally developed by CaseWare International Inc. for the Canadian Court of Auditors.

Gap analysis

IDEA provides a number of different analysis functions. At this point, we wish to mention just two of these functions—namely, gap analysis and Benford's Law. You can use *gap analysis* to check documents for completeness. If documents are missing from the dataset, you receive a message to this effect. This may indicate to the tax auditor that documents were either knowingly archived and deleted before the DART extracts were created or there was a system malfunction when the documents were updated and, as a result, the document numbers were not assigned consecutively. The tax auditor will then query this with you.

You can use the *Benford's Law* function to examine irregularities in a dataset. This function detects conspicuous numbers that occur very often in a certain constellation and may have already been examined internally and clarified by the tax audit. Figure 1.35 gives you insight into the software interface. Here you see open invoices for debtors.

Benford's Law

Figure 1.35 IDEA User Interface (Source: www.audicon.de)

Many large enterprises have procured licenses for IDEA and therefore regularly check their tax-relevant data for accuracy before this data is handed over to the external auditor. Smaller enterprises generally do not make such an investment and therefore hand over their tax-relevant

Internal preliminary check

data to an external auditor without first performing a preliminary check. In any case, it is always very good to have the option to perform a preliminary analysis of the data contained in DART in preparation for upcoming tax audits.

ACL

Another worldwide leader in audit software is ACL Services Ltd., which is also based in Canada. ACL Analytics has a similar structure to IDEA and also provides various data analysis functions. However, it goes without saying that the final decision rests with you, if you prefer IDEA or ACL.

1.7 Interfaces in the SAP Landscape

SAP landscapes differ greatly

In most cases, an SAP landscape comprises more than just one development system, test system, and production system. In the following section, we will introduce you to some examples of the typical SAP landscapes used in the course of our SAP data archiving projects. Depending on the configuration of the SAP landscape, a special approach is necessary in the context of data archiving. At the start of the project, it is important to obtain a rough overview of the interfaces that exist between the IT systems. Such interfaces may exist not only between SAP systems but also between SAP and non-SAP systems. In the sections that follow, we will provide some examples of SAP system landscapes and interfaces:

▸ **Simple SAP landscapes**
A simple SAP landscape comprises one development system, one test system, and one production system. This form of system landscape is used in smaller enterprises, in particular. It is the easiest environment in which to implement data archiving. Here the data archiving objects are set up in the development system, tested in the test system, and then used in the production system for archiving purposes.

▸ **Enhanced SAP landscapes**
In an enhanced SAP landscape, another system is used in addition to SAP ERP. This is often, for example, *SAP Business Warehouse* (SAP BW), which is used as a data source for reporting. In this case, data is

regularly uploaded from the SAP ERP system into SAP BW and made available for faster reporting. Therefore, it is important that you, as the person responsible for SAP data archiving, cooperate with the SAP BW team in order to harmonize the procedure. Since a complete upload of data into SAP BW is no longer possible after SAP data archiving, data archiving must not take place before the data is uploaded into the SAP BW system. However, the data already loaded into SAP BW is also available in SAP BW for queries after data archiving has taken place in the source system (SAP ERP).

▸ **Complex SAP landscapes**
In the case of complex SAP landscapes, several SAP production systems are used. For example, you may have an SAP system for Finance and Controlling only, which is linked, by means of an interface, to another SAP system for Production and Logistics (distributed SAP systems). Furthermore, several non-SAP systems may be connected to these SAP systems. In the context of SAP data archiving, such SAP landscapes require a special approach.

Table 1.7 provides a compact overview of the three forms of SAP landscapes described earlier, as well as their interfaces to other SAP and non-SAP systems. In the *Complex SAP Landscapes* column, you see that, in such a scenario, at least four IT systems and the interfaces between each of these systems need to be taken into consideration.

Overview

We recommend that you create a list of all interfaces that exist in your SAP landscape and update it on a regular basis. Critical interfaces and the potential effects of interface malfunctions on business operations are particularly important here. This list should contain not only the main contact person for each interface but also suitable representatives.

Interface checklist

IT Systems Involved (Interfaces)	Simple SAP Landscapes	Enhanced SAP Landscapes	Complex SAP Landscapes
Standard SAP ERP systems	✓	✓	✓
SAP BW		✓	✓
Distributed SAP systems			✓
Non-SAP systems	✓	✓	✓

Table 1.7 Overview of Various SAP Landscapes and the IT Systems Involved (Interfaces)

[Ex] **Data Records for Barcode Labels**

We wish to emphasize the relevance of this procedure by means of a practical example: An enterprise needs barcode labels for the storage and shipment of its products. When placing these products in storage, the enterprise wants the barcode labels to be printed promptly and affixed to the packaging material (cardboard boxes, pallets, and so on). In very exceptional cases (for example, if the affixed barcode labels are lost in the warehouse), the enterprise wants it to be possible to reprint the barcode labels up to six months after placing the products in storage (but prior to shipping the goods), because these barcode labels are important for assigning the goods. In our example, the products can be placed in interim storage for this length of time. A non-SAP system connected to the SAP system is responsible for printing the labels. The relevant data is read from two SAP tables. However, these SAP tables have grown considerably as a result of goods continuously being placed in storage. As a result, it takes a very long time to print the barcode labels. The shipping processes also come to a standstill. By archiving those data records no longer required for the barcode labels of goods that have already been shipped, you can control the growth of both SAP tables again, thus accelerating the shipping processes.

Interface with a major impact

The interface in this example is a critical interface for the following two reasons:

▸ **Slow shipping processes cause transport bottlenecks and delivery delays**
As a result of slow shipping processes, the products cannot be packaged and transported on time. This inevitably results in a delivery delay and general chaos within the shipping department.

▸ **Reprinting barcode labels requires a residence time of six months**
Some products need to be placed in interim storage for a period of up to six months. In special cases, the barcode labels can be reprinted up to six months after a product has been placed in interim storage. Consequently, the SAP tables must, at the very least, contain label data for the past six months. Therefore, the residence time is already predefined. Having a residence time of less than six months would endanger the smooth operation of the shipping business process.

Before you tackle a data archiving project, you should observe the following steps:

▶ Gain an understanding of the interface and SAP landscapes.

▶ Document all interfaces in the SAP landscape.

▶ Specify a main contact person and a representative for each interface.

▶ Define critical interfaces, their impact, and measures.

▶ Adjust SAP data archiving projects to the SAP landscape.

1.8   Parties and Organizations Involved

The IT department should not implement SAP data archiving projects alone. You should involve other important parties and organizations that are essential to the success of a project (see the next section). In particular, we wish to show you which information you require from the parties and organizations involved (from an SAP data archiving perspective) and which interests these parties and organizations pursue.

1.8.1   In-House Parties and Organizations

In the sections that follow, we will first describe the in-house parties and organizations involved in data archiving.

Top Management

Top management plays a very large role in the context of a data archiving project. Depending on the size of the enterprise, this may be the managing director of a medium-sized *limited liability company* (Ltd), a *senior head of department* of a large public limited company (PLC), or another party who has all of the relevant skills and business resources needed to support the project. Since top management has the greatest authority within the project, they can make key decisions and therefore significantly influence the success of the project. In general, top management and the IT department attend strategic meetings together to

Involving top management

discuss the orientation of IT projects for the enterprise. Top management should also be involved in key questions relating to the archiving project (for example, procuring an archive system or investing in SAP ILM software), because these concern a long-term investment.

IT Department

Central role The IT department plays a central role in implementing the data archiving project. Most of the time, the project is initiated by the IT department because it has the best overview of the respective SAP systems and the technical environment. Therefore, the IT department is the first to notice the early signs of deterioration in performance or a rapid increase in database growth.

The SAP experts within the IT department can quickly make specific recommendations in relation to data archiving. Furthermore, the IT department is responsible for providing IT support for the business strategy. The IT strategy must always be coordinated with top management. One example of how the IT strategy can support the business strategy is, for example, using data archiving to reduce costs in relation to hardware and memory space.

User Departments

No success without the involvement of the user department An SAP data archiving project without the involvement of the relevant user departments is inconceivable. Similar to user departments, an SAP system and the SAP data archiving objects are structured according to different SAP components such as Materials Management (MM), Sales and Distribution (SD), Controlling (CO), and Finance (FI). However, some user departments access data from several SAP components. For example, a person in the Controlling user department requires not only information from the CO component but also information from the MM, SD, and FI components.

Therefore, under no circumstances can you avoid consulting with the right parties at meetings with the user departments. The parties representing the user departments also represent the users of your SAP system. In other words, it is these parties who call transactions and enter business processes and business data into the SAP system on a daily basis. Consequently, they also know which data they require and for how long. Alternatively, they may be able to indicate why a particular query executed by them causes system performance to deteriorate.

As a result, the user departments must be involved in good time. Furthermore, their particular requirements in relation to SAP data archiving must be taken into consideration. This is the only way you can also obtain the mandatory approvals for SAP data archiving from the user departments.

Tax Department

The tax department must use the tax-relevant SAP data to satisfy the enterprise's statutory obligation to report tax-relevant data to the tax office. In addition to monthly VAT returns, the annual financial statement is the main focus of their work. Consequently, the tax department is continuously in contact with external parties and organizations. It deals with any requests from the tax office and tax auditors.

SAP data required by the tax department

The tax department also looks after external auditors from the tax office when tax audits take place. They use not only the SAP system but also specialist electronic tools as described in Section 1.6. Therefore, the IT department plays a special role in terms of providing IT support to the tax department. In particular, the tax department and the IT department must communicate about the requirements of the tax auditors in good time and then implement the requirements so that the enterprise does not receive any detrimental tax assessments. Furthermore, an IT employee should always be available to provide information and answer any quick queries that may arise during a tax audit.

The tax department works very closely with the other departments within the enterprise, especially the IT department, the finance department, and top management. If, due to its size, an enterprise does not have a tax department, the finance (accounting) user department will undertake those tasks.

Internal Auditing

In public limited companies, the *internal auditing* (IA) department plays an important function that can be fulfilled by both in-house personnel and, if certain activities are outsourced, by external personnel (for example, an auditing company). Top management is supported by the auditing, check, and monitoring activities of this independent and objective auditing and consulting unit within an enterprise. Its purpose is to continuously improve business processes and to add value. In the area of SAP data archiving, internal auditing can ensure, for example, the reliability and integrity of the information made available. This department can also evaluate the data protection concept.

Legal Department

Most of the time, a separate legal department exists in larger enterprises only. Smaller enterprises use local law firms with the relevant expertise. The legal department can support SAP data archiving through its specialist knowledge of, for example, statutory retention periods or product liability.

Table 1.8 provides an overview of the information that you can obtain from in-house parties and organizations involved in an SAP data archiving project, as well as the interests that they pursue themselves and that you should know.

Internal Parties and Organizations	Contribution to the Project	Interests Pursued
Top management	Decisions in special cases	Success of the entire enterprise
IT department	Recommendations for concepts, proposals for residence times, process analysis	Improve performance, check database growth
User departments	Approval for SAP data archiving	Performance, maintain access quality

Table 1.8 Contribution of Internal Parties and Interests Pursued

Internal Parties and Organizations	Contribution to the Project	Interests Pursued
Tax department	Tax-based effects of SAP data archiving, provision of extracts for the tax audit	Proper creation of tax returns, support for tax auditors
Internal auditing	Independent feedback, suggestions for improvement	Improve business processes, add value
Legal department	Specialist knowledge of the legal situation	Avoid complaints and legal cases

Table 1.8 Contribution of Internal Parties and Interests Pursued (Cont.)

1.8.2 External Parties and Organizations

In the following sections, we will discuss the various external parties and organizations involved in SAP data archiving.

External Auditor

External auditors provide auditing and consulting services. An auditing company must not and should not audit the financial statement of an enterprise while simultaneously acting as a consultant for the enterprise. For this reason alone, it is necessary to clarify what role an external auditor can play in an SAP data archiving project and if another auditing company should undertake the task. Always clarify the relevant details with the auditing company.

External auditors can also advise

The primary task of an external auditor is to audit and test the financial statement created for the enterprise. In the context of a data archiving project, external auditors very often provide support during a quality inspection. They also provide support in international projects in terms of providing the various statutory requirements that relate to data archiving in different countries.

Tax Consultant

If the enterprise does not have its own tax department, tax consultants assume responsibility for the enterprise's statutory obligation to report tax-relevant data to the tax office and are available to answer any tax-related questions. External tax consultants can also advise in-house tax departments.

Similar to an external auditor, a tax consultant can, in the context of SAP data archiving projects, determine the statutory requirements in the various countries and advise the IT department in terms of defining tax-relevant data.

Tax Auditor

Tax auditors from the tax office have the task of checking the figures reported by the enterprise. Several options are available to them. The tax auditor can perform an audit on-site at the enterprise or use appropriate software to audit the tax-relevant data provided by the enterprise. In practice, a combination of both options is frequently used. Tax auditors give the enterprise sufficient notice of an upcoming audit date.

In return, they also expect that they will have sufficient access to the SAP system and data media when the audit commences.

User Groups

Involvement of SAP user groups

SAP user groups have a direct voice to SAP. In the United States, the main organization is the *Americas SAP Users Group* (ASUG). Within this organization, there are various regional chapters and special interest groups (SIGs). In ASUG, SAP data archiving is organized into the *Archiving and Information Lifecycle Management SIG*. This SIG provides an ideal opportunity to exchange information on SAP data archiving with other enterprises both online and at various events.

Having direct contact with the relevant persons responsible at SAP ensures optimum knowledge transfer. Any missing functions within SAP data archiving objects are assigned a priority by the working group and then forwarded directly to SAP in the form of development requests. In recent years, many of these development requests have actually been realized.

Service Provider

External service providers may be involved in SAP data archiving. If an enterprise does not have specialist knowledge of SAP data archiving in-house, it should always enlist the services of an expert. External service providers provide not only consulting services but also support to the IT department (during periodic archiving and by handling support queries from user departments) and the tax department with regard to managing SAP data archiving after the project ends.

Service providers have specialist knowledge

Depending on the size and structure of your enterprise, one central service provider or several local service providers may be involved. Furthermore, SAP data archiving is very often performed by an in-house or external SAP Basis team.

Hardware Provider

For SAP data archiving, the archive medium is, without a doubt, the most importance piece of hardware. In most cases, the hardware provider also supplies the relevant software for managing the archive medium. In real life, you very often have a scenario whereby the hardware provider supplies only the archive medium and another provider supplies the software. The price, quality, and availability of the hardware are important here. As a result of new technical capabilities, some hardware providers also provide memory space on their own servers (*cloud computing*). However, due to statutory and in-house requirements, you must clarify if business data can and should be stored on external servers.

Software Provider

SAP software plays the most important role in SAP data archiving projects. However, it is not the only software that we must take into consideration. Within the tax department, other important software is used for electronic tax audits. The software for the archive medium is also very important in SAP data archiving. For transport management within Logistics, you can also use other software with an interface to the SAP system. Furthermore, other specialist software may be used within production.

Depending on the level of complexity of the SAP landscape, the list of software providers with an interface to the SAP system may be very long. Each piece of software that has a direct impact on SAP data archiving must be analyzed and evaluated in detail. If there are any potential weak points, you can work directly with the software provider to develop a solution.

Overview Table 1.9 provides an overview of essential information and interests pursued by external parties and organizations.

External Parties and Organizations	Information Required for the Project	Interests Pursued
External auditor	Certificate for the financial statement, statutory obligation to retain data	Independent audit and consulting
Tax consultant	Statutory obligation to retain data, definition of tax-relevant data	Correct tax return for the tax office
Tax auditor	Access to the SAP system, data media for the electronic audit	Check figures for accuracy
User groups	Attendance at events, involvement in Internet forums	Support, influence SAP
Service providers	Specialist knowledge of SAP data archiving and SAP data extraction	Consult, support, archive administration
Hardware provider	Select suitable archive media	Archive media and software provider for archive administration
Software provider	Effects of SAP data archiving on software	Sell supplementary software, optimum access to the archive

Table 1.9 Information Required Externally and Interests Pursued

1.9   Summary

In this chapter, we took a close look at the principles and framework conditions of SAP data archiving from various perspectives. You now know the potential sources of error associated with SAP data archiving projects and why it is essential to safeguard the performance of an SAP system. You are now also familiar with the individual phases of ILM and the typical activities within each phase. In this chapter, we also provided a detailed description of the ADK, which is the technological basis for SAP data archiving and the most important transactions. You also obtained a good overview of the laws currently applicable in the United States and internationally. Finally, we introduced you to the IT tools used in electronic tax audits, the various interfaces in an IT landscape, and the parties and organizations involved in SAP data archiving projects.

In the next chapter, we will build on this basic knowledge and take a detailed look at the various storage options available for archive files.

You have different options to store archived data. Technical information, cost considerations, and recommendations for various scenarios support your decision.

2   Storage Options for Archived Data

Storing archive files for legal purposes is vital in an SAP data archiving project. The archive files must be stored on a secure and cost-efficient storage media and retained according to the legally defined retention time. Besides the archive files, you must also store the associated documents, DART extracts, and print lists accordingly. Even if this chapter primarily focuses on archive files, the storage methods discussed here are also suitable for other document types.

Various options are available for storage, which are detailed in Section 2.3. The *ArchiveLink* interface, which is provided by the SAP system, forms the technical basis for data storage. An archive system with Web-DAV function is additionally required if you want to use SAP Information Lifecycle Management (SAP ILM). WebDAV stands for *Web-based Distributed Authoring and Versioning* and is an advanced form of the Hypertext Transfer Protocol (HTTP), which is used to design websites. These two interfaces and their special features with regard to SAP data archiving are outlined in Section 2.1 and Section 2.2. We round this chapter off with a cost analysis for the individual archiving options and a recommendation for various scenarios. They are supposed to help you choose the optimal storage variant for your archive files.

In Figure 2.1, you can see four possible locations for file storage and the various forms of storage media:

Storage locations

▶ **Database**
You can store data in contents tables in the internal database for SAP ERP. Another storage option is the SAP Content Server with one or

more instances of the databases SAP MaxDB or SAP IQ for using the *storage on the database for SAP ILM (external databases)* function. Additional information on this topic is available in Section 2.3.1.

▸ **File system**
The file system is subdivided into the directories (folders) in the file system and the SAP Content Server for managing content repositories in the file system (see Section 2.3.2).

▸ **Archive system**
An external archive system is another option for data storage. In this context, Section 2.3.3 also presents the ArchiveLink and WebDAV interfaces.

▸ **External media**
The fourth storage option involves optical data carriers, such as discs or magnetic tapes, which are primarily used for data backups after archiving (see Section 2.3.4).

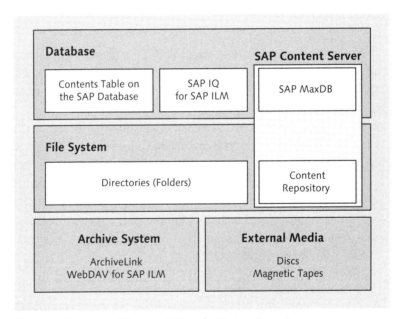

Figure 2.1 Overview of Storage Options for Various Scenarios

These four options reflect the current approach for archiving in enterprises.

2.1   ArchiveLink Interface

The ArchiveLink interface is a service within the SAP NetWeaver Application Server AS ABAP and requires a *content repository* for storage. Content repositories are logical storage areas on the hard disk in which you can store the files in a structured manner. A content repository can be set up for storage in the database, file system, and, particularly, in an archive system. Here it is important that the archive system is certified for the ArchiveLink interface. This ensures the technical communication between the SAP system and the archive system without additional developments. Providers of archive systems have their systems certified for the current version of the ArchiveLink interface at regular intervals. You can use the *SAP Content Server* that is provided by SAP and the ArchiveLink interface for storage in the database or file system. The SAP Content Server is available free of charge, but requires one or more instances of SAP MaxDB or the file system to manage the content repositories. However, SAP recommends not using the SAP Content Server for long-term archiving. Instead an archive system should be deployed. The SAP Content Server is primarily suited for minor amounts of data and short-term storage.

Content repository

By means of ArchiveLink, you can link (inbound and outbound) documents with the corresponding application documents in the SAP system and store them in defined storage areas (content repositories). ArchiveLink can also be utilized for print lists, DART extracts, and archive files in our case. Further in this book, we'll only deal with the storage of archive files using the ArchiveLink interface. Please note that archive files, for example, inbound and outbound documents, DART extracts, and print lists are also referred to as *documents* in the context of ArchiveLink.

Functional scope

Link entries between the documents and the application documents are stored in the link tables defined in Customizing. Link tables manage the reference between the stored documents and the business object in the SAP system. Figure 2.2 illustrates this principle. Without this reference, you can't uniquely identify and find the documents. The link tables assume the role of a bridge between the database and the archive.

Link tables

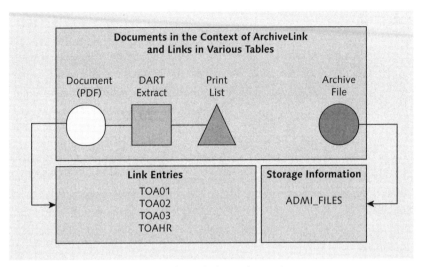

Figure 2.2 Document Types and Links with the ArchiveLink

The following four link tables are provided by default in the SAP system:

- TOA1 (used most frequently)
- TOA2
- TOA3
- TOAHR (reserved for Human Resources)

In most cases, only table TOA1 is used in Customizing. To optimize performance or undo the link between link entries if required, you can distribute the link entries for documents, print lists, and DART extracts to the other two tables TOA2 and TOA3 and use them in Customizing (see also Figure 2.7). This way, you can use table TOA1 for documents, table TOA2 for print lists, and table TOA3 for DART extracts.

Exception for print lists
Table TOADL, however, forms an exception. It is automatically filled in the background explicitly for print lists. You can't select this table directly in Customizing. Instead, you select tables TOA01 or TOA02, for example. During storage, the information is then updated to the print list in table TOADL.

A data record with the fields illustrated in Table 2.1 is created in the link tables for each document to be stored, for example, a PDF file, a print list, or a DART extract.

Field	Remark	Example
CLIENT		100
SAP ARCHIVELINK: OBJECT TYPE OF THE BUSINESS OBJECT	One or more document types exist for an object type.	DRAW (document) or BUS4010 (DART extracts)
SAP ARCHIVELINK: OBJECT ID (OBJECT IDENTIFIER)	Uniquely identifies the object in the SAP system.	Document numbers
CONTENT REPOSITORY IDENTIFICATION	Storage area.	AT
SAP ARCHIVELINK: DOCUMENT ID	Uniquely identifies the object in the content repository.	Document key
DOCUMENT TYPE (DOCUMENT CLASS)	Print list or DART extract.	D01 (ALF) or DART_EXTR (BIN)
SAP ARCHIVELINK: STORAGE DATE	Date on which the entry was generated.	01/01/2014
ARCHIVELINK RESERVE FOR FUTURE APPLICATION CASES	Document class.	ALF or BIN
EXPIRY DATE	Defined based on the retention period. The retention period specifies how many months must pass before you can archive the entry from the link table.	A retention period of one month results in an expiry date of 02/01/2014 if the storage date is 01/01/2014

Table fields

Table 2.1 Examples of Field Content in Link Tables TOA01/02/03

The fields of table TOADL deviate slightly from the fields described in Table 2.1 and are not listed explicitly here.

Another exception exists for the storage information of archive files. Since release 4.6C, this information is not managed in the link tables of

Table for archive files

ArchiveLink, but in table ADMI_FILES (archive files of archiving sessions). Refer to SAP Note 395766 to learn more on this topic. The logic of the interface is identical to the principle of link tables. You can determine the archive file using the document ID in the archive and the content repository. Table 2.2 describes the fields of table ADMI_FILES in detail.

Field	Remark	Example
DOCUMENT	Number of the archiving session	000001
ARCHIV_KEY	Key of an archive file	000001-001IDOC
CREAT_DATE	Creation date of an archive file	08/14/2014
CREAT_TIME	Creation time of the archive file	13:29:45
OBJ_COUNT	Number of objects in an archive file	1
FILE_SIZE	Size of an archive file in byte	Value in byte
FILENAME	File name of the archive file	BC_IDOC_20140814 _132945_0.ARCHIVE
STATUS_OPT	Status of an archive with regard to the storage	Stored
STATUS_FIL	Status of an individual archive file of an archiving session	Deletion complete
COMMENTS	Comment on an archive file	Comments on the archiving session
STATUS_IDX	Status of an archive for index	No index
PATHINTERN	Logical path name	Empty after storage
CREP	Storage location for physical documents	AT
ARCH_DOCID	Document ID of the stored file (ArchiveLink or CMS)	53B233C701A2FF2 E10000003547508F
DELETING	Delete running or scheduled	Empty after deletion

Table 2.2 Fields within ADMI_FILES

File names   You can determine the file name of the archive file in the FILENAME field. You maintained this name in Customizing of the archiving object. After you've stored the file name in a content repository, the system removes it again from this field. Subsequently, the archive file can only be identified using the ID in the ARCH_DOCID field. If you reload the archive file from the archive system to the file system, the system will assign a new deviating file name. The archive file is then temporarily named *RETRIEVED_000001-001IDOC_0*.

To be able to use the ArchiveLink interface, you must perform basic Customizing or check if the corresponding settings have already been made. The following sections describe which settings must be made.

2.1.1 Creating and Maintaining Content Repositories

You can create or maintain content repositories using Transaction OAC0. It makes sense for storage to create several content repositories. You can create them separately according to your requirements. In common practice, separate content repositories are often created for the various retention periods and document classes.

Several repositories

You must at least define the STORAGE TYPE for each content repository. This entry ultimately specifies where to store the archive files. The following two values usually qualify for this purpose:

Storage type

▶ SAP SYSTEM DATABASE

▶ HTTP CONTENT SERVER

You definitely require a contents table if you select SAP SYSTEM DATABASE. This table is also located in the database of the SAP system. If you select HTTP CONTENT SERVER, you must specify, among other things, the address of the external archive server so that you can ensure the communication between the SAP system and the storage. The SAP Content Server and the SAP IQ database also belong to this area. The HTTP CONTENT SERVER is used in most cases.

LOGICAL REPOSITORY, RFC ARCHIVE, and STRUCTURE STORAGE are further options that do not play a significant role within the scope of SAP data archiving.

To maintain a content repository, proceed as follows:

Maintain content repository

1. Call Transaction OAC0.

2. Select a content repository, for example, the first entry FILESYSTEM (available by default) and click on the DETAIL button in the toolbar 🗔 (see Figure 2.3) to view additional properties for this content repository, which is illustrated in Figure 2.4.

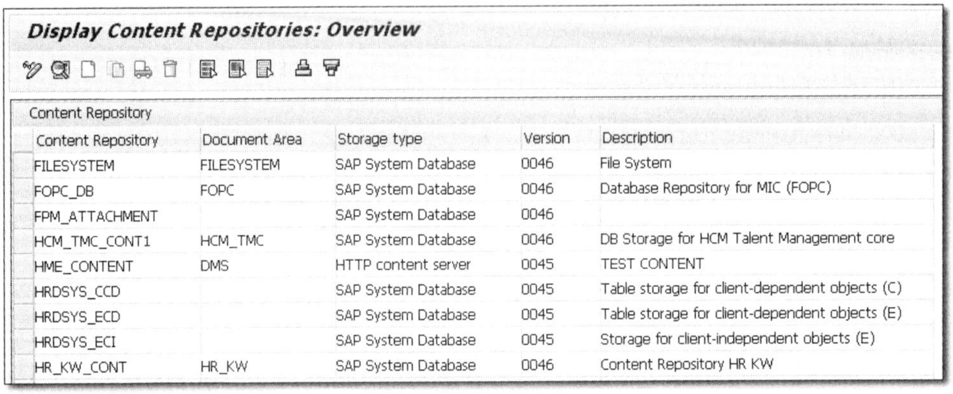

Display Content Repositories: Overview

Content Repository	Document Area	Storage type	Version	Description
FILESYSTEM	FILESYSTEM	SAP System Database	0046	File System
FOPC_DB	FOPC	SAP System Database	0046	Database Repository for MIC (FOPC)
FPM_ATTACHMENT		SAP System Database	0046	
HCM_TMC_CONT1	HCM_TMC	SAP System Database	0046	DB Storage for HCM Talent Management core
HME_CONTENT	DMS	HTTP content server	0045	TEST CONTENT
HRDSYS_CCD		SAP System Database	0045	Table storage for client-dependent objects (C)
HRDSYS_ECD		SAP System Database	0045	Table storage for client-dependent objects (E)
HRDSYS_ECI		SAP System Database	0045	Storage for client-independent objects (E)
HR_KW_CONT	HR_KW	SAP System Database	0046	Content Repository HR KW

Figure 2.3 Overview of Existing Content Repositories in Transaction OAC0

3. In the DOCUMENT AREA field you can see that the documents that are stored in this content repository are managed in the FILE SYSTEM document area. You can view the document area in the Knowledge Provider's Customizing in the SAP system (Transaction SKPR03). Within the scope of SAP data archiving, however, you don't need to maintain any new Customizing entries here. The existing entries in the SAP system are fully sufficient to set up the content repositories to meet the storage's requirements.

[»] **Right Selection of the Document Area**

Table 2.3 provides the most critical entries for storage using ArchiveLink:

▶ To store documents, DART extracts, and print lists, you must use the ARCH-LINK DOCUMENT AREA for your content repository.

▶ The FILESYSTEM DOCUMENT AREA prevents the utilization of this content repository for ArchiveLink.

▶ The content repositories with the ARCHLINK DOCUMENT AREA are stored in table TOAAR. A check takes place when you create links in Transaction OAC3, which specifies if the entered content repository exists in table TOAAR. If this is not the case, you can't create a link, and you must change your content repository to ARCHLINK in the DOCUMENT AREA field.

▶ The DATAARCH DOCUMENT AREA enables you to select a content repository when you are customizing the archiving object in Transaction SARA.

If you leave the document area empty, you can use a content repository both for documents and for archive files, that is, across document types.

Document Area	Description	Comment
ARCHLINK	ArchiveLink	Mandatory
DATAARCH	Data archiving	Mandatory
FILESYSTEM	File system	Unsuitable
–	Empty selection	Optional

Table 2.3 Sample Entries for the Document Area in Transaction SKPR02

Identifying Storage Areas [«]

To determine which documents are stored in which storage areas in the SAP system, you can analyze the link tables with regard to the DOCUMENT CLASS and CONTENT REPOSITORY IDENTIFICATION fields using Transaction TAANA.

4. The SAP SYSTEM DATABASE option is selected in the STORAGE TYPE field. So a CONTENTS TABLE is absolutely required (see Figure 2.4).

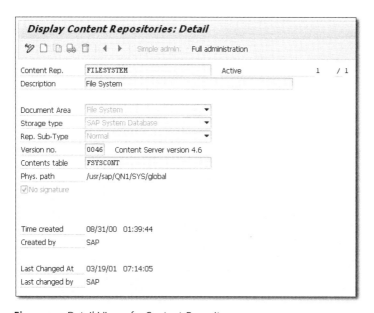

Figure 2.4 Detail View of a Content Repository

5. You can see table FSYSCONT in the CONTENTS TABLE field.

You can also create your own new contents table and use it for your new content repository. In doing so, you must copy and activate the new contents table in Transaction SE11 from the standard SAP table FSY-SCONT or SDOKCONT1.

Can You Use the Content Repository FILESYSTEM for ArchiveLink?

Figure 2.4 shows an example of the already existing FILESYSTEM content repository from the SAP system in which a contents table is used. However, you can't use such a content repository with this configuration for ArchiveLink for two reasons:

▸ There is no two-digit alphanumerical content repository identification.

▸ The document area is not ARCHLINK.

So you can't use existing content repositories with corresponding configuration for ArchiveLink, but you must create new ones.

Create content repository

The following shows how to create an appropriate content repository.

1. Call Transaction OAC0.

2. Use the DISPLAY <-> CHANGE button 🖉 to switch from DISPLAY view to CHANGE mode.

3. Click on the CREATE button 🗋.

4. Enter a two-digit alphanumeric ID in the CONTENT REP. field and a DESCRIPTION (see Figure 2.5).

Figure 2.5 Creating a New Content Repository with the "HTTP Content Server" Storage Type

5. Select DATA ARCHIVING (for archive files) or ARCHIVELINK (for documents) in the DOCUMENT AREA field. You also have the option to leave this field empty so that the content repository can be used for both document areas.

6. Select HTTP CONTENT SERVER in the STORAGE TYPE field.

7. In the VERSIONS NO. field, choose the current version of the content server that you require for the storage system.

8. The HTTP SERVER and HTTP SCRIPT fields are mandatory because the storage type is an HTTP CONTENT SERVER. Here you require the exact address of the server and the directory of the corresponding script.

9. You can adapt the PORT NUMBER and SSL PORT NUMBER if required.

10. After you've completed your entries, you can save the content repository 🖫. Subsequently, your user name will be stored as the creator in the SAP system.

11. Then test the connection to the storage system using the 🖾 button.

12. If not done yet, you must send a certificate to the storage system at least once for each SAP system to ensure smooth communication. To do so, click on the SEND CERTIFICATE button 🖩. The certificate must also be confirmed on the storage system side.

After you've successfully created the content repository in the SAP system and also maintained it identically in the archive system, you can link it with the document types and use it in Transaction OAC3.

Creating Content Repositories for ArchiveLink	[+]

When you set up new content repositories, you should always consider the following questions:

▸ **How many content repositories do you require?**
The number depends on various criteria. In principle, you can either create one content repository for a specific period of time or two content repositories for the same period of time that are separated by document types (for example, archive files and DART extracts).

▸ **How long should the retention period be for each content repository?**
It has proven useful in real life to create several content repositories with different runtimes. It is possible, for example, that you create repositories

with a retention period of one to 15 years. This enables you to distribute the document types to the various content repositories if required.

▶ **How should IDs be assigned?**
The IDs must only comprise two alphanumerical values. For this reason, you should come up with a sound logic so that you can easily allocate the IDs later on.

It is conceivable that you use the first digit in the form of letters to code the regions, business units, or company codes. By means of the second digit of the ID, you can code the retention period in years using numbers (0–9).

There are no limits to your imagination here. It is important, however, that you assign the IDs uniquely if different SAP systems are linked with the storage system.

▶ **Which document areas should be selected?**
To store documents using the ArchiveLink interface, you must set the ARCHLINK DOCUMENT AREA for the content repository or leave the selection field empty.

To store archive files, you must select the DATAARCH DOCUMENT AREA or leave the field empty.

2.1.2 Creating and Maintaining Document Types and Document Classes

Transactions OAC2, OAD2, and OAC3

You can specify the document type and their classes in Transaction OAC2 (see Figure 2.6). D01 is used as the document type and ALF as the document class for print lists. The DART_EXTR document type and the BIN document class (for binary files) are assigned to DART extracts.

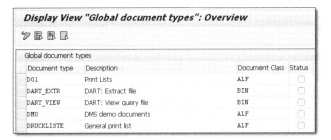

Figure 2.6 Document Types in Transaction OAC2

You can view the document types in Transaction OAC2. The document types and document classes are preset sufficiently in the SAP system so that you should maintain new entries for new customer-specific document types only. This can be required particularly if you want to store an enterprise-specific document and assign a name that is different to the standard documents. Prior to storage, each document (OBJECT TYPE) is assigned to exactly one document class in Transaction OAC3 according to the entries in Customizing (see Figure 2.7).

2.1.3 Creating and Maintaining Links

Object type, document type, content repository, and the link table are ultimately linked in Transaction OAC3. With this link, you ensure that you determine the relevant link table and the content repository for each document to be stored. In Figure 2.7, the content repository with the ID A2 and the table TOA01 link were assigned to the DRAW OBJECT TYPE (document) and the D01 DOCUMENT TYPE (print list). Nevertheless, the SAP system updates table TOADL with information for print lists in the background. This only applies to print lists and is not relevant for other document types.

Display View "Links for Content Repositories": Overview

Links for Content Repositories

ObjectType	Doc. Type	L	Cont.Rep.ID	Link	Retent.Period
BUS4010	DART_EXTR		D3		0
BUS4011	DART_VIEW		D3		0
CERTIFPAYD	HROBWFORM	X	D3	TOAHR	0
DRAW	D01	X	00	TOA01	0
DRAW	DMO	X	A2	TOA01	0
DRAW	DRW	X	A2	TOA01	0
DRAW	PI_CHARGE	X	D3	TOA01	0
EKKO	MEOACKNOWL	X	A2	TOA01	0
EKKO	MEOAGREEM	X	A2	TOA01	0
EKKO	MEOORDER	X	A2	TOA01	0

Figure 2.7 Overview of Links for Content Repositories in Transaction OAC3

In the RETENTION PERIOD column, the value 0 is defined by default. The retention period specifies after how many months the system can archive the entry from the link table (for instance, table TOA01) with the

Retention period

109

SAP data archiving object `ARCHIVELNK` (the link entries of ArchiveLink). The retention period for an SAP data archiving object and the retention periods for the corresponding object types should be identical.

2.2 WebDAV Interface

Enhanced interface
for ILM

Besides the ArchiveLink interface, the WebDAV interface is also required for using SAP ILM and storing archive files. Here storage is possible via an ILM-certified archive system or via the SAP IQ database. For this reason, archive system providers not only need to certify for the ArchiveLink interface but also for the ILM-enhanced WebDAV interface. The ArchiveLink interface is still the only interface required for classic SAP data archiving. Documents are still stored using the ArchiveLink interface if you deploy SAP ILM. References to the link entries of the link table entries (table `TOA*`) are generated by ArchiveLink in the WebDAV environment.

New functions

You may ask yourself why you need a new interface and technology. We'd like to answer this question by describing its new functions and options in the following sections.

2.2.1 Metadata

Properties

Metadata contains information about information. In the WebDAV environment, this metadata is also referred to as *properties*. You can supplement the stored archive files with metadata by means of the WebDAV interface. Among others, the following metadata is provided within the scope of ILM:

- ▶ Minimal retention period
- ▶ Maximum retention period
- ▶ Deletion lock

Metadata help you to control the lifecycle of a stored archive file more efficiently and individually. With the classic storage in a content repository via ArchiveLink, the retention period only applies generally across all archive files that are stored in a content repository. To enable storage according to the ILM principle, the archive system must be able to understand and apply such metadata.

2.2.2 Archive Hierarchy

Another important function that is available in the ILM-enhanced Web-DAV interface is the mapping of an archive hierarchy. You can imagine an archive hierarchy as a directory with many subfolders. These subfolders are also referred to as *hierarchy nodes*.

File structure with hierarchy nodes

You can call an archive hierarchy in SAP ILM using the *ILM Store Browser* function. This tool provides you with a full overview of the files stored in the archive and you can quickly view the details of the metadata.

ILM Store Browser

This hierarchy is built as a folder structure starting with the system ID, client, and right through to the following lowest hierarchy nodes:

▸ AD (archived data)

▸ SN (snapshots of data that is still open and cannot be archived)

▸ AL (documents)

▸ DL (print lists)

You can transfer specific properties, for example, the start and end of the retention period for each hierarchy node or archive file or document contained therein. If you store archive files or documents using SAP ILM, the relevant information is stored in the corresponding directories within this archive hierarchy. The archive hierarchy thus contains the management entries both for structured information in the AD (archive files) and SN (snapshots) nodes and for unstructured information in the AL (documents, attachments) and DL (print lists) nodes, the latter in the form of links from the ArchiveLink interface. Unstructured information (documents, attachments, and print lists) is stored using the ArchiveLink interface even if SAP ILM is deployed. The special feature of the archive hierarchy is that unstructured data is managed together with the structured data and also inherits its metadata although two different interfaces are used. Figure 2.8 illustrates the structure of the hierarchy.

Archive Files and Snapshots

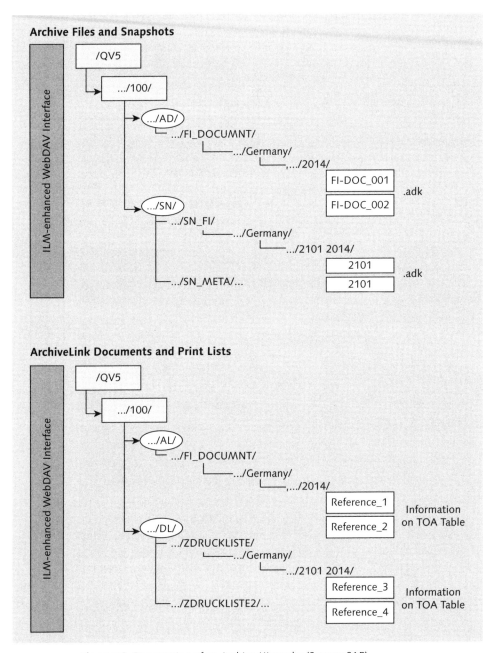

ArchiveLink Documents and Print Lists

Figure 2.8 Presentation of an Archive Hierarchy (Source: SAP)

If you use the WebDAV interface, archive files are stored and managed
as resources using a separate *Uniform Resource Identifier* (URI). A URI is
a unique address of the archive file and the links to the documents in the
archive (white boxes in Figure 2.8). This principle facilitates special
functions for searching and destroying archive files and documents.

Chapter 8 provides concrete examples to describe further specifics and
how to use an ILM-enabled WebDAV storage for SAP ILM.

2.3   Data Storage Locations

You can choose from various locations to store your data. Technical
progress always requires new storage options. In real life, it is almost
impossible to categorize one of the options as the absolutely best option.
One option is ideal for one enterprise, but not for another one. So our
goal should be to define the optimal retention strategy from the myriad
of possible storage locations for your specific SAP data archiving project
and the respective archiving scenario.

To simplify the decision-making process, you should evaluate each storage option based on the following criteria:

▸ Storage security

▸ Access performance and quality

▸ Technology

We'll consider costs separately in Section 2.4, as another important cri-
terion.

2.3.1   Storage in the Database

Storage in the database can be made with two approaches:

▸ **Contents table**
  On the one hand, it is possible to generate a contents table from the
  database of the SAP ERP system and store documents in the contents
  table. When you create a new contents table in Transaction SE11, you
  can use the standard SAP tables `FSYSCONT` or `SDOKCONT1` as templates.
  After you've copied the new table, you only need to activate it.

Storage in the contents table, however, should not replace an archive system. The contents table is very well suited for a low number of documents. If the number of documents to be generated is higher, you should deploy an archive system in order to avoid putting too much load on the SAP system. A contents table is not suited to store archive files and DART extracts with a size of several gigabytes. For this reason, we consider this option only as a storage for a few documents with little memory requirement, for example, in the form of PDF files. Please also refer to SAP Note 595563 (Database Storage for ArchiveLink).

▶ **ILM database storage**
On the other hand, secondary external databases can be used for storage. As mentioned in the introduction of this chapter, you can use an instance of the SAP MaxDB with the SAP Content Server.

In addition, a new option, SAP NetWeaver 7.4, exists for SAP ILM to also store archive files in a separate secondary analytical database (*data warehouse*). This new function called *ILM database storage* is only possible if you deploy the SAP IQ database (formerly SAP Sybase IQ).

Column-based database
The SAP IQ database is based on technology other than that used for the traditional relational databases. Although the data is also stored on hard disks, access is not line-based, but column-based. This column-based technology is also used for SAP HANA. In contrast to SAP IQ, however, SAP HANA doesn't use any hard disks as storage media but very fast memories (in-memory) to further boost performance. Chapter 9 provides more details on these trends.

SAP IQ promises better performance
In SAP IQ, the interface standard WebDAV is deployed to transfer all important information to the archive file when it is stored. In the case of ILM database storage, the data still remains in the SAP landscape after data archiving. This approach can be one reason for enterprises to switch from classic SAP data archiving to SAP ILM. Additionally, SAP IQ can also be used for SAP BW as a *nearline storage* (NLS). This way, you only have one storage for two application cases. Besides the archive files, you can also store archive information structures on SAP IQ. This additionally relieves the SAP system database. A Guinness world record was achieved with SAP IQ Version 16 for loading and indexing large amounts of data (big data). SAP IQ thus provides performance that is better compared with the storage of a traditional archive system.

2.3.2   Storage in the File System

Archive files are always stored in a directory on the SAP system's file system   Exchange directory
first. In this context, this directory is often referred to as *exchange directory*.
So an exchange directory is a temporary storage location in the file system
while archive data is transported to the archive system. But what happens
if you don't want to use an archive system for SAP data archiving but only
have a file system for storage? In this case, the storage in the file system is
no longer an intermediate stop but the final destination for your archive
files. So the file system is used as a final storage option.

Storing Archive Files in Any Directory   [Ex]

Chapter 1, Section 1.4.5 described how to define physical path names using
Transaction FILE. This way, you may store the archive files of an archiving
object in a directory that is specifically designated for this purpose.

Let's assume, for example, you want to archive data using the SAP data
archiving objects RV_LIKP (deliveries) and BC_SBAL (application logs). Separate subdirectories and module levels are supposed to be created and used
for these two archiving objects. In this case, you can set the directory structure in all SAP systems according to this logic:

1. Create DIR_ARCHIV directory as the first level:
   ▸ /Archive

2. As the second level, create subdirectories for each system ID:
   ▸ /Archive/P01
   ▸ /Archive/Q01
   ▸ /Archive/E01

3. On the third level, you can split the subdirectories by clients:
   ▸ /Archive/P01/100
   ▸ /Archive/P01/200

4. As the fourth level, you can create additional subdirectories for the SAP
   components:
   ▸ /Archive/P01/100/SD
   ▸ /Archive/P01/100/BC

The corresponding physical path name must therefore read as follows:

/Archive/<SYSID>/<CLIENT>/<PARAM_1>/<FILENAME>

The following steps are necessary to use the file system for storing   Set up file system
archive files: for storage

1. Initially, create all directories required in the file system. Depending on the operating system used (for example, Unix or Windows), you must follow different procedures. It is useful to get support from the SAP Basis team that can provide the required knowledge of the operating system used. Create a folder structure as described in the example box.

2. After you've created the directories in the file system, you must create them analogously in the SAP system using Transaction AL11. Here it is important that you create the directories in all SAP systems and make sure that the correct system ID is used so that the directories can be used during SAP data archiving.

3. In the physical path name's Customizing in Transaction FILE, you must check whether or not its structure fully corresponds with directories that have already been created. Also check in the SAP data archiving objects Customizing in Transaction SARA to determine if the correct logical file names have been defined. This is important because the physical path name is ultimately derived from these file names.

4. Users and administrators can have different authorizations both in the SAP system and at the file system level. If archive files have been stored in the file system, you must therefore check and adapt the authorizations to ensure that it is not possible to manipulate or accidentally delete archive files. Otherwise, revision security is no longer provided.

[+] **Creating Backups**

You must protect archive files in the file system. The best way to achieve this is to create corresponding backups on external media after each archiving session. You ideally keep these backups in multiple copies at different locations under appropriate conditions.

In real life, storage in the file system is a very common option. You can ensure revision security by taking appropriate measures, for example, adapting authorizations of users and administrators and regular backups of archive files on external media after each archiving session.

2.3.3 Storage in the Archive System

Revision security and certification

In real life, using an external archive system is by far the most frequently used option for storing archive files. Numerous manufacturers and providers of storage media and archiving solutions have specialized on SAP data archiving and are certified by SAP. The interfaces, ArchiveLink and WebDAV, are always available for a certified archive system. Additionally, the archive systems are advertised as *audit-proof* to emphasize that the archive system fully meets legal requirements. For example, premature deletion of stored archive files before the defined period has expired is not possible with these archive systems.

Selecting an Archive System Provider	[«]
Selecting an appropriate archive system is not the subject matter of this section. The criteria of procurement are very versatile and can only be defined and evaluated by you. Rather, we'd like to discuss the specific features of the archive system as a storage option.	

Enterprise Information Management

In most enterprises, an archive system is deployed to store all enterprise-wide critical information (data, files, documents, emails, etc.). In this context, this is also referred to as *SAP Enterprise Information Management (SAP EIM)*—a topic that is allocated to Information Lifecycle Management. So storing archive files from an SAP system is only one of many different scenarios within SAP EIM. Enterprises usually use further IT systems in addition to their SAP system. These systems also contain information objects that must be preserved for legal reasons and must be stored in the same or a separate archive using appropriate procedures.

Content repository in the archive system

When you set up a content repository for storing archive files in the SAP system, you must also set up a corresponding content repository in the archive system. You must record the link between the two repositories in a mapping table of the archive system. The lifecycle of the stored archive files in a content repository is managed exclusively in the archive system. The SAP system can only manage the lifecycle of the link entries in accordance with the retention time specified in Customizing.

Connection to the SAP system

An important prerequisite for using the archive system is the technical connection to the SAP system. Here certificates must mutually be exchanged between and installed on the SAP system and the archive system to ensure smooth communication. Usually, this connection only needs to be set up once when you create the first content repository.

In Section 2.1.1, you learned how to test this connection to the archive system and send a certificate. If no certificates have been deposited in the SAP system at all, you must first import the corresponding certificate lists in Transaction STRUST (Trust Manager). You must then restart the Internet Communication Manager in Transaction SMICM (ICM Monitor).

We can tell from our own experience gained in customer projects that the storage of archive data in an archive system has established itself in practical use and is first choice for enterprises when it comes to storage of archive files.

2.3.4　Using External Optical Storage Media

Besides the archive system, other very cost-efficient external storage media are available on the market that are partially also used in private solutions. These include, among other things, external hard disks, USB flash drives, and optical data carriers, such as discs and magnetic tapes. For data and revision security reasons, however, the only media that qualify for an SAP data archiving project are writable only once. We'll take a look at discs and magnet types as a small selection of options, because experience has shown that enterprises use these two external media for special scenarios.

Discs

Let's first take a look at write-once discs, for example, a CD (compact disc), a DVD (digital versatile disc), or a BD (Blu-Ray Disc). These discs are marked with the addition *recordable* or *R* to emphasize the property of once-only writability. Table 2.4 shows an overview of commonly used disc formats and their typical properties.

Property	CD	DVD/HD DVD	BD
Average lifetime	5–10 years	10 years	30–50 years
Capacity per disc	540–900 MB	min. 4.7 GB/ min. 15 GB	min. 25 GB

Table 2.4 Common Discs and Their Properties

Technological development continuously advances in the area of discs. Among others, the HVD (holographic versatile disc), with a capacity in the range of terabytes, was introduced as the successor of BD. Many manufacturers are working on placing the next generation of BDs on the market. So in the future, discs will exhibit an ever-increasing capacity and longer average lifetime. Particularly, BDs with a longer than average lifetime and storage capacity foster the idea in some IT departments to take advantage of this technology, which is also within the scope of SAP data archiving.

Technical further development

Using a BD for Data Archiving

[Ex]

An IT employee at a US enterprise had already started with the archiving of a technical SAP data archiving object BC_SBAL (application logs) when suddenly the tables became extremely large and soon occupied most of the memory in the database. However, no archive system was available for storage. The IT employee therefore came up with the idea of burning the archive files on BD and retaining them in the IT department. He believed that he could delete the archive files from the corresponding directories in the file system after burning because hardly anyone ever accessed this data. In the short run, the IT employee was able to celebrate a success with this measure. The database's growth could be reduced. The database's memory didn't have to be enhanced for several months. However, he didn't consider many minor, yet important, details that can result in more severe problems for the enterprise in the long term:

► There was no coordination with the user department and the tax or legal department as to how long the residence time would be set and which retention period was required in the various countries.

► Archive access in accordance with the user departments' requirements was not taken into account and was not set up in the SAP system. Because the archive files were also deleted from the file system, users could only access the data on the database.

► The BDs' storage location was not secure enough, and colleagues were not informed sufficiently about the actual location. Keeping an additional copy at a separate location would have been more secure.

Section 2.5 provides a detailed recommendation for this scenario.

You should always consider the following points when using the various discs:

Rules for archiving on discs

- Discs require manual administration, documentation, and management.
- You must ensure secure storage of discs in appropriate rooms and under suitable conditions; otherwise, you considerably minimize the lifetime of the data carriers.
- For revision reasons, you must only use once-writable blank discs.
- Discs are frequently touched by hands and must by no means be scratched or soiled; otherwise, they may no longer be read.
- Discs are only used for data backup measures. Direct access to the archive files from the SAP system is not possible.

Using Discs within the Scope of Electronic Tax Inspections
Using DART

Within the scope of electronic tax inspections, auditors often request excerpts of specific tables (views) from the SAP system. In real life, there are many options to provide these views to tax auditors. If the tax auditors don't conduct the check personally at the enterprise and can't access the view files, you can burn them on a discs and provide them to the tax auditors.

Magnetic Tapes

Magnetic tapes are another medium for storage. They are frequently used in real life, and magnetic tapes are ideal media for storage because of a lifetime of approximately thirty years. Even if this involves a rather old technology, market leaders, such as HP, IBM, Fujifilm, and Sony, continuously work on new options to improve this technology. In May 2014, for example, Fujifilm and IBM introduced a prototype with 154 TB on LTO (Linear Tape-Open), which they developed jointly. This corresponds to a 62-fold capacity of today's magnetic tape storage cassette of this sixth generation LTO6.

[Ex] **Using Magnetic Tapes for Data Archiving**

We'd also like to share a real-life example for using magnetic tapes: Another US enterprise faced the challenge of starting SAP data archiving for its foreign enterprise. An archive system for storage was not available, and procurement was not possible in the short term. Here special focus was on archiving objects that must be preserved for legal reasons, for instance, RV_LIKP (deliveries) or FI_DOCUMNT (FI documents). The enterprise decided to keep archive files in the file system after archiving and to additionally back them up on magnetic tapes, because the relevant technology was already available at the foreign enterprise. So the magnetic tapes were primarily used as a data backup measure, because possible loss of archive files from the file system had to be prevented by all means.

You must always consider the following points when using magnetic tapes:

Rules for archiving on magnetic tapes

▸ Magnetic tapes require manual administration, documentation, and management.

▸ You must ensure secure storage of magnetic tapes in appropriate rooms and under suitable conditions; otherwise, you considerably minimize the lifetime of the magnetic tapes.

▸ For revision reasons, you must only use once-writable magnetic tapes.

▸ Magnetic tapes are primarily used for data backup measures. Direct access to the archive files from the SAP system is not possible.

Restricted Access to Archive Files When Using External Media (Discs and Magnetic Tapes) [«]

Magnetic tapes and discs provide very cost-efficient options for storing archive files. However, the two media are rather suited for data backup measures, because no read access on magnetic tapes or discs is possible from the SAP system and thus you cannot access the archive files. If you want to access the archive files, you must first copy them to the corresponding directories of the SAP system's file system and you must not remove them from the file system.

2.4   Cost Considerations

Costs arise in different areas within the scope of an SAP data archiving project. Compared with personnel costs, the costs for storage play a rather minor role, because they only represent a fraction of the overall project costs.

Costs depend on
the amount of data

Costs can vary considerably depending on which storage option and scenario you choose. To calculate the costs, however, it is important to provide an estimate about the amount of data that is expected to be archived. The general rule of thumb for archiving objects is:

If the amount of data to be archived is 10 GB, you generate approximately 2 GB of archive files. This corresponds to a compression of about 80%. So if you delete 10 GB from the database, you simultaneously generate 2 GB of archive files, which you must store again. Particularly, a compression rate that is set too low or too high will result in unnecessary additional costs later on. If you provide insufficient storage space and more archive files are generated, you cannot store them immediately, but must first extend the storage space. If you generated fewer archive files than expected and allowed for too much storage space, you must pay for the unused storage space. So you must make an important decision based on an assumption.

Example of cost
evaluation

In real life, the storage space required is generously calculated and provided in the long term. The idea behind it is the following: due to regular data archiving sessions, new archive files are created and stored on a continuous basis. The storage space is not supposed to be extended too frequently, because each extension of the storage space also entails personnel costs. Based on the cost items, licenses, maintenance, hardware, and personnel, which only refer to the storage of archive files, Table 2.5 provides a rough evaluation using school grades. An A+ (excellent) corresponds to negligible or no costs, and an F (failure) corresponds to highest costs.

Cost Item	Storage in the Database	Storage in the File System	Storage in the Archive System	Usage of External Media
Licenses	A+	A+	D	A+
Maintenance	A+	A+	B	A+
Hardware	D	C	A+	A+
Personnel	A+	B	B	D
Average	A	A	B	A

Table 2.5 Grading of Cost Items By Storage Option

License and maintenance fees are incurred only for storage in the archive   Cost items
system. They may differ depending on the manufacturer. Very high costs
arise particularly for group licenses. Maintenance is then calculated based
on a predefined percentage of the license costs. No costs are incurred for
these two items if you store in the database, in the file system, or on external media. But if you use SAP IQ for ILM database storage, additional costs
may arise for software when you store in the database.

The storage space in the database is the most expensive investment in
terms of hardware. Here you deploy high-availability storage and several system copies of the live system exist. In comparison, the storage in
the file system is somewhat more cost-efficient, because the system copies require less storage space. Archive systems and external media incur
the lowest costs per gigabyte. Using external media, however, involves
a very high employment of staff for administration, which can offset the
savings in the areas of hardware, maintenance, and licenses. In summary, there are no real winners or losers when you consider the costs.
Even if the storage in the archive system received a slightly poorer
grade of B due to the simple evaluation that is based on the cost items of
Table 2.5, it is still the best choice for storage in enterprises. Base your
individual decision on the frequency of archiving and the amount of
data. In the following section, we provide a summary of all critical factors and our personal recommendations for storage strategies in different scenarios.

2.5   Recommendations for Storage Strategies

We've faced many different storage strategies during SAP data archiving
projects that we supervised at various enterprises. There are many pros
and cons for every option depending on the enterprise's requirements
and situation. In this section, we'd like to present five classic scenarios and
report which decision enterprises made under the given conditions. These
examples are not best practice recommendations but rather reflect individual decisions from real life. You can use these examples as a basis when
you define and implement your own storage strategy.

Questions
for a storage
strategy The following points are important when defining a storage strategy:

▸ What is the residence time for the respective SAP archiving object on the database?

▸ Is the data to be archived relevant for inspection, and when does the inspection take place?

▸ Might the data that is to be archived be required for other purposes, for example, legal disputes, after inspections?

▸ What is the legal retention period?

The access frequency and probability of access after data archiving are determined based on these points. On this basis, you can define an optimal storage strategy.

Example In Table 2.6, we answer these questions for two SAP data archiving objects. The example is supposed to illustrate the decision-making process.

Archiving Object	RV_LIKP (Deliveries)	BC_SBAL (Application Log)
Residence time	18 months	3 months
Relevance for inspection	Yes	No
Inspection period	5 years	Not relevant
Relevance for legal disputes	No	No
Retention period	10 years	10 years
Access frequency and probability	Frequently up to 5 years	Frequently up to 3 months

Table 2.6 Example of Selecting the Optimal Storage Strategy

Both SAP data archiving objects have a retention period of ten years. However, they have different residence times. The relevant user department wants to access the delivery data directly on the database for a longer period of time before the data is archived (residence time). Also within the scope of inspections, for example, customs inspections, direct access to delivery data is supposed to be possible for up to five years after archiving. Although the application logs have the same retention period, they become less important three months after archiving so that access to the archive is required less frequently. In real life, there are many application logs that don't need to be archived at all and can be deleted immediately after their validity expires. In our example, we assume that the application logs, must be preserved for legal reasons and have been classified accordingly. Archived application logs are retrieved in very rare cases only within the scope of inspections or legal disputes. Using these two SAP data archiving objects as examples, we can evaluate the following five scenarios.

Scenario 1: Storage in the Database

Our first sample enterprise doesn't have an archive system and doesn't plan to acquire one. Storage in the file system or data backup on optical data carriers for archive files is not in the focus either. The enterprise rather opted to deploy SAP ILM in connection with the secondary database SAP IQ and uses the new function of the ILM database storage for archive files. This technological investment is supposed to be state of the art. At the same time, the enterprise uses the SAP IQ database for Business Warehouse. The enterprise thus assumes a leading role. For this reason, the evaluation must be made based on assumptions. In contrast to archive files that are stored on SAP IQ, the documents must still be stored in contents tables on the primary database of the SAP system.

ILM database storage

| Pros and Cons of Scenario 1 | |

Deciding for scenario 1 can involve the following pros and cons:

- Pros:
  - Very fast access to archive files is possible, because they are stored within the SAP environment.
  - No external archive system and no external media are used, which can lead to cost savings.
- Cons:
  - The scenario is not suited for storing documents. For this reason, you still require content tables on the SAP system database or an archive system.

> ▶ At present, SAP ILM only supports the SAP IQ database, which SAP purchased with the acquisition of Sybase. This database is not yet commonly used in enterprises. For this reason, you must consider the additional costs for SAP IQ against alternative storage options.

Fast access relevant for business?

Let's use the two archiving objects RV_LIKP (deliveries) and BC_SBAL (application logs) as examples again, because archiving objects are used not only within the scope of classic data archiving but also for SAP ILM. A significant benefit of this procedure is that SAP ILM database storage allows for very fast access to deliveries, which still need to be accessed frequently after archiving. Because application logs hardly ever need to be accessed, this argument is less important for this archiving object. You should therefore check with your enterprise how important fast access to archived data is so that your business-relevant processes run smoothly.

Necessary investment

This database storage scenario definitely requires the usage of SAP ILM and new database software. For this reason, this scenario is not an alternative for every enterprise, especially in the short term. Our personal recommendation is to not select this scenario if you use classic SAP data archiving in your enterprise and you don't plan to switch to SAP ILM or even invest in new database software. But if you already use SAP ILM or plan to implement this solution, this scenario is a good opportunity, which entails benefits in the area of access speed, system simplification, and cost savings.

Scenario 2: Storage in the File System

Low amount of data, simple system landscape

The enterprise of scenario 2 also has no archive system available and doesn't plan to implement one. Data backup on external data carriers is not in the focus either. Archive files are to be stored in the file system without additional costs, because the amount of data to be archived will be low. The enterprise rules out any risk that the archive files are manipulated by renaming, for example, or that data could get lost in the file system because the number of users is manageable and authorizations for accessing files are granted to a few experienced IT employees only. These framework conditions exist only in rare cases in real life and usually for smaller enterprises with small amounts of data and a simple system landscape.

Pros and Cons of Scenario 2

Deciding for scenario 2 can involve the following pros and cons:

▶ Pros:

  ▶ Very fast access to archive files is possible, because they are available directly in the file system.

  ▶ No archive system and no external media are used, which can lead to considerable cost savings.

▶ Cons:

  ▶ Storage space in the file system can be extended to a limited extent only and is considerably more expensive than alternative storage media.

  ▶ Only authorized users may access the file system in order to not jeopardize data security.

  ▶ Checking and possible adapting authorizations involves additional personnel costs.

  ▶ A missing backup jeopardizes the revision security of data!

If you archive data as described in this scenario, the missing data backup potentially risks revision security. Let's take a closer look at this aspect based on our two sample archiving objects, RV_LIKP (deliveries) and BC_SBAL (application logs). The application logs are not relevant for inspection and files are hardly ever accessed after a few months. But if the archive files for the deliveries get lost, the user department can't continue with their work, because access to archived data is still required frequently within a period of five years. Moreover, auditors cannot access this data any longer. So the enterprise quickly faces a major problem.

Consider revision and access relevance

Although the enterprise can save time and money for data backup, they must still weigh the benefits against the risks in terms of revision security. For this reason, we most strongly advise you against implementing this scenario in your enterprise. You should not save money at the wrong places. Only for data that is not relevant for revision and access may you consider this scenario. Scenario 3, which is described in the following section, is a better alternative.

Scenario 3: Storage in the File System and Data Backup on Optical Data Carriers (Discs or Magnetic Tapes)

The enterprise of the third scenario doesn't have an archive system either and doesn't plan to implement one. It stores the archive files in

More secure variant

the file system but additionally uses optical data carriers for data backup to protect itself against possible manipulations or loss of archive files. Scenario 3 is thus the secure variant of scenario 2. Archived data from the file system is backed up on optical data carriers, such as discs or magnetic tapes, after each archiving session. In practical use, this scenario is implemented both in smaller enterprises and in very large corporations.

[◉]

Pros and Cons of Scenario 3

Deciding for scenario 3 can involve the following pros and cons:

▸ Pros:
  ▸ Very fast access to archive files is possible because they are available directly in the file system.
  ▸ No archive system is used, which can result in cost savings.
  ▸ Optical data carriers are significantly more cost-efficient than an archive system.
  ▸ Additional data backups ensure higher security storing archive files in the file system.

▸ Cons:
  ▸ Storage space in the file system can be extended to a limited extent only and is considerably more expensive than alternative storage media.
  ▸ Only authorized users may access the file system so as not to jeopardize data security.
  ▸ Manual activities by administrator are required for data backup on optical data carriers.
  ▸ The administration of optical data carriers also requires personnel and is thus cost intensive.

Minimize personnel costs

The backup scenario helps to ensure that the archive files that must be preserved for legal reasons (in our example deliveries and application logs) can't be manipulated or lost. This guarantees revision security, which is required by law within the scope of archiving. In order to reduce the most significant disadvantage of this scenario—personnel-intensive manual tasks—our recommendation is to archive once per year and then directly back up the archive files. If you archive at shorter intervals, for example, quarterly or monthly, you must create a backup four to twelve times per year.

Scenario 4: Storage in an Archive System

In contrast to the enterprises presented so far, the enterprise of scenario 4 already has an archive system that can be used for storing archived data. This archive system is certified for SAP data archiving. In practical use, a certified archive system is the most commonly used scenario and is highly appreciated by many enterprises.

Pros and Cons of Scenario 4	[◉]

Deciding for scenario 4 can involve the following pros and cons:

► Pros:

  ► An archive system is a secure, scalable, and stable storage medium.

  ► Storage space can be extended with relatively low costs.

  ► Many archive system providers are certified by SAP.

  ► The certified archive systems support both ArchiveLink and WebDAV interfaces.

► Cons:

  ► Usually, high one-time procurement costs are incurred for licenses and hardware for the archive system. Additionally, current license fees may also apply depending on the provider.

  ► Maintenance costs arise during the running operation of the archive system.

  ► Access to data in the archive system is slower than to data in a file system.

In practical use, an archive system is not only used for storing archive files. Documents that have been generated in the SAP system as well as inbound (for instance, scanned) documents must also be retained securely and linked with the corresponding data records. For this reason, an archive system is the first choice for enterprises when it comes to the storage of data and documents that must be preserved for legal reasons. In general, an archive system is equally suited for all archiving objects with long retention periods and for our sample objects, RV_LIKP (deliveries) and BC_SBAL (application logs). However, archived data from the SAP system sometimes cannot be accessed with the desired speed. Scenario 5, which is discussed in the next section, is well suited to remedy this problem.

Regular archiving

If you must archive at weekly or monthly intervals due to high data growth in your SAP system, an archive system is the best choice. You must make Customizing settings in your SAP system once and can then store the archive files automatically in the desired content repository. Moreover, you don't need to worry about manual backups on optical data carriers. In the long run, your investment in an archive server certainly amortizes after just a few years.

Scenario 5: Storage in a File System (and in an Archive System)

Just like the enterprise of scenario 4, the enterprise of our last example already deploys an archive system. In contrast to the enterprise of scenario 4, however, it attaches great importance on faster access to archived data. For this reason, this enterprise copied the archived data from the archive system and additionally provided it in the file system for faster access.

[◉] **Pros and Cons of Scenario 5**

Deciding for scenario 5 can involve the following pros and cons:

▶ Pros:
- ▶ Very fast access to archive files is possible, because they are accessed in the file system and not directly in the archive system.
- ▶ The archive system also represents a secure, scalable, and stable storage medium for the enterprise.
- ▶ Storage space can be extended with relatively low costs.
- ▶ Many archive system providers are certified by SAP.
- ▶ These archive systems support the ArchiveLink and WebDAV interface.

▶ Cons:
- ▶ The archive files are available redundantly in the archive and in the file system.
- ▶ Manual work of the administrator is required to copy the archive files from the archive system and then delete them from the file system if they no longer need to be accessed.
- ▶ An archive system usually requires high one-time procurement costs (licenses).
- ▶ Furthermore, you must add running operating costs (maintenance fees).

In practical use, scenario 5 is frequently used if you require evaluations of archive data, which take too long or are canceled. In these cases, you should therefore first recheck the residence time specified for the SAP data archiving object and the selection criteria selected by the users for evaluation. In practice, the residence time is often too short and therefore frequently requires an archive access, which then results in long runtimes or cancellations. We have noted that many users have not adapted their selection templates yet and thus unintentionally selected data that is already several years old.

Check reasons for long runtimes

You should note that archive files of scenario 5 exist redundantly in the file system and in the archive system and therefore occupy some of the storage space in the file system you freed up previously. For this reason, you should consider scenario 5 only if you can exclude the two causes mentioned and can no longer counteract the long runtimes by increasing the residence time or adapting the selection criteria.

> **Decision-Making Process for Storage** [+]
>
> To make a sound decision about the available storage options, you should list your individual requirements in detail and evaluate them. In general, all options presented in this section are conceivable as described or can also be combined. For example, you can use an archive system (scenario 4) and only copy the archive files for the SAP archiving object FI_DOCUMNT (FI documents) to the file system (scenario 5) to enable faster access to these files. Or you can store all archive files in the file system (scenario 2) and only back up critical archive files to external media (scenario 3).

2.6 Summary

In practice, various options are feasible and possible for storing your archive files. Selecting the optimal method depends on the data volume that you want to archive on a regular basis. Enterprise and database size are highly significant in this context. Primarily larger enterprises usually deploy an archive system for storage. These enterprises face high data growth so that an archive system most likely meets their requirements. In the ideal case, the archive system supports both the ArchiveLink interface and the ILM-enabled WebDAV interface and is thus suited for using SAP ILM.

You are now familiar with the various options for storing archive files. There are also various options for accessing these archive files, which are discussed in the following chapter.

Like for data storage, you have many selection options available for accessing archived data. Depending on the respective SAP data archiving object, there are some specifics that you should observe.

3   Access Options for Archived Data

Accessing archived data after SAP data archiving is highly significant within the archiving process. Archiving SAP data doesn't make much sense if you don't have the option to appropriately access the archive. However, the quality of the display from the archive is usually not as good as the display from the database. Depending on the SAP archiving object used, the corresponding transactions cannot display the data from the archive in the format that users are accustomed to. Either not all information in archived documents is displayed or certain transactions are not able to read from the archive. Also, the alternative access options for archive access are not very user-friendly in many cases. As a result, users may be dissatisfied with the archive access and ultimately decide against SAP data archiving.

For this reason you should evaluate all possible access options to optimally define archive access for the user. Only then can you convince the users and obtain approval for data archiving. In this chapter, we'll take a closer look at the various options using examples and find out which alternative access options you can revert to if individual solutions exhibit weak points. The goal of SAP data archiving is to provide access in such a way that the users can support data archiving.

3.1   Read Programs

Read programs provide sequential access to archive files. In other words, you can access archive files in sequence until you've found the

Sequential data access

133

document numbers that have been entered in the selection criteria. In case of direct access, however, you would access an individual document using an archive infostructure. In Transaction AOBJ, you can display the read program that was defined for the respective archiving object. Figure 3.1 shows the read program that was assigned to the SD_ VBAK archiving object.

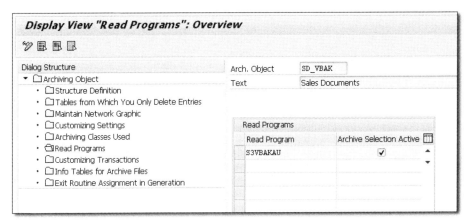

Figure 3.1 Displaying Assigned Read Programs in Transaction AOBJ

Display and maintenance via Transaction AOBJ

For the SAP data archiving object SD_VBAK, for example, the S3VBAKAU READ PROGRAM is used in the SAP standard. Alternatively, you can also develop your own read programs and store them at this location in Customizing. If you select the ARCHIVE SELECTION ACTIVE column in the overview of the read programs, you enable the users to restrict their selection to specific archive files or archiving runs when executing the program. This accelerates the display. This procedure assumes, however, that a descriptive note for an archiving run is available to determine the archive files that contain the desired documents. Otherwise, no results will be returned by the search if it is restricted to the wrong files. In the following, we'll discuss the read program using an example.

Entry via Transaction SARA

To utilize the read program, call Transaction SARA:

1. Again, enter the "SD_VBAK" ARCHIVING OBJECT in the corresponding field as an example, and select the READ action (see Figure 3.2).

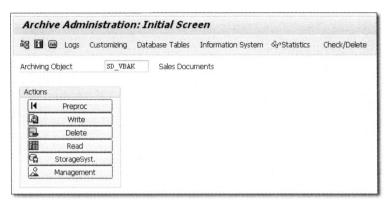

Figure 3.2 Actions for the SD_VBAK Archiving Object in Transaction SARA

2. In the subsequent dialog window, you can start the S3VBAKAU read program in the background or in DIALOG mode. To be able to run the read program in the background, choose the value BATCH in the BACKGROUND/DIALOG field (see Figure 3.3). Because the selection using read programs can take some time, the benefit of running it as a background is that you can schedule this job at any point in time. In our example, we opt for the value DIALOG.

Figure 3.3 Starting the Read Program S3VBAKAU in Dialog Mode

3. Click on the EXECUTE button ⊕. Because we selected DIALOG mode, the system displays a selection screen (see Figure 3.4).

Figure 3.4 Selecting Archived Orders

4. In the DOCUMENT SELECTION field, use a document number to choose a specific order, for example, 3030143440, and click on the EXECUTE button ⊕ (see Figure 3.4).

5. This opens a dialog window for selecting files (see Figure 3.5). Note that the DOCUMENT SELECTION of the previous step doesn't impact the file selection. The system displays all files that match the selected archiving object. In this dialog window, you must now indicate the SESSIONS AND FILES that contain the documents you are looking for. Otherwise, the result list will be empty (see Figure 3.6).

Figure 3.5 Selecting Archive Runs and Files

Figure 3.6 Empty Result List in the Read Program

Selecting the Correct Sessions and Files

To be able to select the correct sessions and files at this point, the sessions must have been provided with a descriptive NOTE during archiving (for instance, fiscal year, organizational unit, document number intervals, etc.), which you can use to simplify the selection of files. You can enter a note for the session and for each individual file. You can update and change notes at any time in Transaction SARA using the MANAGEMENT ACTION (see Figure 3.2). For this purpose, you must select the relevant session or files and click on the DETAIL button ☜. In the NOTES field, you can enter any text to roughly describe the file's content (see Figure 3.7).

Figure 3.7 Maintaining Notes for a File

6. Alternatively, you can also select all sessions and files (see Figure 3.5). This way you can ensure that your document is included in one of the files. However, this considerably prolongs the runtime of the read program.

7. After the document has been read from the archive, the evaluation of Figure 3.8 is displayed as the result.

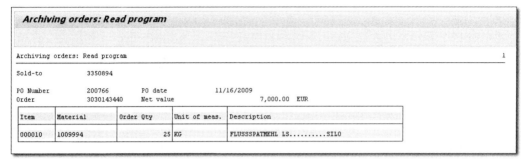

Figure 3.8 Result of the Read Program for Archived SD Orders

Display in the read program

The evaluation differs considerably from the display via Transaction VA03 (Display SD Order). The read program provides only a minor subset of available information from the SD order.

In summary, read programs require a certain level of accuracy from the user during selection so that the user can access the archived data. If you mark sessions and archive files incorrectly, you run the risk of causing long runtimes for access or that no data is displayed at all. Read programs are no longer first choice for archiving objects that are used very frequently. The archive access has been optimized for many archiving objects in previous years and now presents itself in the form of direct access; that is, the users access the archive directly from the display transactions. User interaction is not required in most cases because automatic archive access can be defined as a default value in Customizing.

3.2   Direct Access

Access using a transaction

Direct access is an option for accessing archived data, which is much more convenient compared to the read programs. This is discussed in more detail in this section. Direct access takes place within an SAP transaction and is the most frequently used method for displaying data in an SAP system. Many transactions can read data not only from the database but also from the archive. Transaction VA03 is an example for displaying sales documents.

Although Transaction VA03 can read data from the archive, some restrictions still apply to this process. These restrictions are listed in SAP Note 577162 (Display Archived Orders via VA03) and can also be found in the SAP documentation for the SD_VBAK archiving object. We'd like to point out two critical restrictions that you'll encounter when displaying archive data in the subsequent example:

Access restrictions

- ▶ Display the document flow
- ▶ Display texts

To illustrate the restrictions, we call an archived SD order in Transaction VA03:

Display archived data

1. Call Transaction VA03, and enter the name of the archived SD order, for example, "3030143440," in the ORDER field (see Figure 3.9). Press Enter to confirm.

Figure 3.9 Calling the Archived Sales Order

2. The following error message is displayed in the status bar: *"SD document 3030143440 is not in the database or has been archived"* (see Figure 3.10). You receive this message whenever the SD order does not exist in the database.

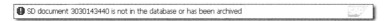

Figure 3.10 Error Message When Displaying an Archived SD Order in Transaction VA03

3. To be able to access archived documents via direct access, you must build and activate an archive infostructure. This process is described in Section "Archive Information System" on page 144. If this structure is not built, the said error message appears.

4. Let's assume that the archive infostructure is active and built. If you search for the archived object in this case, you receive the same message in the status bar (but not marked as an error message): SD document 3030143440 is not in the database or has been archived. So the SD document was read from the archive and is displayed (see Figure 3.11).

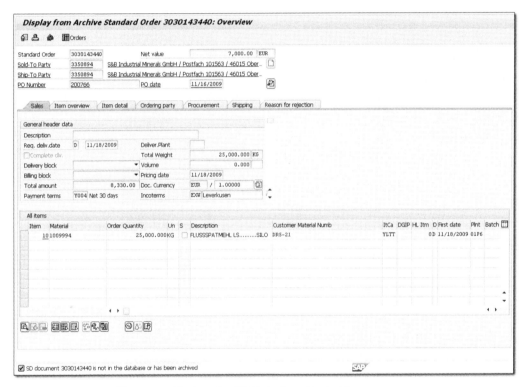

Figure 3.11 Display of an SD Order from the Archive

[»]

Missing Display of the Document Flow in Transaction VA03

In the sales overview, you can determine at the top left that the document flow button 🕞 (see Figure 3.9) does not exist, which means that you can no longer navigate directly from the SD order display to the document flow.

Since release SAP R/3 4.7, you can use Transaction VA03 to read from the archive. Prior to that, only the S3VBAKAU read program was available. Unfortunately, the document flow button has not been implemented by SAP. But the document flow is an important source for the user, for example, to view the linked documents of financial accounting and their statuses. Deliveries and billing documents for the SD order, which are essential for the user, are displayed in the document flow.

5. Now double-click item 10 to navigate to the item data. Here, the TEXTS tab for the SD orders that have already been archived can no longer be opened (see Figure 3.12). Texts are usually subdivided into various text types and languages. In these fields, you can, for example, save important notes on a customer or granted discounts, which the administrator will be able to view. You should also factor this restriction in when you consider the archiving of the SD_VBAK object.

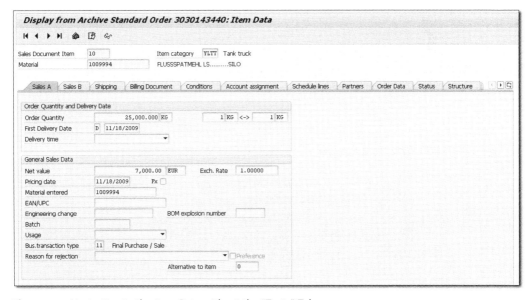

Figure 3.12 Navigating to the Item Data without the "Texts" Tab

[»] **Comparison with the Display of Non-Archived Data**

By contrast, a non-archived SD order that displays the TEXTS tab, including various text types and languages, looks as shown in Figure 3.13.

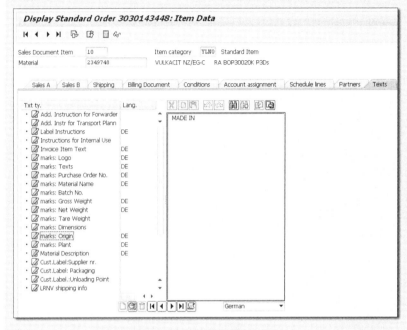

Figure 3.13 Texts Tab in a Nonarchived SD Order

Alternative access options

But which options are available to bypass such weak points and to provide full, user-friendly access to data? We'll continue our example of document flows and texts. SAP provides an alternative access option in the SAP standard to display the document flow. The *Document Relationship Browser* (DRB) is available for this purpose. It is discussed in more detail in Section "Document Relationship Browser" on page 157. SAP doesn't yet provide any convenient default solution for displaying texts in the SD order. If you can't omit the display of texts after SAP data archiving, you can choose from the following three options:

▸ Develop your own transaction for displaying from the archive

▸ Use archive add-ons (see Section 3.6)

▸ Utilize the technical view in Archive Explorer (see Section 3.3.1)

With the example of Transaction VA03, you learned that a transaction with automatic archive access doesn't necessarily provide the same functions for accessing archived data as for accessing non-archived data. It is essential to discuss weak points of important transactions with the user department at an early stage and take appropriate measures if the weak points involve critical functions. We recommend checking all display transactions for weak points, for instance, missing or restricted archive access prior to archiving. The restrictions with regard to archive access are documented for all data archiving objects in the SAP documentation and in SAP Notes. Therefore, by all means, take the time and read the SAP Notes to prepare appropriate measures.

Coordinate critical functions with the user department

You can archive various SD document categories using the SD_VBAK archiving object. By default, some SD document categories are displayed in a transaction other than VA03, which can't access the archive at all or only with restrictions (see Table 3.1). Here too you must take appropriate measures to convince the user department of the necessity of archiving.

Further restrictions

SD Document Category	Description	Display Transaction
A	Query	VA13
B	Offer	VA23
C	Order	VA03
E	Scheduling agreement	VA33
G	Contract	VA43

Table 3.1 SD Document Categories with Restrictions for Archive Access

If the amount of data is not very high, you can exclude SD document categories with major archive access restrictions from archiving by adapting the selection variant for the SD_VBAK archiving object accordingly. Alternatively, you can also implement archiving as planned and utilize another access method. The archive information system for archive access, which is presented in the following section, is available for all SAP data archiving objects.

3.3 Archive Information System

The archive information system (AS) indexes the archive files and uses them to generate archive infostructures for displaying archived data records. You can't access your archived data without generating archive infostructures. For this reason, the AS must be set up immediately after the archive files have been created.

Transaction SARI — You can call the AS using Transaction SARI. You can see the initial screen in Figure 3.14.

Figure 3.14 Central Management of the Archive Information System in Transaction SARI

The AS is subdivided into the following three areas, which we'll discuss in more detail in the following sections:

▶ Archive Explorer

▶ Status (status management)

▶ Customizing (Archive Retrieval Configurator)

3.3.1 Archive Explorer

Requirements — The Archive Explorer is the central entry point for displaying archived data of all SAP data archiving objects. Before you can use the Archive Explorer, however, you must first check the Customizing settings and adapt them if necessary. This procedure is described in Section 3.3.3. Additionally, you must activate and build at least one archive infostructure for each SAP data archiving object used. This is outlined in Section 3.3.2.

Area of use — In real life, the Archive Explorer is deployed whenever no direct access or read programs are provided for the data archiving object used. The Archive Explorer is thus the only access option for such data archiving objects. The quality of display varies considerably for each SAP data archiving object. In most cases, however, it is sufficient for the user department's requirements.

To call, for example, an archived sales document via the Archive Explorer, proceed as follows:

Archive access via the Archive Explorer

1. Call the Archive Explorer using Transaction SARE. Figure 3.15 shows the initial screen.

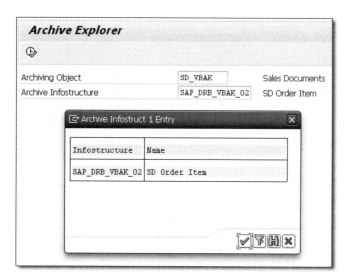

Figure 3.15 Entry via Transaction SARE (Archive Explorer)

2. Initially, enter the ARCHIVING OBJECT "SD_VBAK" that you want to access, and press ⎡Enter⎤ to confirm.

3. An active archive infostructure is displayed immediately in the ARCHIVE INFOSTRUCTURE field. If several activated archive infostructures exist for the data archiving object, you must pick one archive infostructure. In our example, only the SAP_DRB_VBAK_02 infostructure is active. You can only choose one archive infostructure in this field, because the archive infostructure determines the selection screen. To navigate to the selection screen for the archive infostructures (see Figure 3.16), click on the EXECUTE button ⊕.

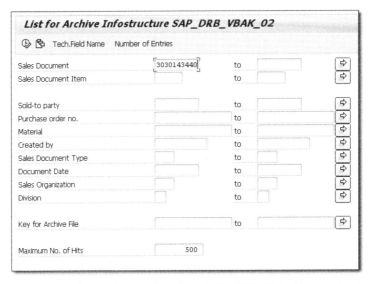

Figure 3.16 Selection Screen of the SAP_DRB_VBAK_02 Archive Infostructure

4. You can enhance this selection screen with optional fields in Customizing, which we'll discuss in Section 3.3.3. However, you should restrict the display to relevant fields so that the archive infostructure, displayed as an index table in the SAP system, doesn't become unnecessarily large.

5. For example, enter the desired SD order "3030143440" in the SALES DOCUMENT field, and confirm your entry by clicking the EXECUTE button ⊕. You receive a list according to the selection criteria from the archive information structure. Figure 3.17 shows an example.

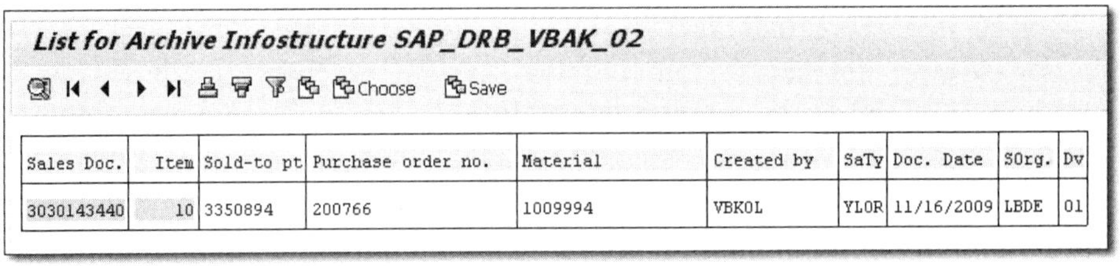

List for Archive Infostructure SAP_DRB_VBAK_02

Sales Doc.	Item	Sold-to pt	Purchase order no.	Material	Created by	SaTy	Doc. Date	SOrg.	Dv
3030143440	10	3350894	200766	1009994	VBKOL	YLOR	11/16/2009	LBDE	01

Figure 3.17 Result List from the Archive Information Structure

6. If you double-click the 3030143440 sales document, the dialog window of Figure 3.18 is displayed, which provides the following options for displaying the archived SD order:

▶ SALES DOCUMENT: Navigates to Transaction VA03

▶ DISPLAY ORIGINALS: Displays attachments of the sales document

▶ DRB: SD ORDER: Document flow display in the Document Relationship Browser

▶ TECHNICAL VIEW: Displays individual tables of the SD order

By means of the first three display functions for the SD order, you can readily view the sales document in Transaction VA03, the attached documents, or the document flow.

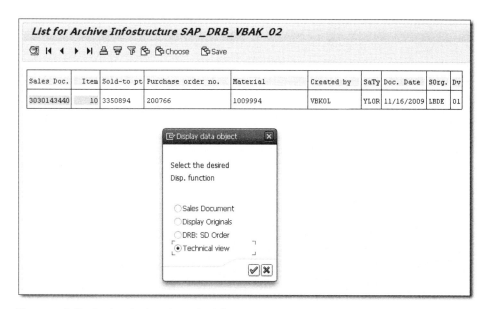

Figure 3.18 Navigation Options from the Infostructure

Another option is to display the archived data using the TECHNICAL VIEW display function. The technical view provides all tables from which the data was archived. You can use this function, for example, as a workaround to display texts of the sales documents that we couldn't call using the direct access in Transaction VA03 (see Section 3.2).

Data access via the technical view

1. After you've selected the TECHNICAL VIEW option, you can view an overview of various tables (see Figure 3.19). To display the texts for an SD order, you can use tables THEAD (Header Line) and TLINE (Text Lines) in which this information is stored.

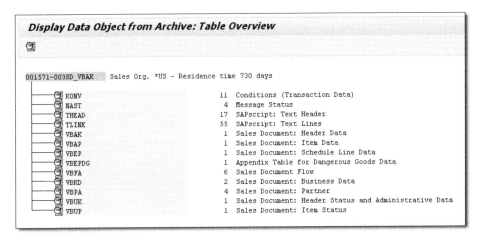

Figure 3.19 Table Overview of an Archived SD Order

2. Open table TLINE by clicking on the DETAIL button. The content is displayed as illustrated in Figure 3.20.

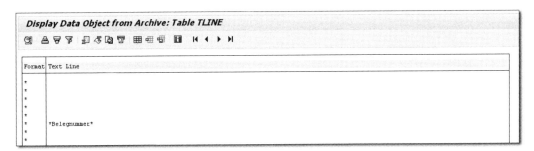

Figure 3.20 Text Information in Table TLINE

3. You can now view all texts of the archived SD order. Because the presentation in the table is very unstructured, the table doesn't inform you about the original text fields of the texts, that is, which text type they have respectively.

Usage of Transaction SARE by the Users [◉]

This section detailed the various options of Transaction SARE to display information about an archived data record from the infostructure. Transaction SARE offers very good support in real life. It is a very good alternative, particularly for archiving objects without acceptable direct access or read programs.

An important factor is that Transaction SARE can access archived documents only. So if the users deploy this transaction, they know exactly that they are checking the archive. With the TECHNICAL VIEW display function, you have the option to retrieve missing texts from archived SD orders. Optimal usage of Transaction SARE is possible within a short period of time thanks to the appropriate documentation and user instructions.

3.3.2 Status Management

Within status management, you can view the status of an infostructure for each SAP archiving object either separately by individual archiving sessions or as a whole. Additionally, in the status management you fill and delete infostructures that have already been activated in Customizing. For this purpose, select the STATUS button on the initial screen of the archive information system. You are still in Transaction SARI during this process. Then proceed as follows:

Call status information

1. Enter the desired SAP data archiving object in the ARCHIVING OBJECT field, for instance, SD_VBAK (SALES DOCUMENTS; see Figure 3.21).

Archive Information System: Status Management

Status Per Archive   Status Per Infostructure

Archiving Object   SD_VBAK   Sales Documents

Figure 3.21 Status Management in Transaction SARI

2. Then either click STATUS PER ARCHIVE or STATUS PER INFOSTRUCTURE to go to the detail view. Figure 3.22 shows the status display per archive.

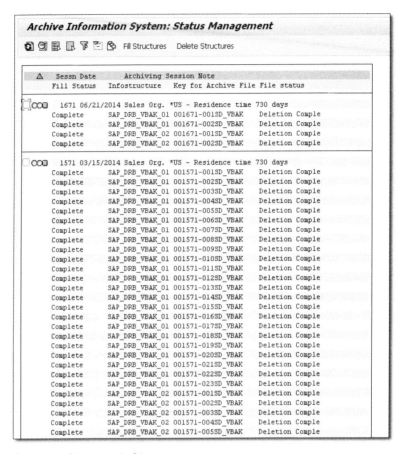

Figure 3.22 Status per Archive

3. Here you can fill or delete the archive infostructure per archiving session (Sessn column). To do so, select an archiving session and click the Fill Structures button or Delete Structures button. Successfully filled infostructures are indicated with a green icon. Infostructures that have not been filled are marked with a red icon, and partially filled infostructures are provided with a yellow icon. Our example shows two infostructures, SAP_DRB_VBAK_01 and SAP_DRB_VBAK_02. Additionally, you can see the Archiving Session Note, the individual archive files (Key for Archive File), and the File status. Successfully filled archive files are marked as Complete.

Status Management per Archive [«]

The benefit of status management per archive is that you can delete the data records within the archive infostructure of a very old archiving session and thus keep a lean archive infostructure if no archive access is required for the time slice of this archiving session. In contrast to the status management per archive, the status management per infostructure doesn't differentiate by archiving sessions but only by the archive infostructures used.

In real life, more than one archive infostructure is frequently used for an SAP data archiving object. In this case, too, you can select all infostructures for this object via the corresponding SESSION in the STATUS MANAGEMENT PER ARCHIVE and fill or delete them in one step.

4. If you switch to the STATUS PER INFOSTRUCTURE area (see Figure 3.21), you can no longer view the individual archive files and sessions but only the INFOSTRUCTURE (see Figure 3.23). Here, as well, a green icon indicates that the infostructure was filled for all archiving sessions. If you partially deleted the infostructure using older archiving sessions in the STATUS PER ARCHIVE area, a yellow icon would be displayed. If you want to fill or delete a complete infostructure independent of the archiving sessions, this area of status management is ideally suited for this purpose.

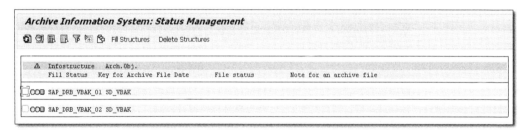

Figure 3.23 Status Management per Infostructure

Note, however, that you can only fill infostructures after they have been activated in Customizing. The following section shows which settings you can make in Customizing and how to activate the infostructure.

3.3.3 Customizing

The SAP standard includes appropriate, defined archive infostructures for almost all data archiving objects. You can either use them directly or adapt them to your requirements via Customizing. If the SAP standard should not meet your requirements, you can also create completely new archive infostructures. When you activate an infostructure, you generate a table in the SAP database in the background. You can then fill this table with information from the infostructure's fields as described in Section 3.2. This enables you to access archived data. Let's now display an existing infostructure and adapt it slightly.

Archive Retrieval Configurator

For this purpose, select the CUSTOMIZING button on the initial screen of the archive information system. This takes you to the *Archive Retrieval Configurator*. Alternatively, you can also use Transaction SARJ to access Customizing. You can see the initial screen in Figure 3.24.

Figure 3.24 Customizing in the Archive Retrieval Configurator (Transaction SARJ)

Within Transaction SARJ, the following functions are available via the toolbar:

- CREATE □
- CHANGE ✎
- DISPLAY ✎
- ACTIVATE ▮
- DELETE 🗑

Adapt the infostructure

To make Customizing settings for an existing archive infostructure, proceed as follows:

1. Enter the name of an infostructure in the ARCHIVE INFOSTRUCTURE field, for example, the SAP_DRB_VBAK_02 structure (SD ORDER ITEM) for the SD_VBAK data archiving object.

2. Call the detail view by clicking the DISPLAY button ✎.

3. Here you can see that the infostructure is based on the SAP_SD_VBAK_002 FIELD CATALOG. The SAP standard provides field catalogs for an

archive infostructure. They contain fields from different tables (for instance, VBAK, sales header and VBAP, document items), which you can use for the infostructure and the selection screen. They meet requirements in most cases and you should only enhance them with additional fields from the corresponding tables in exceptional cases. To do so, in the initial screen of Transaction SARJ, you can call the corresponding FIELD CATALOG from the menu (ENVIRONMENT • FIELD CATALOG) and adapt it to your requirements (see Figure 3.25). If you want to make changes to the field catalog, you should copy it to your own namespace and then assign it to a new infostructure. This way you ensure that you retain the original form of the standard SAP field catalog and the infostructure and that updates to SAP software do not overwrite them.

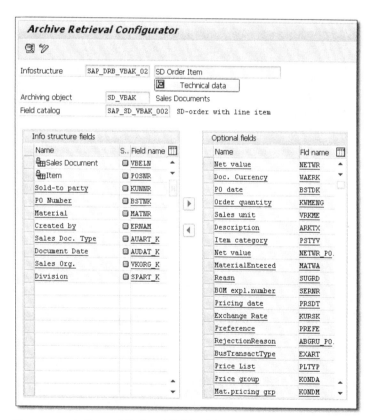

Figure 3.25 Active and Optional Fields of the Archive Infostructure

[Ex] **Adapting the Field Catalog**

In some of our projects, one requirement was, for example, to add three new fields to the PR_ORDER archiving object (process orders). The user department requested them:

► Basic start date (GSTRP)

► Basic finish date (GLTRP)

► Resource/work center (ARBPL)

For the user department, it made work much easier, because they were now able to select by these additional fields in Transaction SARE. Such additional fields must first be added to a new field catalog so that they can then be used in a new archive infostructure.

4. On the left side, you can view all active INFO STRUCTURE FIELDS. On the right-hand side, you are provided with a list of OPTIONAL FIELDS with additional optional fields from the field catalog. You should check these optional fields in detail to decide whether to add one or more of them to the infostructure.

5. If you now switch from the DISPLAY mode to the CHANGE mode, you can make changes to the infostructure. In Figure 3.25, we have already transferred two fields from the OPTIONAL FIELDS area to the area on the left: SALES ORG. and DIVISION. Users often use these criteria in Transaction SARE to browse the archive.

6. To use the infostructure, you must first activate it. To do so, click on the ACTIVATE button ⓘ. Activating the infostructure creates a new table in the background (see Figure 3.26).

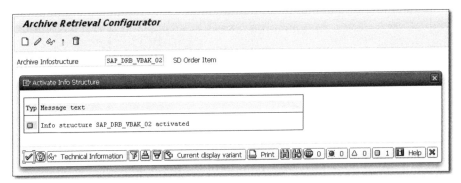

Figure 3.26 Archive Infostructure SAP_DRB_VBAK_02 Activated

Tables for Infostructures **[«]**

The table is the infostructure at the same time, and you can only fill it in the status management via the FILL STRUCTURES function. The naming of the tables follows a predefined pattern: It always starts with a prefix, followed by the SAP component of the archiving object, and is incremented numerically, for example:

▸ Prefix: ZARIX

▸ Component: SD, MM, FI etc.

▸ Counter: 1 to n

7. Our table (infostructure) is named ZARIXSD1 (see Figure 3.27) because we've activated an infostructure in the SD ERP component for the first time.

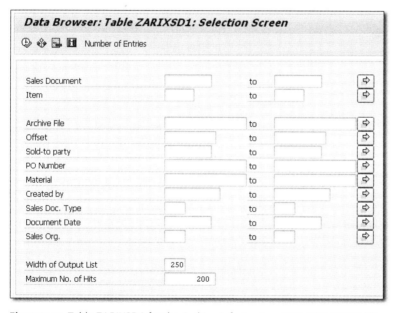

Figure 3.27 Table ZARIXSD1 for the Archive Infostructure SAP_DRB_VBAK_02

8. You can also display the assigned table by clicking the TECHNICAL DATA button (see Figure 3.28).

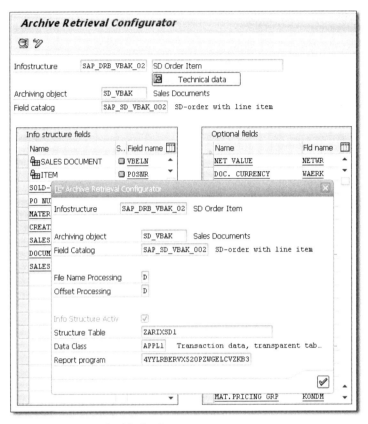

Figure 3.28 Assigned Table for the Structure

9. In the STRUCTURE TABLE field, you can see table ZARIXSD1, which we've generated by activating the infostructure. This table is located in the SAP database and forms the bridge to the archive.

Create a new infostructure

So far you've learned how to display and adapt an existing infostructure. To create a new infostructure, proceed as follows:

1. First, create a new field catalog because you require it later on when you create the new infostructure. To keep this section less complex, we'll omit a detailed description on how to create a new field catalog. We will assume that experts considering the customer namespaces created a corresponding new field catalog.

2. Call Transaction SARJ, and enter the new name for the infostructure in the INFOSTRUCTURE field (for instance, NEW_INFOSTRUCTURE, see Figure 3.29). Consider the namespaces in your SAP system in doing so.

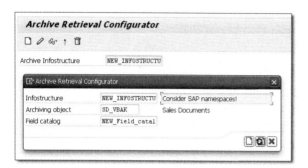

Figure 3.29 Creating a New Infostructure

3. Select the appropriate archiving object.

4. Then select the newly created field catalog and click on the CREATE button.

This creates the new infostructure and it can be individually set, activated, and used as described by selecting the fields.

The archive information system is the core of archive access. It allows for direct access and is the central entry point for accessing all data archiving objects. The *Document Relationship Browser (DRB)*, presented in the following section, also requires these infostructures. For this reason, you should perform Customizing thoroughly and define the infostructures together with the user department. If you really need to enhance the standard field catalogs, we recommend consulting experts who have the relevant technical know-how. To ensure smooth access, you must not forget to fill the infostructures after each archiving session. This is an important task in administration, which we discuss in greater detail in Chapter 7.

The core of archive access

3.4   Document Relationship Browser

You can use the DRB to display linked documents from the database or archive. The following points of entry assigned with the corresponding documents, structure the DRB (see Figure 3.30):

Points of entry

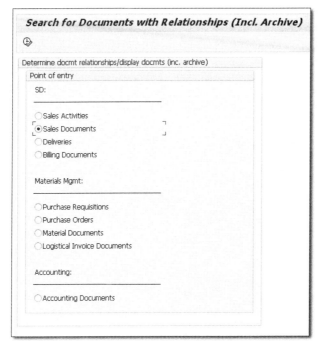

Figure 3.30 Document Relationship Browser (Transaction ALO1)

- Sales
- Materials Management
- Accounting

You can call the DRB using Transaction ALO1. You can then select which documents you want to determine relationships.

Display document flows

The DRB is essential within the scope of SAP data archiving, because you can use this tool to determine all relationships between archived and non-archived data and display them as a document flow. Activating and filling the corresponding archive infostructures for the archived data records is a prerequisite.

1. For example, choose SALES DOCUMENTS in the SD area as the POINT OF ENTRY. Then click the EXECUTE button ⊕.

2. This opens the view shown in Figure 3.31. Here you can restrict your search based on various selection criteria. You want to display the

already archived SALES DOCUMENT 3030143440. It is particularly important to determine which areas you want to perform your search. The following three options are available for the search:

▹ Search in database

▹ Search in database and SAP AS

▹ Search DB, SAP AS, and archive

The second option is very well suited for quick archive access, because data is read from the database and the archive information system only. Although the data from the archive information system are located in the database too, it contains only a subset of archived data as defined in Customizing. Choose the third option if you require full archive access. In this case, the runtime may be somewhat longer than for the second option.

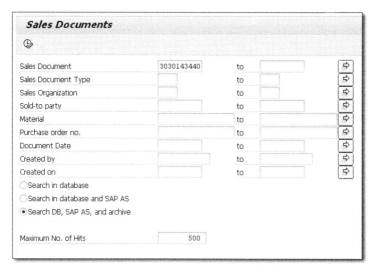

Figure 3.31 Selection Screen for Sales Documents in the Document Relationship Browser

3. Depending on which option you've picked, you receive an empty (see Figure 3.32), possibly incomplete (see Figure 3.33), or complete list (see Figure 3.34) of sales documents according to your selection. You should run the selection once per option to see the differences. Then click on the EXECUTE button ⊕.

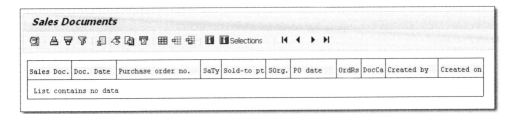

Figure 3.32 Empty List If "Search in Database" Is Selected

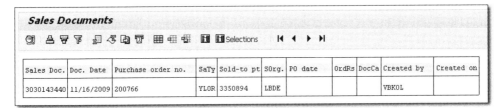

Figure 3.33 Incomplete List If "Search in Database and SAP AS" Is Selected

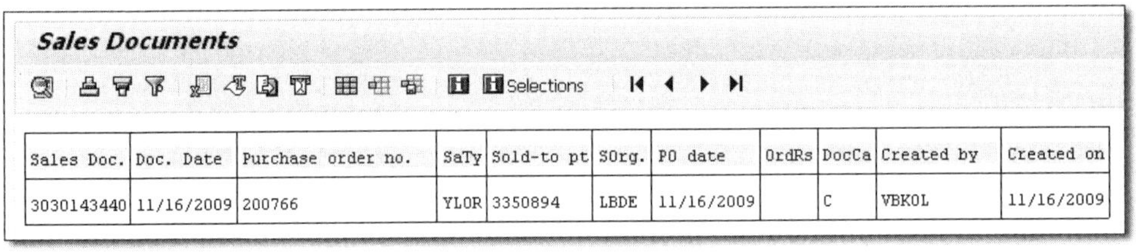

Sales Documents

Sales Doc.	Doc. Date	Purchase order no.	SaTy	Sold-to pt	SOrg.	PO date	OrdRs	DocCa	Created by	Created on
3030143440	11/16/2009	200766	YLOR	3350894	LBDE	11/16/2009		C	VBKOL	11/16/2009

Figure 3.34 Complete List If "Search DB, SAP AS, and Archive" Is Selected

[+]   **Enhancing the Infostructure**

The fields, PO DATE, DOCCA, CREATED BY, and CREATED ON, can only be read from the archive using the third option (SEARCH DB, SAP AS, AND ARCHIVE). To also obtain a full display using the second option (SEARCH IN DATABASE AND SAP AS), which is more beneficial considering performance aspects, you can enhance your infostructure to include all fields from the DRB selection screen if required.

4. When you double-click the sales document (3030143440), you navigate to the document flow of the DRB, where you can view the relationships for this document (see Figure 3.35).

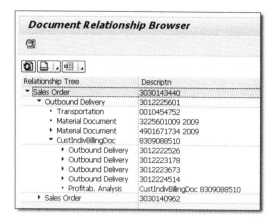

Figure 3.35 Document Relationships (Alternative Document Flow) without Display of the Data Origin

5. You can see all document relationships in the RELATIONSHIP TREE for the SALES ORDER. It is possible to branch to the individual documents.

6. In our example, we adapt the layout so that the origin of data is displayed immediately. You can determine straight away if the documents are read from the ARCHIVE or DATABASE. For this purpose, click on the CHANGE LAYOUT button [⊞], select the ORIGINS OF DATA and ORIGIN (DESCRIPTION) fields from the COLUMN SET, and move them to the DISPLAYED COLUMNS box on the left (see Figure 3.36).

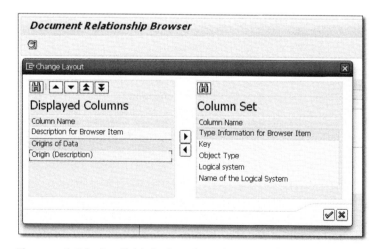

Figure 3.36 Selecting Fields for Describing the Origin of Data

7. As a result, you can now see the document relationships, including information of the data's origin (see Figure 3.37).

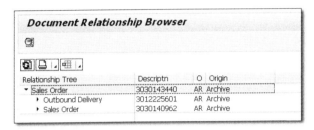

Figure 3.37 Document Relationships (Alternative Document Flow) and Display of the Data Origin

By means of the DRB functions, we mitigated another restriction mentioned in Section 3.2, which concerned the missing display of the document flow for archived SD documents in Transaction VA03.

3.5 Print Lists

Within the scope of SAP data archiving, print lists play a minor role, which is still important in some cases. In two special cases it pays off to also archive print lists before and after SAP data archiving.

Print lists before archiving | Specific evaluation programs create print lists and prepare evaluation results for printing. Particularly in accounting, print lists are created and stored with the following programs, among others:

▶ RFBILA00 (financial statement/profit and loss statement, P&L)

▶ FAGL_CL_REGROUP (balance sheet supplement, analysis)

▶ FAGL_FC_VALUATION (foreign currency valuation)

The FAGL_FC_VALUATION program should be specifically mentioned as an example, which reads data from table FAGL_BSBW_HISTRY (Valuation History of Documents). The FI_DOCUMNT archiving object also archives this table. So this program can no longer create any valuations for the previously archived period.

In case of print list archiving prior to SAP data archiving, you can store these print lists and revert to them quickly at a later point in time—particularly if data is archived and affected by the valuation as described in our example. So, on the one hand, the benefit of print list archiving is that you don't have to restart these evaluation programs every time to obtain the same valuation results. This helps you to save time. On the other hand, some evaluation programs can't access archived data. For such purposes, you must definitely create and store the print list prior to SAP data archiving if you still need to access them later on.

Print list archiving after SAP data archiving is interesting for documenting jobs during archiving. Each job generates a spool file within the scope of SAP data archiving. Because spool files can be deleted again from the SAP system after a few days, you should store the spool files as print lists.

Print lists after data archiving

The best way to store the spool files for the respective jobs is to directly use Transaction SARA in the job overview. Alternatively, you can also call Transaction SP01 (Spool Requests) and store the corresponding spool files from there. Here it is important to perform the following steps:

Archiving spool files

1. In Transaction SP01, select the desired spool file, and click on the PRINT WITH CHANGED PARAMETERS button 🖨 in the toolbar to open the ARCHIVE PARAMETER window (see Figure 3.38).

2. Choose DRAW (Document) in the OBJECT TYPE field and D01 (Print Lists) in the DOCUMENT TYPE field. You can find these values in Transactions OAC2 and OAC3 (see also Section 2.1.2).

3. Subsequently, you can add descriptive information in the INFORMATION and TEXT fields to retrieve spool requests later on. It is helpful, for example, to use the abbreviation ARC behind the INFORMATION field for spool files from SAP data archiving. There are no limits to your creativity here. In the INFORMATION field, you can also provide information on the SAP data archiving object, the type of job, organizational units, and time slices.

4. Click on the ARCHIVE button to confirm your settings and to archive the print lists in the corresponding content repository.

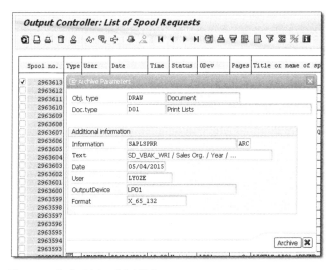

Figure 3.38 Archiving Print Lists

You can access print lists using Transaction OADR (*see* Figure 3.39).

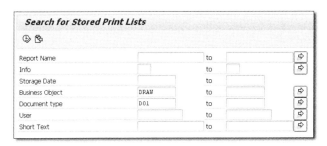

Figure 3.39 Search for Stored Print Lists

Enter object type "DRAW" in the BUSINESS OBJECT field and "D01" for DOCUMENT TYPE. You can also refine your search using the SHORT TEXT or INFO fields.

3.6   Third-Party Add-ons

Due to the fact that not all transactions can read data from the archive with the same high quality after SAP data archiving, several enterprises have specialized in this field and offer add-ons for displaying from the archive.

3.6.1   PBS Transactions

PBS Software is a leading provider with add-ons deployed at many enterprises. The PBS add-ons are grouped by SAP components and data archiving objects. PBS offers an add-on called CSD, which has been developed for the SD component. This add-on includes PBS transactions for archive access to the following SAP data archiving objects:

▶ LE_HU (handling units)

▶ RV_LIKP (deliveries)

▶ SD_VBAK (sales documents)

▶ SD_VFKK (freight costs)

▶ SD_VTTK (transports)

The PBS transactions are copies of original SAP transactions. To display sales documents in Transaction VA03, PBS offers a corresponding fully archivable transaction named /PBS/VA03. This PBS transaction removes, among other things, the restrictions with regard to document flow and text display discussed in Section 3.2.

Better access, additional costs

To utilize the PBS transactions, they must be integrated with your user role concept after installation. The standard SAP authorization check is also performed for the PBS transactions.

Installation and setup

Deploying add-ons entails pros and cons that each enterprise must consider carefully. In real life, we have worked both with customers who opted for add-ons and also decided against them. One reason in favor of add-ons is, for example, that the quality of archive access is much better. In the meantime, however, the standard SAP transactions offer archive access that is considerably better than in the past, which is why add-ons become less important in some SAP components. Costs are one argument against their usage. You must consider both the costs for one-time investment as well as the ongoing support fees. We recommend first checking all options of the SAP standard for archive access. These options are usually sufficient in most cases. Only if you cannot access your archived data using the SAP transaction should you look for alternatives.

Pros and cons

Another interesting
provider

Besides PBS Software, we'd like to introduce further providers and scenarios, which don't directly refer to the display of archive files using SAP transactions but can still be interesting within the scope of archiving projects.

3.6.2   Creating DART Extracts from Archive Files

In Section 3.6.1, you learned that DART can only extract from the SAP database. For archived documents, DART only offers an option to reload to appropriate DART tables for some important tables.

To save you the effort of reloading, several providers offer additional software for data extraction to enable you to generate DART extracts from archive files. Here the benefit is that you save the time for reloading and that your DART extracts are complete. Another reason for deploying such additional software is, for example, that you can start with SAP data archiving independent of the DART extraction and can access your additional software when you actually require DART extracts.

Extraction from
the archive

As a result, you don't need to provide any data redundantly in the form of DART extracts. Providers that deal with this topic include, among others:

▶ TJC Software SA with the *Audit Extraction Cockpit* (AEC)

▶ PBS Software GmbH with the *CDART* add-on

▶ Fujitsu TDS GmbH with the *AIS TDS SAPconnect* solution

We'd like to point out that you can also generate DART extracts from archived data using SAP ILM. We will discuss this function in more detail in Chapter 8.

3.6.3   Creating Structured Data from SAP Print Lists

Convert print lists
to tables

Another option can be interesting in practical use: the transfer of unstructured data, such as SAP print lists, into structured data in the form of tables. Let's assume, for example, that several SAP systems were shut down completely during a project. It was agreed with the local financial authorities that important information that must be preserved for legal reasons will be stored in the form of SAP print lists. If required, it should be possible to convert these print lists to tables in a structured form and provide them to the auditors for electronic tax inspections. For this purpose, you can use DATAWATCH's *Monarch Professional* software.

The add-ons presented here are just a few examples of additional software available to support archiving projects and to simplify access to archived data.

3.7   Summary

This chapter described the various options for accessing archived data. In this context, you should particularly note that restrictions apply to archive access after data archiving and that it is not a matter of course that all transactions work just like before. One of your biggest challenges is to provide archive access with different options (with or without additional costs) that meet users' requirements while you continue with data archiving.

PART II
Implementing Data Archiving Projects

Tackle your SAP data archiving project by developing an individual strategy. Document your decisions and approach in concepts easily understood by everyone involved.

4   Developing a Data Archiving Strategy

You use a strategy to generally determine the goal you want to achieve and the path you need to take in order to reach it. A major goal of data archiving is to ensure the performance of an SAP system, as you already learned in Chapter 1, Section 1.1. The path to better performance comes via data archiving with SAP data archiving objects in order to relieve large tables. In addition to performance, you can achieve secondary goals using SAP data archiving. Appropriate strategies are also required in order to determine the optimal path to each goal. Secondary goals include such things as the master data cleanup or the completion of information object lifecycles.

For companies, there is a specific time, as well as specific drivers, for the introduction of an archiving project. Regardless of the time, a successful strategy is based in particular on an archiving concept that can be easily understood by everyone involved. In the second part of this chapter, we will provide you with a detailed description of the possible appearance and structure of such an archiving concept.

4.1   Choosing the Right Time

The length of this path is of course significant for the practical implementation of archiving. If it is a short path, you can take your time initially, for example, and then speed up. Alternatively, you can complete this short path comfortably at a steady pace.

Acting with foresight

How do you reach your goal, however, if the path is very long? Can you still take your time and then speed up for the remainder of the long path? Probably not. Thus it is advisable to start planning SAP data archiving for large projects and databases at an early stage. Nevertheless, if you have miscalculated and have only sped up later, you must note some important points, which we will present in Section 4.1.2, so that you do not run out of steam. However, remember that the path is not always straight and may also involve obstacles. Thus you must sometimes take detours or overcome hurdles. Flexibility and a future-oriented perspective are thus required.

Team influences project duration

In reality, it can easily happen that, although you may think that you have started the project in time and have also scheduled the time required for its implementation, the collaboration with the user department does not work as expected, and you need far more time than originally planned. Alternatively, you have not involved the relevant decision-makers in the project and thus do not receive their support or only receive it at a very late stage, which leads to delays in turn. In this case, you have to hold workshops and meetings again, that is, take detours. We can thus state that the composition of your archiving project team can significantly affect the duration of the project. This may apply in a positive sense; that is, they may adhere to or exceed the schedule through good cooperation. It may also apply in a negative sense; that is, they may end up under time pressure and thus also endanger the long-term performance of the SAP system.

4.1.1 Early Planning

Gaining time

The ideal prerequisite for ensuring good long-term performance of an SAP system is an early start in planning an SAP data archiving project. Early planning enables you to primarily gain an important resource: time. How do we now define *early*? Figure 4.1 shows different times for getting started with SAP data archiving. The following two times are suitable for early planning:

- Before the go-live (*template phase*)
- After the go-live (up to three years in the short term)

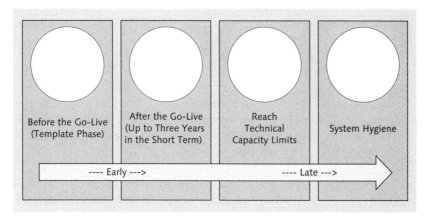

Figure 4.1 Start Times for the Path to Data Archiving

Before the Go-Live

In our opinion and experience, the ideal time to start thinking about data archiving is at a very early stage before the go-live of the SAP system. In reality, however, such an early discussion of the topic is very rare. The same significance and weight are not attached to data archiving as to implementing the processes at this very early stage of the system introduction.

It would be ideal to define the data archiving strategy during the implementation of the processes, because it is precisely in these processes that one intervenes with data archiving. When considering data archiving at this early stage, you can also contact the users directly very early on and prepare them for the impending SAP data archiving. This approach improves the acceptance of the archiving concept, because the discussions on the topic have already taken place and users and the IT department are aware of the requirements. In addition, the developers and those responsible for IT interfaces can take measures and precautions for archiving in the event of early integration. When developing customer-specific transactions and reports, it is possible to check directly if an archive access will be needed later and, if this is the case, it can be taken into account directly. This saves you the time spent coordinating and subsequent adjustments at a later date. Those responsible for the interfaces already know at an early stage the IT systems that may be affected by data archiving.

Greater acceptance and success

Strategy Development before the Go-Live

A leading US automobile manufacturer has decided to introduce a central SAP system with the component SAP Treasury and Risk Management. All subsidiaries are also supposed to handle their banking transactions via this SAP system. This global treasury platform reflects, on the one hand, in-house banking within which, for example, the subsidiaries can lend to each other, while on the other hand, it is connected to external banks. All requests for payment or bank statements of individual companies are exchanged with the connected banks via this central treasury system.

The enterprise defined and documented the IT landscape and the interfaces to other IT systems during the template phase. Thus it was known even before the go-live that a lot of IDocs had to be sent via this business-critical SAP system and also that the number of financial accounting documents would be extremely high. Due to the major importance of the treasury system for the group, the enterprise could not risk its performance and stability on any account.

The SAP data archiving objects eligible for the SAP system were thus determined and a technical concept was written. Intensive discussions on the two most critical data archiving objects IDOC (Intermediate Document) and FI_DOCUMNT (financial accounting documents) were held with the user department to determine the period of time after which archiving may be performed and how the archive access could be ensured. Thus the company was ready even before the go-live to start SAP data archiving at any time after the go-live. It was possible to define a suitable tailored strategy as a result of this proactive approach. Thus both the goal and the path were known in advance.

[+] **Don't Put Off until Tomorrow What You Can Do Today!**

The following also applies to SAP data archiving: the sooner you start developing your individual strategy, the more relaxed you will be as you look toward the future due to this head start.

After the Go-Live

Rapidly determining critical tables

Another good time to start data archiving is up to three years after the go-live of the SAP system. The database grows rapidly in this phase, and the tables that grow the fastest are easily recognizable and thus particularly critical. In the first three years after the go-live, the memory is large enough and performance is usually acceptable and in the normal range.

After this period, there are frequent first questions put to the IT department as to how to get the steady growth of stored data under control and thus ensure performance in the long term. Experienced IT employees are usually already aware that using data archiving at this point will counteract the growth in stored data. Such past experiences can be both positive and negative. It is important to derive best practices based on the positive experiences and to compile a list of lessons learned based on the negative experiences.

Strategy Development after the Go-Live   [Ex]

A leading company from the chemical industry has carried out a very large consolidation project that will document all global business processes in a central SAP ERP system in future. Thus the enterprise can expect a very large growth in data. New companies are also continuously being connected to the new SAP system through rollouts, thus it is a very dynamic environment.

In the older SAP systems, which are still used and have different releases, archived data was sometimes archived in the past with different SAP archiving objects. Thus the users and IT employees had already come in contact with the data archiving topic. Within the first three years after the go-live of the new system, the company performs archiving with such rapidly growing data archiving objects as BC_SBAL (application logs), IDOC (IDocs), and BC_DBLOGS (changes to tables). This data has a very short residence time (less than one year) and generates a very large volume of data in the database.

At the same time, the company uses the three-year period after the go-live to prepare the archiving of the component-related SAP data archiving objects with very frequent access. These archiving objects usually have a significantly longer residence time of between 24 and 36 months and can be archived at the earliest two to three years after the go-live because the relevant data must be initially created. If an enterprise introduced SAP ERP in 2011, for example, and an archiving object has a residence time of thirty-six months, the data records for this archiving object for 2011 can only be archived after a period of three years, thus early 2015. The fiscal years 2012, 2013, and 2014 must remain available in the database. Thus the company can successfully introduce SAP data archiving in two parallel phases.

In the first three years after the go-live of an SAP system, it is only the SAP data archiving objects that require little or no archive access and are unaffected by tax data extraction with DART that are mostly used. These archiving objects usually have a very short residence time. The component-related archiving objects, for example, from the financial or sales

Taking full advantage of time

area with significantly longer residence times, should be already pre-pared in parallel and also promptly used in live operations. The parallel approach enables you to take full advantage of time and achieve your goal faster.

4.1.2 Late Setup

Late is not necessarily late
The time most widely used for implementing SAP data archiving proj-ects is a late setup several years after the go-live. This is usually a period of over three years and can even extend to over ten years. Starting data archiving late does not always signify being under time pressure. Depending on the scenario, you can still have enough time to imple-ment data archiving. The following times or occasions are suitable for a late setting up of data archiving:

▶ Reaching technical capacity limits

▶ System hygiene

If a system has already reached its technical capacity limits, the imple-mentation of archiving is definitely under time pressure. If the system hygiene is involved, however, it is more likely to be an archiving project without time pressure, because the focus here is not primarily on perfor-mance but on an increase in the quality of data in the SAP system. In the following sections, we will look at some practical examples of the late setting up of data archiving projects.

Reaching Technical Capacity Limits

Client server architecture
The infrastructure of of an SAP system consists of different layers and different hardware. Generally, we can distinguish the following layers in a very simplified model (see Figure 4.2):

▶ **Presentation layer**
Client, PC, notebook, etc.

▶ **Application layer**
Server, memory and processor/CPU

▶ **Database layer**
Database management software and memory

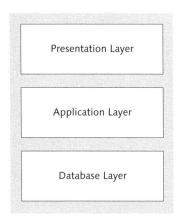

Figure 4.2 Different Layers of an SAP Landscape

In the presentation layer, you access the SAP system using the SAP GUI or via the web browser. The application server (application layer) processes your requests and is able to store information in the database (database layer) as well as retrieve information that is stored. We will use three examples from companies to illustrate how you can reach the technical capacity limits in the various layers of such an infrastructure.

Database Layer

A company from the automotive industry is on the verge of occupying the maximum memory in the database. During the introduction of the SAP system, the company assumed that a database size of 2 terabytes (TB) would be completely sufficient. The enterprise created a too small infrastructure at that time and now it no longer meets the requirements. They cannot simply extend the memory, as the existing hardware is not designed for this purpose.

Too small database

The company thus faces an important decision: Should it start archiving data rapidly and bring the growth of the database under control and free space, or should it make a costly investment in a new database server? The IT department has calculated that the memory will be fully occupied after three months at the latest. Due to the very high cost of a new database server and the relatively brief period for its procurement and installation, the company opts for data archiving. A consultant who not only advises conceptually but is also actively involved in implementing archiving can achieve a turnaround in this short period of time. After a detailed analysis of the SAP system, he calculates that a large amount of data can already be archived in the short term with just a few data archiving objects. The company prepares the archiving objects in close cooperation with the relevant departments and uses them in live operations. Those responsible in the company are reassured and the database can be relieved in time.

[+] **Procedure for Small Databases**

You should not wait until the last minute to start data archiving in small databases that cannot be extended infinitely. As soon as the freely available memory is below 50%, you should immediately prepare appropriate measures and initiate a corresponding project.

Application Layer

Continuously extending the database

Another company waits a very long time before implementing data archiving. Instead of initiating data archiving in a timely manner, it continuously extends the database. Thus the dataset generated in the last eight years in the SAP system is currently available.

The real problem arises for this company in the application layer, rather than in the database layer. The first complaints about performance deficits come from Controlling. Many transactions terminated during the month-end closing because the available memory could not process the selected large datasets within the available time frame. Time-outs occur repeatedly, which is why the month-end closing took much longer and the user department had to perform it in several smaller steps. The reporting in Controlling also does not work properly. Users no longer use the SAP ERP system for reporting but frequently change to SAP BW, which promises better performance and thus attempts to compensate for the missing reporting option in the SAP ERP system.

Defining residence time

After intensive discussions with the user department, an external consultant can define the optimal residence time for the data from Controlling, which should be 36 months. The data from the previous five years is thus stored unnecessarily in the database and may be archived.

After data archiving, the database is relieved and the month-end closing can be performed quickly and reporting can also be carried out with the usual quality and speed. Due to this success and following the archiving of Controlling data, the company decides to also set up the relevant archiving objects for all other components of the SAP system. Thus an important foundation was laid to avoid further problems in the future.

Quickly Archiving Unnecessary Data	[+]
Data that you no longer have to access frequently after a few months or years should be archived very quickly. You thus avoid future problems with performance.	

Software Update

As a last example of a late setup of an SAP data archiving project, we will discuss the *upgrading* of a system with a newer software version. In most cases, a higher processor or CPU capacity, as well as more memory and disk space, is required for such an upgrade. In particular, the upgrade of an SAP system from version R/3 4.7 to version ECC 6.0 requires a significantly higher disk space as the number of tables greatly increases.

For this reason, many companies tend to keep the database as lean as possible by means of SAP data archiving before such a change. Often a company does not realize until a later stage that a data archiving project requires a thorough analysis and planning, as well as sufficient time for its implementation. If you do not take this into account, you may fall behind schedule for the SAP software update or the employees from the archiving project have to work under extreme time pressure.

Archiving before upgrade

Archiving Before a Software Update (Upgrade)	[+]
SAP data archiving is a stand-alone project. You should give archiving high priority in advance in order to perform your upgrade project in a successful and timely manner.	

System Hygiene

Data archiving may be required at a later date even for an SAP system with good performance and sufficient memory. In these specific cases, system hygiene is the goal of archiving. We would like to present such scenarios using three practical examples.

Completion of the Information Lifecycle

A medium-sized company with a very simple SAP landscape has decided to archive all data from the SAP system after the statutory retention period of ten years has expired and to finally destroy it immediately afterward, because there is no other legal or internal obligation to retain it. The database is relatively small (approximately 400 GB) and its growth is also very manageable. Furthermore, there are no signs of any loss in performance. All tax inspections based on data that is older than ten years have already been performed. There is also no likelihood of any judicial dispute that would require further retention of the data.

Most important archiving objects

In such a case, it is advisable to choose only the most important from the multitude of data archiving objects. To be able to remove all data from the database, you would need to set up and use a very large number of archiving objects, which is not in the proper cost/benefit ratio in this situation.

This requirement for data archiving is hardly ever the case in reality. However, you can see very clearly from this example that the time will come at some point for every company to dispose of the old and no longer required data and complete the information lifecycle.

Varying phase duration

In Figure 4.3, you can see an exemplary presentation of the ILM phases of an archiving object for different countries in which a company may be active. An archiving object can thus have a different residence time and retention time in the archive in each country. After the retention period in the archive has expired, however, the deletion phase starts in any case to actually complete the lifecycle.

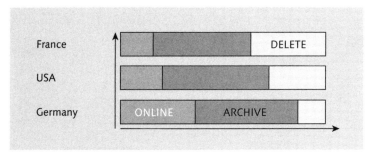

Figure 4.3 ILM Phases for Different Countries

Archiving for Completion of the Information Lifecycle [+]

First, determine all archiving objects that are required for the complete removal of the relevant data. Next, start with the most important archiving objects. Then gradually introduce the other archiving objects.

Archiving Master Data

The archiving of master data is a topic that is increasingly on company agendas. We can distinguish between the master data for vendors, customers, and materials. In contrast to transaction data, however, master data remains for a very long time in an SAP system. Furthermore, you can only archive master data after archiving all related transaction data.

When archiving master data, there are thus restrictions (criteria for archivability) that must be observed. Let's take a look at the archiving object FI_ACCPAYB (Vendors) as an example. If you use the network graphic in Transaction SARA (see Chapter 1, Section 1.4.4) to display the dependent archiving objects, you will obtain the following sequence:

Criteria for archivability

- ▶ MM_EKKO (Purchasing Documents)
- ▶ FI_TF_CRE (Vendor Transaction Figures)
- ▶ CA_BUPA (Business Partner)
- ▶ FI_DOCUMNT (FI Documents)
- ▶ MM_EINA (Purchasing Info Records)

Thus you must first archive all transaction data for a vendor with these five archiving objects before you can eventually archive the vendor data itself. Additional archiving objects are required for customers or materials in order to archive their transaction data completely.

Master Data without Transaction Data [+]

There is also master data in an SAP system not assigned to any transaction data (see Figure 4.4). Perhaps the company incorrectly created or duplicated the data. There may also be manually created vendors or vendors in the context of a migration in the SAP system with whom no business relationship developed and thus there is no transaction data. From a technical point of view, you can start archiving such master data immediately. Note, however, that the user department still requires some master data without transaction data. For this reason, you should always consult the employees in the user department as to the data that must remain in the database and the archivable data.

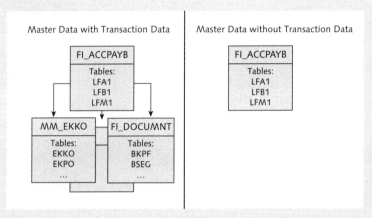

Figure 4.4 Master Data (Vendors) with and without Transaction Data

Archive access restrictions

After archiving master data, archive access to the archived transaction data is restricted significantly. After you have archived the master data for a vendor, for example, you can no longer display the line items or balances with the relevant archive-enabled Transaction FBL1N (Display Items) or Transaction FK10N (View Balances). For this reason, you should use master data archiving only in the following two scenarios:

▶ Archiving and deleting of master data that was never used or required

▶ Archiving and deleting of master data at the end of the information lifecycle

Even if you have already archived all transaction data for a vendor, you should archive the master data of this vendor only after the statutory retention period has expired. In two of our projects, there was major disagreement in the company as to when vendor data with transaction data may be archived. The recommendations of the IT department and the user department diverged as follows:

▶ **IT department**
All vendors that have not generated any transaction data for three years

▶ **User department**
All vendors that have not generated any transaction data for ten years (end of the statutory retention period)

The user department prevailed with their requirement. It bears the responsibility and knows the processes best as the data owner.

> **Master Data with Transaction Data** [+]
>
> You should be particularly careful when archiving master data with transaction data. We recommend that you archive it only after the statutory retention period has expired and retain it in the database until then.

Data Cleansing

As the last application scenario for system hygiene, we'd like to present *data cleansing*. The reasons for data cleansing include the following:

Reasons for data cleansing

▶ Sale of a company (system copy)

▶ Partial migration of data (legacy system/system shutdown)

When a company is sold, the relevant data for a company code is handed over to the buyer. If, however, the company division to be sold does not have its own SAP system and the data is retained in a superordinate system, first create a system copy. Then delete the nonrelevant data from the system copy, leaving only the data of the sold company division. Figure 4.5 illustrates this procedure. In this context, this is also referred to as *deleting of company codes*.

Sale of a company

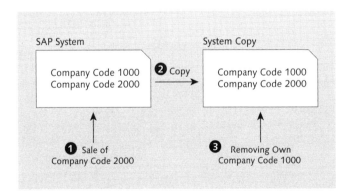

Figure 4.5 Exemplary Procedure for Sale and Handing Over of a Company Code

SAP SE has its own consulting unit named *System Landscape Optimization* (SLO), which provides you with fee-based support with the appropriate tools precisely in this area. Alternatively, you can also archive and delete

System Landscape Optimization

this data using SAP data archiving. Note that a very large number of archiving objects are required in this case, however, and you cannot remove all data completely. This is due to the fact that a lot of data does not have the correct status and is not considered by the standard writing programs of the archiving objects. You thus have to create your own writing programs and remove the relevant tests to increase the archiving success.

[+] **Get Experts on Board**

The removal of data for a particular company code from an SAP system is a complex technical procedure. The complexity of this procedure is very high and should not be underestimated, particularly if the organizational units do not have direct one-to-one links. This requires not only knowledge at a technical level but also extensive business and SAP Customizing knowledge. For these types of tasks, we recommend that you include consultants who already have experience in implementing such projects or that you contact the SAP SLO consulting team directly.

Legacy systems

The new installation of an SAP system also requires a partial migration of specific data from a legacy system. This may be master data and transaction data of business transactions that are still open. From a legal perspective, however, the data from a legacy system must be available during the entire statutory retention period. How do you now deal with this legacy system? Do you wait until the statutory retention period has expired and then finally shut down the legacy system or do you archive the data of the oldest time slice from the legacy system each year to reduce the memory in use? Do you choose a completely different option to shut down the legacy system? If the legacy system is still to be used for other SAP components, the data that is no longer required can be removed with archiving objects after the statutory retention period has expired.

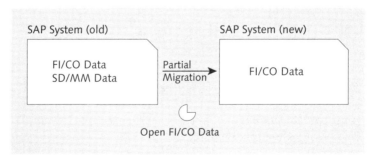

Figure 4.6 Partial Migration of Data to a New SAP System

On the left side in Figure 4.6, you will see a legacy SAP system with data from the components FI/CO and SD/MM. However, the FI/CO data for open business processes will ultimately be migrated to the new FI/CO system. The legacy SAP system will be available from now on only for information and inspection purposes. Its operation still gives rise to significant costs for a company. For this reason, a company will try in reality to shut down the legacy SAP system quickly and conveniently. There are different approaches to this in reality, which we will not consider in detail here. In Chapter 8, we'll take a detailed look at one option where data archiving functions can shut down legacy systems.

Starting Points in Data Archiving

In summary, we can say that the start of the SAP data archiving project can have different drivers. If your focus is on performance optimization and memory, you should start to plan and implement archiving as soon as possible.

The practical examples in this section have given you an insight into the problems that may occur in the environment of SAP data archiving. When developing your strategy and concepts, you should consider the issues addressed in the various sections. You can thus develop concepts that are flexible and can be adapted to changing circumstances. This flexibility and adaptability differentiates simple strategies from good strategies.

4.2   Developing an Archiving Concept

When you start SAP data archiving without an archiving concept, you run the risk of ending up in a dead end sooner or later. An archiving concept provides you with a complete overview of the IT systems, processes, and departments that are affected in your company and also meets the legal requirements for appropriate documentation (*system documentation*). The archiving concept is similar to a city map that includes all-important information about a city. A third-party must be able to gain a good overview of SAP data archiving in your company in a relatively short time.

System overview and documentation

How should an archiving concept for SAP data actually look so that it can meet these requirements exactly? It is useful to divide the archiving concept into the three levels displayed in Figure 4.7 to enable it to be viewed from different angles:

Concept levels

▸ **Strategic level**
At the strategic level, you make far-reaching decisions for your archiving concept. We will provide further details in Section 4.2.1.

▸ **Operational level**
The operational level of the archiving concept includes help and tips for the efficient performance of ongoing archiving. We'll take a close look at this in Section 4.2.2.

▸ **Conceptual level**
The conceptual level is divided into two areas or columns, the "archiving object" area and the "country" area in an SAP system. You will learn how to create your concepts at the conceptual level in Section 4.2.3.

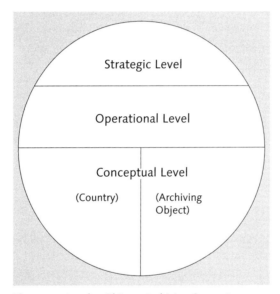

Figure 4.7 Levels within an Archiving Concept

Best practices The distinction between strategy, operational implementation, and conceptual level has proven itself in reality. For this reason, we recommend that you create your archiving concept in a similar manner or, if an archiving concept is already available, that you adapt the existing concept to this structure.

Creating a Concept and Building a House	[Ex]

The development of an archiving concept requires as much planning and care as the building of a house. You first create a well-conceived floor plan and blueprints (strategic level), you then start with the foundation and the shell (conceptual level), and finally complete your home with interior design and furnishings in order to live in it (operational level).

4.2.1 Strategic Level

At the start of this chapter, we said that you define your goal and determine the path to it using a strategy. At the strategic level, you can specify your goal and calculate the route to it. In doing so, you must consider several factors:

Strategic issues

- With which archiving objects should I start?
- Where will the archived data be stored?
- Will I make investments in fee-based add-ons to optimize archive access?
- How does the company's future IT landscape look?
- Is there a plan to use SAP ILM or the SAP HANA platform at a later date?
- In what period of time is the project to be completed?
- Are corporate acquisitions or sales pending?

These are just some of the many issues you will confront at the strategic level of concept development. You are unlikely to be able to answer all of these questions yourself. You need feedback from various decision-makers so that everyone involved supports the archiving strategy. Furthermore, certain questions cannot be answered at all when creating the archiving concept, because there are as yet no plans for the future for these topic areas. However, you should work in these cases with assumptions and probabilities and develop strategic options. Decisions at the strategic level have a long-term character and usually cover the procedure for a period of five years. Thus it is particularly important in this phase to refrain from making hasty decisions that may be difficult or almost impossible to revise later.

Section 4.1 introduced you to the various start times for an archiving project. Different strategies are required depending on the scenario. Thus it makes no sense to perform a technical table analysis in the template phase since no data will be generated here in the live SAP system. If, however, the system reached the technical capacity limits, you must perform a technical table analysis using Transaction DB02 (see also Chapter 1, Section 1.4.1).

However, consider the following aspects, regardless of the start time, in order to strategically plan an archiving project.

Overview of the SAP Landscape

A complete overview of the SAP landscape enables you to achieve, above all, transparency. As already noted in Chapter 1, Section 1.7, the transparency of existing IT systems and interfaces is very important. If you do not have an overview of your IT landscape, you should create such a visual overview. Clarify immediately the points that are of major importance for SAP data archiving:

- What data from the SAP system will be distributed in other systems (SAP and non-SAP systems)? For example, can the system distribute newly created master data automatically via IDoc to other systems?

- Which IT systems have read access to the tables of the SAP system? How often does this access occur and how far back does the accessed data go? What are the names of the accessed tables and to which data archiving objects are they assigned?

- What is the expected impact of data archiving in these IT systems? What measures can be taken here?

After you have gained an overview of your SAP landscape, you can base your strategy on it.

Technological Trends

Additional influencing factors on archiving, which you should consider at the strategic level, include new technological trends such as SAP HANA or SAP ILM. We will discuss these topics in detail in Chapter 8 and Chapter

9. If you intend to upgrade to the SAP HANA platform or to introduce the SAP ILM solution in the near future, you must make the appropriate preparations. On the one hand, new knowledge on the implementation of data archiving is required in such cases and, on the other hand, the tasks of the administrator change (also see Chapter 7).

Storage of Archive Files

Chapter 2 describes the storage of archived data. You have already learned about the various storage options. At the strategic level of concept development, you must opt for one of these options and define the appropriate storage locations for the next few years.

Defining storage locations

If, as in most cases, you opt for an archive system, you must select a suitable vendor for such a system. Here there are numerous well-known manufacturers that specialize in archive systems. Groups may already have a group license, thus you only have to provide access to the archive system. However, remember to take care of the procurement of the archive system in time. It is precisely this task that is often associated with a lot of time and effort in reality.

Selecting archive system

Access to Data

Chapter 3 focuses on access to archived data. You have already learned about the various access options. During the strategic conception of data archiving, you must decide whether the standard SAP version meets your needs or should be extended via add-ons.

You cannot make this decision without knowledge of individual transactions and their archive access quality. At the strategic level, however, you must make a decision on behalf of the user at a very early stage. Before you do so, the administrator for SAP data archiving should perform small tests for the various SAP data archiving objects together with the users, where the users can also evaluate the quality of access. By setting the residence time to a high level, you can satisfy the users and testers even with worse archive access over a long period of time.

Testing archive access with users

Road Map for Data Archiving

Long-term road map

The road map for data archiving is a strategic plan that leads you on the optimal path to your goal. You must use data archiving objects and data extraction in live operations in a defined time for the various countries involved. In doing so, it is of major importance to specify the priorities correctly. It is useful, for example, to first tackle the concepts for important countries and archiving objects in order to be able to promptly start live archiving and extraction. If you start with the concepts for archiving objects with low data volume and without performance impact, you will lose time that you should first invest in important archiving objects.

Team for Data Archiving

External consultants

Giving thought to the composition of the data archiving team at an early stage is a prerequisite for future success. Is, for example, the expertise available internally or must an external consultant be hired? The provision of human resources is a very important issue in addition to financial resources. SAP consultants are in high demand on the market, and it can take some time to find specialists for data archiving. For this reason, you should seek suitable consultants at an early stage.

Internal project team

The core team should also have a common understanding of the archiving project, and the members should share their knowledge with each other. To this end, the team can create a mind map for getting started on the topic, which can lead especially to promoting the creativity of the core team and can be useful in strategic decisions.

[+] **Creating a Mind Map**

Create a mind map as in Figure 4.8 in order to make your decisions at the strategic level. Try to identify important points in essential questions for which a long-term decision must be made. The question of *when* takes you, for example, to a long-term road map, including a project and milestone plan. The question of *who* leads you to putting together an ideal team composed of internal and external persons. The more questions you can clarify and answer at the strategic level, the sooner you can concentrate on the conceptual level.

Figure 4.8 Mind Map for Strategic Decisions

4.2.2 Operational Level

You must ensure the optimal operation of SAP data archiving at the operational level. The most important question that needs to be answered here is as follows:

Who performs when, which tasks, how and where?

However, this relatively simple question usually poses significant problems in reality. Responsibilities are often unknown and the relevant authorizations and powers are missing. Furthermore, it is not always obvious when SAP data archiving may start, because there are important features here that must be observed so that no unwanted situations occur.

Thus divide the question according to the included essential questions, and use these key points to create documentation that answers all of these questions. We will go through the following essential questions individually.

Key points for documentation

Who Performs the Task?

In reality, a person from the SAP Basis team, who is also responsible for the administration of the SAP system, usually performs operational data archiving. We call this person the *administrator for SAP data archiving*.

Administrator for data archiving

Employees in user
departments In rare cases, trained employees from the user departments perform an archiving run. This can be useful if the person from the user department is the *data owner*. Thus, for example, the employees from the finance department can take care of the archiving of financial accounting documents using the archiving object `FI_DOCUMNT`.

In addition, it is possible that external consultants and companies perform archiving in the form of maintenance contracts. Ideally, you have already decided who will ultimately handle this task for your SAP system and have documented it according to individual criteria at the strategic level.

Selecting competent administrators In this context, it is important to learn about the expertise of the administrator for SAP data archiving and, where appropriate, to ask for references. The administrator usually has comprehensive authorizations for performing data archiving and thus bears a great responsibility. Incorrectly created selection variants within the write job of an SAP data archiving object caused by a simple typing error can result in serious problems, for example. Of course, if the administrator is sick or absent, another suitable administrator or IT employee with similar knowledge can represent him or her.

When?

Time zones The time, that is, the time of day for the implementation of SAP data archiving is also of major importance, especially if users on different continents and in different time zones access the SAP system from which the data is to be archived. When selecting the appropriate time, coordinated universal time UTC (*Universal Time Coordinated*) assists you. By means of the UTC, you can calculate—starting from each time—how late it is at the moment in a different country. In addition, you either add or subtract whole numbers. UTC-4 applies to New York, for example. Istanbul (Turkey), on the other hand, has a coordinated universal time of UTC+3. Thus the time difference between these two cities is seven hours. Figure 4.9 shows how great the time difference between certain countries can be.

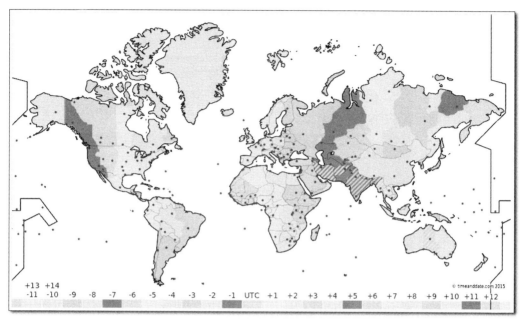

Figure 4.9 Time Differences Around the World (Source: http://www.timeanddate.com/)

In SAP systems used in only one country or on one continent, it is easier to schedule the times for the implementation of SAP data archiving. Here you know when users start to work in the SAP system and when they log off from the SAP system. Administrators usually prefer evenings or public holidays or weekends for SAP data archiving. This is due to the fact that there are no users or hardly any users logged on to the SAP system at these times, and they can perform SAP data archiving without any loss in performance. You should have your eye on the right time for archiving when it comes to archiving large amounts of data. On the other hand, you can schedule archiving of small amounts of data in addition to the day-to-day operations of the SAP system if there is no reason to fear an impact on performance.

Times of low system use

As an example, we have created a table to determine the optimal time frame for the implementation of data archiving. Maintain UTC+1 as standard time and UTC+2 as daylight saving time for Germany, UTC+8 for China, and UTC-5 as standard time and UTC-4 as daylight saving time for the United States. The working hours extend in each case from 09:00

Example: Defining time frame

to 18:00 local time. Since different time zones exist for the United States in contrast to Germany and China, we have decided on New York's time zone in this example. You gain insight into when overlap occurs and when, according to Table 4.1, completely free time frames are available.

UTC Time	USA, New York (UTC-5)/(UTC-4)	Germany (UTC+1)/(UTC+2)	China (Beijing) (UTC+8)
00:00	free	free	free
01:00			09:00
02:00			10:00
03:00			11:00
04:00			12:00
05:00			13:00
06:00			14:00
07:00		08:00/09:00	15:00
08:00		09:00/10:00	16:00
09:00		10:00/11:00	17:00
10:00		11:00/12:00	18:00
11:00		12:00/13:00	
12:00		13:00/14:00	
13:00	08:00/09:00	14:00/15:00	
14:00	09:00/10:00	15:00/16:00	
15:00	10:00/11:00	16:00/17:00	
16:00	11:00/12:00	17:00/18:00	
17:00	12:00/13:00	18:00/19:00	
18:00	13:00/14:00		
19:00	14:00/15:00		
20:00	15:00/16:00		
21:00	16:00/17:00		
22:00	17:00/18:00		
23:00	18:00/19:00		

Table 4.1 Determination of a Time Frame for SAP Data Archiving

You can quickly see that work stops only around 00:00 UCT in all three countries or cities. This time can be ideal for the implementation of SAP data archiving. However, you should not interpret this example as meaning that you must archive only between 00:00 and 01:00 UCT. Another good time frame would be, for example, between 11:00 and 12:00 UCT. At this time, employees have already finished work in China, colleagues have not yet started work in the United States, and most employees are on their lunch breaks in Germany. Of course, it is also possible to start archiving from 21:00 UCT when it is known that most employees finish work earlier in the United States.

Another important point for the determination of the optimal time frame is the cooperation of the international teams. If you would like to have a teleconference from New York with your colleagues in Germany to agree personally on the SAP data archiving activities, you have a time frame from 14:00 to 17:00 UCT during standard time and from 13:00 to 16:00 UCT during daylight saving time. Thus when you are about to start work in New York, your colleagues in Germany are just finishing work.

International teams

You can also maintain all-important national and international holidays with a transnational calendar in order to obtain a better overview of other possible time frames in addition to weekends. Public holidays and weekends are usually suitable time frames for performing large archiving runs in an SAP system. The question as to *when* is thus a very important question that has to be agreed on for each individual SAP data archiving object.

International public holidays in the calendar

After an archiving and deletion run, you must ensure in particular that the archive information structures are built in a timely manner so that the user can access the archived data even after SAP data archiving.

Timely building of archive infostructures

Missing Archive Infostructures

 [Ex]

Over the weekend, a company archived and deleted very large amounts of data, but the archive infostructures are not available at the start of work at 09:00 local time on Monday. Thus there are temporary restrictions on archive access, which is confusing for users and should always be avoided.

What Tasks?

The operational tasks within SAP data archiving are very wide-ranging. We will give a detailed description of the most important tasks that the administrator assumes in Chapter 7. Here we will mention only the main areas:

▶ System analysis

▶ Communication

▶ Operations

▶ Monitoring

▶ Documentation

These five points are essential for optimal operational implementation of SAP data archiving.

How?

The different tasks of the operational level are performed manually to some extent but are performed automatically as far as possible. The administrator can perform the system analysis, for example, either manually via individual transactions or automatically via a report. Communication, on the other hand, should primarily be prepared and performed manually. The degree of automation is almost zero for this task. The documentation is also a purely manual activity. The operation and monitoring of SAP data archiving, however, can be performed manually or partially automated as required. The goal in answering the question *how* should be to design the administrator's workflow as efficiently as possible.

Where?

The administrator usually performs his or her activities from a local workspace. If the administrator comes from the United States, his or her workplace will thus be in an American city. However, it is no longer rare nowadays to perform tasks in an SAP system *remotely*. It is also possible for an external company in the United States or abroad to perform the administration. The external administrator then accesses the system remotely in this case also. The *where* is not of importance at the operational level as long as the administrator always has access to the SAP system.

Planning Operational Tasks

In short, the answer to our question, *Who performs when, which tasks, how and where*, is the administrator for SAP data archiving performs, either manually or largely automatically, the precise tasks described in Chapter 7 from any workplace, while taking into account the UTC in the countries concerned and the optimal time frame.

You can use a simple Excel file to plan your work as an administrator more effectively and keep track of the countries and the SAP data archiving objects in your SAP system. You can also quickly see for which country the tax data extraction with DART is required by law and which archiving objects this affects. This Excel file should contain the following plans, for each of which you can use one spreadsheet:

Increasing effectiveness

▶ Integrated long-term data archiving and extraction plan (LDAEP)

▶ Long-term data archiving plan (LDAP)

▶ Long-term data extraction plan (LDEP)

We'll describe these plans in detail in the following sections. At *www.sap-press.com/3928*, you can download a sample file in the area "Materials for the Book."

Integrated Long-Term Data Archiving and Extraction Plan (LDAEP)

We look at all countries that access an SAP system within the Excel sheet LDAEP. For each of these countries, we require a separate concept, and we answer the question according to the DART relevance. The detailed description of the content of these concepts is part of the conceptual level, which is discussed in detail in Section 4.2.3. At the operational level and as an administrator, you need only the information that a concept exists. The data for a country may not be archived without such a concept, because the retention periods and other country-specific features have still not been clarified. In the LDAEP, you also see immediately whether or not data extraction is required for each country. In Table 4.2, you see, for

Basic data for countries involved

example, that a concept exists only for the United States and that data extracts must be created for this country. On the archiving page, only such SAP data archiving objects for which a concept exists may be used live for the United States.

Country Code	Country	UTC	Concept Status	DART Relevance
DE	Germany	UTC+1 UTC+2	In process (10–90)	Yes
US	USA	Various	Created (100)	Yes
CN	China	UTC+8	Open (0)	To be clarified

Table 4.2 Countries in the SAP System

Overview of archiving objects

In Table 4.3, you can see, for example, the archiving object FI_DOCUMNT (financial accounting documents) with a concept. Since a concept has been created only for this archiving object, only this archiving object may be used for the United States. Since the archiving object FI_DOCUMNT is relevant to DART, it may be used only if the data extract has been created completely for the period to be archived.

Overview of DART extracts

The overview of completely created DART extracts is maintained on an additional Excel sheet *Long-term data extraction plan* (LDEP), which we'll take a look at in the following section. The archiving object IDOC (Intermediate Document) in Table 4.3 is not indicated as DART-relevant because it does not contain any data relevant to the electronic tax inspection. The archiving of this object can be started for the United States, thus independent of the DART extraction, as soon as its concept exists.

Archiving Object	Description	Concept Status	DART Relevance
FI_DOCUMNT	Financial accounting documents	Created (100)	Yes
IDOC	Intermediate Document	In process (10–90)	No
RV_LIKP	Deliveries	Open (0)	Yes

Table 4.3 Archiving Objects in the SAP System

In the following section we'll look at the countries Germany, the United States, and China and consider how the status of these country-specific concepts can be set in each case. Possible values for the status, particularly if the concept for the country or extraction is still in process, are as follows:

Setting concept status per country

▸ **Open**

   ▹ *0 – Open*

   A concept is required for each country from which the SAP system is used live. You set the *open* status if a concept has not yet been created for a country. In order to create a concept, the legal requirements and, in particular, the retention requirements and the use of DART must be clarified, among other things.

▸ **In Process**

   If you notice that DART must be used for the country involved, divide the *in process* status into smaller milestones in order to have better control of the implementation progress. You can use the milestones suggested here or define a new status according to the circumstances of your specific company.

   ▹ *10 – Candidate for an Extraction*

   The country for which an extraction is required by law and where you also want to actually start the introduction is a candidate for the extraction.

   ▹ *20 – Creation of the Concept Paper*

   Within the concept paper, you document the legal requirements as well as the retention periods for the country concerned. If DART has to be set up, document exactly how it can be set up and used.

   ▹ *30 – Workshop*

   The DART requirements are specified more precisely via workshops with the user department and IT.

   ▹ *40 – Customizing*

   Perform customizing in the development system according to the concept paper and the discussions in the workshops with the user department. In particular, you must include additional tables and fields, which are not extracted by DART in the standard system within the scope of the extraction.

► *50 – Test in the Development System*
Create and present first data extracts to the user department through tests in the development system.

► *60 – Adjustment and Optimization*
Any adjustments and optimizations in accordance with the feedback from the user department are implemented in the development system.

► *70 – Presentation and Release for Transport*
The final results are presented to the user department to obtain the release for the transport in the quality assurance system.

► *80 – Test in Quality Assurance System*
The transport is imported in the quality assurance system and checked. DART is tested extensively via different test scenarios.

► *90 – Release for Go-Live*
The user department then performs the release for the go-live in the live system. Document the releases of the user department in appropriate templates and store them.

► **Created**
100 – Concept Created or Live Extraction
Finally, you reach the *created* status with the live extraction and regularly perform the extraction in the SAP system on the predefined dates.

Setting status for archiving objects

You proceed almost identically for archiving objects. You can define different statuses here also.

Possible values for the status, particularly if the concept for the archiving object is still in process, are as follows:

► **Open**

► *0 – Open*
A concept is required for each archiving object that is to be used live in the SAP system. You thus set the *open* status if a concept has not yet been created for an object. The concept must include answers to the questions about the requirements of the user department, particularly with regard to archive access and residence times in the SAP system.

▶ **In Process**

If, after a database analysis, you notice that an archiving object is to be used, divide the *in process* status into smaller milestones in order to have better control of the implementation progress. You can use the milestones suggested here or define your own status according to the requirements of your specific company.

▸ *10 – Candidate for Data Archiving*
The archiving object that you would actually like to introduce after the database analysis is a candidate for data archiving.

▸ *20 – Creation of the Concept Paper*
Within the concept paper, you document the requirements of the user department as well as the various archive access options. You also make suggestions for Customizing and the residence time here.

▸ *30 – Workshop with the User Department and IT*
The requirements for the data archiving object are specified more precisely via workshops with the user department and IT.

▸ *40 – Customizing*
Perform Customizing in the development system according to the concept paper and the discussions in the workshops with the user department.

▸ *50 – Test in Development System*
After small tests in the development system, create and show the first archive files to the user department.

▸ *60 – Adjustment and Optimization*
Any adjustments and optimizations in accordance with the feedback from the user department are implemented in the development system.

▸ *70 – Presentation and Release for Transport*
The final results are presented to the user department to obtain the release for the transport in the quality assurance system.

▸ *80 – Test in the Quality Assurance System*
After being imported in the quality assurance system, the transport is checked. The data archiving object is tested extensively via different test scenarios.

> ▸ *90 – Release for Go-Live*
> The release is then performed for the go-live in the live system. Afterward, document releases of the user department in appropriate templates and store them.

▸ **Created**
100 – Concept Created or Live Archiving
Finally, you reach the *created* status with live archiving and regularly perform data archiving in the SAP system on the predefined dates.

Long-Term Data Archiving Plan (LDAP)

Overview of archiving objects

The long-term data archiving plan contains all active and future data archiving objects (see Table 4.4). This plan shows which archiving objects will be started when and for which countries. A column for the DART relevance indicates that the DART extracts must be fully created before archiving.

Archiving Object	Description	Archiving Time Frame	DART Relevance
FI_DOCUMNT	Financial accounting documents	USA: 00:00 UTC, Sunday monthly	Yes, for US
		In process	Yes, for DE
IDOC	Intermediate Document	In process	No
RV_LIKP	Deliveries	In process	Yes

Table 4.4 Archiving Objects in the Archiving Plan

Rules for archiving

During the operational implementation of archiving, you must observe the following key points:

▸ Only archiving objects with a concept may be started.

▸ The time frame as to when and for how long archiving may be performed must be defined.

▸ Archiving objects with DART relevance may be started only after the DART extract has been created.

▸ Archiving objects may be started only for the countries for which the requirements were documented in a concept and released.

Long-Term Data Extraction Plan (LDEP)

The long-term data extraction plan contains all company codes from the various SAP systems from which DART extracts must be created. This list quickly shows the countries for which the DART extract is still open or partially or completely created or stored (see Table 4.5).

Overview of
company codes

System ID	Client	Company Code	Fiscal Year	DART Extract
P01	100	1000	2013	Created
P01	100	1000	2014	Created
P01	100	1000	2015	Open
P20	200	2000	2013	Created
P20	200	2000	2014	Open
P20	200	2000	2015	Open

Table 4.5 Created and Still Open DART Extracts for the Respective Company Codes in the Different SAP Systems

During the operational implementation of data extraction, you must observe the following key points:

Rules for the
extraction

▸ Open DART extracts are to be created promptly so that the archiving of dependent archiving objects can start.

▸ You create an extraction per company code and fiscal year.

The documents described here are important resources during the administration of SAP data archiving, which we'll look at in detail in Chapter 7. Due to the compact overview, not only you as administrator but also your colleagues obtain a quick overview of the regular operational tasks within archiving.

4.2.3 Conceptual Level

The conceptual level forms the foundation of our archiving concept. It is divided into the area of the data archiving object and the area of legal requirements in the country where archiving is to be performed. Each SAP data archiving object requires its own concept in which key points are extensively documented, for example, the residence times, Customizing, and archive access. For each country that works with the data in

Stable foundation

the SAP system, you must also identify, document, and implement the respective statutory requirements. In particular, the retention periods and the storage place of archive files are documented here with the corresponding legal texts. We'll now examine two examples in detail to see how such concepts can look. On the one hand, you'll learn how to document a concept for an archiving object while, on the other hand, we'll take a look at a concept for a country. These concepts are templates that you can customize and use for your archiving project.

Pooling knowledge centrally

In large corporate groups, we have often experienced the fact that there is no central contact person for SAP data archiving and, for this reason, various projects and concepts are designed by different departments. On the one hand, this is due to the fact that the corporate organization is very complex and, on the other hand, that subsidiaries, particularly abroad, do not interact regularly with the IT department of the company headquarters. For this reason, we recommend that large corporate groups establish a company-wide pool for archiving concepts in which reusable templates are stored for other departments or that they strengthen the unity of the various teams. By having a central team for SAP data archiving in the corporate group, you achieve synergy and thus save resources.

Concepts per Archiving Object

Example: Concept for FI documents

This section contains a sample concept for an archiving object. This concept is divided into different sections.

Description of Archiving Object

In the first section of the concept, you enter a short description of the archiving object. The SAP documentation pages in the SAP Help Portal, from which you can copy the main content, are useful.

[Ex] **Archiving Object FI_DOCUMNT (FI Documents)**

Financial accounting documents (FI documents) are archived with the archiving object FI_DOCUMNT and deleted. The archivable documents including their change documents, form texts, and ArchiveLink link entries are written in one or more archive files during document archiving. To ensure that only no longer needed documents are archived from the system, several conditions must be met. The write program checks the archivability at document header and document item level.

Criteria for Archivability

The criteria for archivability specify when you can archive a data record. You should analyze the data quality in advance and, if necessary, specify activities in the concept that the user department must perform before data archiving, for example, setting the status of a document to *completed*.

Conditions for archiving

Conditions for Archiving FI Documents [Ex]

To ensure that you archive only no longer needed documents from the system, several conditions must be met, which are defined in Table 4.6. The write program checks the archivability at document header and document item level. If one of the requirements for a document is not satisfied in the tests, the entire document is not archived.

Check Level	Check
Document header	The document type runtime must be exceeded.
	The document must be more than the minimum number of days in the system.
	Documents with withholding tax remain at least 455 days in the system.
	Recurring entry documents, parked documents, or sample documents are not considered.
Document item	The document must not contain any open items. The system considers only cleared items or those without open item management.
	The account type runtime must be exceeded.
Additional checks	Can be set up using business add-ins (BAdIs): FI_DOCUMNT_CHECK (Archiving FI documents: additional archivability check)

Table 4.6 Checks in Accordance with SAP Documentation

Customizing

Customizing is divided into different areas. You include in this documentation all areas for which you maintain corresponding settings. Thus you can always trace adjustments. You also document for which SAP sys-

Customizing areas

tems you have set up Customizing—that is, for which systems this concept is valid.

[Ex] **Customizing for the Archiving Object FI_DOCUMNT**

The SAP systems listed in Table 4.7 have identical Customizing for this archiving object.

SAP System	Client	Company Code	Modules
P01	100	1000 (Portland)	FI/CO
P03	200	2000 (Chicago)	All

Table 4.7 SAP Systems for the Archiving Object

The Customizing settings for the archiving object FI_DOCUMNT are made in the following areas:

► **Cross-archiving-object Customizing**
Not required.

► **Archiving-object-specific Customizing**
Technical settings are made in accordance with Table 4.8.

Field	Value
Object Name	FI_DOCUMNT
Logical File Name	ARCHIVE_DATA_FILE
Maximum Size in MB	100 MB
Maximum Number of Data Objects	Blank
Test Mode Variant	SAP&TEST
Live Mode Variant	SAP&PROD
Deletion Jobs	Automatic Start
Settings for Postprocessing Program	SAP&PROD Automatic Start
Content Repository	C1 (Archive Routing) Automatic Start
Sequence	Storage before Deletion Phase

Table 4.8 Technical Settings for the Archiving Object

▶ **Archive routing**
The archive files of the two company codes are stored in two different content repositories in the archive system as defined in Table 4.9. In the examples in the table, the data is stored directly in the content repository when condition one is met.

Rule No.	Condition 1/ Company Code	Condition 2/ Fiscal Year	Content Repository	Logical File Name
1	1000		C1	
2	2000		C2	

Table 4.9 Rules and Conditions for Archive Routing

▶ **Basis Customizing**
Cross-client file names/paths (see Table 4.10).

Field	Description
Log. Path	*ARCHIVE_GLOBAL_PATH*
Phy. Path	*<P=DIR_GLOBAL>/<FILENAME>*
Log. Name	*ARCHIVE_DATA_FILE*
Phy. Name	*<PARAM_1>_<PARAM_3>_ <DATE>_<TIME>_<PARAM_2>. ARCHIVE*

Table 4.10 Overview of the Links of Path and File Names

▶ **Cross-client file names**
No Customizing required.

▶ **Application-specific Customizing**
Maintenance of account type runtimes. The runtime of 730 days (two years) was set as the residence time and 4015 days (eleven years) was set for the secondary indexes in the tables BSIS/BSAS, etc. (see Table 4.11).

CoCd	A/C Type	From Account	To A/C	Runtime	Secondary Index Runtime
*	*	*	*	730	4.015

Table 4.11 Account Type Runtimes

▸ Maintenance of document type runtimes as defined in Table 4.12.

CoCd	Doc. Type	Doc. Runtime	FBRA Check
*	*	730	blank

Table 4.12 Document Type Runtimes

Dependencies

Dependencies usually exist between an archiving object and other archiving objects that must first be archived. An archiving object can also affect processes in the SAP system or connected IT systems. Thus document possible dependencies extensively.

[Ex]

Dependencies of the Archiving Object FI_DOCUMNT

There is no dependency on other archiving objects.

There is no dependency on connected IT systems, which could possibly be affected after data archiving.

Archive Access

Accessing transactions

Archive access is very important. Here document the transactions that have restricted, full, or no archive access after SAP data archiving. If archive excess is to be extended by add-ons, you should also document this aspect accordingly. Table 4.13 shows an example of such documentation.

Transaction before Archiving	Transaction after Archiving	Restrictions	Alternatives
FB03	FB03	None	SARE
FAGLB03	FAGLB03	Yes, automatic archive access can be established using SAP Notes	Not required
FAGLL03	FAGLL03	None	Not required
...	...	...	...

Table 4.13 Excerpt of Transactions for Archive Access

In this table, you include, for example, all transactions that are used to display FI documents. The example contains only three possible transactions. If you have only restricted access or no access to the data with a transaction after archiving, document in this section of the concept whether there are proposed solutions or alternatives such as SAP Notes or the Archive Explorer (Transaction SARE).

SAP Notes

There are a variety of SAP Notes for archiving objects. SAP Notes are published regularly, not only for troubleshooting but also with recommendations. In a table similar to Table 4.14, insert relevant SAP Notes in this section of the concept. If you read or implement new SAP Notes, you should update this section.

Relevant Notes

SAP Note	Description	Released On	Relevance	Comment
2072407	Reloading Archive Data	09/26/2014	Yes	Information
204426	RFUMSV00: Read Archive Data	07/09/2014	Yes	Implement
...	...	...	...	...

Table 4.14 SAP Notes for the Archiving Object FI_DOCUMNT

Customer-Specific Extensions (Tables, Transactions, Reports, Interfaces, etc.)

The standard SAP version is almost always adapted via customer-specific extensions. For tables, transactions, and reports, you maintain in a table similar to Table 4.15 information as to whether appropriate measures must be taken or already have been taken.

Documenting measures

Extension Type	Sample Name	Access to Table(s)	Measure Required
Transaction	ZFITRANSACTION	BSIS	No
Table	ZFITABLE	n. a.	Archive also

Table 4.15 Examples of Customer-Specific Extensions with a Dependency on the Archiving Object FI_DOCUMNT

Extension Type	Sample Name	Access to Table(s)	Measure Required
Report	ZFIREPORT	BKPF	Adjust code with regard to archive access
Interface	ZFI0001	BSEG	No
...	...	...	...

Table 4.15 Examples of Customer-Specific Extensions with a Dependency on the Archiving Object FI_DOCUMNT (Cont.)

All customer-specific extensions that need to access the tables affected by archiving must be assessed accordingly to determine if a measure must be taken to enable access. If measures are required, also document them in this section of the concept.

Operational Implementation

Procedures   The operational implementation of data archiving is an administrator task that we will introduce in Chapter 7. This section of the concept specifies the requirements for the administrator in terms of how the operational implementation must ultimately look, for example, the maintenance of selection variants, which we introduced in Chapter 1, Section 1.4.4 (see Table 4.16).

Fields in the Selection Variant	Values during First Archiving	Values during Second Archiving
Company codes from	1000	2000
Company codes to	Blank	Blank
Document numbers from	Blank	Blank
Document numbers to	Blank	Blank
Fiscal year from	2012	2012
Fiscal year to	2012	2012
Period from	01	01
Period to	16	16

Table 4.16 Selection Criteria in the Variant

Fields in the Selection Variant	Values during First Archiving	Values during Second Archiving
Document type from	Blank	Blank
Document type to	Blank	Blank
Minimum number of days in the system	Blank	Blank
Key date	System proposal	System proposal
Flow control	Live mode	Live mode
Detailed log	Complete	Complete
Log output	List and application log	List and application log
Note on the archiving run	CoCd 1000 FY 2012	CoCd 2000 FY 2012

Table 4.16 Selection Criteria in the Variant (Cont.)

The administrator can see from the table how he or she must set up the variants for the first two archiving runs. The next archiving runs are then based on this model and can be adjusted if necessary.

Retention of Archive Files

Storage locations

In addition to archive access, the retention of archive files is a very important point of the archiving concept and is discussed in detail in Chapter 2. You enter the selected option or options in this section of the concept. In particular, you document the content repository with the corresponding runtime and storage location or locations—if several countries are involved.

Content Repositories for FI Accounting Documents   [Ex]

The archive files are stored in two different content repositories in an archive system in the United States, as displayed in Table 4.17.

Content Repository ID	Description	Runtime
C1	FI data CoCd 1000	11 years
C2	FI data CoCd 2000	11 years

Table 4.17 Active Content Repositories in the Archive System

Information Lifecycle

Basic data of lifecycle

The goal after archiving is to destroy the archive files after the end of the lifecycle. In this section of the concept, you document how the information lifecycle for an archiving object looks specifically and if manual deletion locks are set.

[Ex]

Information Lifecycle for the Object FI_DOCUMNT

The archiving object FI_DOCUMNT is retained with a residence time of 730 days and a retention period of 11 years (see Table 4.18). It is then deleted automatically in the archive system unless the archive files are explicitly locked by the user department to prevent deletion.

Archiving Object	System ID (Client)	Company Code	Residence Time	Retention Period
FI_DOCUMNT	P01(100)	1000	730 days	11 years
FI_DOCUMNT	P03(200)	3000	730 days	11 years

Table 4.18 Overview of the Information Lifecycle

Contacts

Contact data

You document the main contacts who have been involved in the development of the concept, noting the contact data as in Table 4.19, to enable quick answers to questions.

Name	Phone Number	Email	Department	Involved in Areas
Ahmet Türk			External	Overall concept
John Cooper			Taxes	Inspections/laws for the United States
Michelle Connor			Accounting	Inspections/laws for the United States
...	...	...	...	...

Table 4.19 Contacts for the Concept

Publishing Concepts

You can use the sample concept shown here for the archiving object FI_ DOCUMNT (financial accounting documents) as a template for all other archiving objects in your project. This structure has proven itself in real life during our archiving projects, but you can adapt and extend it of course at any time according to your own needs.

In addition to the creation of concepts, access to these concepts is also of major importance. Store these concepts in suitable IT systems in your company. You will find examples in Chapter 7, Section 7.5.

Storage of concepts

Concepts per Country

Now that we have looked at a specific sample concept for an archiving object, we would like to introduce another one for a country. We have chosen the United States as an example. Your concept should contain the following sections:

Example: Concept for the United States

Description of the Companies in the United States

The individual companies in the documented country as well as the relevant SAP organizational units (client, company code, etc.) in existing SAP systems are presented clearly in this section.

Companies and organizational units

Sample Software Corporation   **[Ex]**

Sample Software Corporation has its headquarters in Portland and a sales and marketing company in Chicago (see Table 4.20).

SAP System	Client	Company Code	Modules
P01	100	1000 (Portland)	FI/CO
P02	100	1000 (Portland)	SD/MM
P03	200	2000 (Chicago)	All

Table 4.20 Overview of a Company on SAP Systems

Sample Software Corporation is using three live SAP systems but only two legally independent business units, which have also been created as two separate company codes (1000 and 2000).

Company code 1000 is created in not only one but also two SAP systems (P01 and P02). This is due to the fact that the finance and controlling processes for company code 1000 are mapped only in SAP system P01. The corporation has its headquarters in Portland and is inspected by the Portland tax office.

Extract of Laws Relating to Archiving

You will find laws relating to archiving and retention of documents in the United States particularly in the Revenue Procedure 98-25 (Rev. Proc. 98-25) from the IRS. There are some guidelines that you should also observe. You will find an extract in Chapter 1, Section 1.5.

[Ex] **Legal Requirements for Archiving in the United States**

The requirements for archiving can be derived from the following laws and guidelines:

▶ 26 US Code, Sec. 6001

▶ 26 CFR, Regs. Sec. 1.6001-1(a)/(e)

▶ Rev. Rul. 71-20

▶ Revenue Procedure 98-25

Retention Location

The retention location of archive files can be derived from the laws. Answer, in particular, questions about whether data may be stored abroad or on external servers.

[Ex] **Retention Location for Archive Files in the United States**

Pursuant to Section 26 CFR 31.6001-1 Code of Federal Regulations (CFR), paragraphs (e), (1), and (2), the archive files are retained in one or more safe locations. Here is an excerpt from the legal text:

"All records required by the regulations in this part shall be kept, by the person required to keep them, at one or more convenient and safe locations accessible to internal revenue officers, and shall at all times be available for inspections by such officers."

Retention Periods

The retention periods for archive files can be derived from the laws. In this section of the concept, you should clarify the minimum and maximum periods during which the data may be retained.

Retention Periods for Archive Files in the United States [Ex]

Sample Software Corporation has, as an American company pursuant to internal and external requirements, defined the retention periods from Table 4.21.

Business Object	SAP Data Archiving Object	Retention Period	DART Relevance
FI document	FI_DOCUMNT	11 years	Yes
Sales order	SD_VBAK	11 years	Yes
Deliveries	RV_LIKP	11 years	Yes
…	…	…	…

Table 4.21 Retention Periods for Sample Software Corporation

Electronic Tax Inspection

The electronic tax inspection is carried out in different ways. The provision of tax-relevant data from an SAP system is a basic prerequisite for it. Document the process for the electronic tax inspection in this section of the concept.

Electronic Tax Inspection of Sample Software Corporation [Ex]

Sample Software Corporation is obliged, as an American company, to provide the data from the SAP system for the electronic tax inspection. To this end, the company has defined the following processes:

► DART extraction process:
  ► Creation of DART extracts by the administrator shortly after the annual financial statements in June of each year
  ► Inspection of the DART extracts by the administrator to ensure they are correct
  ► Securing of DART extracts on an appropriate storage medium (archive system)
► View provision process:
  ► Notification of inspection dates and scope to the administrator by the tax department
  ► Provision of view files by the administrator
  ► Review and, if necessary, new request for the view files
  ► Transfer of the view files to the auditor by the tax department

- ▸ Provision process for access:
  - ▸ Notification of inspection dates and scope to the administrator by the tax department
  - ▸ Ensuring the various requested access types for the inspection period
  - ▸ Adaptation of authorizations if necessary

Data Retention Tool (DART)

If DART is to be used, you should document the relevant Customizing settings and customer-specific extensions in this section.

[Ex] | **DART Settings**

Sample Software Corporation has made the following settings:

- ▸ All available transaction and master data is extracted with DART.
- ▸ The data catalog for the United States is already automatically determined and taken during the extraction.
- ▸ Customer-specific fields that are added to the standard SAP tables are also included within the scope of the extraction.

SAP Notes

There are also many SAP Notes for electronic tax inspections published not only to correct errors but also to provide recommendations relating to the tax inspection. In a table similar to Table 4.22, insert relevant SAP Notes for your country. If you implement or become aware of new SAP Notes, update this table.

SAP Note	Description	Released On	Relevance	Comment
2066693	DART: Control totals for FI documents are wrong	10/14/2014	Yes	Implement
2002469	DART 2.7e: Extension of the data catalog	05/09/2014	Yes	Implement
...	...	...	...	...

Table 4.22 SAP Notes for Electronic Tax Inspection

Access Types

Access must be ensued for auditors during the course of tax inspections and not just electronic inspections. You document the access types and how you can implement them in this section of the concept.

Access Types at Sample Software Corporation   **[Ex]**

The legislators distinguish three access types:

▸ **Direct access (A1 access)**
Direct access takes place in the SAP system. The auditor role ZAUDITOR was set up for this purpose. The role may be requested via a ticket to the administrator. Validity periods and restrictions on certain modules can be implemented upon request.

▸ **Indirect access (A2 access)**
Indirect access also takes place in the SAP system. For this purpose, the administrator assists the auditor. Here the administrator must be informed in a timely manner, about four weeks prior to the audit.

▸ **Immediate access (A3 access)**
Immediate access takes place using the provision of view files via DART. The tax department applies to the administrator for the appropriate files, which are provided on optical data carriers, such as a CD, or on the desired drive.

Inspection Periods and Types

Different inspections (customs inspection, tax inspection, etc.) take place at different intervals. An overview of previous audits as in Table 4.23 also gives a view of the future.

Inspection Type	Interval	Period of Last Inspections
General company audit	Every 2 years	2014
Special VAT audit	Every 4 years	2012
External audit of employee income tax	Every 2 years	2014
Customs inspection	Every three years	2013
Other inspections	Varies	2010

Table 4.23 Inspection Types and Periods According to Interval

Dependencies of SAP Data Archiving Objects

You use data archiving objects to archive information that must be preserved for legal reasons. There are archiving objects that you may archive only after a DART extraction because you cannot create complete DART extracts otherwise. Thus list important archiving objects from your archiving project in tabular form as in Table 4.24 and comment on them.

Archiving Object	Description	Affected DART Segments	Affected Tables
FI_DOCUMNT	Financial accounting documents	TXW_FI_HD TXW_FI_POS TXW_BSET	BKPF BSEG BSET
RV_LIKP	Deliveries	TXW_DL_HD TXW_DL_POS	LIKP LIPS
MM_MATBEL	Material documents	TXW_MM_HD TXW_MM_POS	MKPF MSEG
SD_VBAK	Sales orders	TXW_SD_HD TXW_HD_POS	VBAK VBAP
...	...	...	...

Table 4.24 Archiving Objects with Dependencies on DART

Contacts

You document the main contacts who have been involved in the development of the concept, noting the contact data as in Table 4.25, to enable questions to be posed to the right people.

Name	Phone Number	Email	Department	Involved in Areas
Ahmet Türk			External	Overall concept
John Cooper			Taxes	Inspections/laws for the United States
Michelle Connor			Accounting	Inspections/laws for the United States
...	...	...	...	...

Table 4.25 Contacts for the Concept

4.3 Summary

After looking at two examples of concepts, you can design such a concept for each individual data archiving object and for any country that is affected by SAP data archiving in your SAP system.

If you have not created a concept for a country, we advise you to refrain from starting SAP data archiving in that country. In particular, archiving objects affected by the DART extraction should not be archived under any circumstances until you have clarified if electronic tax inspections are performed in this country.

No archiving without a concept

Although DART has been standard in the United States and Germany for several years, the electronic tax inspection has only recently become a topic in countries such as Portugal, Belgium, and France. Since more reliable empirical values are often missing here and data is sometimes required in a different format, you will spare yourself a lot of effort in technical and organizational terms if you do not start SAP data archiving here until you have resolved all content-related questions with the tax authority. SAP also regularly provides SAP Notes on this topic, which you should read and observe. As an example of a country-specific format, we would like to mention only France at this point and give you a brief overview of the relevant SAP Notes in Table 4.26.

Other approaches abroad

SAP Note	Description	Relevant Country
1943727	DART: View file creation for France legal requirement	France
1951943	DART: France legal requirement FAQ note	France
1463497	DART: Use in various countries	Various

Table 4.26 SAP Notes for France in Area of Electronic Tax Inspection

We would like to encourage you at this point to search at regular intervals for current SAP Notes for the countries relevant to your SAP systems and to stay in constant contact with the local user departments. This is because it is the only way in which you can professionally and technically implement the requirements of the respective countries in relation to the electronic tax inspection.

You lay the foundation for the optimal planning and implementation of SAP data archiving projects with professional change management and good communication with everyone involved.

5 Planning Archiving Projects

After dealing with the creation of an archiving concept in the previous chapter, we can now focus on planning archiving projects. As with every project, archiving also requires professional change management and appropriate communication mechanisms between those involved. We will describe these two aspects in detail in Section 5.2. Archiving projects usually involves a change, for example, access to the archived data changes in most cases. Primarily, these changes affect users. Thus they must be prepared for the change and sufficiently informed so that archiving is accepted and possible resistance is eliminated.

In order to illustrate the approach in archiving projects, we'll take a look at three sample archiving projects in three different industries. We will present these examples in Section 5.1. The three sample industries include an automotive industry, a chemical industry, and an energy sector, in which we have been largely involved in projects with during previous years. The sample companies from these three industries can exemplify various other companies that have almost the same archiving objects in use. You'll learn about the similarities as well as the differences between the sample industries.

Sample industries

An important part of planning is the definition of the persons who are responsible. During your archiving project, decisions have to be made continuously so that you can proceed with the next task. We'll focus on this in Section 5.3. If all concepts are defined and the persons involved are clarified, a project plan and schedule can be created, which is the focus of Section 5.4.

Defining decision-makers

5.1   Archiving Projects in Three Sample Industries

SAP data archiving as a technical solution for ensuring performance and controlling data growth in SAP systems is relevant for all industries and is thus also in use in all industries. For your archiving project, it is important not only to be familiar, in technical terms, with SAP data archiving but also to be familiar with the specific requirements of the industry in which your company operates. If you become familiar with the specifics of your industry, you will gain valuable insights into your company's processes and can use them to your benefit for the planning and subsequent implementation of SAP data archiving.

Focus on three leading industries

This book focuses on the following three sample industries:

- The automotive industry represents all *manufacturing companies* here, that is, including those that do not manufacture cars.

- The chemical industry represents companies that are located in the *process industries*, for example, pharmaceutical or food manufacturers.

- The energy sector represents companies of the *utilities industry* (electricity, gas, and water), which often use the industry-specific SAP solution SAP for Utilities (SAP IS-U).

Examples are universal

If your company operates in another industry, the examples presented here will still be of interest to you. You can also copy the archiving objects, which are considered in detail in the examples, for your SAP system if they are relevant to it.

5.1.1   Automotive Industry

The automotive industry is a mainstay of the economy of most countries. Its economic importance is clear, for example, in campaigns such as the introduction of the "scrappage allowance" (allowance when purchasing a new car while scrapping the old car) in 2009, with which the automotive industry was supported financially by different governments in response to the economic crisis in order to secure jobs. This value chain not only includes car manufacturers but also lots of suppliers.

The world's leading car manufacturers from the United States or Germany, for example, not only produce locally today but also produce increasingly abroad. The car manufacturers are thereby relying on the *BRIC countries* (Brazil, Russia, India and China), which have very large populations on the one hand and offer very high growth opportunities on the other hand. You might be wondering what relevance it has for SAP data archiving if the board of directors of an automotive group decides to build new plants or even new independent companies abroad. For each of these countries, you must develop concepts for SAP data archiving, which take into account the respective statutory retention periods and so on.

International locations

For a leading car manufacturer, we had to deal with, for example, the general framework for SAP data archiving in China, because the sales figures there had surpassed the domestic figures by then, and this fact had led not only to high sales but also to very high data growth at the same time. Globalization has led to a trend where you will need to deal increasingly with how SAP data archiving can be set up for foreign companies.

In order to illustrate this trend, Table 5.1 shows three well-known international companies with large plants abroad.

Leading car manufacturers

Group	Well-Known Brands	Large Foreign Plants
Ford Motor Company	Ford and Lincoln	▸ China ▸ Germany ▸ Turkey
General Motors	Chevrolet, Buick, GMC, Cadillac, Opel, and so on	▸ Brazil ▸ USA ▸ South Africa
Volkswagen AG	Volkswagen, Audi, Skoda, Seat, Bentley, Lamborghini, and so on	▸ China ▸ India ▸ Russia ▸ Hungary

Table 5.1 Leading International Car Manufacturers and Their Plants

Leading international car manufacturers have built global production plants. Depending on the size of the foreign plant, it may be necessary to install an SAP system locally. However, there is also the variant according to which the SAP systems are operated centrally at the headquarters. Regardless of whether the SAP system is installed at the headquarters or abroad, the plants are always foreign companies, which are subject to foreign laws and retention requirements. Thus you must document the retention periods of the respective country in a concept before you start archiving, for example, financial accounting data with the archiving object `FI_DOCUMNT`.

Important suppliers   A car consists of several thousand individual parts. The car manufacturer no longer manufactures the important components itself; instead, several hundred suppliers manufacture and deliver the parts. You undoubtedly know the products of the leading manufacturers listed in Table 5.2.

Early planning   After this brief overview of the automotive industry, we'll take an in-depth look at the special features relating to SAP data archiving. For this purpose, we'll consider an example of a car manufacturer that manufactures vehicles worldwide in different plants and is supplied by several suppliers. Due to the size of the company and the large number of SAP systems in the group, we must first obtain an overview of SAP data archiving in the group at the start of the planning phase. In all our examples in this chapter, we assume that the individual SAP systems do not operate for more than three years (early planning, also see Chapter 4, Section 4.1.1).

Group	Well-known Products
Robert Bosch GmbH	Antilock braking system (ABS), diesel injection pump, and so on
MAHLE GmbH	Pistons for the engines and so on
Valeo S.A.	Windshield wipers and so on
Mann+Hummel GmbH	Filters and so on
ZF Friedrichshafen AG	Gears and so on
Continental AG	Tires and so on

Table 5.2 Leading Automotive Suppliers

Create an Overview of the Global Companies with Their SAP Systems **[+]**

Even if you are only responsible for SAP data archiving in a certain country or SAP system, you should always obtain an overview of the companies and SAP systems worldwide. By doing so, you can find out if SAP data archiving was already set up in one of these SAP systems and consult the administrators responsible. On the other hand, you can see how much memory each SAP system is using and which ones to expect loss in performance from in the future.

Our example of a car manufacturer, Road Cruiser Inc. operates the plants shown in Figure 5.1 and is supplied by different suppliers. Figure 5.1 shows an excerpt of live SAP systems in the business areas of cars and commercial vehicles.

Obtaining an overview

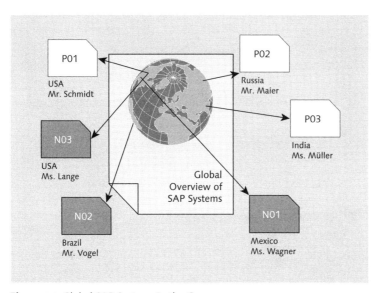

Figure 5.1 Global SAP Systems in the Group

The contact person for each country can provide us with information that data archiving has already been set up for SAP systems P01 and N03 only in the United States. We document this information in a table.

Table 5.3 shows the SAP systems of the individual companies and lists whether or not SAP data archiving is in use in these SAP systems. If data archiving is used actively, the relevant data archiving objects are documented.

Exchanging experience

Business Area	SAP System(s)	Contact Person (Country)	Is Data Archiving Active? (Objects)
Cars	P01	Mr. Schmidt (USA)	Yes BC_DBLOGS BC_SBAL IDOC
	P02	Mr. Maier (Russia)	No
	P03	Ms. Müller (India)	No
Commercial vehicles	N01	Ms. Wagner (Mexico)	No
	N02	Mr. Vogel (Brazil)	No
	N03	Ms. Lange (USA)	Yes MM_MATBEL FI_DOCUMNT

Table 5.3 SAP Systems in the Business Areas with Active SAP Data Archiving Objects

In the cars business area, three SAP data archiving objects are actively used in SAP system P01. The commercial vehicles business area also uses two SAP data archiving objects in SAP system N03. You can reach out to the contact person to discuss experiences and consider his or her findings in the planning phase. Other business areas have often traveled long paths, for example, when selecting the suitable storage option, which you can spare yourself by discussing it and thus saving valuable time.

Creating questionnaire

In order to discover all SAP systems in the group, the contact persons, and the already used data archiving objects, you first create an overview of all live SAP systems in your company. You can extend this list through the current size of the database and the contact person responsible. Then send this contact person, for example, a questionnaire to obtain feedback as to whether data archiving is active or scheduled for a later date and if preparations may already have been taken.

You can create such a questionnaire based on the template in Table 5.4.

Sample questionnaire

No.	Question	Answer	Example(s)
1	SAP system ID	<Input>	P01
2	Do you already archive data in your SAP system?	<Input>	▸ Yes ▸ No ▸ Planned from 2015
3	At what intervals do you archive data?	<Input>	▸ Daily ▸ Weekly ▸ Monthly ▸ Quarterly ▸ Annually
4	What archiving objects do you use?	<Input>	▸ `FI_DOCUMNT` ▸ `IDOC`
5	Do you have an archiving concept?	<Input>	▸ Yes ▸ No
6	Is the creation of an archiving concept planned?	<Input>	▸ Yes ▸ No
7	What residence times have you defined?	<Input>	▸ 12 months ▸ 36 months
8	Do you use add-ons for data archiving?	<Input>	▸ Yes ▸ No
9	Where do you store the archived data?	<Input>	▸ Databases ▸ File system ▸ Archive system ▸ Optical data carriers
10	Do you use the DART tool?	<Input>	▸ Yes ▸ No
11	...	<Input>	...

Table 5.4 Sample Questionnaire for the Contact Persons of SAP Systems in the Company

Workshops

You can add your own questions to this questionnaire. It is important to determine for which SAP systems SAP data archiving was set up and in which form within your own company. Once you have determined if there is a contact person with whom you can interact, you should set up joint workshops to exchange knowledge. If no one in the company archives, you can assume the leading role in this area and set up a company-wide service center for data archiving.

Grouping SAP systems

Next, it is important to organize the SAP systems in the group. In most cases, there are several templates in a group in which only certain modules and processes have been set up. Thus it is quite common to have an SAP system for finance and controlling and another one for sales and logistics.

Detecting data growth

You should also analyze typical processes in the company that can lead to major data growth. The following core processes usually take place for a car manufacturer:

▸ **Design, research, and development**
The data for design, research, and development is usually not generated in the SAP system but in other IT systems, such as CAD programs (CAD = computer-aided design). However, the bills of material that contain the individual materials and components of the products are subsequently transferred to SAP ERP so that they can be used for production and costing. Thus you may have to introduce the archiving object CS_BOM (PP BOMs) from the production planning (PP) module if the data in the relevant tables grows.

▸ **Production and logistics**
A vehicle is usually manufactured in a customized manner upon receiving a sales order. The company may also create orders itself so that the production lines are at full capacity; that is, the company only produces for the warehouse stock. Ideally, these vehicles are sold promptly. Regardless of which model is produced and whether the vehicle is sold immediately or later, the following data is usually created:

  ▹ *Archiving Objects in the Area of Purchase Requisitions and Purchase Orders:*

    – MM_EBAN (Purchase Requisitions)

    – MM_EKKO (Purchase Orders)

▶ *Archiving Objects in the Area of Deliveries (Internal and External):*

   – RV_LIKP (Deliveries)

   – JITO_CALL (JIT Calls Outbound)

   – RL_TA (MM-WM Warehouse Management: Transport Requests)

▶ *Archiving Objects in the Area of Production:*

   – PP_ORDER (Production Order)

   – PP_CONF (PP Confirmations)

▶ **Sales and after sales**

The sales and after sales area primarily take care of the sale of vehicles. The sale of new vehicles takes place in the sales centers (car dealerships) of the group, where the group usually sells cars directly to its subsidiaries (services companies) after the orders. The service company, mostly a leasing or finance company, then deals with the end customer. From a group perspective, first a SD order and subsequently a billing document are entered in the SAP system, that is, the following archiving objects are used:

▶ SD_VBAK (SD Order)

▶ SD_VBRK (Billing Document)

In addition, financial accounting and material documents and the relevant documents in Controlling are always generated by balance sheet–related goods movements, which also need to be considered with the relevant archiving objects.

Vehicle Management System (IS-A-VMS)	[«]
For the automotive industry, the automotive industry solution can be used in the sales and after sales area. There is a special archiving object, VEHICLE (Archiving of Vehicles, VMS), for it. Since many car manufacturers create numerous customer-specific tables in the SAP system, you usually cannot use this archiving object without a thorough analysis of the processes and table structures. We recommend that you perform a thorough analysis, integrate the additional tables in the archiving object VEHICLE if necessary, and only then start SAP data archiving. Otherwise, the customer-specific tables remain in the SAP system, which will lead to unnecessary data growth over time and will require an adjustment of your archiving concept.	

Archiving concept
You have now obtained a first overview of the SAP system and the typical processes in the group and will start planning SAP data archiving step by step. Remember the three levels of the archiving concept, which were discussed in Chapter 4 and consider the required activities during planning.

Strategic level
At the strategic level, we must answer the following questions in our first example:

▶ In which SAP systems is SAP data archiving to be set up?

▶ Which archiving objects can be used for archiving after a table analysis in Transaction DB02?

▶ Where are the archive files from SAP systems P01 and N03 stored in the United States? Can this storage be created or does a new strategy have to be defined for the storage?

▶ Can the existing concepts be used directly for the archiving objects?

Operational level
At the operational level, the following questions, at least, must be answered:

▶ Who is responsible for the administration of SAP data archiving?

▶ Who assumes which tasks?

Conceptual level
This example involves five different countries:

▶ United States

▶ Brazil

▶ Russia

▶ Mexico

▶ India

For these countries, we already need an approach during the planning phase for the creation of the concept. A possible approach could be as follows:

1. Sending a letter to the local managing director or country representative so that persons responsible can be nominated.

2. Providing templates as to how to fill in and complete a concept together with the local persons responsible.

3. Planning joint workshops or telephone conferences for long distances in order to clarify open questions promptly.

For the archiving objects, we also require appropriate concepts that may be structured as described in Chapter 4, Section 4.2.3. We can assign the archiving objects to three groups:

▶ Active objects (already set up SAP systems)

▶ Necessary objects (must always be set up)

▶ Future objects (should be introduced in the future if necessary)

In Road Cruiser Inc., we identified the following active archiving objects:

Active archiving objects

▶ BC_DBLOGS (Archiving of Changes to Customizing Tables)

▶ BC_SBAL (Archiving Object for Application Log)

▶ IDOC (iDoc: Intermediate Document)

▶ MM_MATBEL (Materials Management: Material Documents)

▶ FI_DOCUMNT (FI Documents)

These include the necessary archiving objects, which we have to expect due to the processes in the automotive industry. In addition to the active and necessary archiving objects, we recommend that you take a close look at the following archiving objects that could also be used for an introduction:

Future archiving objects

▶ CHANGEDOCU **(Change Documents)**
Change documents are created in all SAP systems. Especially for such master data objects as materials whose master data records are almost never archived or only archived after several years, you can use the archiving object CHANGEDOCU to archive only the change documents in advance separately from the master data records and thus relieve the database.

▶ WORKITEM **(Work Items from the Workflow System)**
Different workflows are active in an SAP system, for example, to release authorizations or purchase orders. These workflows, which are promptly processed by the user, then have no great significance for the day-to-day business and can also be archived at short notice.

▶ MM_ACCTIT **(MM Subsequent Posting Data for Accounting Interface)**
The MM subsequent posting data is generated only if the update of the ACCT* tables is active. Since enormous amounts of data are generated in reality in these tables, we recommend that you archive these data records promptly until a decision is made as to if the update may even be disabled because no one accesses this data.

Thus we have exactly 18 archiving objects that can be used for SAP data archiving. You do not have to introduce all archiving objects at the same time in all SAP systems. However, you do have some idea of the data archiving objects that you have to keep an eye on in future.

[⊙]

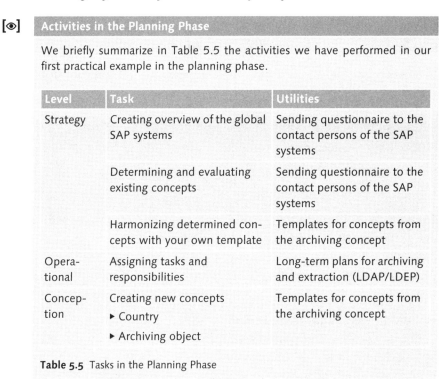

Activities in the Planning Phase

We briefly summarize in Table 5.5 the activities we have performed in our first practical example in the planning phase.

Level	Task	Utilities
Strategy	Creating overview of the global SAP systems	Sending questionnaire to the contact persons of the SAP systems
	Determining and evaluating existing concepts	Sending questionnaire to the contact persons of the SAP systems
	Harmonizing determined concepts with your own template	Templates for concepts from the archiving concept
Operational	Assigning tasks and responsibilities	Long-term plans for archiving and extraction (LDAP/LDEP)
Conception	Creating new concepts ▸ Country ▸ Archiving object	Templates for concepts from the archiving concept

Table 5.5 Tasks in the Planning Phase

Setting up archiving objects

In Chapter 6, we will set up two of these archiving objects as an example. Unfortunately, we cannot discuss the setting up of all archiving objects in detail because that would go beyond the scope of this book. However, Appendix B provides a short summary of each archiving object. You can look up important information there.

5.1.2 Chemical Industry

The chemical industry is omnipresent in our lives, with its countless products and areas of application. If you take a headache pill or change your car tires, for example, you come in contact with its products. How does a chemical company differ from a car manufacturer? A tablet is not composed of individual numerable pieces and the rubber for the tire is not assembled as an intermediate product from numerable products. In comparison with the car manufacturer, there are two distinguishing features:

- Processes instead of assembly
- Recipe instead of bills of material

We are primarily involved with processes in the chemical industry. The products are created in the SAP system as recipes and thus already differ by name from bills of material. You know the term *recipe* from the kitchen, where we can cook or bake something according to a recipe. We also have similar processes in the chemical industry, where certain products are manufactured according to predefined processes and recipes.

Demarcation of the chemical industry

Table 5.6 shows leading international groups in the chemical industry that also have large plants abroad like the leading companies in the automotive industry.

Group	Well-Known Products	Large Foreign Plants
BASF SE	Chemicals, plastics, crop protection, and so on	- China - Germany - Turkey - India - Mexico
Dow Chemical Company	Chemicals, plastics, performance chemicals, catalysts, coatings, crop technology, crude oil and natural gas exploration and production, and so on	- Germany - China - The Netherlands
DuPont	Chemicals, plastics, and so on	- Belgium - China

Table 5.6 Leading International Companies from the Chemical Industry

The globalization phenomenon thus applies in the same way to the chemical industry. We can thus build on our first example in Section 5.1.1 and no longer have to pay attention to archiving conditions in individual countries but concentrate instead on the archiving objects that can be added in the chemical industry in addition to the archiving objects already presented in the first example.

Archiving Process Orders

Archiving objects in the chemical industry

Since we are primarily involved with processes in the chemical industry, it is not a production order (PP_ORDER) that we need to manufacture products as in the automotive industry, but a *process order*. The archiving object is thus PR_ORDER. The difference between a production order and a process order is minimal and lies especially in the terminology of certain fields, transactions, and so on. From a Controlling point of view, both order types are cost objects, which we can post with costs and settle during the manufacture of the product.

Process orders

Nevertheless, there is a different transaction for displaying process orders (COR3) than for displaying production orders (CO03). Thus, Transaction COR3 must be evaluated in terms of if the archive access meets the requirements of the user. *Batches* are another special feature of the chemical industry. A batch number is assigned to the manufactured products during each new manufacturing process. Thus the products can be quickly identified if a batch does not meet the quality requirements of the company. Batches can also be archived if necessary. However, the amount of data in relation to the process orders is very low here; also the dependencies on other archiving objects are very high.

Displaying process order

Let's take a detailed look at the special features of the archiving project PR_ORDER (Process Order):

1. As already mentioned, you display a process order via Transaction COR3 (see Figure 5.2).

Figure 5.2 Initial Screen of Transaction COR3

2. In the PROCESS ORDER field, enter the desired order number, for example, 1000140, and confirm by pressing [Enter] to display the order. One of the following three cases may occur:

  ▷ The process order is stored in the database and displayed directly.

  ▷ If the process order is already archived, the error message, "Order 1000140 not found" is displayed, but does not refer to the archiving.

  ▷ If you have mistyped or entered an incorrect order number, the same error message, "Order <order number> not found," is displayed.

Since this error message does not refer to the archiving, it is advisable to make a small adjustment by adding "or already archived (Use trans. SARE)" to the existing error message. The resulting error message gives the user the chance to think about the archived process orders (see Figure 5.3). The user is thus informed directly that the order he is looking for may be an archived process order (typos are the exception), which can be called only via Transaction SARE (Archive Explorer).

Figure 5.3 Adjusted Error Message in Transaction COR3

You adjust the error messages in Transaction SE91 (Message Maintenance) as follows:

Adjusting error message

1. Call Transaction SE91 and enter "CO" for MESSAGE CLASS. Under MESSAGES and next to NUMBER enter "017" (see Figure 5.4).

Figure 5.4 Initial Screen in Transaction SE91 for Message Maintenance

2. Click on the DISPLAY button.

3. The system then displays a list as shown in Figure 5.5 in which you can select and adjust the corresponding row for MESSAGE 017.

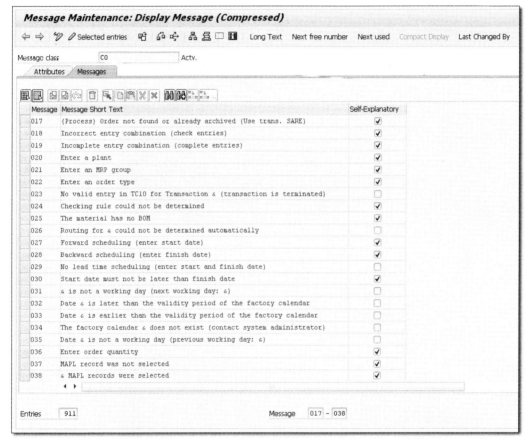

Figure 5.5 Adjusting Messages in Transaction SE91

Translations — Remember to adjust the messages for the relevant languages in an international SAP system. In Table 5.7, you will find a brief overview that we created with the support of local colleagues during a project. The translations are of course subject to change and should be checked again by you.

Language key	Language	Message Short Text
DE	Deutsch	(Prozess-)Auftrag nicht vorhanden oder bereits archiviert (Trans. SARE nutzen)
EN	English	(Process) Order not found or already archived (Use trans. SARE)
FR	French	Ordre (de fabrication) pas trouvé ou déjà archivé (Utilisez trans. SARE)
IT	Italian	(Processo) Ordine non trovato o già archiviato (Usare la transazione SARE)
NL	Dutch	(Proces) Order niet gevonden of al gearchiveerd (Gebruik trans. SARE)
PT	Portuguese	(Processo) Ordem não encontrada ou já arquivada (Usar trans. SARE)
ES	Spanish	(Proceso) Orden no encontrada o ya archivada (Utiliza trans. SARE)
ZH	Chinese	（过程）订单不存在或已归档（使用指令 SARE）

Table 5.7 Translation of Message Texts into Different Languages

After having made Transaction COR3 somewhat more user-friendly, it is important to make the infostructure user-friendly also. The standard infostructure for the archiving object PR_ORDER is SAP_PR_ORDER001 and contains only a few fields for selection. However, it has proved positive to also include the fields from Table 5.8 in this infostructure, because users often select a process order according to these fields.

Adapting the infostructure

Field	Description
PRCTR	Profit center
VERID	ProdVersion
GSTRI	Actual start date
GLTRI	Actual finish date
ERNAM	Creator
ERDAT	Entry date

Table 5.8 Important Additional Fields for the Infostructure

Field	Description
GSTRP	Order start date
GLTRP	Order finish date
ARBPL	Resource/work center

Table 5.8 Important Additional Fields for the Infostructure (Cont.)

Optimizing archive display

Finally, we optimize the display in Transaction SARE so that users can display important information despite restricted archive access. Proceed as follows:

1. First, call Transaction COISN (Order Information System: Overall Profiles) in which we can adjust the overall profile of the display in Transaction SARE (see Figure 5.6).

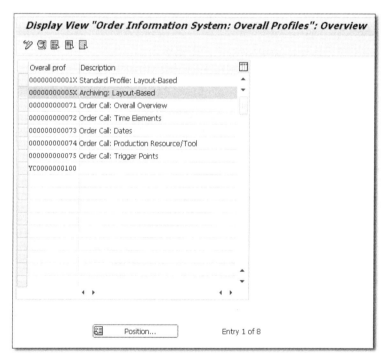

Figure 5.6 Overall Profiles in Transaction COISN

2. Select the overall profile, ARCHIVING LAYOUT-BASED, and click the DETAILS button ⬚.

3. In the details view, you can make the following Customizing settings (see Figure 5.7): In the ITEM column, you can see that the ORDER HEADERS and the ITEMS are at ITEM 1 and 2. DOCUMENTED GOODS MOVEMENTS have ITEM 0, on the other hand, and thus are not displayed directly in Transaction SARE when they are called. This object can be displayed manually, however, which we'll take a look at soon. In order for this object to be displayed directly when Transaction SARE is called (if desired by users), just enter the value "3" in the ITEM column.

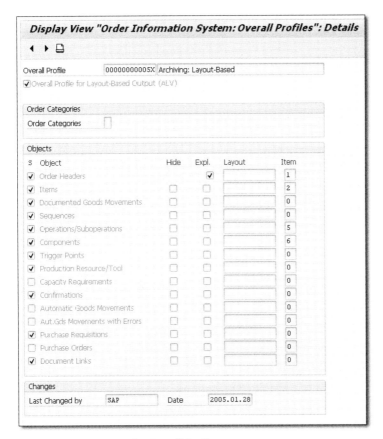

Figure 5.7 Customizing the Overall Profile

4. You have the option of customizing the display according to your requirements by selecting other objects (check mark in the S) column or hiding them (check mark in the HIDE column).

5. Let's now take a look at it in Transaction SARE. In Figure 5.8, we called an archived process order. You see immediately that the display differs from the display in Transaction COR3.

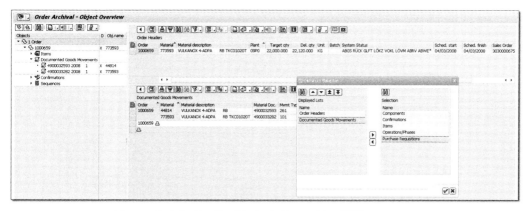

Figure 5.8 Adjusting the Display in Transaction SARE

6. You can use the menu SETTINGS • INDIVIDUAL LISTS to call the DETAIL LIST SELECTION.

7. From the SELECTION area on the right side of the dialog box, you can move the object DOCUMENTED GOODS MOVEMENTS to the DISPLAYED LISTS area on the left side. You have thus displayed the object manually, as already addressed in the third bullet point.

8. In the table DOCUMENTED GOODS MOVEMENTS, you also see the MATERIAL DOCUMENT as a result. You can navigate to a material document by double-clicking a document.

9. You can further refine the table DOCUMENTED GOODS MOVEMENTS by showing additional columns. To do so, choose the arrow button ▶ to activate the ALV functions.

10. You will see a number of new buttons that were previously hidden (see Figure 5.9).

11. To insert additional columns, choose ⊞.

Figure 5.9 Toolbar with ALV Functions

12. The system displays the window from Figure 5.10 in which, for example, you can select the columns PURCHASE ORDER and SALES ORDER and move them to the left side. Thus the user also has the option in the individual list DOCUMENTED GOODS MOVEMENTS to display the PURCHASE ORDER or SALES ORDER for an archived process order in Transaction SARE.

Figure 5.10 Selecting New Columns for a Table

We'd like to complete this example with a note on the residence times and the automatic completion of process orders with a background job. You can see from the application-specific Customizing that for the reorganization (archiving) of process orders for each order type, you have to maintain a residence time 1 (time interval between setting the deletion flag and the deletion indicator) and a residence time 2 (time interval between setting the deletion indicator and the implementation of archiving) (see Figure 5.11). A value of 18 months is usually in these fields, which would mean that you can archive a process order at the earliest after 36 months. This is due to the fact that we first set a deletion flag for the process order and then a deletion indicator. If you start initially with archiving and would like to archive old process orders very

Preparing archivability

quickly, we recommend that you first remove the existing values before entering any new values. You can then set the residence time at will via the selection variant of the write job while archiving.

Figure 5.11 Maintaining Residence Times per Order Type

Noting sequence After the initial archiving, you can decide if you would like to continue controlling the residence time via the selection variant in the write job or work with the residence times 1 and 2. Note the following requirements in order to be able to archive process orders at all:

1. Process orders must have the *completed* status. You can set this manually or automatically via a background job.

2. You must set a deletion flag. You can perform this manually or automatically with the preprocessing job.

3. You must set a deletion indicator. You can perform this manually or also automatically with the preprocessing job. If you maintained residence time 1, this time must first elapse.

4. You can then start directly with the archiving if you are not maintaining residence time 2. If a value was also stored here, this time must expire before you can archive.

The entries in the fields RESIDENCE TIME1 and RESIDENCE TIME2 can thus intentionally or unintentionally delay the start of archiving. Consider this aspect in time in the planning phase of data archiving.

Completing Old Process Orders Automatically [+]

You can use Transaction COHVPI (Mass Processing Process Orders) to schedule a background job in order to automatically complete process orders according to a selection profile. Select according to such criteria as plant, date, and so on. You thus make subsequent archiving of these orders easier because the deletion flag can be set directly.

Controlling of process orders

Also note, however, that a process order is not only required for the manufacture of products, but is also a cost unit at the same time in terms of Controlling. Thus the users from Controlling also regularly access the process orders and perform variance analysis in terms of material consumption and costs. You must also consider their requirements sufficiently in terms of archive access.

Transaction KOB1

The controller can use the archive-enabled Transaction KOB1 (Order Actual Line Items) to perform relevant analyses. It is also possible to navigate via Transaction SARE to the cost view.

Archiving Process Orders

In summary, we can say the following about the archiving of process orders:

▸ Access via Transaction COR3 is no longer possible after archiving.

▸ An adjustment of the error message in Transaction COR3 helps the user to switch to Transaction SARE.

▸ You can optimize the archive display in Transaction SARE.

▸ Residence time 1 and residence time 2 must be chosen carefully so that initial archiving does not have to be delayed.

▸ You can set the status of old process orders to *completed* by an automated job.

▸ In any case, you must include the Controlling department in the workshops because a process order is used as a cost object for analyses in Controlling.

Archiving Handling Units

Handling units

After the products are manufactured and stored, shipping or transport also plays a very important role in the chemical industry. In this context, we would like to present another archiving object that we find very often in the chemical industry. A *handling unit* is archived with the archiving object LE_HU (Handling Units) and is, put simply, always a combination of the material and packaging (cardboard box, barrel, and so on). A handling unit can be nested, which means you can, as shown in Figure 5.12, form a pallet from a package and form a container from several pallets. Thus you have a hierarchically constructed shipping unit. In Figure 5.12, you can see a truck with a container as a handling unit, which contains two other pallets as another two handling units. These palettes in turn each contain another two handling units. Thus such materials as granules or paint are stored in multiple units in cardboard boxes or barrels on pallets up to a maximum weight. A unit in this case may be 100 kilograms or 50 liters. If a customer now orders 400 kilograms or 200 liters of a material, two pallets must be combined in a new unit in this example. The movements of the pallets in the warehouse and company generate lots of data records, which ultimately result in it not being possible to avoid archiving with the archiving object LE_HU (Handling Units).

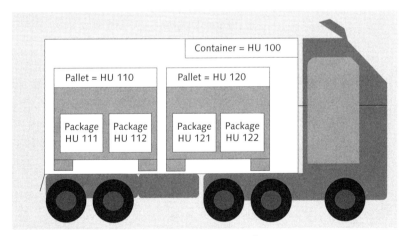

Figure 5.12 Example of Handling Units (Source: SAP)

Archiving conditions

You can only archive handling units if you have archived the corresponding preceding documents. In this context, we recommend that you analyze the field VPOBJ (Packing Object) in the table VEKP (Handling Unit Header Table). Table 5.9 shows possible values.

Packing Object	Short Description
00	No object assignment
01	Delivery
02	Sales document
03	Inbound delivery
04	Transport
05	Free handling unit
06	Free handling unit
07	Repetitive manufacturing
08	Work order components
09	Work order end product
12	Free handling unit
21	Outbound delivery – general
23	Inbound delivery – general

Table 5.9 Packing Objects for Handling Units

Exceptions

However, free handling units (05, 06) and those that are not assigned (00) can be archived directly as exceptions, because there aren't any preceding documents there. For this reason, it is advisable to first determine the number of handling units per packing object in order to decide with which packing object you should start. We also analyze the status of the handling unit in terms of its archivability. In table VEKP, the status must have a value of at least 0050 to enable the handling units to be archived in the first place.

Status Correction for External Transport Management Systems   [«]

If the status of a handling unit is not updated correctly through the use of an external transport management system, which can certainly happen in reality, you can either adjust the corresponding interface (if possible) or create a small correction program that you schedule and run in your SAP system at regular intervals. You can create the code for a correction program according to the following template:

▶ **Field** VBUK-TRSTA **(Transport Status)**
Set "C" directly if LIKP-WADAT_IST is filled.

▶ **Field** VEKP-STATUS **(Handing Unit Status)**
Set "0050" directly if LIKP-WADAT_IST is filled.

Thus you have created an important prerequisite for the subsequent archiving of deliveries and handling units.

[+]   **SAP Note**

For archiving object LE_HU, there is the very useful SAP Note 1694788 (HU Archiving—Frequently Asked Questions) in which many questions are compiled and answered. We recommend that you read this Note before archiving handling units.

Archive access not required

Archived handling units are virtually not accessed at all in reality. After a residence time of 24 months, users in our projects have confirmed that archive access is not really required. For this reason, we recommend that you do not fill any infostructures here in order to save memory space. Nevertheless, it is always the decision of each individual company as to whether access to archived handling units should be made available or not after the residence time has expired. It is even possible to delete the data directly after the residence time of 24 months and not store it in the archive at all. Again, this is a decision that has to be made individually.

Considering Transport Management Systems

Transport management systems

Transport and shipping are next in line after packaging. The transport of chemical products is a complex and time-consuming task. These products are usually subject to increased dangerous goods and export restrictions. Thus many companies use external IT systems for transport management. These IT systems calculate optimum routes and transport routes and assign the transfer orders automatically to the relevant carriers. Thus there is a strong dependency between data and deliveries in the SAP system. If you would like to archive with the archiving object RV_LIKP (Deliveries) in your SAP system, make sure that you check the impact, which is to be expected, on the connected transport management systems. Data and documents that must be preserved for legal reasons, for example, transport dispatch notes, are also stored only in these external IT systems and thus must also be considered in your archiving concept.

Observing Retention Requirements **[Ex]**

One of our customers was using external IT systems for transport management. However, the software supplier insisted on deleting the data in the system after two years. He was unaware of retention requirements in the international context, and he also did not offer a relevant archiving solution. Thus our customer was required to develop an alternative. The only solution that we were able to implement was to load the data and documents that were older than two years from the external IT systems and set up our own archive for them.

Special Features in the Chemical Industry **[◉]**

In summary, we can say the following about the chemical industry:

▶ Process orders are used for the manufacture of products in the chemical industry. The relevant data is archived using the archiving object PR_ORDER.

▶ The archiving object PR_ORDER must be very well prepared during the planning phase, because many points have to be considered.

▶ An outbound delivery usually consists of several pallets combined into a single unit and referred to as *handling units*. The large amount of data generated is kept under control using the archiving object LE_HU.

▶ Complex transports in the chemical industry require a sophisticated transport management system. You must check in particular for any impact on the external interfaces due to SAP data archiving.

▶ In the chemical industry, there are legal and regulatory requirements that you must observe.

5.1.3 Energy Sector

Our third and last industry example concerns the energy sector. You'll learn about industry-specific archiving objects in this section also. The energy sector, as a subarea of the utilities industry, accompanies us every day with its main product: electricity. Although electricity is invisible, it is an indispensable product. Not only companies and households need electricity; for several years, for example, electric vehicles have been a topic via which global electricity consumption could increase dramatically in the future, as soon as these vehicles are suitable for mass production and displace fuel-powered engines from the market.

Core processes   Primarily, the following core processes characterize the energy sector:

- Generating electricity
- Supplying electricity
- Billing consumption

Let's take a quick look at these areas. In particular, the billing area is of major importance for SAP data archiving, because it is here that the most data records are generated.

- **Generating electricity**
  Nowadays electricity is generated in different ways. While nuclear power plants dominated up to a few years ago, renewable energy sources, in particular wind turbines and solar systems, have been continually progressing in the meantime. They are state-funded and it is intended that their share will grow even further in the future. For most consumers, however, it is primarily the price and less the origin of electricity that is decisive.

  Households have also become electricity producers in the meantime. Through a solar system on the roof, the electricity generated can be used for personal use or can even be supplied to the electricity grids in exchange for appropriate remuneration. Thus not only consumption but also supplying to the electricity grid is measured at this point. This fact has enormous impact on the core process "billing consumption." An additional electricity meter is required for the supply of electricity in order to calculate and settle the amount of electricity generated. This increases the number of settlements and thus also the data records in SAP IS-U.

- **Supplying electricity**
  Electricity is an invisible commodity. It can be neither packed nor stored. It is transported via visible power lines or invisible underground cables into our households. We can cover our consumption with corresponding devices using a socket.

  We see increasing numbers of electric charging stations for electric vehicles in cities. A socket is also the end of the supply chain there. This fact also leads us to have additional consumption points apart from the traditional electricity meters in homes and companies, which also increases the number of billings. Since electricity is not packaged and physically delivered, no archiving objects for deliveries, transport, etc., must be considered as we know it from the automotive industry or the chemical industry.

▶ **Billing consumption**
In addition to the generation and supply of electricity, the regular billing of consumption is also a very important process in the energy sector. In order to bill consumption, you require a consumption point (households, companies, electric charging stations, or mains supply), which takes the form of an electricity meter. This electricity meter calculates how much electricity was consumed in kilowatt-hours (KWh) at the consumption point. The billing takes place according to the agreed prices and payment intervals (monthly or annually). Since payments are made (advance payments or installments) in addition to the billing, however, the payments are compared with consumption and a final annual invoice is created. In the SAP system, meter readings are logged for this purpose, payments are entered in the accounts, and credit memos are created. The billing also takes place here.

Other Industry Solutions: For Example, IS-T (Telecommunications)	[«]
In the telecommunications industry, the billing mainly takes place on a monthly basis for contract customers. Thus, an even greater amount of data is produced in the telecommunications industry than in the energy sector where billing usually takes place only once per year.	

Table 5.10 shows the leading providers in the energy sector in the world.

Group	Extract of Business Areas	Major Locations
Duke Energy	Nuclear power, renewable energies, and so on	▶ United States ▶ Latin America ▶ Saudi Arabia
ENGIE	Nuclear power, renewable energies, and so on	▶ Germany ▶ United Kingdom ▶ Turkey
National Grid	Transmission network, nuclear power, renewable energies, and so on	▶ United States ▶ United Kingdom ▶ Australia

Table 5.10 Leading Companies in the Energy Sector in the World

Now that we have an overview of the energy sector and its special features, let's take another look at the SAP solution SAP IS-U for the energy sector.

SAP Solution for the Energy Sector

Industry-specific functions can be added to SAP Business Suite via industry solutions, such as SAP IS-U in our example. This enables mapping of the exact processes required by a company from the energy sector. The specific functions involve new transactions, and the new transactions lead to additional reports, which ultimately store data in tables that are specific to SAP IS-U and differ significantly from the standard tables in the SAP system.

Special Archiving Objects

SAP IS-U stores the data from the energy sector in these special tables. Specific archiving objects are also necessary for this purpose. We'll present additional archiving objects in the following section, which you'll need especially in an SAP IS-U system. In order to obtain an initial overview, however, we'll take a closer look at only some of these archiving objects.

Overview Table 5.11 shows the archiving objects that are currently available in an SAP IS-U system.

Archiving Object	Description
ISU_EABL	Archiving Meter Reading Results
ISU_PROFV	Archiving Profile Values
ISU_EUFASS	Profile Assignments and Usage Factors
ISU_SETTLB	Settlement Document
ISU_BILLZ	Billing Document Line Items
ISU_BILL	Billing Document Headers
ISU_FACTS	Installation Facts
ISU_PRDOCL	Print Document Line Items

Table 5.11 Archiving Objects for SAP IS-U

Archiving Object	Description
ISU_PRDOCH	Print Document Headers
ISU_BBP	Budget Billing Plans
ISU_PPM	Cash in Advance Documents
ISU_INSPEC	Campaigns for Inspection List
ISU_ROUTE	Route
ISU_EORDER	Waste Disposal Order
ISU_SWTDOC	Switch Document
INV_REMADV	Invoice Documents
INV_TRANSF	Transfer Table for Invoice Data
FI_MKKDOC	FI-CA: Document

Table 5.11 Archiving Objects for SAP IS-U (Cont.)

Table 5.11 introduces 18 additional archiving objects. The number of archiving objects that you have already seen in this section and the previous sections is still small compared to the total number of archiving objects in SAP systems, which is approximately 500. You do not implement all 500 archiving objects in any project, only as many in each case as are actually required in order to ensure performance. This may be ten archiving objects in one SAP system, while it is 20 in another SAP system. In the course of planning an archiving project, it is important to first define a subset of the available archiving objects often used and that generates the largest amounts of data.

We have frequently used the following 7 archiving objects in our previous projects in the SAP IS-U environment. In this example, we'll present the archiving objects in a slightly different form. In the first example, we started the planning with a top-down approach (from top to bottom). We took a look from a bird's-eye view at the processes of a car manufacturer and then proposed potential archiving objects. In the second example, we started directly using the specific scenarios in a chemical company and selected the archiving objects that were critical for performance. In the third example, we tackle the planning from a bottom-up perspective, by starting from the bottom—that is, from the available SAP data archiving objects. You can also apply these three different

Bottom-up planning

approaches in a combined manner during a project. The common goal of all three approaches is to select the archiving objects that are most relevant for your SAP system.

In the following sections, we'll create a compact overview per the archiving object that specifies the documents for which the object can be used. We'll also enter information in a table about the optimal residence time, important SAP Notes, transactions for archive access, and so on (see Table 5.12). Practical tips will complete the compact overview.

In Figure 5.13, you can see the rough flow of the core process *billing consumption* from billing to the printing of the invoice. It is important for SAP data archiving that billing documents and print documents are generated in this process. In the following sections, we'll present suitable archiving objects with which the billing and print documents can be archived after the defined residence time.

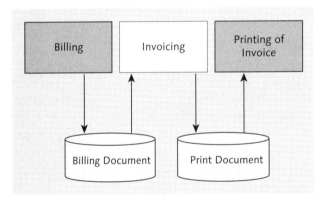

Figure 5.13 Flow of Billing Consumption and the Generated Documents (Source: www.help.sap.com)

Archiving Print Documents

Print document header and line items

A print document is created when billing a contract account. This print document contains a print document header and print document line items that are archived with different SAP archiving objects:

▶ ISU_PRDOCL (Print Document Line Items)

▶ ISU_PRDOCH (Print Document Header)

You archive print document line items before the print document headers. The print document line items have no preceding archiving objects. Table 5.12 contains the compact overview for this archiving object.

Characteristic	Description/Recommendation
Preceding archiving object	None
Leading table(s) for table analysis	▸ DBERDL (Print Document Line Items) ▸ DBERDLB (Reference to a Billing Document Line Item) ▸ DBERDZ (Database Table Single Lines Print Document)
Optimal residence time	▸ 36 months
Archive access and archive infostructure	▸ Standard Transaction EA40 (Display Print Document) ▸ Archive infostructure: SAP_ISU_PRDOCL
Current SAP Notes (Excerpt)	▸ 2048949 (EABICO: *No list of reversals for archived print document lines*) ▸ 2045623 (IDE: Print documents archived before REDISND1/MEER)
Relevance for DART	Yes, special extraction required
Archiving interval	Monthly or quarterly
Practical tips	▸ The preprocessing job REPDAR_ ANALYSE_LINES can be extended by additional checks with the function module EXIT_REPDAR_ANALYSE_HEAD_ 002. ▸ Enter a meaningful comment for the write job.

Table 5.12 Compact Overview of Archiving Object ISU_PRDOCL

After you have archived the print document line items, you can continue with archiving the print document headers (see Table 5.13).

Characteristic	Description/Recommendation
Preceding archiving object	ISU_PRDOCL (Print Document Line Items) You archive print document headers after the print document line items. The print document headers thus have only one preceding archiving object
Leading table(s) for table analysis	▶ ERDK (Print Document/Header Data) ▶ ERDB (Documents for a Print Document (ERDK))
Optimal residence time	▶ 36 months ▶ 24 months for reversed documents
Archive access and archive infostructure	▶ Standard Transaction EA40 (Display Print Document) ▶ Archive infostructure: SAP_ISU_PRDOCH
Important SAP Notes	▶ 1519651 (ARC: Incorrect statistics for deleted objects (ISU_PRDOC*)) ▶ 668797 (ARC: Extension of archiving for GDPdU)
Relevance for DART	Yes, special extraction required
Archiving interval	Monthly or quarterly
Practical tips	▶ You can define the residence time for reversed documents shorter than the residence time for the remaining documents ▶ The preprocessing job REPDAR_ANALYSE_HEAD can be extended by additional checks with the function module EXIT_REPDAR_ANALYSE_HEAD_001 ▶ Specify a meaningful comment for the write job

Table 5.13 Compact Overview of Archiving Object ISU_PRDOCH

Archiving Budget Billing Plans

A budget billing plan must first be deactivated before it can be archived. The corresponding print document (print document header and print document line items) must have been archived completely. This ensures that neither the budget billing plan nor the print document (which is already archived and cannot be activated) can be reactivated and processed. The archiving object for the budget billing plan is called ISU_BBP. Table 5.14 provides a compact overview of this archiving object.

Archiving prerequisites

Characteristic	Description/Recommendation
Preceding archiving object	▸ ISU_PRDOCL (Print Document Line Items) ▸ ISU_PRDOCH (Print Document Header)
Leading table(s) for table analysis	EABP (Budget Billing Plan)
Optimal residence time	36 months
Archive access and archive infostructure	▸ Standard Transaction EA63 (Display Budget Billing Plan) ▸ Archive infostructure: SAP_ISU_BBP
Important SAP Notes	▸ 1595046 (BBP: Archived budget billing plans are displayed incorrectly) ▸ 1316058 (IS-U Archiving: Reset archiving status for BBP)
Relevance for DART	Yes, special extraction required
Archiving interval	Monthly or quarterly
Practical tips	If you archive statistical budget billing plans (Statistical Budget Billing Procedure 1), you must also use the archiving object FI_MKKDOC to archive the items

Table 5.14 Compact Overview of Archiving Object ISU_BBP

Archiving Billing Documents

A billing document is created when billing a contract account. This billing document contains a billing document header as well as billing document line items, each of which are archived with an SAP archiving object:

Billing the contract account

- ISU_BILLZ (Billing Document Line Item)

- ISU_BILL (Billing Document Header)

Archiving billing document line items

You can archive billing document line items only if you have already archived the print document line items and then the print document headers. Further information on the archiving object ISU_BILLZ is available in Table 5.15.

Characteristic	Description/Recommendation
Preceding archiving objects	▸ ISU_PRDOCL (Print Document Line Items) ▸ ISU_PRDOCH (Print Document Header)
Leading table(s) for table analysis	DBERCHZ (Individual Line Items)
Optimal residence time	36 months
Archive access and archive infostructure	▸ Standard Transaction EA22 (Display Billing Document) ▸ Archive infostructure: SAP_ISU_BILLZ
Important SAP Notes	▸ 1803395 (EA20: Billing document before archived period reversed) ▸ 1649553 (ARC: ISU_BILLZ delete program with update error ERCHARC)
Relevance for DART	Yes, special extraction required
Archiving interval	Monthly or quarterly
Practical tips	▸ The preprocessing job REAARCH_ANAL-YSE_LINE can be extended by additional checks with the function module EXIT_REAARCH_ANALYSE_LINE_001 ▸ Enter a meaningful comment for the write job

Table 5.15 Compact Overview of Archiving Object ISU_BILLZ

Archiving billing document headers

After you have archived the billing document line items, you can continue with archiving the billing document headers. Table 5.16 contains the most important information on the archiving object ISU_BILL.

Characteristic	Description/Recommendation
Preceding archiving objects	▶ `ISU_PRDOCL` (Print Document Line Items) ▶ `ISU_PRDOCH` (Print Document Header) ▶ `ISU_BILLZ` (Billing Document Line Item)
Leading table(s) for table analysis	`ERCH` (Invoice Document Data)
Optimal residence time	▶ 36 months ▶ 24 months for reversed documents
Archive access and archive infostructure	▶ Standard Transaction EA22 (Display Billing Document) ▶ Archive infostructure: `SAP_ISU_BILL`
Important SAP Notes	▶ 1908506 (EARETPER: An error dialog box opens when saving the retention period for `ISU_BILL`) ▶ 1673995 (SARI: Incorrect billing document is displayed)
Relevance for DART	Yes, special extraction required
Archiving interval	Monthly or quarterly
Practical tips	▶ You can define the residence time for reversed documents shorter than the residence time for the remaining documents ▶ The preprocessing job `REEARCH_ANAL-YSE_HEAD` can be extended by additional checks with the function module `EXIT_REAARCH_ANALYSE_HEAD_001` ▶ Enter a meaningful comment for the write job

Table 5.16 Compact Overview of Archiving Object ISU_BILL

Archiving FI-CA Documents

All postings for subledger accounting from the SAP IS-U area are stored in the Contract Accounts Receivable and Payable. This data is subsequently transferred to the general ledger accounting in the FI module. The archiving object for FI-CA documents is called `FI_MKKDOC`. These documents from Contract Accounts Receivable and Payable can be archived directly.

Subledger accounting documents

257

Characteristic	Description/Recommendation
Preceding archiving object	None
Leading table(s) for table analysis	DFKKKO (Header Data for the Contract A/R & A/P Documents)
Optimal residence time	36 months
Archive access and archive infostructure	▸ Standard Transaction FPL3 (Display Document)
	▸ Standard Transaction FPL9 (Display Account Balance)
	▸ Archive infostructure: SAP_FICA_DOC001
Important SAP Notes	▸ 1992978 (Transactions FP07/FP08/FP09 with error message >A015 (Document &1 is possibly being archived)
	▸ 1919163 (FPL9: Performance optimization for reading archives II)
Relevance for DART	Yes, special extraction required.
Archiving interval	Monthly or quarterly
Practical tips	The archive access can take a long time and affect performance. Restrict by fiscal years.

Table 5.17 Compact Overview of Archiving Object FI_MKKDOC

Archiving Settlement Documents

Consumption data   With the settlement, the consumption data—for example, the consumption at a point of delivery (electricity meter) within a specific period—is determined and transferred to the customer for billing. The archiving object for settlement documents is called ISU_SETTLB. It can be implemented directly (see Table 5.18).

Characteristic	Description/Recommendation
Preceding archiving objects	None
Leading table(s) for table analysis	EEDMSETTLDOC (Settlement Document Header Data)
Optimal residence time	36 months

Table 5.18 Compact Overview of Archiving Object ISU_SETTLB

Characteristic	Description/Recommendation
Archive access and archive infostructure	▸ Transaction SARE (Archive Explorer) ▸ Archive infostructure: SAP_ISU_SETTLB
Important SAP Notes	▸ 1867418 (ARC: MESSAGE_TYPE_X ARCH_PROT-111 for ISU_SETTLB) ▸ 1800050 (ISU_SETTLB: Runtime error TSV_TNEW_PAGE_ALLOC_FAILED 2)
Relevance for DART	Yes, special extraction required
Archiving interval	Monthly or quarterly
Practical tips	With the Business-Add-in (BAdI) ISU_EDM_SETTL_ARCHIV, additional checks for archivability can be defined

Table 5.18 Compact Overview of Archiving Object ISU_SETTLB (Cont.)

We recommend that you analyze your SAP IS-U system with a table analysis in Transaction DB02 and check if the 7 archiving objects can be of importance to you. The optimal residence time of 24 to 36 months is an average value that emerged in all of our projects in the energy sector. You should check the specified SAP Notes for your release and also search the SAP Support Portal for current Notes at regular intervals.

Data Extraction in SAP IS-U Systems   [«]

A special feature results in the creation of extracts from SAP IS-U. Since SAP IS-U is a system for processing mass data, DART is not designed for extractions of this scale. However, SAP IS-U has its own approach to enable you to extract the data. There are various reports available, for example, the report RFKK_DOC_EXTR_EXP (FI-CA Documents) or the report RERD_DOC_EXTR_EXP (Print Documents), to extract tax-relevant data from the SAP IS-U system. In the AUDITING area of the SAP IS-U documentation, you will also find instructions on the best way to proceed with the extraction.

We have looked at three different industries in this section and you have learned about several useful SAP data archiving objects. In Appendix B, you will find a short overview of each archiving object.

Before we proceed with the implementation of SAP data archiving and set up examples of SAP data archiving objects in Chapter 6, we would like to give you additional important information and tips for the planning phase in the next sections. Good planning not only involves the selection of industry-specific archiving objects but also includes a strategy for change management and communication in order to consider the persons involved and decision-makers. If you have a well-conceived project plan and schedule, you will pave the way for the implementation of SAP data archiving.

5.2   Change Management and Communication

Change management, as a generic term for handling changes, applies to different areas in a company. Thus it may be necessary, for example, to reconcile different corporate cultures through a corporate acquisition. The introduction of new software, for example, changing to a different email application provider, can pose challenges for users. The common denominator of all *successful* changes is the willingness among the parties concerned to achieve a change. There are different approaches to getting everyone involved, such as the three-phase model from Kurt Lewin, which we'll take a closer look at in Section 5.2.1.

Changes due to archiving
SAP data archiving projects also involve changes. In this case, the change brought on by archiving particularly affects the processes in an SAP system. This affects users because they document the business processes in the company daily using transactions in the SAP system. You have already learned in Chapter 2 that certain restrictions in accessing data are to be expected after SAP data archiving.

Allaying fears
It is of particular importance in the planning phase to reduce these user concerns so that users do not respond negatively to these restrictions and make the implementation of data archiving more difficult. To do so, you must not only know these concerns in order to define proposed solutions, but also communicate them in an appropriate form. You will

learn in the next two sections how to prepare the user and other persons concerned in the company for the change and the best choice in terms of means of communication for this purpose. If you neglect change management and communication in your SAP data archiving project, it will be difficult for you to adhere to your project plan and schedule.

5.2.1 Preparing for the Change

Changes in a company are natural events that no one can or should oppose. You must gain the necessary acceptance, however, before starting the change. In adopting changes, you need to note that we have to deal with the *ability to change* (knowledge and skills) and with the *willingness to change* (want and should) of the people involved. You will have little success if you inform everyone in your company in advance about the upcoming SAP data archiving. Know that your team has the ability to implement the project but fail to inspire enthusiasm for this project on the part of the people involved.

Ability and willingness to change

SWOT Analysis

Every change involves opportunities as well as risks, which need to be estimated exactly before the change is triggered. In terms of SAP data archiving, the opportunities would be, for example, much better performance and the optimal use of IT resources. The threat would be poorer archive access and, in a worst-case scenario, the loss of archive files if they were not stored in an audit-proof manner. Before you start SAP data archiving, you must determine not only its opportunities and threats but also its strengths and weaknesses. A SWOT analysis is particularly suitable for this purpose. SWOT is an acronym for *strengths*, *weaknesses*, *opportunities*, and *threats*. In Figure 5.14, you can see two aspects of data archiving, the archive system and archive access for the archiving object SD_VBAK (Sales Documents), which are to be analyzed within a matrix using SWOT analysis.

Identifying weaknesses and threats

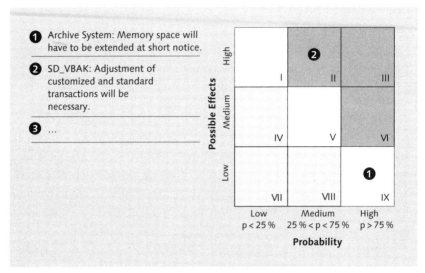

Figure 5.14 Risk Assessment in Terms of Weaknesses and Threats

Creating action plan We have divided the matrix into nine quadrants. The X-axis (probability) and Y-axis (possible effects) are each divided into the areas of low, medium, and high. You can now place the aspects of data archiving in these quadrants according to your own assessment of the situation. You have to deal in this manner with the potential weaknesses and threats and thus prepare yourself for their occurrence.

Point ❶ symbolizes the threat that the memory space in the archive system will have to be extended at short notice. In our example, this will occur with a high probability, because the memory space is too small. However, the possible effects on the archiving project are classified here as rather low because the memory space can be quickly extended.

Point ❷ symbolizes the threat that an adjustment of customized and standard transactions will be necessary. Here the probability of occurrence is assessed with a medium value. If the situation were to occur, however, this would have serious effects on our archiving project. We already know in advance the weaknesses in the archive access for the archiving object SD_VBAK and thus set the effects to the high level.

After you have included all essential points of your archiving project in this matrix, you can create an action plan outlining how you can eliminate the threats and weaknesses of the project. You can see an example of such an action plan in Table 5.19. In this table, you can add more fields, for example, target date, persons responsible, and status to enable you to coordinate and track the processing of these points in a better manner.

No.	Description	Solution
1	Archive system: Memory space must be extended at short notice.	The SAP Basis team has ordered the necessary hard disks from the suppliers and will extend the memory space in time in CW 42.
2	SD_VBAK: Adjustment of the customized and standard transactions is required.	As, after SAP data archiving, Transaction VA03 cannot display the texts in particular, our developer, Mr. Müller, will create a new archive transaction in consultation with the user department.
3	...	...

Table 5.19 Action Plan for the Identified Weaknesses and Threats

You should prepare for discussions with users so that you can respond to all possible questions and reservations with an appropriate solution and convincing arguments. This is how you gain trust among users. If, before a change, trust exists between the parties involved and you exude confidence due to your competence, you will quickly and easily get users on board. If you fail to achieve this—that is, if you avoid questions or cannot give a satisfactory answer—you will have to invest much more energy than you want in the planning phase.

Gaining confidence through competence

Note the Following Points before You Meet with Users [+]

Before you personally meet with users in workshops or meetings, note the following points for the successful implementation of a change:

▶ Make sure that you prepare a SWOT analysis.
▶ Define an action plan to eliminate the threats and weaknesses.
▶ Define a specific schedule as well as the persons responsible.
▶ Inquire in advance about users' expectations of the new solution.

▸ Be 100 percent prepared. Ideally, explain not only the theory of your solution in the discussion but also demonstrate practical examples of archive access in a sandbox or test system.

▸ Create a "we" feeling because the users are your future team members.

▸ Do not create any pressure in relation to decisions. The users must be in favor of SAP data archiving based on their own convictions.

If you observe these tips, you will find discussions with users a lot easier.

Three-Phase Model

You should know in which phases a change is usually made. In describing these phases, we rely on the three-phase model by Kurt Lewin, who developed the model in 1947. There are other change management models that are based in part on the three-phase model by Lewin or that break down change management using a different division in phases or stages. However, the goal of these models is virtually identical, and the three-phase model continues to be widespread. Lewin divides a change into three phases that must be completed for the change to succeed:

1. Unfreezing

2. Changing/Moving

3. (Re)freezing

Achieving group consensus The idea underlying Lewin's model is that a change can be achieved and sustained best by a group consensus. Individual decisions, on the other hand, have a lower success rate. We'll take a closer look at the three phases in the following sections.

Unfreezing Phase

Preparation and information In the course of a change, you invest the most energy in the first phase. You explain the need for SAP data archiving in meetings to the people involved and explain the benefits that every single user will have as a result. You respond competently to any objections or questions with your insights from the SWOT analysis and the corresponding action plan; that is, you explain how you will mitigate the potential threats and weaknesses. Your goal is to achieve group consensus that SAP data archiving should be implemented so that you can proceed to the second phase.

Changing/Moving Phase

The actual change takes place in the second phase. You create the first archiving sessions in the sandbox or test system and present the new archive access to users. You respond promptly to user queries, offer professional assistance, and, if necessary, also provide user manuals for archive access with the relevant transactions. You dispel uncertainties and gain confidence as a result. Even after the go-live in the live system, you support users with the usual high quality if there are queries regarding archive access.

Actual change

(Re)freezing Phase

The last phase ensures that the already achieved status is also retained in the long term. Transfer to SAP data archiving, perform the archiving sessions on the specified dates, and manage the lifecycle of data in the future. At regular intervals, you can inform users about the benefits that the company has achieved as a result of the change. For this purpose, for example, you could send a short info email and express your thanks. This increases user motivation in the long term and also ensures good cooperation.

> **Preparing for the Change** [◉]
>
> Each SAP data archiving project involves a change. The users who are affected must become the persons involved from the outset. In order to allay possible fears and gain the trust of users, you should prepare carefully, for example, by performing a SWOT analysis and creating an action plan for the identified weaknesses and threats. According to the three-phase model by Kurt Lewin, our goal is always to achieve group consensus and to secure the achieved status in the long term.

5.2.2 Choosing the Right Means of Communication

Communication between the persons involved is an integral part of any successful change management. In order for you to successfully perform your archiving project, you must make those affected become those involved. What is the best way to do this? How do you communicate with the users to get their attention? We'll give you some practical tips and tricks in this section so that you can effectively use proven means of communication for this purpose. We'll present some useful means of communication and assess them in terms of strengths and weaknesses.

Making those affected become those involved

Intranet

The Intranet is an excellent information platform for the employees of a company. Every employee can retrieve valuable information here. In particular, a current news area directly on the homepage ensures that a large group of people perceive this information. Departments such as the IT or tax department can also have their own page on the Intranet to provide important information for their area.

Creating intranet page

In the course of SAP data archiving, we recommend that you set up an area for SAP data archiving on the IT department's page on the Intranet in which employees can access all-important information. You should not only describe the project itself but also such ongoing activities as the long-term data archiving plan, the active and future archiving objects, and so on. An overview of residence times and access to the concepts for the individual archiving objects are also very helpful. Thus, you enable all users to regularly obtain an overview of SAP data archiving in the company. Users can easily trace the ongoing activities within the course of SAP data archiving as a long-term topic on one page of the Intranet.

Example of Intranet presence

You can design your presence for SAP data archiving on the Intranet according to the following template:

- Main page
  - Project
    - Goals
    - Project plan and schedule
    - Newsletter
    - Meetings
    - Team
  - Data archiving
    - SAP system(s)
    - Archiving object(s)
    - Long-term data archiving plan (LDAP)
    - Contacts
  - Data extraction
    - SAP system(s)
    - Country or countries

- Long-term data extraction plan (LDEP)
- Contacts

In this example, the presence is divided into three areas. In the first area, project, you provide general information about the project. The areas data archiving and data extraction, on the other hand, provide specific information about the SAP systems that are affected and how the implementation of archiving and extraction takes place as planned. This example should serve only as a starting point for you. You can use it as a basis and design your customized page on the Intranet. An expensively maintained page for data archiving on the Intranet is of little use, however, if only very few employees are aware of it. In order to promote your page, we recommend that you include it in the newsletters that are sent out regularly and in the presentations on data archiving to increase its usefulness among users.

Newsletter

A newsletter sent by email can be used to reach selected recipients in the company via distribution lists. This requires that you maintain distribution lists in your company and know the addressees included in them. Newsletters provide the advantage of allowing you to write specifically to those persons for whom the information is of the utmost importance. In the course of SAP data archiving, you can use newsletters effectively as follows:

Send an info email in advance to all SAP users who are directly affected by the implementation of an SAP data archiving object. Ideally, you can identify this group of users by the SAP user IDs, which have authorizations for the relevant transactions. You will find an example of this in Chapter 6, Section 6.3.1. If you, for example, archive the process orders with the archiving object PR_ORDER, you can determine and inform all users of Transaction COR3 (Display Process Order).

An info email may look like the following:

Example of info email

> *Dear Colleagues,*
>
> *In order to increase the performance of the SAP system <SYS-ID>, we are going to start archiving process orders for the fiscal year <year> as of <date>. If you require access to archived process orders, please use the*

archive information system with Transaction SARE (Archive Explorer). You cannot use SAP Transaction COR3 (Display Process Order) for archived documents. A user manual for archive access is available in four different languages and shows you how to use Transaction SARE. You will find the user manual on the Intranet at the following link <link>.

Best regards,
SAP Basis/Administrator

Storing info email on the Intranet

After you have sent an info email, you can store it on the relevant Newsletter subpage on the Intranet for documentation purposes. This enables users to read the history of sent info emails at any time. You defuse a major disadvantage of a newsletter in this manner. It is not uncommon for users to fail to read the newsletter or to delete it directly due to the flood of emails in their inboxes.

Meetings

Meetings are excellent opportunities to discuss topics personally and intensively, either on-site in a meeting room or virtually via a video conference. Here specific issues from the agenda are dealt with and timely decisions are made. Meetings are also the best platform to advance the project together with the decision-makers. Often a specific group will already have regular meetings scheduled to discuss certain topics. The name assigned to such meetings differs from company to company.

Types of meetings

During our projects, we encountered the following names for meetings:

- Integration Meeting (consultation between various areas of SAP, for example, SAP Basis, Development, Processes, and so on)

- IT and User Department Fixed Day (user departments such as Tax, Accounting, and so on meet with IT)

- Rollout Manager Meeting (responsible for the implementation of rollouts in other countries)

- Department Meeting

- Team Meeting (members of the archiving project)

- Steering Committee (sponsors and decision-makers from top management)

In the course of the SAP data archiving project, participation in these various meetings is very beneficial and even a prerequisite for success. For this reason, we recommend that you determine all of the important meetings in your organization and decide which meetings you can participate in and the frequency in which you will attend.

Create an overview for yourself in the calendar as to when exactly the individual meetings take place. It is, for example, very useful to go into a Rollout Manager Meeting in order to introduce SAP data archiving at an early stage to the countries for which an SAP system is to be implemented in the future. If you want to introduce archiving objects in sales, for example, deliveries, invoices, or sales orders, you should participate in the IT and Sales Fixed Day. There you can optimally introduce the archiving objects and gather important feedback from the users.

Creating a calendar

Means of Communication

Intranet, newsletters, and the various meetings are excellent means to optimize communication in the context of change management. While you communicate unilaterally on the Intranet and via newsletters, discussions and exchanges take place in meetings. Meetings are also an opportunity to come in contact with decision-makers or to make decisions.

5.3   Defining Decision-Makers

We make decisions consciously or unconsciously every day. At times, a decision is particularly easy or difficult for us to make. We're sure you have heard the saying that even the worst decision is better than not deciding at all. Does this pearl of wisdom also apply to the decisions within data archiving? Without decisions, you will not progress in your SAP data archiving project. You will pay for a bad decision, however, after a certain amount of time in any case. This is why it should be your goal to define the right decision-makers who make the right decisions. In the following sections, we will present important decision-makers in the course of SAP data archiving projects. You will then learn the decisions that these people make and how you can achieve a workable consensus with everyone involved.

Decisions are crucial

Decision-makers are required, of course, to make decisions. The most important decision-makers in an SAP data archiving project are as follows:

- The *sponsor* usually comes from the top management (for example, department head, managing director, and so on) and is the main driver of the SAP data archiving project. The sponsor often participates in steering committees and makes decisions at the management level, for example, finance, personnel, and budget.

- The *experts* (for example, user department, module consultants, archiving specialists, and so on) contribute in terms of content with their special knowledge to the success of the project. The experts are represented in various meetings and are indispensable in making decisions at the user department level.

- *Change agents* (for example, moderators, project managers, and so on) are communications experts and help the team to achieve the project goals. Change agents make decisions at project level, for example, in terms of the project plan and schedule.

- *Employees* (for example, a key user or users) are the persons primarily affected by SAP data archiving. They make decisions at the user level, for example, to assess archive access.

Now that you have learned about the four key decision-makers, we would like to describe the decisions that these people usually make during an SAP data archiving project:

- *Financial decisions and budget allocation* are topics with which the sponsor deals.

- *Concepts per archiving object and country* are created by experts together with employees. The experts and employees usually make the decision on the release jointly.

- *Daily decisions for project management* come solely from the change agents. In making these decisions, they take into account the different opinions of the team. The sponsor can also specify the direction on major decisions.

- *Storage options* the experts present to the sponsor include an assessment of costs. As the sponsor is responsible for the finances and budget, he alone makes the decision.

▸ Since *archive access* can be optimized via fee-based add-ons, the sponsor must also be included, in addition to the employees, in the question of if a financial budget would be provided for it.

▸ For the application of *future trends*, the expert prepares the arguments for the decision-making process and presents them to the sponsor. Since long-term decisions are involved, such a decision is usually not made immediately. An example of such a decision is the introduction of SAP ILM.

Table 5.20 presents the decisions and decision-makers in a matrix.

Decision-maker matrix

	Sponsor	Experts	Change Agents	Employees
Finances and budget	✓			
Concepts		✓		✓
Project management	✓		✓	
Storage options	✓	Prepare the decision		
Archive access	✓	Prepare the decision		✓
Trends	✓	Prepare the decision		

Table 5.20 Persons Responsible for Different Decisions

You can add other decision-makers and decisions to this matrix. It is important to analyze in detail the interests of individual stakeholders and to develop coordinated strategies.

Decision on Archive Access	[Ex]
The experts know best how to optimally design archive access. Their goal is to convince the users (employees) as well as management (sponsor) of their recommendation.
The user would usually prefer that all transactions also continue as before to access the data in the archive. The sponsor expects the experts and users to agree on an optimal solution that will not involve any additional costs at best. These three stakeholders have different interests. If you accommodate the users too much as an expert, this can annoy the sponsor. If the expert acts

very much according to the specifications of the sponsor because he wants to keep the costs low, this can confuse users and lead them to reject the project. All interests must be reconciled in this triangle.

5.4 Creating a Project Plan and Schedule

A project is usually a one off undertaking with a specific goal that is subject to certain restrictions, such as time, personnel, and costs. When we refer to a project plan and schedule in this section, we assume that the areas of personnel and costs have already been clarified for our archiving project. In this section, we focus primarily on the individual tasks that must be done by specified dates so that we can successfully complete our project.

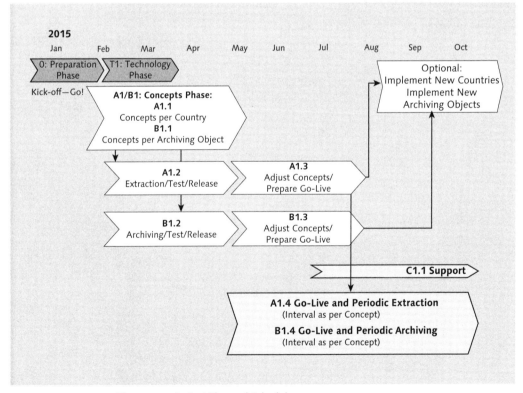

Figure 5.15 Project Plan and Schedule

A project is often divided into several phases. If a phase is successfully completed, we also refer to it as reaching a *milestone*. There may be dependencies between the individual phases. You cannot, for example, start archiving until you have created a concept and obtained the release.

Dividing projects into phases

In Figure 5.15, we divide our project into the following five phases:

Possible project phases

▶ **0 – Preparation**
The preparation phase is assigned to the strategic level (also see Chapter 4, Section 4.2.1). You start here with a kick-off meeting in which you obtain the *Go!* — that is, the release for SAP data archiving. You then create an archiving concept in which you document the results of the database analysis and the archiving objects sorted by sequence.

▶ **T – Technology**
In the technology phase, you create the basis for SAP data archiving by customizing your authorizations, creating the directories on the file system, and creating the necessary workbench and transfer orders for the subsequent Customizing. Finally, you create the required content repositories and connect the archive system to the SAP system.

▶ **A – Concept per country**
A concept is required for each country that is affected by SAP data archiving. If data extraction is required by law in this country, DART is also set up and implemented. You also have the option of using another phase (A2) for other countries. In this new phase, you can introduce only a single country or several countries. New phases can be incremented alphanumerically, for example, A2, A3, and so on.

▶ **B – Concept for SAP data archiving object**
A concept is required for each SAP data archiving object. Before an archiving object may go-live, you perform user tests and obtain the release for the go-live. You also have the option of using another phase (B2) for other SAP data archiving objects. In this new phase, you can introduce only a single archiving object or several archiving objects. New phases can be incremented alphanumerically, for example, B, B2, B3, and so on.

▶ **C – Support**
The last phase is the support phase, which continues even after the end of the implementation project. Even if a project has an end date,

data archiving is a regular task for which no specific end date can be set. The data extracts are created on the specified dates and the periodic archiving sessions are scheduled for the live data archiving objects.

In the following sections, we'll describe the individual phases in detail.

5.4.1 Preparation

Preparation phase   In Table 5.21, you will find an overview of tasks that arise in the *preparation* phase and are to be assigned to the strategic level.

ID	Topic	Responsible	Document
0.0	Prepare project/Kick-Off – Go!	All	Presentation
0.1	Create archiving concept	Experts	Concept
0.2	Analyze database (DB02)	Experts/ Administrator	Excel file
0.3	Select archiving objects and specify sequence	Experts/ Administrators	Presentation

Table 5.21 Tasks in the Preparation Phase

We'll describe these tasks more comprehensively in the following list:

▶ **0.0**
With a kick-off event and a meaningful presentation, you set the course for the data archiving project in the preparation phase. Invite all decision-makers to this event and try to create a "we" feeling among those involved.

▶ **0.1**
Then start to create the archiving concept, which includes all important topics of the strategic, operational, and conceptual levels (see Chapter 4, Section 4.2). Define your goal and determine with which strategy you can achieve your goal.

▶ **0.2**
As a result of a timely database analysis via Transaction DB02, you obtain important information about extensive tables (see Chapter 1, Section 1.4.1).

▶ **0.3**

Based on this information, you determine the relevant archiving objects in Transaction DB15 and specify the sequence as in with which archiving objects you would like to go-live first (see Chapter 1, Section 1.4.2).

5.4.2 Technology

In Table 5.22 you will find an overview of tasks that arise in the *technology* phase and are to be assigned to the operational level. Mainly, the administrator for SAP data archiving performs these tasks.

Technology phase

ID	Topic	Responsible	Document
T1.1	Assign authorizations for archiving	Administrators	Role concept
T1.2	Create directories for storage in the file system	Administrators	File system concept
T1.3	Create workbench and Customizing request	Administrators	Customizing
T1.4	Set up content repositories and connect archive system	Administrators	Archive connection

Table 5.22 Tasks in the Technology Phase

In the following list, we'll describe the individual tasks in the technology phase more comprehensively:

▶ **T1.1**

Check and customize the authorizations, not only for the administrator but also for the user. The authorizations for Transactions SARE and ALO1 are usually not included in the user roles but are essential for users after SAP data archiving.

▶ **T1.2**

In the file system, you create the various directories that you regard as necessary for the implementation of your storage strategy (storage options).

▶ **T1.3**

For the various archiving objects, we recommend that you create separate workbench and Customizing requests. You thus have the flexibility to transport a data archiving object separately from the others.

▶ **T1.4**

For storage in the archive system, you set up the relevant content repositories and establish the connection to the archive system.

5.4.3 Concept per Country

Concept per country phase

In Table 5.23, you will find an overview of tasks that arise in the *concept per country* phase and are to be assigned to the conceptual level.

ID	Topic	Responsible	Document
A1.1	Document legal requirements in terms of retention and extraction	Experts/ Users	Concept
A1.1.1	Determine and document relevant laws	Experts	Concept
A1.1.2	Specify tax-relevant data	Experts	Concept
A1.1.3	Document processes during the checks	Experts	Concept
A1.2	Release and tests	Users	Released
A1.2.1	Extract data per company code	Administrators	LDEP
A1.2.2	Create various view files	Experts/ Administrators	View files
A1.2.3	Check, test, and release the data extraction	Experts/ Users	Released
A1.3	Check and complete the concept	Experts	Concept
A1.4	Go-live: Extraction in the live system	Administrators	LDEP

Table 5.23 Project Plan for the Concepts per Country Phase

The individual tasks in the concepts per country phase are as follows:

▶ **A1.1**

A concept is created for every country that creates live data as a company in the SAP system (see Chapter 4, Section 4.2.3). Depending on the number of countries, you can track other tasks in the project plan with your own ID. The concept includes, in particular, such topics as laws, as well as the definition of tax-relevant data and processes during the company audit.

▸ **A1.2**

After you have created the concept, proceed with the user tests. You also create DART extracts and view files. As a result of the feedback of users, you obtain important information as to if adjustments are required for the concept. Your goal is to obtain the release for the go-live.

▸ **A1.3**

Ensure that the results from the tests are included in the revision of the concept and, after obtaining the release, file the concept in the relevant documentation systems, which you will learn about in Chapter 7, Section 7.5.2.

▸ **A1.4**

You can then go-live with the DART extraction, as defined in the concept. You update your activities in the long-term data extraction plan (LDEP; also Chapter 4, see Section 4.2.2).

5.4.4 Concept per Archiving Object

In Table 5.24, you will find an overview of tasks that arise in the *concept per data archiving object* phase. These are also assigned to the conceptual level.

Concept per archiving object phase

ID	Topic	Responsible	Document
B1.1	Create concepts for the archiving objects	Experts/ Users	Concept
B1.1.1	Archiving object 1	Experts	Concept 1
B1.1.2	Archiving object n	Experts	Concept n
B1.2	Release and tests	Users	Released
B1.2.1	Archiving object 1	Users	Release 1
B1.2.2	Archiving object n	Users	Release n
B1.3	Check and complete the concept	Experts	Concept
B1.3.1	Archiving object 1	Experts	Concept 1
B1.3.2	Archiving object n	Experts	Concept 2
B1.4	Go-live: Archiving in the live system	Administrators	LDAP

Table 5.24 Project Plan per SAP Data Archiving Object

The individual tasks in the concept per SAP data archiving object phase are as follows:

▶ **B1.1**

A concept is created for each individual data archiving object (see Chapter 4, Section 4.2.3). Depending on the number of data archiving objects, you can track other tasks with your own ID.

▶ **B1.2**

After you have created the concept, proceed with the user tests. You make the Customizing settings and start to test the created archive files. As a result of user feedback, you then obtain important information as to if adjustments are required for the concept. Your goal is to obtain the release for the go-live.

▶ **B1.3**

You can revise the concept while taking the results of the test into account. After obtaining the release, you can then store it in the relevant documentation systems.

▶ **B1.4**

You can then go-live with the SAP data archiving object, as defined in the concept. You update your activities in the long-term data archiving plan (LDAP; see Chapter 4, Section 4.2.2).

5.4.5 Support

Support phase The last phase within our archiving project is the *support* phase. This phase is to be assigned to the operational level. The tasks assigned to it are listed in Table 5.25 and are performed by the administrator for SAP data archiving.

ID	Topic	Responsible	Document
C1.1	Hypercare and support	Administrators	Ticket
A1.5	Periodic extraction	Administrators	LDEP
B1.5	Periodic archiving	Administrators	LDAP

Table 5.25 Project Plan for the Tasks in the Support Phase

We'll describe the individual tasks in the support phase in the following list:

▸ **C1.1**

The administrator is responsible for observing abnormalities in the SAP system after the go-live and thus provides an extended on-call service (*hypercare*). If there is a need for action in the course of data archiving, the requirement and the documentation are each documented via a ticket, which is created, for example, in SAP Solution Manager.

▸ **A1.5**

After the successful go-live of data extraction for a country, the administrator is responsible for the periodic implementation of data extraction. He or she maintains the long-term data extraction plan for this purpose.

▸ **B1.5**

After the successful go-live of an archiving object, the administrator is responsible for the periodic implementation of archiving sessions. He or she maintains the long-term data archiving plan for this purpose.

5.5 Summary

Planning archiving projects is a challenging task. On the basis of three sample industries and different archiving objects, we have tried to share valuable information from our professional experiences. Planning ultimately involves defining how to implement the strategy in reality, the drafting of which we discussed in Chapter 4. In business administration, planning is described as follows: "*Planning is the mental anticipation of a future situation.*" In Chapter 6, we will deal with this future situation and implement an example of the drafted strategy using two archiving objects.

*Adopting a structured procedure during the implementation
phase of SAP data archiving projects will not only ensure that
your go-live will be low key, but that you will be best prepared to
deal with potential support requests.*

6　Implementing Archiving Projects

In Chapter 5, we took a closer look at three sample industries, namely
the automotive, chemical, and energy industries. We introduced you to
several archiving objects, some of which are industry-specific archiving
objects and some of which are relevant for most SAP systems. In this
chapter, we will discuss two of these archiving objects in greater detail.

Archiving projects may vary in size and scope. Implementing a single
archiving object is as much a project as implementing several archiving
objects at once. In this chapter, we will demonstrate, step by step, how
you can set up two archiving objects, namely RL_TA (Warehouse Management: Transfer Orders) and IDOC (IDoc = Intermediate Document), in
a sample SAP system and use them in live operation. The archiving
object RL_TA is well suited to the requirements of the automotive and
chemical industries, because these producing industries have more
warehouse-based processes than the energy sector. On the other hand,
the archiving object IDOC is used in almost all SAP systems.

The instructions that follow will serve as a guide for using archiving
objects in live operation as they can also be used for other archiving
objects.

Guide for data
archiving

6.1　Implementation Phase

In Chapter 4, we discussed developing an archiving strategy and creating an archiving concept. We then used the methods and key points
described in Chapter 5 to plan our archiving project, which brings us

seamlessly on to implementing a data archiving project. First, we will discuss the implementation phase, followed by two more phases—namely, final preparation and go-live.

Tasks in the implementation phase

The implementation phase essentially comprises the following two tasks:

▸ **Selecting the archiving objects**
In this phase, you initially select (from the total volume of archiving objects defined in the strategy and planning phase) those archiving objects that you first want to use in live operation. If, for example, your plan comprises 30 archiving objects, you can start with a much smaller volume and initially select only the five archiving objects that are most important for your project. The number of archiving objects selected determines the size of your archiving project. In real life, the project scope may vary greatly. In our experience, we have known one corporate group to implement only one archiving object in its archiving project (for example, FI_DOCUMNT) and another corporate group to implement almost twenty archiving objects at once. On average, however, approximately 5 to 10 archiving objects are implemented in an archiving project. It goes without saying that a recommendation concerning the initial number of archiving objects to be implemented must comply with the circumstances in which you use your SAP system.

▸ **Kick-off**
Once you have selected your archiving objects, you can host kick-off workshops and meetings until all decisions and approvals pertaining to each archiving object have been made or obtained. The concept for each individual archiving object must also include information from discussions with users and decision-makers so that the archiving object can be completed and used in live operation.

The implementation phase is therefore a very time-intensive phase within the project. In particular, the kick-off workshops and meetings require thorough preparation and planning.

Getting to know the archiving object

First, you must familiarize yourself with the possibilities associated with an archiving object, especially if confronted with a completely new archiving object that you have not encountered previously. No one can expect you to know every single SAP data archiving object inside out, including their various strengths and weaknesses. There are simply too many archiving objects in an SAP system.

If you are focusing on archiving objects from several components (for example, FI, CO, SD, and MM), we recommend that you host separate kick-off workshops and meetings for each component. In the case of archiving objects that concern several components, you should always invite those persons responsible for each individual component. Otherwise, you run the risk of implementing only the requirements of one user department and completely forgetting the other user departments or not involving them until much later. You should avoid such a one-sided consideration in the implementation phase at all costs. Otherwise, you may run the risk of flagging the concept as complete even if the requirements are incomplete. If, for example, you want to obtain information about the archiving object PR_ORDER (Process Order), you should involve not only decision-makers from production but also from controlling, because both user departments use different transactions to access the data contained in the process order. In a meeting, a controller will have very different archiving requirements than a decision-maker from production planning.

Involving the right user departments

Start the Project with a Small Number of Archiving Objects [+]

To start the archiving project quickly, we recommend that you start the project with a small number of archiving objects. Even if you possibly intend to implement 30 archiving objects in the long term, the *big bang approach* (that is, implementing all objects simultaneously) is not advisable, because doing so would result in a very long project runtime. You would also have to forgo any possibility of achieving fast success.

It is better to divide the archiving project into several archiving phases known as *waves*. By doing so, you can use the first wave to deal, for example, with performance-critical archiving objects or archiving objects that concern a large volume of data and a short residence time. Then, following this initial success, you can proceed with the next wave.

In the next section, you will learn how to assign archiving objects to the various phases in order to start with the right archiving objects.

6.1.1 Selecting the Right Archiving Objects

Given the multitude of data archiving with SAP objects available, it is not always easy to select the right archiving objects for the first wave of the project. Therefore, the objects selected depend on the driving force behind your data archiving project. For this reason, you learned various approaches in Chapter 4, Section 4.1.

Procedure   Depending on whether you want to archive for performance reasons or you want to use archiving for system hygiene only, you can proceed as follows when selecting your archiving objects:

> **Goal: Safeguard the performance of your SAP system**
> If you want to restore system performance, there is generally an acute need for action. If poor performance by your SAP system impacts on your day-to-day activities, you can quickly determine which tables are the culprits.

[Ex]   **Archiving Objects RL_TA and SD_AGREEM**

In our projects, we have frequently worked with the archiving objects RL_TA (Warehouse Management: Transfer Orders) and SD_AGREEM (Agreements and Conditions) in this area. Fortunately, neither of these archiving objects has any preceding archiving objects that you need to set up first. You can therefore invest your time directly into setting up these performance-critical archiving objects. Since neither of these archiving objects is characterized by large volumes of data, you should also use them in live operation if you have a large number of warehouse-based business processes and if you enter into agreements with your customers and vendors on a regular basis and settle these periodically.

> **Goal: Optimize IT resources (memory space, etc.)**
> You can use Transaction DB02 to quickly determine which tables occupy the most memory space and grow the fastest. Here it is important to determine the associated archiving objects and to check whether or not these archiving objects have preceding objects.

[Ex]   **Archiving Object LE_HU**

The tables for the handling units in the system of an enterprise from the chemical industry experience strong growth. However, the associated archiving object LE_HU has several preceding archiving objects (for example, the material documents and the deliveries). Consequently, for the first archiving object, you must not select only the archiving object LE_HU but also the objects MM_MATBEL, RV_LIKP, and so on. Therefore, if you have identified a critical archiving object, you may have to do some preparatory work before you can use the actual archiving object in live operation. You can do this in one large wave or in two smaller waves. You therefore decide how many archiving objects you want to process within a wave.

▶ **Goal: System hygiene**
Sooner or later, data archiving at the end of the information lifecycle becomes a necessary task for each SAP system. For this task, you require a very large number of archiving objects, because data is to be archived from all modules.

In real life, this task is willingly bypassed by installing a new SAP system that operates alongside the legacy system. However, this merely enables you to change the type of task that you need to perform. In other words, you now need to consider how you can deactivate the legacy system in the future. One possibility here is SAP ILM, which we will discuss in Chapter 8.

▶ **Goal: Remove master data that is no longer required**
Archiving objects exist not only for transaction data but also for master data (for example, vendors, customers, materials, and so on). In reality, creditor data (vendors), in particular, is frequently archived. However, as you already learned in Chapter 4, Section 4.1.2, it is not so easy to remove creditor master data from an SAP system as soon as transaction data has been assigned to it. Nevertheless, you should also make preparations for archiving master data because, sooner or later, you will definitely be faced with the task of archiving master data.

The next step is to use an overview to assign those archiving objects that are generally eligible for your SAP system to various phases known as waves. For example, you can divide your project into the following three phases:

Assignment to archiving phases

▶ **Phase 1**
In phase 1, you implement archiving objects with a short residence time (for example, IDOC) or those that are critical for performance (for example, RL_TA). If an archiving object is both relevant for DART and critical for performance (SD_AGREEM), you must immediately clarify if a DART extraction is necessary beforehand for those countries that access the associated SAP system. If this is the case, you implement the DART phase as the first project implementation phase. You then start the process of archiving DART-relevant objects.

▶ **Phase 2**

In the second phase, you implement archiving objects that have a somewhat longer residence time or have one or more preceding archiving objects.

▶ **Phase 3**

The third phase and all subsequent phases comply with the long-term road map. The archiving object FI_ACCRECV (Customer Master Data) has, for example, several preceding archiving objects and therefore you can only use it in live operation later. Therefore, you should plan its use for one of the later phases.

Sample division into waves
We have already divided the archiving objects frequently mentioned in this book into possible archiving phases within a project (see Table 6.1). This assignment reflects our experiences with various projects in different enterprises. However, your individual approach may, of course, deviate from this example, depending on the circumstances and goals of your enterprise.

Industry Sector	Phase (Wave) 1	Phase (Wave) 2	Phase (Wave) 3
General	IDOC	RV_LIKP	LE_HU
	BC_SBAL	SD_VBRK	PM_ORDER
	BC_DBLOGS	SD_VBAK	FI_ACCRECV
	CHANGEDOCU	MM_EKKO	
	WORKITEM	MM_EBAN	
	MM_ACCTIT		
	RL_TA		
	MM_MATBEL		
	SD_AGREEM		
Automotive	VEHICLE		
Chemical	PR_ORDER		

Table 6.1 Sample Assignment of Archiving Objects to Various Phases (Waves)

Sample implementation
In the example shown in Table 6.1, let's assume that there are acute performance problems during the read access to transfer orders. Therefore, a basic prerequisite is that we must urgently implement the archiving

object `RL_TA`. Let's also assume that the IDocs tables on the database have experienced very large data growth that we need to tackle, ideally using the archiving object `IDOC`. For these reasons, we will start the first phase of this project with precisely these two archiving objects.

6.1.2 Hosting Kick-Off Workshops

Once you have decided which archiving objects will form the basis for your project, invite the relevant decision-makers to a kick-off workshop. Of course, it goes without saying that you have already given some thought to which decision-makers you want to involve (see Chapter 5, Section 5.3).

The first meeting held with decision-makers is the kick-off workshop. Ideally, all key players will be in attendance. For this reason, choose a suitable date (in other words, a day when all decision-makers can attend the kick-off workshop). Following the kick-off workshop, you will hold meetings for smaller teams specifically to clarify certain issues.

Choosing a suitable date

In Chapter 5, you learned how to carefully prepare for these workshops. Ideally, you can also use various archivable transactions in a sandbox system or test system to demonstrate the archive access, which will be implemented later. This first live demonstration gives colleagues an early insight into the world of data archiving and makes it easier for them to make the necessary decisions and grant the requisite approvals. This procedure contributes to fast and productive implementation of the archiving object.

The majority of the time that you need to estimate for an archiving project is devoted to hosting workshops. Here a large number of details need to be thoroughly clarified in order to reach a consensus within the team and to successfully implement the necessary changes. Therefore, observe the following points when hosting kick-off workshops:

Reaching a consensus

- Specify decision-makers
- Create a SWOT analysis
- Document decisions
- Prepare the archive access in a demo system
- Define an approval procedure

Different process
flow possible

It goes without saying that the process flow for a kick-off workshop differs for each individual archiving object. For the archiving object RL_TA, you must adopt a completely different process flow than the one that you may need to adopt for the archiving object IDOC, because RL_TA directly influences warehouse-based business processes in which not only data records but also documents are generated.

Visiting user
departments

In order to familiarize yourself with the associated business processes, we recommend that you tour the warehouse and speak with the user department on-site if it is feasible for you to do so within your enterprise. This enables you to not only keep the name of this warehouse in mind when archiving warehouse-generated data records in your SAP system but also the physical building in which the relevant goods are placed in storage and removed from storage on the basis of the transfer orders.

IDOC, on the other hand, is an archiving object that generally requires little or no coordination and communication with the user departments in question. IDoc transfers data from one system to another. The only option available to you here is to view the relevant systems and the interface overview. Nevertheless, it is also necessary to clarify in detail at the kick-off workshop which message types are sent between the systems as IDocs and how you can handle these individual message types. We will now take a look at this in the following example.

Examples

In the sections that follow, you will learn what a sample kick-off workshop may entail in real life for the two archiving objects mentioned earlier.

Kick-Off Workshop for the Archiving Object RL_TA

In Chapter 5, Section 5.3, you learned about potential decision-makers and the types of decisions made by these parties.

Specifying
decision-makers

In the case of an archiving object such as RL_TA, which has major effects on day-to-day activities, it is absolutely necessary that you invite the experts and employees from the relevant departments to the kick-off workshops. Ideally, you have already recorded the names of these parties in the archiving object concept as contact persons. These parties are best able to judge which transactions and reports are used to control the business processes in the SAP system.

You should not, on the other hand, invite a sponsor from top management to such kick-off workshops at the archiving object level, because for the multitude of archiving objects being focused on and the time needed to host these workshops, top management would be too heavily involved in working out the necessary details. Of course, there are always exceptions. If the archiving object RL_TA can, as is the case in our example, significantly influence performance and therefore the overall operation of the SAP system, you should invite top management because they will want to follow the topic intensively.

Sponsors in special cases only

The experts and employees from the departments in question can, after a brief *round of introductions* at the start of the kick-off workshop, discuss the reasons, the planned procedure, and the potential effects of archiving in detail and try to reach a consensus. Therefore, it is best to start by presenting the archiving object RL_TA and guiding the workshop participants through the topic of data archiving. Try to obtain feedback from all participants and integrate this feedback into the workshop, because each party will have a different viewpoint and bring different experiences to the table.

Obtaining feedback from all participants

At the end of the workshop, all general questions (for example, which warehouses are affected by archiving) should be clarified as much as possible so that only specific questions need to be handled in the smaller teams. If, for example, you have identified a critical customer-specific transaction or such a program, do not deal with the associated program code in detail in the first kick-off workshop. Add this task to your list of open items and specify a person responsible and a target deadline. By doing so, you avoid turning the kick-off workshop into a meeting in which only a handful of participants with technical knowledge can have a say while all other participants become bystanders.

Clarifying the details in follow-up meetings

Ideally, end the kick-off workshop by proposing a follow-up meeting at which the findings of all items still outstanding can be presented in the form of an interim result. Specify a day when all participants are available again and by which all open items can be completed.

Specifying a date for an interim result

Kick-Off Workshop for the Archiving Object IDOC

For the archiving object IDOC, the kick-off workshop can have a simpler format. As a first step, it more than suffices to invite one expert and one employee from the IT department to the kick-off workshop in order to define the procedure for using the archiving object IDOC for data archiving. IDocs have a relatively short lifetime in an SAP system. Furthermore, users call them from the archive in only extremely rare circumstances.

Handling message types differently
You can also determine whether all types of IDocs are archived in accordance with the same procedure or certain messages types (field MESTYP) are to be deleted immediately. Therefore, defining the residence time is not the only decision that you need to make in this kick-off workshop and in follow-up meetings. You also need to make a decision in relation to which message types you want to archive. If you are considering using the archiving object IDOC separately for different message types, you should always involve those user departments that send and receive such IDocs.

SWOT analysis
As a basis for discussion during the kick-off workshop, we recommend that you use Transaction TAANA to analyze the leading tables for the archiving object. During the meeting, you will then have a good basis for discussing and making decisions in relation to certain items. In Figure 6.1, we analyzed table EDI40 for the archiving object IDOC in detail with regard to the fields ARCHIVABLE and MESSAGE TYPE. You see, for example, that the MESSAGE TYPE INTERNAL_ORDER has more than 25,000 entries, but this has not been flagged as ARCHIVABLE (no X). In the kick-off meeting, you could discuss the reason for this with the decision-makers, along with which measures you should define in this case.

Documenting decisions
Using the example of IDocs, Table 6.2 provides an overview of the decisions participants in a kick-off workshop are responsible for making and documenting. You should then discuss these topics and decisions with the decision-makers and incorporate them into the concept for the archiving object.

Figure 6.1 Analyzing Message Types in Transaction TAANA

Topic	Description
Residence time	▸ Confirmation of the residence time is necessary for the concept. In the kick-off workshop, you can make a recommendation and obtain the opinions of experts and employees. ▸ You can configure a different residence time for each message type, if required.
Retention period	▸ You must also make a decision in relation to the retention period. ▸ Many IDocs (message types) are generally not subject to a retention obligation and could be deleted immediately or retained for only a very short time.
Archiving scope	▸ You can archive IDocs separately according to message type, or you can even fully exclude certain message types from archiving. ▸ In this context, it is important to reach agreement on the archiving scope.

Table 6.2 Decisions That Need to Be Made and Documented

Topic	Description
Storage of archive files	▶ In the case of IDocs that are subject to a retention obligation, you can store them in an audit-compliant manner in accordance with the retention period. ▶ You can define a different storage strategy for IDocs that are not subject to a retention obligation.
Archive access	▶ Present and evaluate the archive access. ▶ If the archive access is to be expanded further, specific activities and persons responsible must be specified until such time as the new archive access is set up.

Table 6.2 Decisions That Need to Be Made and Documented (Cont.)

Demonstrating the archive access

For successful kick-off workshops, it is both helpful and highly recommended to demonstrate an archive access immediately. Test archiving in a suitable SAP system (for example, a sandbox system) enables you to give participants an insight into productive archiving even at a very early stage. Meeting participants can evaluate the strengths and weaknesses of this access and the results incorporated into their archiving decisions. In this way, you can demonstrate, for example, the archivable Transaction WE09 (IDoc Search for Business Content) for the archiving object IDOC (see Figure 6.2).

Figure 6.2 Selecting a Data Source in Transaction WE09

All decision-makers present at the kick-off workshop will therefore learn how to use Transaction WE09, which is already familiar to them, to access the archive directly. To do this, they must choose DATA SOURCE... and then select the ARCHIVE and ARCHIVE INFORMATION SYSTEM options for an automatic search across the archive infostructure. In this way, the number of steps that an employee needs to execute in Transaction WE09 to access the archive is immediately apparent to all parties present. Therefore, this demonstration makes it considerably easier to reach a decision.

In discussions within the kick-off workshops, you also need to define an approval procedure for productive data archiving. The decision-makers present will see that you will document every key decision made and, only after explicit approval, move from one step to another. In Chapter 4, Section 4.2.2, Operational Level, you learned about the various statuses that may be assigned to an archiving concept. In the kick-off workshop, you provide an accurate presentation of this procedure and you explain the milestones according to which you expect decision-makers to grant final approval for using archiving objects in live operation. This final approval will ultimately result in you being able to declare the concept for the archiving object as "created" and assigning it status 100. You can then archive it as approved documentation.

Defining an approval procedure

6.2 Final Preparation

As soon as you have completed the concept for an archiving object, you can prepare the object, step by step, for use in live operation. Here you always comply with those concept-based specifications that define each individual step. Consequently, for the go-live, you implement the requirements that you discussed, determined, and documented in discussions within the kick-off workshops and meetings held with decision-makers.

Implementing specifications from the concept

Before you can commence archiving in the production system, you must prepare each archiving object carefully, because an SAP data archiving object already exists in the standard SAP system and is available for use with general settings. Usually, however, these settings do not satisfy your particular requirements. Specifically, you need to maintain the residence times, file names, path names, and content repositories in Customizing. For these Customizing settings, the concept developed for the archiving object is available to you as a guide, because, in this concept, you have ideally answered all open issues on the basis of the decisions made in the workshops held with the decision-makers.

The long journey until an archiving object goes live starts in a development system in which the relevant Customizing settings are made. The archiving object then moves to the test system where you schedule the first archiving sessions and conduct user tests. The journey ultimately ends in the production system where you use prepared, successfully tested archiving objects in live operation and run them periodically.

6.2.1 Preparing Archiving Objects

In addition to Customizing, preparing an archiving object generally involves implementing various SAP Notes, depending on your system release. Therefore, check the SAP Notes specified in the concept for the archiving object and check if the SAP Support Portal now has other SAP Notes that have become relevant. If relevant SAP Notes exist, implement them. Then continue with Customizing. In the concept for the archiving object, you have also made specifications in this regard. In the following section, we will show you, step by step, how to set up and use an archiving object. Since, in our example, we have selected two archiving objects, we will first start by preparing the archiving object RL_TA and then continue our example with the archiving object IDOC in order to integrate both archiving objects into the guide. Essentially, the preparatory steps do not differ.

To set up the two archiving objects from our example, namely RL_TA and IDOC, proceed as described in the following text. First, define the file names and path names in Transaction FILE. For information about the relationship between file names and path names, see Chapter 1, Section 1.4.5. We will show you this using the example of the archiving object RL_TA:

1. As soon as you call Transaction FILE, you receive the information message "Caution: The table is cross-client" (see Figure 6.3). To confirm this information message stating that our changes in the tables for path names and file names are cross-client changes, select the check mark ✔ or press Enter .

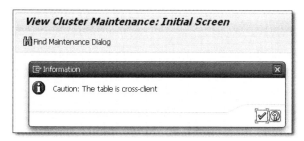

Figure 6.3 Information Message on Initial Screen for Transaction FILE

Separate the Exchange Directory According to Client [«]

Transaction FILE was designed for cross-client maintenance. You must therefore understand this information message as follows: If you use several clients in an SAP system, your entries for the path names and file names are visible in all clients and therefore can also be used in all clients. To ensure that the archive files from different clients are not located in the same directory, we will show you, in the steps that follow, how you can use a suitable definition of the physical path to separate the exchange directories according to client.

2. After you confirm this information message, you access the overview of all logical file paths in your SAP system (see Figure 6.4).

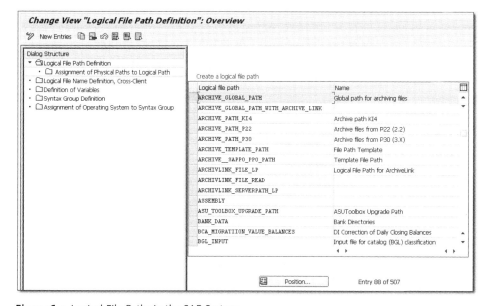

Figure 6.4 Logical File Paths in the SAP System

3. Select the standard SAP entry `ARCHIVE_GLOBAL_PATH` (Global Path for Archiving Files) for archiving objects as a template and choose COPY 📄 in order to create your own entry according to this copy template.

4. In this example, we entered "Z_ARCHIVE_GLOBAL_PATH_RL_TA" in the LOGICAL FILE PATH column and "Global path for RL_TA archiving files" in the NAME column (see Figure 6.5). You have therefore defined a custom logical file path for the archiving object `RL_TA`. Now choose SAVE 💾 to save this entry.

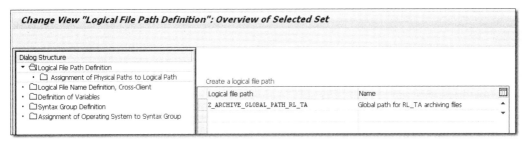

Figure 6.5 Creating an Individual Logical File Path

5. Then assign a physical file path to this newly created logical file path. The physical file path is ultimately the exchange directory in which the archive files are stored temporarily.

6. In our example, the PHYSICAL PATH comprises the following (see Figure 6.6):

/archive/<SYSID>/M<CLIENT>/<PARAM_1>/<FILENAME>

You may recall the reserved words from Chapter 1, Section 1.4.5. In this example, we have used the system ID (SYSID) and the client (CLIENT) so that these can be determined dynamically from any system at runtime when creating the archive file. This dynamic gives us greater flexibility and increases reusability of the physical file path. You can use this physical file path for various clients and SAP systems.

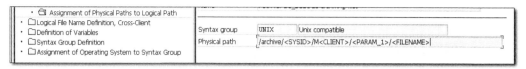

Figure 6.6 Assigning a Logical Path to a Physical Path

It is therefore absolutely imperative that you have already created the corresponding exchange directories in Transaction AL11. In Chapter 2, Section 2.3.2, you learned how to structure exchange directories for storage purposes. In our example, the exchange directories in our SAP system correspond to the directories in Figure 6.7.

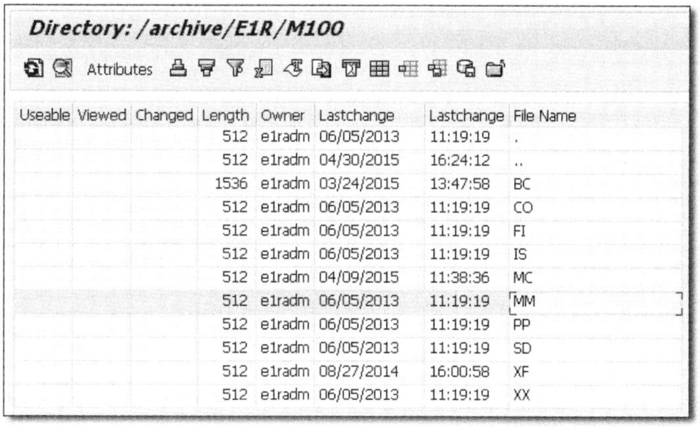

Creating exchange directories

Directory: /archive/E1R/M100

Useable	Viewed	Changed	Length	Owner	Lastchange	Lastchange	File Name
			512	e1radm	06/05/2013	11:19:19	.
			512	e1radm	04/30/2015	16:24:12	..
			1536	e1radm	03/24/2015	13:47:58	BC
			512	e1radm	06/05/2013	11:19:19	CO
			512	e1radm	06/05/2013	11:19:19	FI
			512	e1radm	06/05/2013	11:19:19	IS
			512	e1radm	04/09/2015	11:38:36	MC
			512	e1radm	06/05/2013	11:19:19	MM
			512	e1radm	06/05/2013	11:19:19	PP
			512	e1radm	06/05/2013	11:19:19	SD
			512	e1radm	08/27/2014	16:00:58	XF
			512	e1radm	06/05/2013	11:19:19	XX

Figure 6.7 Exchange Directories in the SAP System for Storing Archive Files

Immediately after creating the client, we created a separate subdirectory for each module so that the archive files for the archiving object RL_TA can be stored in the MM directory. Then we took the archive files for the archiving object IDOC directly from the productive SAP system and stored them in the *BC* directory.

In the next step, we will define a logical file name, which we can also create using the COPY button 🖹. Once again, we have selected the existing standard SAP entry ARCHIVE_DATA_FILE as the copy template (see Figure 6.8).

Defining logical file names

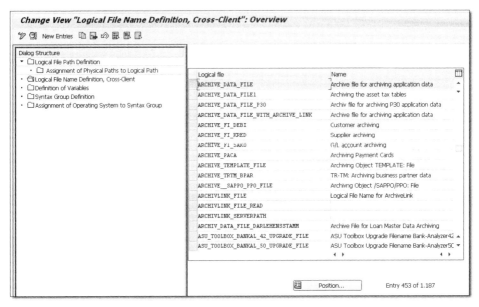

Figure 6.8 Creating a Logical File Name for Each Copy Template

7. Once you have copied the file name template, enter the new logical file name "Z_ARCHIVE_DATA_FILE_RL_TA" in the LOGICAL FILE field, for example (similar to the LOGICAL PATH field). You should also amend the NAME so that it is apparent that it concerns RL_TA application data.

8. The entry in the PHYSICAL FILE field, in which you define the physical file name, is also important here. To ensure that the archive files contain the ID of your SAP system and your client in the file name, you should use the corresponding reserved words again. In our example, we inserted the system ID (SYSID) and the client (CLIENT) in front of the existing reserved words (see Figure 6.9).

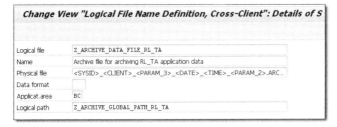

Figure 6.9 Defining Logical File Names

Once you have saved all of the relevant settings, you still need to assign the logical file name to the archiving object RL_TA:

1. Call Transaction SARA and enter "RL_TA" in the ARCHIVING OBJECT field (see Figure 6.10). Then press ⌨Enter to confirm your entry.

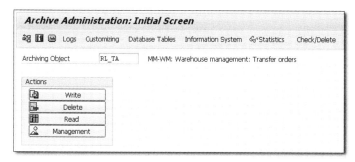

Figure 6.10 Transaction SARA for the Archiving Object RL_TA

2. Choose CUSTOMIZING to access the view shown in Figure 6.11.

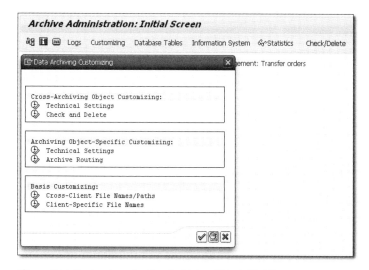

Figure 6.11 Customizing for the Archiving Object RL_TA

3. In the ARCHIVING OBJECT-SPECIFIC CUSTOMIZING area, choose EXECUTE ⊕ next to the TECHNICAL SETTINGS entry.

4. Then in the CUSTOMIZING VIEW FOR ARCHIVING, maintain the previously created logical file name (Z_ARCHIVE_DATA_FILE_RL_TA) in the LOGICAL FILE NAME field (see Figure 6.12).

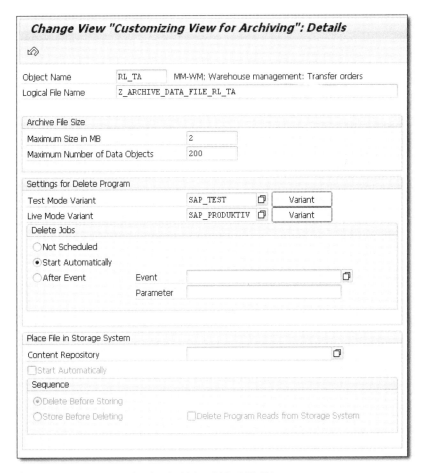

Figure 6.12 Customizing for the Archiving Object RL_TA

Additional settings

Once you have entered the LOGICAL FILE NAME, you must adjust some additional settings in accordance with your concept for the archiving object RL_TA, because the predefined settings are merely suggestions that you need to check and adjust to your own requirements.

1. Table 6.3 contains Customizing recommendations that could originate from the concept for the archiving object RL_TA.

Field	Old Value	New Value	Comment
MAXIMUM SIZE IN MB	2	100	▸ If this value is too small, a large number of small archive files are generated. ▸ If this value is too big, large archive files are generated. ▸ Therefore, you may experience storage problems in the archive system.
MAXIMUM NUMBER OF DATA OBJECTS	200		▸ The SAP system generates a new archive file depending on whether the maximum size in MB or the maximum number of data objects is reached first. ▸ We recommend that you do not enter a value here so that additional archive files are generated only after the maximum size in MB has been reached.
TEST MODE VARIANT	SAP_TEST		▸ Check if the variant is maintained correctly. ▸ If necessary, adjust this variant or define a new variant.
LIVE MODE VARIANT	SAP_ PRODUK- TIV		▸ Check if the variant is maintained correctly. ▸ If necessary, adjust this variant or define a new variant.
DELETE JOBS	START AUTOMATI- CALLY		▸ If you want to start delete jobs manually, select the NOT SCHEDULED option.

Table 6.3 Recommendations for Customizing from the RL_TA Concept

Field	Old Value	New Value	Comment
CONTENT REPOSITORY			▶ Enter a content repository if you do not want the archive files to remain in the exchange directory.
			▶ The storage job can therefore occur automatically.
SEQUENCE	DELETE BEFORE STORING		▶ If you specify a content repository, you can determine the delete phase.
			▶ In our example, we store the archive file in the file system only.

Table 6.3 Recommendations for Customizing from the RL_TA Concept (Cont.)

2. Once you have made your entries for Customizing, choose SAVE 🖫 to save your settings.

3. Use a workbench request to transport the settings to the test system. Here you can test the archiving object RL_TA thoroughly.

To set up the second archiving object, namely, IDOC, perform the same steps as noted earlier.

[»]   **Planning the Transportation of Customizing Settings**

The time it takes to transport Customizing settings may vary in enterprises. In smaller enterprises, we have known a transfer order to take just a few minutes to transport the settings from a development system to a production system (two-system landscape).

In larger corporate groups, however, this is not possible. Generally, there is a transportation calendar that schedules the transportation of settings from one SAP system to another at certain intervals and in accordance with certain specifications (multisystem landscape). You must not transport an object to the production system unless its transportation has been preceded by a successful, documented user test in the test system.

If transportation management in your enterprise is controlled in a similar manner, it is best to reach agreement with a colleague from the SAP Basis team in good time so that your transport is available in the relevant SAP system on the requested date. Of course, there will always be exceptions whereby you can flag a transfer order as urgent in order to bypass the standard procedure. In practice, however, this is not welcomed. For this reason, we recommend that you comply with the transportation calendar and schedule your upcoming activities accordingly.

6.2.2 Archiving Data in a Test System

Since most development systems do not contain any representative data for testing, you transport your Customizing settings directly to the test system and use Transactions SARA and FILE to check them for completeness and accuracy. Then it is time to perform the first archiving sessions in the test system. Once again, the specifications from the concept for the archiving object are crucial here because they specify what you need to do to create the selection variants or whether a preprocessing or postprocessing job is required in addition to the write job.

Write Job

In the case of the write job for our first archiving object (RL_TA), we use the selection screen in the standard system (see Figure 6.13).

Write job
for RL_TA

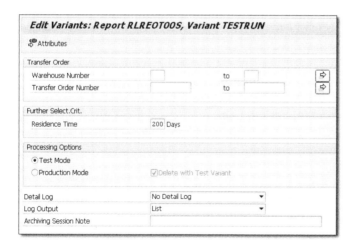

Figure 6.13 Selection Screen in the Write Job for the Object RL_TA

Before you commence archiving in the test system, you should familiarize yourself with the selection criteria for the write job for the archiving object RL_TA so that you can create suitable variants. Note that it is almost impossible to correct errors here (or only with great difficulty). If, for example, in the RESIDENCE TIME field, you enter a lower value than the number of days specified by the user department, you may endanger the processes in your enterprise. Therefore, the RESIDENCE TIME and the WAREHOUSE NUMBER fields are important selection criteria whose values must be specified in the concept for the archiving object RL_TA.

[»] **Maintaining the Residence Time in the Variant**

In the case of some archiving objects, you maintain the residence time directly in Customizing. However, this is not the case for RL_TA. Here the residence time is controlled directly by means of the selection variant. This results in greater flexibility. However, it also means that there is a danger of you being able to quickly and easily change variants.

Transfer order number

The TRANSFER ORDER NUMBER field is very helpful for conducting tests. Entering a transfer order number enables you to archive and test a specific transfer order, thus sparing you from long runtimes and large archive files. In other words, data archiving in the test system can be used specifically for individual transfer orders or for the maximum scope.

Archiving low volumes of data

However, we recommend that, as a first step, you specifically archive individual transfer orders. Archiving the maximum scope makes particular sense if you want to reduce the volume of data in the test system and calculate an approximate runtime for conducting data archiving in the production system. However, the runtimes in the test system and production system may vary (even for the same volume of data) if the hardware for the respective systems has been sized in such a way as to provide different levels of performance.

[»] **Starting the Write Job in Production Mode with the Delete Job**

If you want to start the write job for data archiving in PRODUCTION MODE (PRODUCTION RUN) and, at the same time, you have specified, in Customizing, that you want the system to start delete jobs automatically (see Figure 6.12), the DELETE WITH TEST VARIANT option (see Figure 6.13), which is already selected in the standard SAP system, is active so that a delete run is simulated after the write job ends. However, you must check if the SAP_TEST variant defined in the TEST MODE VARIANT field (as shown in Figure 6.12) has been declared as the corresponding variant in TEST MODE (see Figure 6.14).

If you do not select TEST MODE here, you will unintentionally perform a proper deletion, even though you only want to simulate a delete run. If you deactivate the DELETE WITH TEST VARIANT option, the delete job will be performed using the LIVE MODE VARIANT SAP_PRODUKTIV. Of course, you must also select the right PRODUCTION MODE here. You can use the sample variant SAP_TEST in Figure 6.14 to see how such a variant looks when it is created properly and how to manually check and adjust this variant in the SAP system when developing the concept.

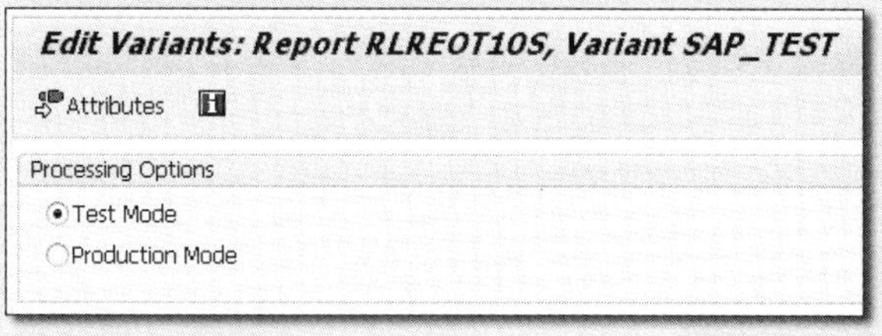

Edit Variants: Report RLREOT10S, Variant SAP_TEST

Attributes

Processing Options
- Test Mode
- Production Mode

Figure 6.14 Checking If Test Mode Is Defined for the SAP_TEST Variant When the Delete Job Is Started Automatically

You call variant maintenance for the delete program in Figure 6.14 by choosing VARIANT next to the variant SAP_TEST or SAP_PRODUKTIV in Figure 6.12.

To create the two variants for the test run and production run associated with the write job, proceed as described in the following text. First, create the variant for the test run:

Creating a variant for the test run

1. Call Transaction SARA, enter "RL_TA" in the ARCHIVING OBJECT field, and press [Enter] to confirm your entry.

2. Then, in the ACTIONS area, choose WRITE to create a variant for the write job.

3. Then enter the variant name "TESTRUN" in the VARIANT field and choose MAINTAIN to maintain the variant with values (see also Figure 6.17).

4. For the archiving object RL_TA in our example, we create the selection variant for the test run of the write job with the values from Table 6.4.

   In our example, we schedule the selection variant for the test run of the write job for WAREHOUSE NUMBER 001 only. This restriction ensures that the test run is performed more quickly. Without this restriction, we would archive all transfer orders that are older than 200 days.

Field	Value(s)
Warehouse Number	001
Transfer Order Number	Blank
Residence Time	200 (in accordance with the concept)
Processing Options	Test Mode
Detail Log	Complete
Log Output	List and Application Log
Archiving Session Note	Testrun Warehouse Number 001

Table 6.4 Values in the Selection Variant for the Test Run

5. Once you have maintained the values for the test run, choose BACK 🔄 to save the variant.

6. Choose YES to confirm the prompt asking you if you want to save the values (see Figure 6.15).

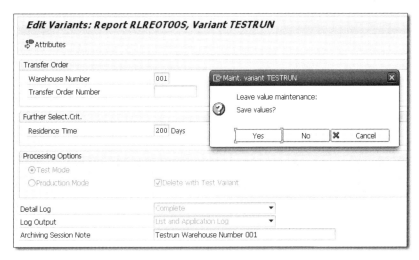

Figure 6.15 Saving the TESTRUN Variant

7. You then access the screen for maintaining variant attributes (see Figure 6.16). In the DESCRIPTION field, you can maintain a short text for the variant. Here we entered "Testrun Warehouse Number 001," for example.

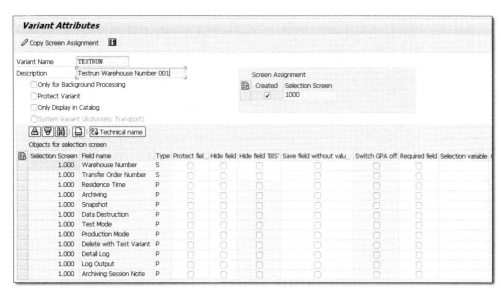

Figure 6.16 Maintaining the Variant Attributes

8. Choose SAVE to save the variant, which you can then use for the write job.

Hidden SAP ILM Functions [«]

In the FIELD NAME column in Figure 6.16, you see fields such as SNAPSHOT or DATA DESTRUCTION, which we did not see on the selection screen in Figure 6.15. These fields already exist in the write job for our archiving object RL_TA and are solely intended for SAP Information Lifecycle Management (SAP ILM). Consequently, they are visible on the selection screen only if you are using SAP ILM. For more information, see Chapter 8.

Apart from some minor differences in comparison to the variant for the test run, we use the same procedure to create the selection variant for the production run for the write job. Table 6.5 contains the values that we will choose in our example.

Variant for the production run

Field	Value(s)
Warehouse Number	001
Transfer Order Number	Blank

Table 6.5 Values in the Selection Variant for the Production Run

Field	Value(s)
Residence Time	200 (in accordance with the concept)
Processing Options	Production Mode
Delete with Test Variant	No (otherwise a delete run is simulated)
Detail Log	Complete
Log Output	List and Application Log
Archiving Session Note	Production run Warehouse Number 001

Table 6.5 Values in the Selection Variant for the Production Run (Cont.)

In the PROCESSING OPTIONS area, however, you select PRODUCTION MODE. You deactivate the default option DELETE WITH TEST VARIANT so that the system does not simulate a delete run after creating the archive file. You adjust the ARCHIVING SESSION NOTE in such a way that it concerns a production run.

Scheduling a write job

Once you have created the two variants TESTRUN and PRODUCTION RUN for our archiving object RL_TA, you can schedule the associated write job in Transaction SARA. To do this, proceed as follows:

1. Call Transaction SARA, enter "RL_TA" in the ARCHIVING OBJECT field, and choose ⌈Enter⌋ to confirm your entry.

2. Then, choose WRITE to schedule the write job.

3. In the VARIANT field, select the TESTRUN variant that we created earlier (see Figure 6.17). If you want to create another variant, enter a new variant name in the VARIANT field and choose MAINTAIN.

Figure 6.17 Scheduling a Write Job for RL_TA

4. You must maintain additional information in the START DATE and SPOOL PARAMS. areas so that the write job can start. As long as a red icon for the status *Not Maintained* is displayed next to the START DATE and SPOOL PARAMS. buttons, the SAP system will be prevented from executing the job. First, choose START DATE to access the maintenance screen shown in Figure 6.18.

Figure 6.18 Maintaining the Start Date Values for the Write Job

5. Here you see various options for the START TIME:

- ▶ IMMEDIATE
- ▶ DATE/TIME
- ▶ AFTER JOB
- ▶ AFTER EVENT
- ▶ AT OPERATION MODE
- ▶ WORKING DAY/TIME (displayed if you choose CONTINUE >..)

In reality, the first three options are used most often. If you choose one of the options, the system displays additional input fields in which you must make some entries. For our test run, it is enough to choose IMMEDIATE as the start time. For the production system (that is, the production run), we recommend that you comply with the specifications from the concept in relation to when the relevant jobs are to be scheduled. The second option (DATE/TIME) is most suitable here. You can specify the DATE and TIME in the SCHEDULED START area as shown in Figure 6.19.

6. If you select the DATE/TIME start option, the system also displays the PERIOD VALUES button at the bottom of the dialog box. If you choose this button, you can specify in which cycle the SAP system is to automatically restart this write job. If you want to activate periodic start times, you must select the PERIODIC JOB option. In accordance with the values in Figure 6.19, our write job would first start on January 01, 2015 at 12:00:00. All subsequent write jobs would then run weekly at the same time. In other words, the next write job would be on January 08, 2015 at 12:00:00.

Figure 6.19 Executing a Job Periodically

7. You can also use the RESTRICTIONS button to determine, on the basis of a factory calendar, whether the job is to be performed on Sundays or public holidays, for example.

8. We opt for an immediate start and choose SAVE 🖫 to confirm our entries. We have now maintained the start time, which is flagged in the overview with a green icon.

9. Next, maintain the spool parameters. To do this, choose SPOOL PARAMS. to open the new BACKGROUND PRINT PARAMETERS window shown in Figure 6.20.

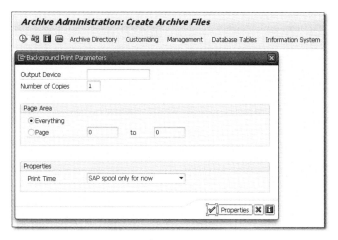

Figure 6.20 Maintaining Spool Parameters

10. In general, you can choose CONTINUE ✔ to confirm the predefined values. We do not recommend creating a paper printout of the spool file. In fact, this should be avoided at all costs, because some spool files may comprise several hundred pages.

11. Note the following: after just a few days, the spool files are deleted from the system again. For more information, choose PROPERTIES (see Figure 6.21).

    The SPOOL RETENTION period is generally eight days. If you require the spool file beyond this time, we recommend that you print it out (if it comprises a small number of pages) or save it as a file or store it in an archive. For information on how to store a print list in an archive, see Chapter 3, Section 3.5.

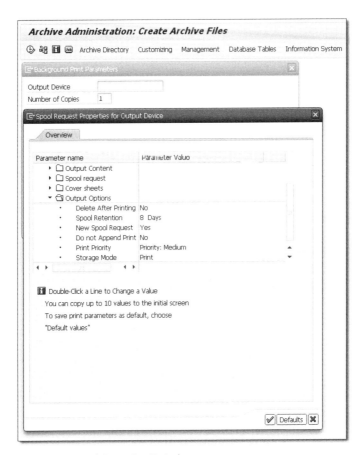

Figure 6.21 Spool Retention Period

[+] **Possible to Repeat a Test Run**

If you did not save the spool file, you can repeat the test run of the write job in order to generate a new spool file. In the case of a production run, however, this is no longer possible, at the latest, after a delete run has deleted the data from the system. Therefore, to ensure that you do not lose important information from the spool files, never neglect to perform this step. Furthermore, make sure that the relevant documentation is comprehensible.

12. If you have selected the green check mark to confirm that the spool parameters have been maintained, a green icon (MAINTAINED) is also displayed in the overview.

13. You can now choose EXECUTE  to start the write job with the TESTRUN variant immediately (see Figure 6.22).

Figure 6.22 All Information Maintained for the Write Job

If you did not encounter any problems while performing the test run, you can continue with the production run. Start the production run in the same way. However, select the PRODUCTION RUN variant in production mode here so that an archive file is actually generated and you can perform the additional steps, execute the delete run, and fill the archive infostructures.

Starting the production run

Archiving Object IDOC   [«]

We demonstrated the previous steps using only the archiving object RL_TA. The procedure is the same for the archiving object IDOC and other archiving objects in an SAP system. In general, the archiving objects differ in terms of the write job and the associated potential selection criteria. The additional steps that we will show you are also identical for all archiving objects. For this reason, we have, as an example, integrated the second archiving object (IDOC) from our example into this guide. We will therefore use the second archiving object (IDOC), which is used across all industries in almost all SAP systems, to show you the job overview and the remaining steps associated with archiving.

Job Overview

Let's assume that we have already performed a production run of the write job for the archiving object IDOC and therefore have already archived an IDoc for demonstration purposes. We now wish to display the associated jobs so that we can view the archiving details.

Displaying jobs

1. To access the job overview (see Figure 6.23), call Transaction SARA and choose JOB 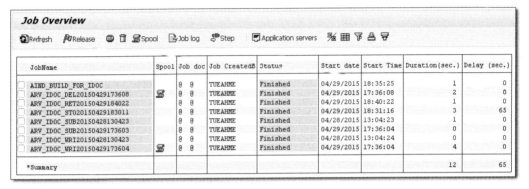. In order to better explain the job overview, we have created not only the write job but also additional jobs for the archiving object IDOC. Therefore, you will also see the delete job, for example.

Figure 6.23 Job Overview for the Archiving Object IDOC

2. In the JOB OVERVIEW, you see the following information in various columns:

  ▹ JOBNAME: The job name for data archiving has a particular structure and therefore always comprises the following:

   – The abbreviation ARV stands for archiving.

   – This is followed by the name of the archiving object (IDOC in this case).

   – Then the job type is listed (an initial job (SUB), write job (WRI), delete job (DEL), storage job (STO), or reload job (RET)).

   – The numbers at the end of the job name reflect the start date and start time.

  In this way, you can quickly identify which type of job is listed in the JOB OVERVIEW.

  ▹ SPOOL: The SPOOL column contains an icon that indicates if a spool file has been created for this job. In particular, spool files are created for the write job and delete job. You should take a detailed look at these spool files to ascertain if the results meet your expectations.

▷ JOB DOC: If, for example, you scheduled the job using SAP Solution Manager, a corresponding icon would be shown here, which you can select to obtain further information. To do this, simply click the icon, log on to SAP Solution Manager via the browser, and view the documentation for the job.

▷ JOB CREATEDB: This is either a basic SAP user or a batch user with extended authorization for performing SAP data archiving.

▷ STATUS: The status should always be colored green (that is, FIN- ISHED). A job may also terminate for various reasons (for example, due to missing authorizations). In this case, the status is colored red. In such cases, clarify the cause and then reschedule the job.

▷ START DATE: The start date specifies the day on which the job was started.

▷ START TIME: The start time specifies the time at which the job was started.

▷ DURATION (SEC.): The duration specifies how long the job ran (in seconds).

▷ DELAY (SEC.): The delay specifies if the job was started with a delay. This may be the case if an overload has occurred on the application server.

Select, as an example, the write job ARV_IDOC_WRI20150429173604 and choose JOB LOG to view the JOB LOG in Figure 6.24 in detail.

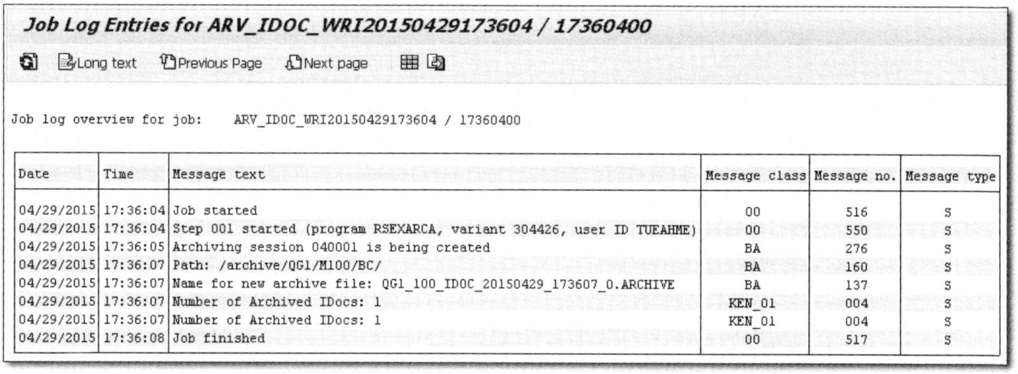

Job Log Entries for ARV_IDOC_WRI20150429173604 / 17360400

🔲 📄Long text 📄Previous Page 📄Next page ⊞ 📄

Job log overview for job: ARV_IDOC_WRI20150429173604 / 17360400

Date	Time	Message text	Message class	Message no.	Message type
04/29/2015	17:36:04	Job started	00	516	S
04/29/2015	17:36:04	Step 001 started (program RSEXARCA, variant 304426, user ID TUEAHME)	00	550	S
04/29/2015	17:36:05	Archiving session 040001 is being created	BA	276	S
04/29/2015	17:36:07	Path: /archive/QG1/M100/BC/	BA	160	S
04/29/2015	17:36:07	Name for new archive file: QG1_100_IDOC_20150429_173607_0.ARCHIVE	BA	137	S
04/29/2015	17:36:07	Number of Archived IDocs: 1	KEN_01	004	S
04/29/2015	17:36:07	Number of Archived IDocs: 1	KEN_01	004	S
04/29/2015	17:36:08	Job finished	00	517	S

Figure 6.24 Job Log for a Write Job

3. The JOB LOG contains different messages in the MESSAGE TEXT column. Here we wish to draw your attention to archiving session 040001, the path */archive/QG1/M100/BC/*, and the name of the archive file *QG1_100_IDOC_20150429_173607_0.ARCHIVE*. In the JOB LOG, you can use this information to check if they meet your expectations and correspond to the definitions in Customizing. You see that, in the *BC* subdirectory, which we created for the archiving object IDOC, we have created a new archive file with the correct name.

4. In the JOB OVERVIEW (see Figure 6.23), select the write job ARV_IDOC_WRI20150429173604 and choose SPOOL to take a detailed look at the spool file.

5. You first access the LIST OF SPOOL REQUESTS (see Figure 6.25). Here you see the SPOOL NO. (46997 in our example) and the number of PAGES (2 in our example). To display the spool file, select SPOOL NO. 46997 and choose DISPLAY CONTENTS 👓 (see Figure 6.26).

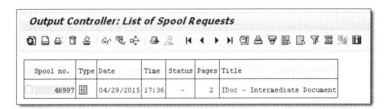

Figure 6.25 List of Spool Requests

6. The spool file contains lots of valuable information (see Figure 6.26). However, we wish to draw your attention to the following only:

▷ PRODUCTION MODE: This area displays whether a test run or production run was performed. In our case, a production run was performed.

▷ ARCHIVE FILE KEY: Here you see the ARCHIVING SESSION NUMBER (040001 in this example). This information is also shown in the SUMMARY area.

▷ TYPE: Here you see the tables or structures affected by archiving (EDIDC, EDIDD, and EDIDS).

Figure 6.26 Displaying the Spool File for the Write Job

▷ SUMMARY: If several archive files are created in a write job, you obtain a summary of all archive files (for example, the SIZE OF ARCHIVING SESSION IN MB).

▷ LOG (SUMMARY) FOR IDOC: Here you see, for example, messages in relation to if a data record could be archived. One OBJECT is displayed as an example. If a data record could not be archived, the reasons for this are generally shown at this point. Here, however, there are only minor differences between the individual archiving objects.

To store the spool file, proceed as described in Chapter 3, Section 3.5.

7. Choose PRINT WITH CHANGED PARAMETERS 🖨 and then ARCHIVE. Then maintain the ARCHIVE PARAMETERS as shown in Figure 6.27.

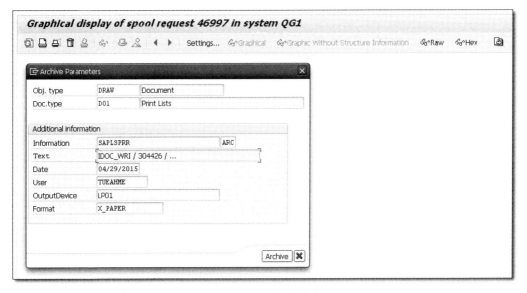

Figure 6.27 Storing a Print List in the SAP System

8. Once you have selected the suitable OBJ. TYPE and DOC.TYPE in accordance with the Customizing setting in Transaction OAC3 (see also Chapter 2, Section 2.1.2), enter the relevant ADDITIONAL INFORMATION and choose ARCHIVE.

9. The spool file is now archived in the relevant content repository.

Delete Job

Scheduling a delete job
The archive file has now been successfully created. Next, you can delete the relevant data records from the tables in the database. This step is essential so that the archiving session is complete. If you do not perform the delete job, the archiving session will be listed as an incomplete

archiving session in the management overview until you mark it as invalid. If you want to delete the data, you must call the DELETE action in Transaction SARA.

In Figure 6.28, you see that not only the START DATE and SPOOL PARAM-ETERS must be maintained for the delete job but that an ARCHIVE SELECTION must occur beforehand. Therefore, you inform the delete program of which archiving session or file you want to delete. The archive files previously created with the write job are available for selection here.

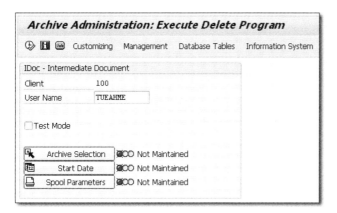

Figure 6.28 Starting the Delete Program

In the start dialog, you also see the TEST MODE option. If you activate this option, the delete run is simulated only. If you have selected one or more archiving sessions and maintained the start date and spool parameters, you can choose EXECUTE ⊕ to start the delete program. The system will then generate at least one delete job, which you can view in the JOB OVERVIEW (see Figure 6.23).

A spool file was also created for the delete job `ARV_IDOC_DEL2015042917` **Spool file**
`3608`. This looks almost like the spool file of the associated write job as shown in Figure 6.29. The TYPE area, however, contains a minor difference in relation to the tables and structures. In the associated write job, the structure `EDIDD` was displayed with two data records. In the delete job, you now see the table `EDID4`, which was concealed behind this structure.

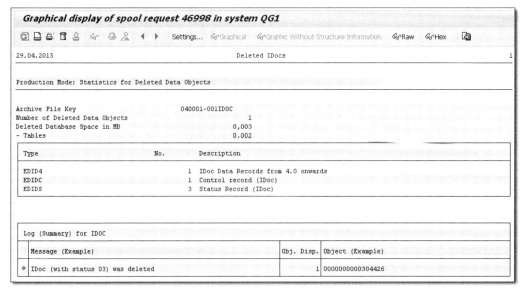

Figure 6.29 Displaying the Spool File for the Delete Job

Storage

Storing or retrieving
the archive file

Once you have scheduled the delete job, you must determine whether the archive file remains in the exchange directory or is archived. You can obtain this information from the archiving object-specific Customizing settings in the technical settings area (see Figure 6.30).

Figure 6.30 Customizing for Placing the File in the Storage System

Proceed as follows:

1. In Figure 6.30, you see that a content repository (NQ) has been maintained in Customizing. The START AUTOMATICALLY option is not activated. This means that you can manually store the archive file in this content repository or it can remain in the exchange directory *BC*.

2. If you want to automate the storage of archive files, you must specify whether you want the delete job or the storage job to start first. In Chapter 1, Section 1.4.4, we explained the differences between both. In the case of important archive files, you should store the files first and then delete them, thus preventing a loss of data under all circumstances. If you delete the data records from the database and the archive file before storage, the data is lost and it would be necessary to perform a costly backup of the database or exchange directory.

3. To store an archive file, call Transaction SARA and choose STORAGE-SYST. in the ACTIONS area (see Figure 6.31).

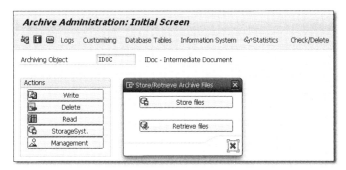

Figure 6.31 Storing or Retrieving Archive Files

4. The system then displays two more buttons:

   ▸ STORE FILES

   ▸ RETRIEVE FILES

   The first button enables you to store archive files manually, while the second button enables you to retrieve archive files from the storage system and return them to the exchange directory. Choose STORE FILES to store the archive files in the content repository NQ. The system creates a storage job again (`ARV_IDOC_STO_20150429183011`), which you can also see in the JOB OVERVIEW in Figure 6.23.

5. Choose RETRIEVE FILES if you want to copy the archive file back to the exchange directory again. A job for retrieving the file is also created again (`ARV_IDOC_RET_20150429184022`). You may need to retrieve files in this way if system performance when accessing the archive system does not meet the user's expectations and it is necessary to retain a copy of the archive files in the faster file system until the cause has been clarified.

6. Irrespective of whether you want to store or retrieve files, you must also maintain an ARCHIVE SELECTION in this step (similar to the delete run) so that the program knows which archive files it concerns (see Figure 6.32). You must also maintain a start date.

Figure 6.32 Retrieving Files

7. Choose ARCHIVE SELECTION. The system displays the RETRIEVE FILES window shown in Figure 6.33.

Figure 6.33 Archive Selection

8. Select the SESSIONS AND FILES that you want to retrieve in the exchange directory and choose the green check mark to confirm your selection.

9. Specify the START DATE (for example, the immediate start date).

10. Once you have maintained the ARCHIVE SELECTION and the START DATE, you can choose EXECUTE 🕓 to start the job for storing or retrieving the archive files.

In the job overview in Figure 6.23, you see the two jobs listed for storing and retrieving the archive files. You now need to check the status of these jobs.

Checking jobs

▸ For storage: `ARV_IDOC_STO20150429183011`

▸ For retrieval: `ARV_IDOC_RET20150429184022`

Once you have stored the archive file and then retrieved it again for demonstration purposes, this archive file is stored in the relevant *BC* exchange directory as a copy. To check the contents of the exchange directory, proceed as follows:

Calling the exchange directory

1. Call Transaction AL11 and navigate to the *BC* subdirectory for the archiving object `IDOC` (see Figure 6.34).

Figure 6.34 Retrieved Archive File in the Exchange Directory

2. In the FILE NAME column, you see the archive file with the prefix *RETRIEVED* before the archive file key (*040001-001IDOC_0*). Therefore, a new name is assigned to the retrieved archive file. In other words, the name is not identical to the original archive file. However, the original archive file still exists in the storage system. The file in the exchange directory is only a copy of the archive file that is retrieved if system performance does not meet expectations in relation to the archive access.

Deleting the file
from the exchange
directory

You can use the program RSARCH_LIST_RETRIEVED (Search via Retrieved Files) to delete the retrieved archive file *RETRIEVED_040001-001IDOC_0* from the exchange directory again once the performance issue when accessing the archive system has been resolved and the archive files are no longer required in the file system.

1. You can call this program either directly in Transaction SA38 (ABAP Program Execution) or in the ADMINISTRATION area in Transaction SARA via GOTO • RETRIEVED FILES (see Figure 6.35).

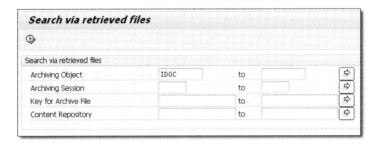

Figure 6.35 Program RSARCH_LIST_RETRIEVED

2. The SEARCH VIA RETRIEVED FILES is performed using various fields (for example, the ARCHIVING OBJECT or CONTENT REPOSITORY fields). Enter the value "IDOC" in the ARCHIVING OBJECT field and choose EXECUTE ⊕.

3. You obtain a list of retrieved files (see Figure 6.36). This list comprises several columns. The STATUS column is particularly important here. You can delete a retrieved archive file only if the STATUS column in the storage system contains the value ONLINE. This ensures that access via the archive system is also possible after you delete the archive file from the exchange directory.

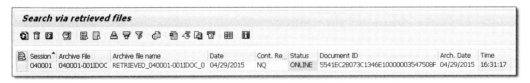

Figure 6.36 List of Retrieved Archive Files

4. To delete the archive file, select the relevant row and choose the trash button 🗑.

5. Choose YES to confirm the prompt asking you if you want to delete the files (see Figure 6.37).

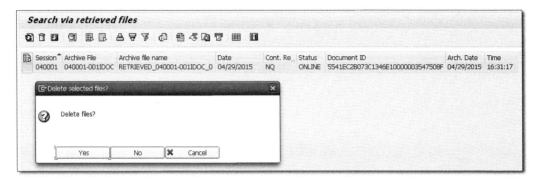

Figure 6.37 Confirming the Deletion of Retrieved Archive Files

6. The archive file is then immediately deleted from the exchange directory and is now available in the content repository (NQ) only.

Archive Access

To access the archive file stored in the archive system, you can now avail of the various options discussed in Chapter 3. For sequential data access via read programs, as described in Chapter 3, Section 3.1, you do not require any archive infostructures. For all other options (for example, direct access via a display transaction or entry via Archive Explorer (Transaction SARE)), you need to activate and fill archive infostructures.

Here we also comply with the specifications from the concept. In our example, we require archive infostructures because we do not want to use read programs to access the archive. Instead, we want to use display transactions and Archive Explorer. In Chapter 3, Section 3.3, we used the archiving object SD_VBAK (Sales Documents) to discuss, in detail, the archive information system in which you use archive infostructures to set up the archive access.

Generating archive infostructures

Now we will discuss the steps involved in setting up the archive access for the archiving object IDOC. You will already be familiar with some of the necessary steps from Chapter 3, Section 3.3. Once we have set up the archive access, we will test it in Section 6.2.3.

Setting up the access archive

To set up the archive access for the archiving object IDOC, proceed as follows:

1. First, activate a suitable archive infostructure for the archiving object IDOC. The standard SAP system already contains two infostructures that you can use directly:

   ▶ SAP_DRB_IDOC001 (specifically for DRB)

   ▶ SAP_IDOC_001 (infostructure for IDOC)

   In this example, we will activate and use the second infostructure (SAP_IDOC_001).

2. Call Transaction SARJ (Archive Retrieval Configurator) and select SAP_IDOC_001 in the ARCHIVE INFOSTRUCTURE field (see Figure 6.38).

Figure 6.38 Activating the Infostructure for IDOC

3. In the application toolbar, choose ACTIVATE 🗑.

4. The system issues a message stating that the infostructure has been activated (see Figure 6.39).

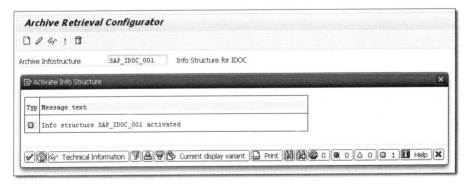

Figure 6.39 Confirming Activation

5. Now call Transaction SARI and choose STATUS to navigate to the STATUS MANAGEMENT area where you can fill the archive infostructure.

326

6. As you learned in Chapter 3, Section 3.3.2, there are two ways to fill an infostructure (see Figure 6.40):

   ▸ STATUS PER ARCHIVE

   ▸ STATUS PER INFOSTRUCTURE

   Since, in this example, we activated only one infostructure, it is irrelevant how you fill the infostructure. If several infostructures are active, but you specifically want to fill only one infostructure, choose the STATUS PER INFOSTRUCTURE option.

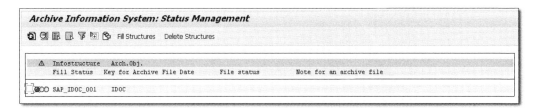

Figure 6.40 Status Management for the Infostructure

7. For our example, choose STATUS PER INFOSTRUCTURE.

8. You now have two options again (see Figure 6.41):

   ▸ FILL STRUCTURES

   ▸ DELETE STRUCTURES

   Since our infostructure has not been filled yet (red icon), you cannot delete it. Therefore, select the infostructure that you want to fill (SAP_IDOC_001) and choose FILL STRUCTURES.

Archive Information System: Status Management

⚠ Infostructure	Arch.Obj.			
Fill Status	Key for Archive File Date	File status	Note for an archive file	
⬜◍◯ SAP_IDOC_001	IDOC			

Figure 6.41 Filling the Infostructure

9. For each job, you will be asked if you want to fill the infostructure using the processing type DIALOG or BACKGROUND (see Figure 6.42). Choose BACKGROUND because long runtimes are generally expected, and this also allows you to specify any start time.

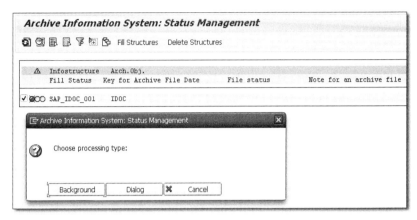

Figure 6.42 Confirming That You Want to Fill the Infostructure

10. Since filling the infostructure in the background involves scheduling a job, you must maintain a START TIME (see Figure 6.43).

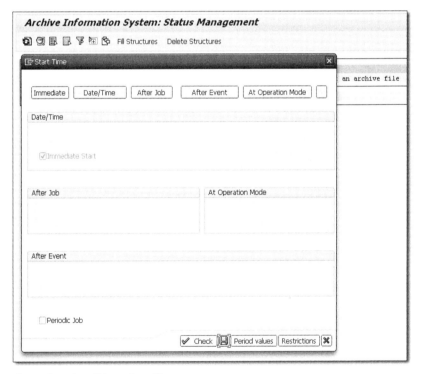

Figure 6.43 Specifying a Start Time

11. Choose IMMEDIATE and then choose SAVE 💾 to save your selection.

12. The status bar then contains a message stating that a job for editing archive infostructures has been scheduled (see Figure 6.44).

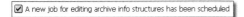

Figure 6.44 Message in the Status Bar

13. In the JOB OVERVIEW (see Figure 6.23) in Transaction SARA, you see the job `AIND_BUILD_FOR_IDOC` for filling the infostructure.

Once the job has successfully ended, the archive infostructure is filled and various options for accessing the archive are available to you. You can use the associated table in Transaction SE16 (Data Browser) to check the infostructure:

Checking the infostructure

1. In our example, table `ZARIXBC4` was assigned to our infostructure `SAP_IDOC_001` (see Figure 6.45).

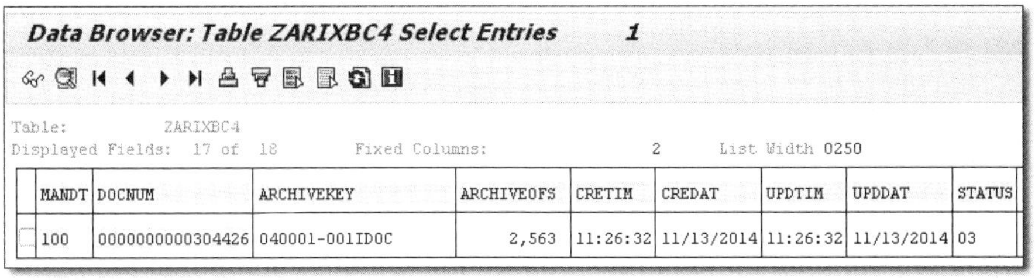

	MANDT	DOCNUM	ARCHIVEKEY	ARCHIVEOFS	CRETIM	CREDAT	UPDTIM	UPDDAT	STATUS
	100	0000000000304426	040001-001IDOC	2,563	11:26:32	11/13/2014	11:26:32	11/13/2014	03

Data Browser: Table ZARIXBC4 Select Entries 1

Table: ZARIXBC4
Displayed Fields: 17 of 18   Fixed Columns: 2   List Width 0250

Figure 6.45 Content of the Infostructure in Transaction SE16

2. In the ARCHIVEKEY column, you see our archiving session 040001 for the archiving object `IDOC` again.

Preparing Archiving Objects

The process of preparing an archiving object comprises a large number of steps, which we examined in detail using screenshots. For final preparation, the specifications from the concept for the archiving object are crucial because they contain all key information in relation to setting up the archiving object.

In this guide, we discussed the preparation of the archiving objects `RL_TA` and `IDOC` step by step. If you have several archiving objects in mind for your archiving project, you will use the same steps to set up each individual archiving object.

6.2.3 Testing Accesses and Interfaces

Once we have successfully created the first archive files for our archiving objects RL_TA and IDOC in the test system, we can test the archive access and the interfaces available.

Archive access for RL_TA

Let's assume that a SWOT analysis (see Chapter 5, Section 5.2.1) has already established that, after we use the archiving object RL_TA to archive transfer orders, we should expect considerable restrictions in relation to the archive access.

Table 6.6 lists those transactions that are no longer available to the user after archiving (extract from the concept for the archiving object).

Transaction	Description	Alternative Archive Access
LT21	Display Transfer Order	▸ SARE (Archive Explorer) ▸ Or via the archivable Transaction LT21
LT22	Transfer Orders for Storage Type	SARE (Archive Explorer)
LT23	Transfer Orders: List of Resident Documents	SARE (Archive Explorer)
LT24	Transfer Orders for Material	SARE (Archive Explorer)
LT25	Transfer Orders for each Group	SARE (Archive Explorer)
LT26	Transfer Orders for Storage Bin	SARE (Archive Explorer)
LT27	Transfer Orders for Storage Unit	SARE (Archive Explorer)
LT31	Print Transfer Order	No longer possible from within the archive

Table 6.6 Transactions for Displaying Transfer Orders

Providing alternative access

To enable us to continue with the archiving process, we provide users (in addition to Transaction LT21) with an alternative archive access via Transaction SARE (Archive Explorer) and document the procedure in a user manual. In our example, let's assume that we have two particularly critical interfaces that we need to evaluate and test. On the one hand, we have an interface for printing labels. On the other hand, we have a barcode scanner that must also have read access to tables LTAK (Transfer Orders: Header Table) and LTAP (Transfer Orders: Items).

Therefore, our test for the archiving object RL_TA focuses on the following: **Focus of the test**

▶ **Scenario 1: Testing the access**
First, we will test the transfer order display in Transactions LT21 and SARE. For the archivable Transaction LT21, you must specify the transfer order (TO NUMBER) and the WAREHOUSE NUMBER (see Figure 6.46).

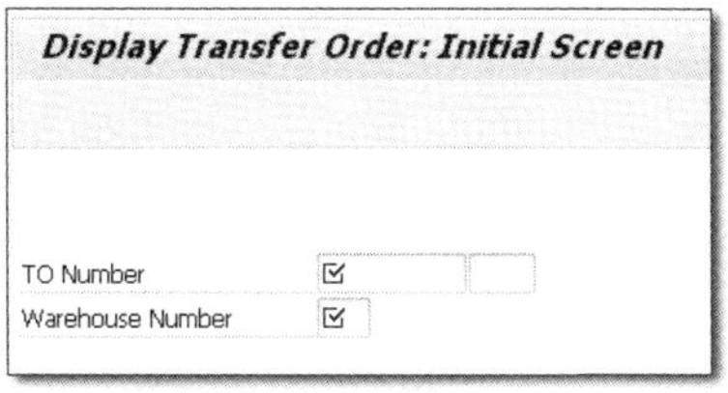

Figure 6.46 Displaying Transfer Orders in Transaction LT21

Since this combination is generally not available to employees, experience has shown that Transaction SARE and its enhanced selection criteria come out on top. To this end, we have, for comparison purposes, activated the infostructure SAP_DRB_RL_TA and called the selection criteria in Transaction SARE (see Figure 6.47).

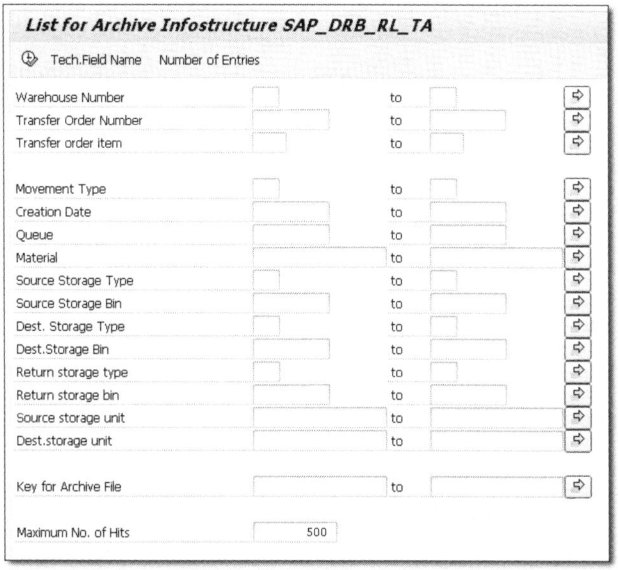

Figure 6.47 Selection Criteria in Transaction SARE for RL_TA via the Infostructure SAP_DRB_RL_TA

The selection criteria for the infostructure SAP_DRB_RL_TA in Transaction SARE contain the MATERIAL field. You can therefore also use this transaction to select transfer orders by material number, even if this transaction has some restrictions compared with Transaction LT24 (Transfer Orders for Material).

▶ **Scenario 2: Printing labels**
In our example, external software is used to print labels and affix them to pallets that contain products for shipping. This software accesses the data records in tables LTAK and LTAP, which we archive using the archiving object RL_TA. Since accessing the archive and reprinting labels for archived transfer orders is no longer possible via this interface, you should test here if a label can be printed during data archiving (write run or delete run) so that data archiving does not restrict the business processes.

If a reprint using the data from the archive is also necessary for goods that have remained in the warehouse for longer than the defined residence time, it is necessary to reprogram the interface so that these archive files can also be read. In this case, you would also have to test label printing for archived transfer orders.

▶ **Scenario 3: Barcode scanner**
In this scenario, you want to test if the barcode scanner can be used without restrictions during data archiving. If problems or delays occur, you must always perform data archiving during those times when neither the label printer nor barcode scanner is in use by employees.

Apart from scenario 1 in which we must always test the archive access, the other scenarios are merely real-life examples of how other test scenarios may look. Your enterprise may also have such interfaces or similar interfaces that must be considered in additional test scenarios alongside the mandatory archive access test.

Archive access for IDOC
For the second archiving object IDOC in our example, the archive access looks a little different (see Table 6.7).

Transaction	Description	Alternative Archive Access
WE09	IDoc Search for Business Content	▶ SARE (Archive Explorer)
WE02	IDoc List	▶ Or via Transaction WE09
BD87	Select IDocs	

Table 6.7 Transactions for Displaying IDocs

After archiving, only Transactions WE09 and SARE are available for displaying archived IDocs. You must therefore test and approve these two transactions. In reality, we have never encountered test scenarios in which the interfaces must be tested in the context of archiving IDocs. However, we cannot completely rule out this possibility. Customer-specific transactions or reports that read or process certain information from IDocs would be conceivable. If this is the case in your enterprise, include these transactions and reports in the test scope as an additional scenario.

6.2.4 Obtaining Approvals

Approvals during data archiving certify that you are permitted to use the archiving object in live operation. There are some rules that you must observe so that the approvals are not only complete but also traceable. First, you must define who is permitted to grant approvals (that is, who is the decision-maker in each specific case). It is also necessary to define what type of decision is made and the steps associated with obtaining the approval.

Since an approval pursues the goal of evaluating the concept for the archiving object as complete and sustainable, it completes the concept. In particular, the archive access and the interfaces that are tested must be documented in a traceable manner on the basis of the corresponding approval. Therefore, we require general approval for the concept along with specific approvals for the subareas of the concept (for example, the archive access). | Approvals complete the concept

The following approvals are necessary prior to the go-live and must be agreed to in writing: | Types of approval

- ▸ **Test the archive access**
  In Section 6.2.3, you looked at various transactions for the archiving objects RL_TA and IDOC. These transactions must be tested in terms of the archive access. Every single tester confirms in writing (either in a test document or by email) that his or her test result meets his or her own expectations as well as the expectations outlined in the concept for the archiving object.

- ▸ **Test the interfaces**
  In Section 6.2.3, you learned about two additional test scenarios that must be tested for interfaces for the archiving object RL_TA. Every single tester confirms in writing (either in a test document or by email)

that his or her test result meets his or her own expectations as well as the expectations outlined in the test document.

▸ **Confirm the residence time**
Ideally, the residence time that you agreed to in the kick-off workshop or in meetings with the decision-makers should be clearly documented in the minutes of the meeting. You can attach the minutes of such meetings to the concept as a document. This ensures that, at all times, you can trace when the decision concerning the residence time was made and by whom.

▸ **Confirm the storage option and retention period**
Similarly, you require documentation in relation to your choice of storage option and retention period. If, for example, you agreed in the kick-off workshops and meetings that the archiving objects RL_TA and IDOC are to be retained in a content repository within an archive system with a retention period of 15 years, you can also trace this in the minutes of the meetings.

Documenting
approvals

You obtain such approvals before the archiving object goes live and record them in the relevant section within the concept.

6.2.5 Documenting Results and Decisions

After the various kick-off workshops, meetings, and extensive tests for data archiving, it is time to document the results and decisions. In Section 6.2.4, we mentioned the results and decisions for which you must obtain approval.

Completing the
concept

The concept for the archiving object is not deemed to be complete until it includes all associated results and decisions. Therefore, it must be finalized before the go-live. In Chapter 4, Section 4.2.2, you learned about the various phases that a concept undergoes and the various statuses that it may be assigned. Let's remind ourselves of the three main phases of concept development:

▸ Open (status 0)

▸ In Process (status 10 to 90)

▸ Created (status 100)

Our goal is to assign status 100 to each concept so that you receive approval to use the relevant archiving object for productive archiving.

When you started the kick-off workshops, the concept was merely a draft. Each additional activity then refined and enhanced the concept to our particular specification. We can also describe this as the *maturity level* of the concept. Only mature concepts are usable concepts in a productive SAP system.

Maturity level of the concept

6.2.6 Creating Data Extracts in the Production System in Good Time

You have learned that certain archiving objects archive data from tax-relevant tables and that this data is then no longer available in the database for a DART extraction. For this reason, it is technically necessary to extract this data first and then proceed to archive the data. To ensure that you do not forget this key point, proceed as follows: in the concept for an archiving object, always declare, in good time, if the archiving object is relevant for DART.

The archiving object RL_TA is not relevant for DART, because the corresponding tables (LTAK and LTAP) do not contain any tax-relevant data.

RL_TA is not relevant for DART

To check if a table has been included in the extraction scope of DART, proceed as follows before the archiving object goes live:

Checking the extraction scope

1. As an example, we will check if table BKPF and the associated archiving object FI_DOCUMNT are relevant for DART. To do this, call Transaction FTWQ (Configure Data Segments) and enter the code for the relevant enterprise in the COMPANY CODE field (see Figure 6.48).

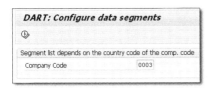

Figure 6.48 Displaying the Segment List

Country Dependency of the Segment List   [«]

Note that the country code of the company code determines which segment list is displayed. You have already learned that in DART a separate data catalog is available for the United States.

2. In our example, we will enter 0003 in the COMPANY CODE field and click EXECUTE ⊕.

3. US indicates that this concerns a US company code (see Figure 6.49). For example, the segment `TXW_FI_HD` stands for the table for the FI document header. We now wish to know precisely which tables are actually concealed behind the individual segments.

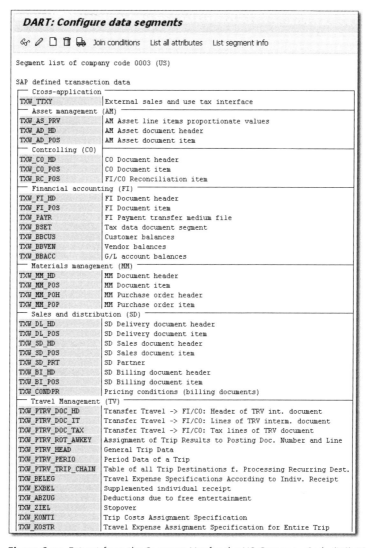

Figure 6.49 Extract from the Segment List for the US Company Code (US) 0003

4. To do this, choose LIST SEGMENT INFO to display the DART segments and their fields (see Figure 6.50).

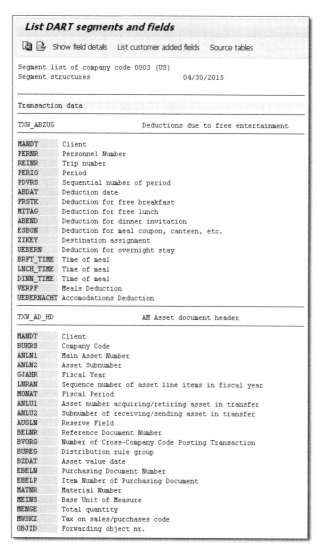

Figure 6.50 DART Segments and Fields

5. To view the tables, choose SOURCE TABLES.

6. On the display screen, scroll down to the table BKPF. You then see that this table is used in the segments TXW_FI_HD (FI DOCUMENT HEADER) and TXW_FI_POS (FI DOCUMENT ITEM) (see Figure 6.51).

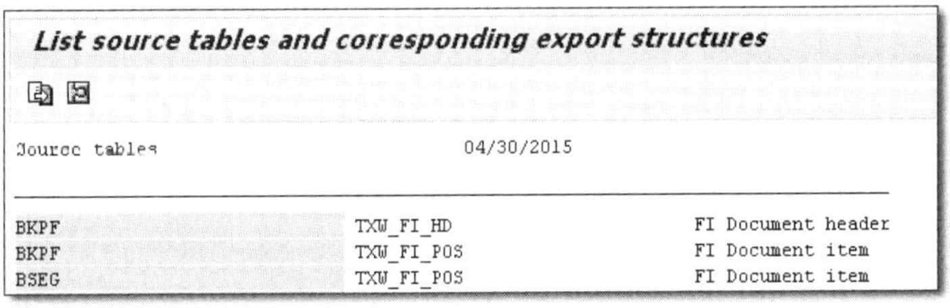

List source tables and corresponding export structures

Source tables		04/30/2015	
BKPF	TXW_FI_HD		FI Document header
BKPF	TXW_FI_POS		FI Document item
BSEG	TXW_FI_POS		FI Document item

Figure 6.51 Source Tables and Associated DART Segments

7. Therefore, it is imperative that you flag the archiving object FI_DOCUMNT, which archives data records from table BKPF, as relevant for DART.

DART-relevant archiving objects

Table 6.8 provides a partial overview of DART-relevant archiving:

Module	Designation	Extraction Scope	Archiving Objects
FI	Financial Accounting	▸ FI documents ▸ Open item list ▸ FI/CO reconciliation ▸ Change documents ▸ Tax data	▸ FI_ACCOUNT ▸ FI_ACCPAYB ▸ FI_ACCRECV ▸ FI_BANKS ▸ FI_DOCUMNT ▸ CHANGEDOCU
MM	Materials Management	▸ Material documents ▸ Purchase orders ▸ Change documents	▸ MM_EKKO ▸ MM_MATBEL ▸ CHANGEDOCU
SD	Sales and Distribution	▸ Sales documents ▸ Delivery documents ▸ Billing documents	▸ SD_VBAK ▸ RV_LIKP ▸ SD_VBRK

Table 6.8 Extract of DART-Relevant Archiving Objects

Creating DART extracts on a regular basis

Even if your initial focus is on archiving objects that are not relevant for DART, we nevertheless advise that, ideally once per year, you perform data extraction in your production system with regard to other archiving objects that are relevant for DART (for example, FI_DOCUMNT (FI documents)). For the country that generates data in the SAP system as an enterprise, you require, in each case, a concept that states if data extraction is required and how this needs to be created so that you can fully respond to requests from the tax auditor in good time.

You can view the current status of the created DART extracts in the long-term data extraction plan (LDEP), which we discussed in Chapter 4, Section 4.2.2.

Obtaining an overview in LDEP

Alternatively, you can also use Transaction FTWL (Display Extract Log) to check if the SAP system contains any DART extracts and, if so, for which company codes and fiscal years. Proceed as follows:

Checking DART extracts in the SAP system

1. Call Transaction FTWL.

2. In the RESTRICT SELECTION OF EXTRACT FILES area, you can enter filter values in the COMPANY CODE and FISCAL YEAR fields (see Figure 6.52).

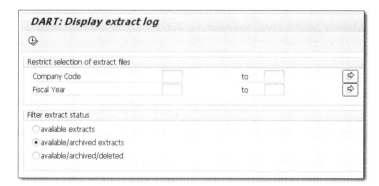

Figure 6.52 Transaction FTWL for Displaying DART Extracts

3. In the FILTER EXTRACT STATUS area, you can also select whether you want to display archived or deleted DART extracts in the overview. Deleted DART extracts are listed as metadata for information purposes only. The files are not physically available.

4. For our example, click EXECUTE ⊕, without making any restrictions, to access the overview shown in Figure 6.53.

Figure 6.53 Overview of DART Extracts Available in the SAP System

5. Our sample system does not have any DART extracts (neither online in the exchange directory within the file system nor in the archive system).

If you require DART extracts for archiving objects selected within your project, you must create these first. Since our two archiving objects RL_TA and IDOC are not contained in the DART extraction scope, nothing else is standing in the way of the go-live.

6.3   Go-Live and Support

After much preparation, you are now at the starting line. In other words, you are almost ready to use an SAP data archiving object within the SAP system in live operation. Bear in mind that an optimum go-live is low key, almost furtive, and does not affect the day-to-day activities of the users. Nevertheless, in the case of important archiving objects such as FI_DOCUMNT or SD_VBAK, it is advisable to send users a brief information mail beforehand.

Performing a low-key go-live

In the sections that follow, we will use an example to demonstrate the best way to inform your users while, at the same time, performing a *low-key* go-live. Thanks to our carefully developed concept for the respective archiving object, our primary goal is to keep support requests to a minimum. The fewer support requests we receive, the more successful the go-live will be.

6.3.1   Informing Users

There are different ways to inform users in your enterprise about an upcoming data archiving activity. In reality, a short yet concise email is frequently sent because, at this point, no further decisions need to be made.

Depending on the archiving object, you need to involve a larger or smaller user base. For example, it does not make sense to inform all system users in the enterprise about an archiving task involving IDocs. The information that you convey in the information mail will also inform those users already involved in the project that you have reached the last milestone and the change will now become a reality.

Defining the recipient group

Therefore, in the sections that follow, we will address the following questions with an example: To *which users* (recipient group) do you send an information mail? *When* (date) do you send the information mail and *in which format* (content) do you send it? Let's use the archiving objects RL_TA and IDOC to examine these three areas in more concrete terms.

Components of the information mail

Recipient Group

You can keep the recipient group as large or as small as you like. However, the recipient group must comprise the members of the project team as well as those employees who, in their user roles, have authorization for the transactions affected.

However, you must consider how your role concept was drawn up within your enterprise. If you usually assign a large number of authorizations to your user roles, users who have never called the transactions affected may also receive an information mail. Despite this, it is still good practice to adopt this approach (see Table 6.9).

Using authorizations as the basis for your decision

Archiving Object RL_TA	Archiving Object IDOC
All employees who can call Transaction LT21 in their user roles	All employees who can call Transactions WE09, WE02, and BD87 in their user roles
Project team members	Project team members

Table 6.9 Recipients of an Information Mail Depending on the Archiving Object

If you want to determine, for example, all relevant SAP system users for Transaction LT21, you can use Transaction SUIM (User Information System) to select them as follows:

Determining the relevant users

1. Call Transaction SUIM.

2. You can use the menu path ADDITIONAL INFORMATION • DISPLAY TRANS-ACTION CODE DISPLAY ON/OF to display the TECHNICAL KEY column.

3. In Figure 6.54, we opened the USERS BY COMPLEX SELECTION CRITERIA directory in the USER area. Here you can search BY TRANSACTION AUTHORIZATIONS. You can also perform this search in Transaction S_BCE_68001398.

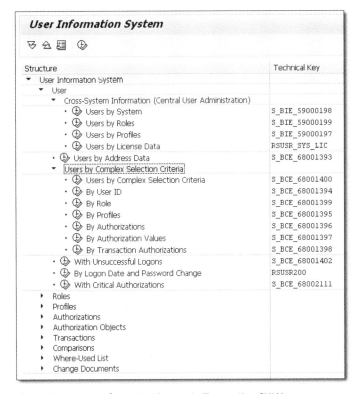

Figure 6.54 User Information System in Transaction SUIM

4. Call Transaction S_BCE_68001398. Here you can restrict your search further.

5. Enter the value "LT21" in the TRANSACTION CODE field (see Figure 6.55).

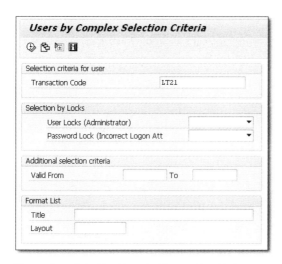

Figure 6.55 Selecting Users by Transaction Code

6. To obtain an overview of those users who have authorizations for Transaction LT21, click EXECUTE ⊕.

7. In the results shown in Figure 6.56, you see that precisely 481 users in this SAP system have authorization for Transaction LT21. Therefore, you should inform them about the upcoming data archiving activity for the archiving object RL_TA.

Figure 6.56 Overview of Users Selected

For the archiving object IDOC, proceed in exactly the same way if you want to determine which SAP system users have authorization for Transaction WE09 and then inform them about an upcoming data archiving activity.

Date

When sending an information mail, you should choose a date that is neither too far in advance, nor a short time beforehand. Generally, it is very unsatisfactory for recipients to receive an information mail either four weeks in advance or only one day beforehand. One to two weeks prior to the go-live has proven itself to be ideal.

Coordinating in good time

Therefore, coordinate, in good time, with those parties within your enterprise who are responsible for sending information mails. If the mail is to be sent to a small recipient group, you can prepare the information mail yourself and send it at the right time. If, however, you want to send the mail to a larger recipient group, you should obtain professional support. In the course of our archiving projects, we have received support from the communications area within the IT department.

Format and Content

You have already seen a sample information mail in Chapter 5, Section 5.2.2. In keeping with this example, you should address the following points in particular:

- Archiving start date (for example, February 23, 2015)
- Periodicity of archiving (for example, annually)
- Archived periods or the residence time (for example, archiving up to fiscal year 2013 or a residence time that includes the current and previous financial year)
- Information about the archive access via the standard transaction or via alternative transactions (for example, Transaction SARE)
- If available, a link to the user manual on the Intranet or to other documentation systems
- Contact details for support requests (for example, a hotline or email address)

Easy to understand

This information should be neither too detailed nor too concise in the information mail. A good information mail contains all-important information about the scheduled archiving session and does not leave the reader with any open questions. However, it should also be easy to understand.

6.3.2   Commencing Data Archiving in the Production System

Starting the production run of the write job for an archiving object in the production system is a significant moment in the archiving project. You question if you have actually taken everything into consideration and not forgotten anything. We recommend that you have a checklist at hand when you are standing at the starting line.

Go-Live Checklist	[+]

Check the following points before you commence archiving:

- ▶ Customizing
  - ▶ Have you maintained the file names and path names correctly?
  - ▶ Have you maintained the right content repository?
  - ▶ Is the residence time correct in Customizing and in the selection variant?
- ▶ Test results (access and interfaces)
  - ▶ Have you successfully tested all test scenarios?
- ▶ Approvals
  - ▶ Do you have all of the necessary approvals?
- ▶ Concept for each archiving object
  - ▶ Has the concept been completed, approved, and stored for the archiving object?
- ▶ Concept for each country
  - ▶ Has the concept been completed, approved, and stored for the relevant countries?
- ▶ Status of DART extraction in the long-term data extraction plan (LDEP)
  - ▶ Are DART extracts necessary for this archiving object and country? Have they already been created?
- ▶ Long-term data archiving plan (LDAP)
  - ▶ Has this archiving object already been included in the long-term data archiving plan?

Once you have checked the most important points again, perform the go-live (for example, for the archiving object IDOC) in a similar way as the production run for data archiving in the test system. First, you must create the selection variant for the write job:

Creating a selection variant

1. Call Transaction SARA in the production system.

2. Enter "IDOC" in the ARCHIVING OBJECT field and choose [Enter] to confirm your entry. The system then displays the possible ACTIONS for the archiving object IDOC as shown in Figure 6.57.

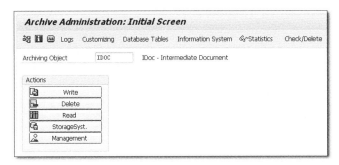

Figure 6.57 Archiving Object IDOC in Transaction SARA

3. Choose WRITE to create a selection variant for the write job.

4. Figure 6.58 shows an information message that you always receive with the WRITE action if there are still incomplete archiving sessions in the SAP system. To ensure that you do not receive such messages, make sure that you always complete an archiving session, either by scheduling a delete run or by marking this write run as invalid.

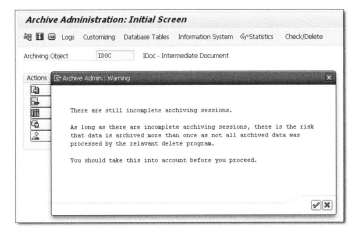

Figure 6.58 Information Message for Incomplete Archiving Sessions in the SAP System

5. To proceed, choose the green check mark to confirm your selection.

6. The system will prompt you to assign a name to the VARIANT (see Figure 6.59). Entering a suitable name here will ensure that you and others retain an overview of the variants used in the production system. If you want to separate the variants according to organizational unit or fiscal year, for example, or even according to test run or production run, you can combine some or all of the naming components from Table 6.10.

Figure 6.59 Creating a Variant for the Archiving Object IDOC

Combinable Characteristics	Example(s)
Test run or production run	T or P
Fiscal year	2014
Period or quarter	01 to 12 or Q1 to Q4
Dynamic selection for write jobs scheduled on a regular basis	Number of days or months (for example, 180 days or 18 months)

Table 6.10 Combinable Characteristics

In our example, we want to create a dynamic VARIANT. The write job will be scheduled once per month for the archiving object IDOC and will archive all IDocs that are older than twelve months. We can therefore assign the following name to the variant: P_12_MONTHS (see Figure 6.60).

347

During the workshops and meetings, we defined the archiving criteria in the concept for the SAP data archiving object IDOC. This concept also specifies how the variants are to be named and in which form the selection variant must be created in the production system.

Figure 6.60 Variant Name

7. Once you have entered the name in the VARIANT field, choose MAINTAIN to specify the selection criteria for this write run.

8. First, the system displays an additional VARIANTS: CHANGE SCREEN ASSIGNMENT window in which you are prompted to select an option (see Figure 6.61):

   ▷ FOR ALL SELECTION SCREENS

   ▷ FOR INDIV. SELECTION SCREENS

We recommend that you select the FOR ALL SELECTION SCREENS option, because you can then proceed in a uniform manner for all additional archiving objects. Alternatively, in the CREATED FOR SELECTION SCREENS area, select the NUMBER on the selection screen in the CREATED column. Since only one selection screen exists in our example, it does not matter which option you select.

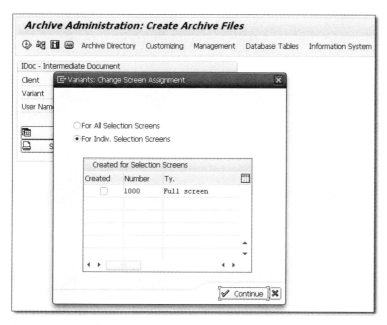

Figure 6.61 Specifying Selection Screens for the Variant

9. For our example, select the FOR ALL SELECTION SCREENS option and choose CONTINUE to access the selection screen.

10. The EDIT VARIANTS screen for the archiving object IDOC is divided into four areas (see Figure 6.62):

   ▷ IDOCS: In this area, you can enter or restrict an IDoc NUMBER. Similar restriction options exist for other archiving objects (for example, by material document number, transfer order number, and so on). In the production system, however, a restriction by IDoc NUMBER is not really practical, because, within a variant, we want to archive not only one IDoc but several IDocs and use the variant repeatedly in order to relieve the SAP system of its load on a regular basis.

   ▷ RESTRICTIONS: In this area, you can use numerous criteria (for example, LOGICAL MESSAGE or CURRENT STATUS) to restrict the IDocs to be archived. Important values (for example, for the DATE or the current status of the IDoc) are maintained here.

349

> ▸ PROCESSING OPTIONS: In this area, you can also schedule the write run in the production system in TEST MODE first and then execute it in PRODUCTION MODE.

> ▸ DETAIL LOG: Here you can specify settings for the spool file.

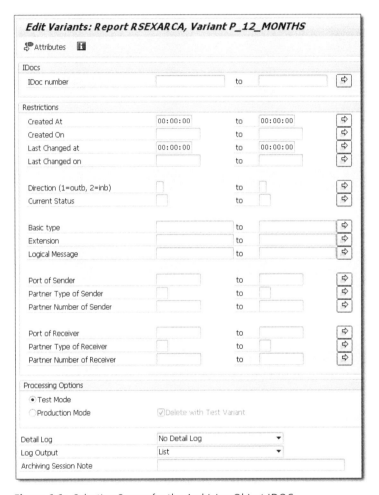

Figure 6.62 Selection Screen for the Archiving Object IDOC

On the EDIT VARIANTS screen, we comply fully with the specifications in the concept for the archiving object IDOC. In our example, the values from Table 6.11 are provided in the concept and must be applied to the variant for the write job (report RSEXARCA).

Fields in the Variant for the Report RSEXARCA	Value(s)
IDoc number (from/to)	
Created At (from/to)	00:00:00
Created On (from/to)	
Last Changed at (from/to)	00:00:00
Last Changed on (from/to)	Dynamic date calculation: current date - 365 days (12 months)
Direction (1 = outb, 2 = inb) (from/to)	
Current Status (from/to)	03 and 53
Basic type (from/to)	
Extension (from/to)	
Logical Message (from/to)	
Port of Sender (from/to)	
Partner Type of Sender (from/to)	
Partner Number of Sender (from/to)	
Port of Receiver (from/to)	
Partner Type of Receiver (from/to)	
Partner Number of Receiver (from/to)	
Processing Options	Production Mode, Delete with Test Variant deactivated
Detail Log	Complete
Log Output	List and Application Log
Archiving Session Note	Archiving IDocs older than 12 months

Table 6.11 Specifications from the Concept for the Variant

Simply enter the values from Table 6.11 in the EDIT VARIANTS screen in Figure 6.62, apart from the dynamic calculation for the LAST CHANGED ON field, which we wish to calculate dynamically.

11. To calculate the data archiving date dynamically, choose ATTRIBUTES.

12. You access the view shown in Figure 6.63. In the DESCRIPTION field, enter a meaningful description for the variant (for example, "IDocs older than 12 months").

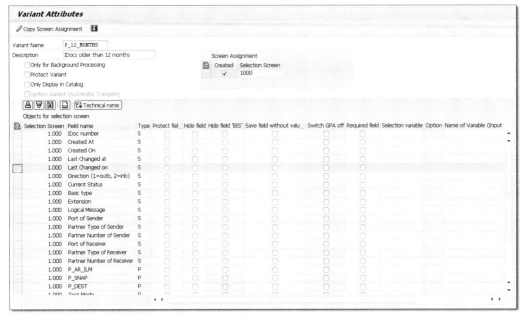

Figure 6.63 Variant Attributes for the Variant

13. To now calculate the residence time (all IDocs older than twelve months) dynamically, select the LAST CHANGED ON field in Figure 6.63.

14. On the right-hand side of the screen, you see the SELECTION VARIABLE column. If you click into this field and select the selection icon [ ], the system opens the selection window shown in Figure 6.64.

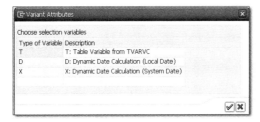

Figure 6.64 Variant Attributes for the Dynamic Date Calculation

15. Here you see the following three options:

    ▶ T: TABLE VARIABLE FROM TVARVC

    ▶ D: DYNAMIC DATE CALCULATION (LOCAL DATE)

    ▶ X: DYNAMIC DATE CALCULATION (SYSTEM DATE)

    Select the second option (D), because in our example the local date will be crucial for the dynamic date calculation.

16. If, in the table shown in Figure 6.63, you scroll completely to the right-hand side of the screen, you will see the NAME OF VARIABLE (INPUT ONLY USING F4) column as shown in Figure 6.65.

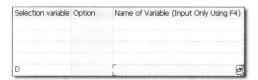

Figure 6.65 Specifying Variables

17. Click this field and select the selection icon 🔲 to open the selection window in Figure 6.66.

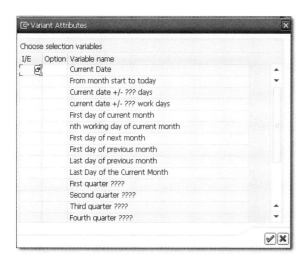

Figure 6.66 Variant Attributes for the Dynamic Date Calculation with the Variables

18. Here you see the following three columns:

▸ I/E: Here you can specify whether the values are to be included or excluded:

 – I (inclusive): If you select the value "I," the specified values are to be included.

 – E (exclusive): If you select the value "E," the specified values are to be excluded. Select the value "I" for CURRENT DATE so that all data records up to the value (that is, the current date) are included.

▸ OPTION: In this column, you can choose between the six options listed in Table 6.12. In this context, the LOW field represents the "from date." In the selection, the SAP system differentiates between LOW (from) and HIGH (to). Here we select the value "LT" so that all data records up to the value (that is, the date) are selected.

Option	Short Description
EQ	Equal: single value
NE	Not Equal: everything except the single value specified
LE	Less or Equal: everything <= to the value in the LOW field
GT	Greater Than: everything > than the value in the LOW field
GE	Greater or Equal: everything >= to the value in the LOW field
LT	Less Than: everything < than the value in the LOW field

Table 6.12 Selection Variable for the Dynamic Date Calculation

▸ VARIABLE NAME: Here you see various options for the dynamic date calculation. We double-click to select the CURRENT DATE +/-??? DAYS variable (or we select it and choose the green check mark) and enter the value "–365" (see Figure 6.67). This enables the SAP system to automatically calculate a residence time of 12 months in the selection variant in the LAST CHANGED ON field.

Figure 6.67 Entering Parameters for the Date Calculation

19. Choose the green check mark to confirm your entry. The write job now considers all data records whose last change date is earlier than the current date minus 365 days and, therefore, last changed more than a year ago (see Figure 6.68).

Figure 6.68 Variables Specified for Selection

20. Now choose SAVE 💾 to save our variant. You now see that the settings have been applied to the LAST CHANGED ON field on the EDIT VARIANTS screen (see Figure 6.69).

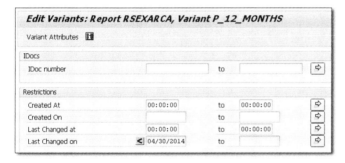

Figure 6.69 Dynamic Date Calculation

In this example, the variant was created on April 30, 2015. In accordance with our setting, the SAP system subtracts exactly 365 days from the current date and automatically maintains the new value (April 30, 2014), including the "Less Than" symbol. All IDocs with a change date of April 30, 2014 or earlier can be archived. We have therefore defined a residence time of exactly 12 months or 365 days dynamically, and we can schedule this selection variant monthly without having to adjust it every time.

Once you have created the variant in accordance with the specifications from the concept and checked it again, you can schedule the write job as specified. To do this, you need to maintain only the START DATE and the

Scheduling the production run of a write job

SPOOL PARAMS.. Then choose EXECUTE ⊕ to start the job. As you already learned in the context of the production run in the test phase, you can run the write job immediately, on a certain date, or after a specific event. We recommend that you comply with the specifications from the concept and that you consider empirical values from the test phase. Ideally, you should execute the write job for large volumes of data at a time when little or no operations are running in the SAP system. This will ensure that the archiving session will not impair system performance and that the go-live will be as low key as desired.

Further steps

Further steps include, for example, the delete run for original data as well as the automatic or manual storage of archive files. They also include activating and filling the archive infostructures as well as storing the spool files. We will not discuss these steps again here because they have already been described in the context of a test run in Section 6.2.2. After the write run, you must also perform all of these steps in the production system in order to complete an archiving session. In the production system, each individual archiving object runs through all of the steps described earlier in exactly the same way.

6.3.3   Responding to Potential Support Requests

A low-key go-live is also a successful go-live, because, in this case, you have documented and implemented all key points in your concept so that no further postprocessing work is required. However, it goes without saying that it is not possible to completely avoid support requests from users, not only immediately after the go-live but also, in all probability, several weeks or months after the go-live.

Be prepared

You can group such support requests together and specifically prepare to not only provide solutions in a timely manner but to also simplify the tasks of other administrators by providing appropriate support instructions.

Examples of support requests

In reality, you generally receive support requests in relation to the topics described in the sections that follow.

Performance of the SAP System and the Archive Access

You generally receive a performance-related support request for the following two reasons:

▶ **Implementing new archiving objects**
Even though you have commenced data archiving, you may have been unable to safeguard performance. In this case, you must analyze your SAP system again and choose and implement additional SAP data archiving objects.

▶ **Optimizing an infostructure**
The tables for the infostructures will grow continuously over time, because, after each archiving session, the system fills the archive infostructures and therefore generates additional data records. Despite data archiving, this may cause system performance to deteriorate in relation to the archive access. You can prevent this by either deleting the data relating to old time intervals from the infostructure by deleting the infostructure or you can partition the infostructure into several tables.

During partitioning, you create several smaller tables from one large table in order to improve performance for the archive access. Let's assume that the large table is called ZARIXBC3 and you want to partition it according to individual fiscal years (retroactively from 2010 to 2014). As of 2015, you also want the system to create a new infostructure table each time the infostructure is filled. To fulfill this task, proceed as follows:

Partitioning the infostructure

1. First, call Transaction SARJ in the development system and enter the name of the relevant ARCHIVE INFOSTRUCTURE (see Figure 6.70). For our example, we have selected the ARCHIVE INFOSTRUCTURE SAP_IDOC_ 001 for the archiving object IDOC.

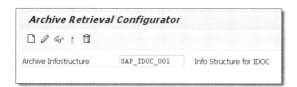

Figure 6.70 Specifying an Archive Infostructure in Transaction SARJ

Consider the Transportation Calendar [+]

Since we need to transport the Customizing settings, consider the transportation calendar in your enterprise and bear in mind how long it will take to transfer your settings from the development system to the production system.

2. Select the menu path GOTO • PARTITIONING. Then select NEW ENTRIES (see Figure 6.71).

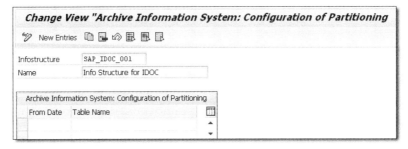

Figure 6.71 Creating New Entries

3. In the FROM DATE column, we define various dates so that, from this date onward, the system creates a new infostructure table (TABLE NAME) each time the infostructure is filled (see Figure 6.72). In accordance with our settings, the system creates a new table, ZARIXBCnn, for the date January 1, 2015 and increments the value for nn numerically.

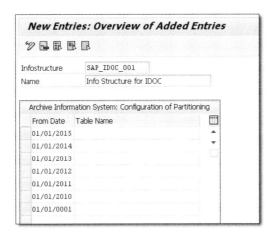

Figure 6.72 Partitioning an Infostructure

To divide the large infostructure table into several small tables (also for the periods that have elapsed), we would have to fully delete the infostructure and then fill it again so that the new settings are applied.

In addition, you can check whether or not an index already exists for the infostructure. If this is not the case, you can create a new index, which may also improve the performance of the archive access: Creating an index

1. To do this, call Transaction SE11 (ABAP Dictionary) and enter the table name for the large infostructure (in our example, the table ZARIXBC3) in the DATABASE TABLE field (see Figure 6.73).

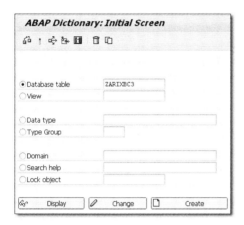

Figure 6.73 Calling the Infostructure in Transaction SE11

2. To display details for this table, choose DISPLAY.

3. You now see the individual fields within the infostructure as shown in Figure 6.74. In the toolbar, choose INDEXES… to check whether an index already exists for this table or if it still needs to be created.

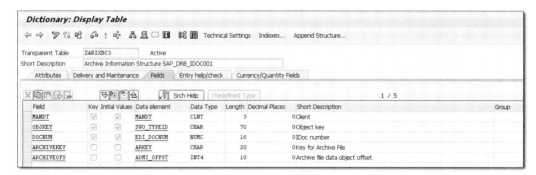

Figure 6.74 Fields in the Table ZARIXBC3 in Transaction SE11

4. The system then displays a new INDICES FOR TABLE ZARIXBC3 window (see Figure 6.75). Here you see that indexes (DB INDEX NAME: ZARIX-BC3~DOC column) already exist for our sample table.

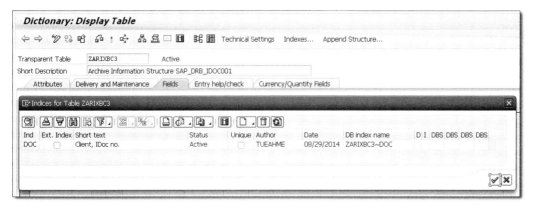

Figure 6.75 Displaying the Indexes for the Table ZARIXBC3

5. Optional: You can now create a new index. To do this, choose CREATE 🗋 and select the CREATE INDEX option. You must define this index beforehand, which we will show you in steps 8 and 9.

6. The system displays an additional small CREATE INDEX window in which you are prompted to enter an INDEX NAME (see Figure 6.76). For our example, we entered ARC as an abbreviation of the word "archiving."

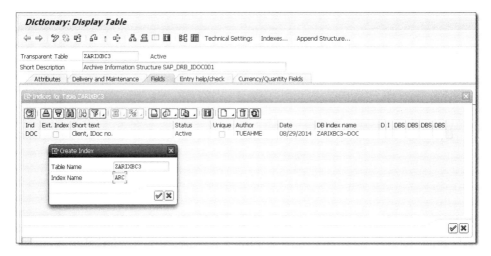

Figure 6.76 Creating an Index and Assigning an Index Name

360

7. Choose the green check mark to confirm your entry so that the index is created and used.

8. As stated in step 5, you must first define this index (in Customizing) with the INDEX NAME ARC before you can create it and use it. To do this, select the following menu path in Transaction SARJ: GOTO • DATABASE INDEX. Then select NEW ENTRIES (see Figure 6.77).

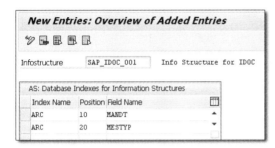

Figure 6.77 Defining Fields for the Index

9. Enter the INDEX NAME in the relevant column as well as the fields from the infostructure SAP_IDOC_001, which are to be taken into consideration for indexing.

Existing Index Names   [«]

If an INDEX NAME has already been defined in the standard SAP system for another infostructure of the archiving object IDOC (for example, SAP_DRB_IDOC001), this index is also created in the SAP system the first time you activate the infostructure SAP_DRB_IDOC001. All active index names for an infostructure are managed in table AIND_STR8 (Archive Information System: Indexes, Fields) and can be viewed in Transaction SE16.

Deterioration in the Performance of the Archive Access   [Ex]

After the FI documents have been archived using the archiving object FI_DOCUMNT, the enterprise initially sees significant improvements in system performance. Nevertheless, after a period of three years, some anomalies are detected. In other words, the performance of the archive access starts to deteriorate. The decision is made to remove the data from past fiscal years (already audited by an external auditor) from the infostructure, to partition the infostructure, and to set up a new index. These three measures will contribute toward improving the performance of the archive access considerably.

Queries Concerning the Archive Access and Documentation

Sending a link to the documentation
You have learned how important it is to inform users about archive access during the test phase and the go-live. It is not uncommon for users to need to access the archive a long time after receiving the information mails. In the interim, users frequently forget the codes for the archivable transactions and the special features of the access. If you receive requests concerning this matter, you can relatively easily direct users (by means of a standardized email) to your page on the Intranet where you have stored all manuals relating to the archive access.

Incomplete archive infostructures
In rare cases, the archive infostructures may not be fully filled or there may be a delay in filling them. As long as the archive infostructures have not been filled for an archiving object, an automatic archive access is not possible. If you have forgotten to check the archive infostructures in good time and you receive a complaint from users stating that the archive access does not work, the first step is to check that the archive infostructures are complete.

Maintaining customizing retroactively
It is even more critical if users are no longer able to execute certain tasks because some functions are missing. Very often (for example, when implementing the archiving object FI_DOCUMNT) the step associated with making a report archivable (for example, RFUMSV00, which is the advance return for tax on sales/purchases) may be forgotten. You may have overlooked this point in the kick-off workshops when developing the concept or during testing.

Example: Maintaining a report retroactively
In general, this requirement is implemented quickly even when it is transported into the production system in a timely manner. To implement this, we recommend that you locate the relevant SAP Notes in SAP Support Portal. SAP Note 204426 (RFUMSV00: Reading Archived Data) would be helpful for our particular example. It states that, depending on the release, the report RFUMSV00 must be entered in table DTINP or ARCH_REPOW so that it can be archived.

In Figure 6.78, you see that, for the archiving object FI_DOCUMT, the report for the advance return for tax on sales/purchases is missing from the table ARCH_REPOW and needs to be maintained. Only three programs exist here. For more information about using Transaction SM30 (Maintain Table Views) to insert report RFUMSV00 in the table ARCH_REPOW, see SAP Note 204426.

Data Browser: Table ARCH_REPOW Select Entries   3

&⁰ 🖩 🖨 🖶 🗐 🗐 🗐 🗐 Check Table...

| Table: | ARCH_REPOW | | | |
| Displayed Fields: | 5 of 5 | Fixed Columns: | 4 | List Width 0250 |

	Client	Arch. Object	ReportTyp	Program Name	ArchiveSelect.Active
☐	100	FI_DOCUMNT		RFITEMAP	
☐	100	FI_DOCUMNT		RFITEMAR	
☐	100	FI_DOCUMNT		RFITEMGL	

Figure 6.78 Example from the Table

In Figure 6.79, you see table DTINP, which is maintained for older releases. The report is also missing here.

Data Browser: Table DTINP Select Entries   13

☐ ✎ &⁰ 🖩 |◀ ◀ ▶ ▶| 🖨 🖶 🗐 🗐 🗐 🗐

| Table: | DTINP | | | |
| Displayed Fields: | 14 of 18 | Fixed Columns: | 1 | List Width 0250 |

Read Prg	Expert mode	Radio	Database use	Database on/off?	DB flag on/off?	Archive use	All archives	Archive on / off?	Archive flag on/off?
J_1AF205	X	X	X	X		X	X	X	
RFBELJ00	X	X	X	X		X	X	X	
RFEP0J00	X	X	X	X		X	X	X	
RFKKET00	X	X	X	X		X	X	X	
RFKLET00	X	X	X	X		X	X	X	
RFKLET01	X	X	X	X		X	X	X	
RFUSVB10	X	X	X	X		X	X	X	
RFUSVS10	X	X	X	X		X	X	X	
SAPF048A	X					X	X	X	X
SAPF048L	X					X	X	X	X
SAPF048S	X					X	X		
SAPF048X	X					X	X	X	X
SAPF048Z	X					X	X	X	X

Figure 6.79 Example from the Table DTINP

A costly issue that may arise here is a failure to take, for example, a customer-specific transaction into consideration when developing the concept and therefore having to make developments retroactively. Here it is necessary to revise the concept promptly so that this requirement can also be fulfilled.

Revising the concept

Content-Related Queries Concerning the Archiving Concept

Relatively often, you will also receive content-related queries in relation to the archiving concept. One typical question could be, how were the residence times maintained for each archiving object? Alternatively, the status of current activities is requested for each country or for extraction purposes. In this case, you can refer directly to the long-term data

Referral to the right page on the Intranet

363

extraction plan (LDEP). For this reason, we recommend that you store such information in a user-friendly format on a page on the Intranet. By doing so, you will not receive any support requests at all or you can draw users' attention directly toward the relevant page on the Intranet.

Authorizations

New archive transactions

The two important transactions for the archive access, namely Transaction SARE and Transaction ALO1, are already integrated into the relevant user roles prior to archiving so that the archive access can also work properly after productive archiving. A large number of SAP transactions can be archived. However, there are some exceptions whereby a completely new transaction is required for the archive access. For example, you can no longer use Transaction VF03 (Display Billing Document) to call archived invoices (for example, archiving object SD_VBRK) (see Figure 6.80).

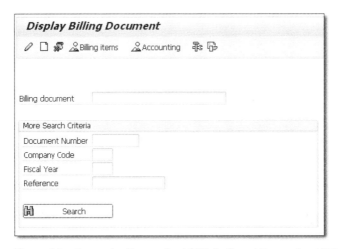

Figure 6.80 Comparing Transaction VF03 (Left) and Transaction VF07 (Right)

Example: Transaction VF07 versus VF03

In this example, you require the archivable Transaction VF07 (Display from Archive Billing Document). If the user roles do not yet contain authorization for this transaction, you must implement this in the relevant user roles before the archiving object SD_VBRK goes live.

> **Documenting Solutions**
>
> In reality, the examples listed in this chapter occur very often despite designing, planning, and performing archiving with care. It is important to learn from all support requests and to document solutions that can be applied in the future.

Errors in IT Interfaces

In conclusion, we wish for you to consider the scenario in which IT interfaces or customer-specific reports no longer work properly after data archiving because data from the relevant tables has already been archived. You should always clarify and rule out this scenario when developing the concept so that such problems do not actually occur in practice. Otherwise, adjusting IT interfaces or customer-specific reports is a very time-consuming and costly exercise.

Interfaces and customer-specific programs

As an initial ad hoc measure, we recommend that you suspend archiving for the relevant data archiving object until all open issues have been clarified. It is absolutely imperative that you revise the concept and implement a test and approval phase before you use the archiving object again in live operation.

6.4 Summary

In this chapter, you learned how to perform classic SAP data archiving using two archiving objects. After the go-live (that is, after initial archiving), you assign the archiving object to administration so that the archiving sessions for this archiving object are started at defined intervals (periodic archiving). In Chapter 7, you will learn about additional tasks in the context of administration.

Periodic archiving

After the go-live of an SAP data archiving object, you as the administrator have to perform various technical and organizational tasks to ensure performance and a reliable operation in the long term.

7   Managing Archiving Systems

The administration of an SAP system and the related IT landscape is a task usually performed by the SAP Basis team. In the area of comprehensive administration tasks, SAP data archiving represents only a small part. This chapter is limited to the area of system administration and details the most important topics.

An archiving system usually includes the following areas:

▸ SAP system

▸ Storage

▸ Scanning (digitization of incoming paper documents and storage of these documents as electronic files)

In this book, we only take a closer look at the first two areas (see Figure 7.1): the SAP system in which we set up and execute SAP data archiving and the storage system for the archive files. As already mentioned in Chapter 2, various options are available here. Depending on the selected storage option, the administration tasks may vary. The administration of the file system, including manual backups on optical storage media, is a little bit more complex than the usage of an audit-proof archive system. If not described otherwise, we assume that you store documents in an external archive system.

Structure of an archiving system

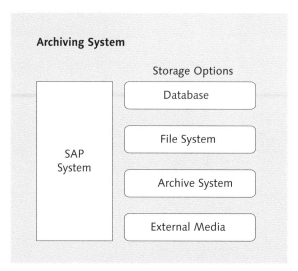

Figure 7.1 Areas of an Archiving System

Digitization of
paper documents

The third area, that is, the scanning of incoming paper documents for digitization and their storage as electronic files in the archive system, is not part of SAP data archiving but of SAP document archiving. Here the digital documents are linked to data records from the SAP system if required; for example, an invoice is linked to the financial accounting document. We mentioned this aspect here to illustrate that an archiving system is not used and managed for data only but also for documents.

The following sections discuss the two areas, SAP system and storage, from different perspectives. You will also learn which transactions enable you to optimally perform your administration tasks within the context of SAP data archiving.

7.1 System Analysis

Focus on the
SAP system

You carry out the system analysis in the SAP system. The storage area, in particular the archive system, is not part of this section. You can analyze the SAP system on the basis of different factors, such as performance or space, using various transactions.

So far, you have been introduced to Transactions TAANA and DB02 (see Chapter 1, Section 1.4) with which you can display the size of the database or tables and analyze these tables using different criteria. You do not need these transactions to determine archiving objects only at the beginning of an archiving project but also to periodically introduce new archiving objects. In addition to these two important transactions, there are other transactions for the analysis of the SAP system. We will discuss these transactions in the following sections. This way you obtain information on abnormalities at an early stage and can counteract them in good time.

Transactions TAANA and DB02

7.1.1 Performance

Our primary goal in this book is to ensure the performance of the SAP system. Therefore, you should also monitor and analyze the performance at regular intervals after the implementation of SAP data archiving. Special analyses enable you to obtain new results, which can again be used in SAP data archiving.

If a specific transaction has a strong negative effect on the performance, you should determine the cause of this. Usually, large tables lead to performance losses. If you have determined a suspicious table, you should use Transaction DB15 for this table to locate the corresponding archiving object.

Because a lot of transactions are available for performance analyses and because they sometimes even provide the same results, Table 7.1 lists only some important transactions.

Performing various analyses

Transaction	Description
ST02	Buffer
ST03	Workload Monitor
ST04	Performance Overview
ST05	Performance Trace
ST06	OS Monitor
ST10	Table Call Statistics
SAT	Runtime Analysis

Table 7.1 Important Transactions for the System Performance Analysis

Transaction ST10 Let's take a look at Transaction ST10 (Table Call Statistics) as an example. Let's assume you want to know how often table ACCTIT (Compressed Data from FI/CO Document) is called in the SAP system, because you determined that this table occupies a large amount of space on the database. The respective archiving object is MM_ACCTIT (MM Subsequent Posting Data for Accounting Interface). Follow these steps:

1. Call Transaction ST10 and click on the SHOW STATISTICS button (see Figure 7.2).

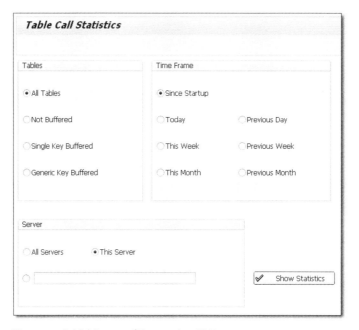

Figure 7.2 Initial Screen of Transaction ST10

2. Ensure that the ALL TABLES option is selected in the TABLES area and the SINCE STARTUP option in the TIME FRAME area.

3. The system then displays an overview of all tables that have been used since the system start. Scroll to table ACCTIT, and click the CHOOSE button.

4. You are then provided with the information shown in Figure 7.3.

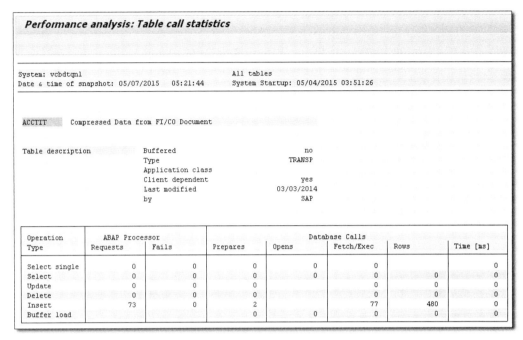

Performance analysis: Table call statistics

System: vcbdtqnl
Date & time of snapshot: 05/07/2015   05:21:44

All tables
System Startup: 05/04/2015 03:51:26

ACCTIT   Compressed Data from FI/CO Document

Table description		
	Buffered	no
	Type	TRANSP
	Application class	
	Client dependent	yes
	Last modified	03/03/2014
	by	SAP

Operation Type	ABAP Processor		Database Calls				
	Requests	Fails	Prepares	Opens	Fetch/Exec	Rows	Time [ms]
Select single	0	0	0	0	0		0
Select	0	0	0	0	0	0	0
Update	0	0	0		0	0	0
Delete	0	0	0		0	0	0
Insert	73	0	2		77	480	0
Buffer load			0	0	0	0	0

Figure 7.3 Table Call Statistics for Table ACCTIT

5. The statistics indicate that this table is not accessed at all (SELECT) but that the system generates data records (INSERT). However, the data records are not buffered (BUFFERED NO), because this is not recommended for these large tables.

6. The information derived from this is that this table—despite its size—does not have a negative effect on the performance but occupies a large amount of space on the database. Nevertheless, you should implement the MM_ACCTIT archiving object soon and even deactivate the update process for this data although the performance in the SAP system doesn't seem to be affected at the moment.

If you keep the large table in the system, because it is not accessed and it does not directly influence the performance during the read access, you will note the consequences somewhere else. In the long term, this table will certainly become a dinosaur and increase the runtimes of backups or recoveries significantly. So the long-term performance of these tasks will diminish.

Buffering of condition tables Transaction ST10 also enables you to determine tables that are accessed very often but are not very large. These tables are interesting for buffering processes. In this case, the data records are fully imported to the main memory when being accessed for the first time. Consequently, database queries are not performed with every new access. This may increase the performance.

[Ex] | **Improving the Performance Using Buffering**

A trading enterprise buffers the condition tables (KOTE*) for Sales and Distribution for the creation of invoices in order to maximize the performance at the month-end closing. Initially, this actually optimizes the performance. Over time, however, due to new data records, these condition tables reach sizes that make them inappropriate for buffering. Here you can see that buffering may have a positive effect on the performance, but this applies to specific scenarios only. At a later stage, you may have to deactivate buffering again.

Transaction ST05 The next example uses Transaction ST05 to analyze the performance. For this purpose, we call an archived SD order via Transaction ST05 and have the system display the respective access results. To do this, proceed as follows:

1. Call Transaction ST05, and click on ACTIVATE TRACE to activate the SQL TRACE (already preset) for the database access (see Figure 7.4).

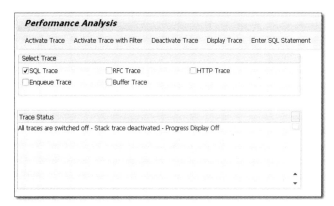

Figure 7.4 Activating the SQL Trace in Transaction ST05

2. Transaction VA03 enables you now to call any archived SD order. The system logs the information on the individual access steps in the background.

3. Then, change to Transaction ST05 again and click on DEACTIVATE TRACE.

4. Click on DISPLAY TRACE. The system opens the window shown in Figure 7.5.

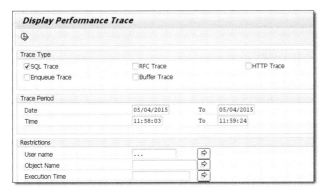

Figure 7.5 Display Trace

5. Specify the TRACE PERIOD and enter your user ID in the USER NAME field to have the system display the information that you have generated. Finally, click on the EXECUTE button ⊕.

6. The system then provides an overview of the individual steps that the trace function logged during the access. We have sorted this list in Figure 7.6 by the EXECUTION TIME (in milliseconds) in descending order to find the objects (OBJECT NAME column) with the longest execution time.

Trace List

⊠ DDIC Information ⚒Explain 📄 🔊 📂 📁

HH:MM:SS.MS Σ	Execution Time	Program Name	Object name	Op.	Curs	Array	ΣHi...	RC	Conn	Statement
11:59:08.246	1,738,043	SAPLV61Z	A099	FETCH	163	1	1	0	R/3	
11:59:09.985	11,309	SAPLV61Z	A099	FETCH	163	1	1	0	R/3	
11:59:08.240	5,446	SAPLV61Z	A099	FETCH	163	1	1	0	R/3	
11:58:58.311	3,783	SAPLMG22	MARC	FETCH	211	56	1	1,403	R/3	
11:58:58.330	2,950	SAPLVMSG	NAST	FETCH	29	74	8	1,403	R/3	
11:58:58.303	2,797	SAPLV61A	KOCLU	FETCH	105	32	1	1,403	R/3	
11:59:06.436	2,686	SAPLVS01	KNVI	FETCH	116	2,500	31	1,403	R/3	
11:58:58.318	2,523	SAPMV45A	VBFA	FETCH	174	273	6	1,403	R/3	
11:59:10.014	2,443	SAPLVFRR	VBAP	FETCH	110	1	0	1,403	R/3	
11:58:22.135	2,228	SAPLSUSM	ADRP	FETCH	248	1	1	0	R/3	
11:58:58.338	2,189	SAPLDG80	VBEPDG	FETCH	185	50	1	1,403	R/3	
11:59:04.802	2,137	CF_ASIT_INTERNAL=========	ZARIXSD4	FETCH	96	492	1	1,403	R/3	
11:59:02.249	2,128	SAPLCLPR	CLPROF	FETCH	201	1	0	1,403	R/3	
11:58:58.316	2,079	SAPFV45P	VBUP	FETCH	135	637	1	1,403	R/3	
11:58:58.323	1,780	SAPLVS01	KNVI	FETCH	116	2,500	34	1,403	R/3	
11:58:58.381	1,623	SAPMV45A	TCVIEW	FETCH	196	226	0	1,403	R/3	

Figure 7.6 Trace List Sorted by Period

7. Select, for example, the first line (Object A099), and click on DDIC INFORMATION to display detailed information on it.

8. You can see in Figure 7.7 that table A099 from Sales and Distribution has a long access time, although it is fully buffered during the archive access.

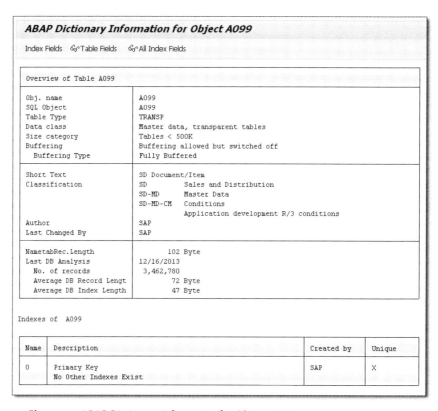

Figure 7.7 ABAP Dictionary Information for Object A099

Recommendation   In this case, you should deactivate buffering to make a comparison and execute the trace again or consider archiving table A099. It would go beyond the scope of this section to describe all transactions listed in Table 7.1. However, please note here that you should regularly analyze the system performance using these transactions to make recommendations for SAP data archiving.

7.1.2 Space

You analyze space via Transaction DB02 (Database Analysis, which we introduced in Chapter 1, Section 1.4.1). Here you trace the development of the space available at database and table level. Both analysis levels provide critical information, which enables you to perform the respective measures. Chapter 1, Section 1.4.1 describes the general overview provided in Transaction DB02 as well as the detailed view for the tables. Here we take a closer look at the database growth.

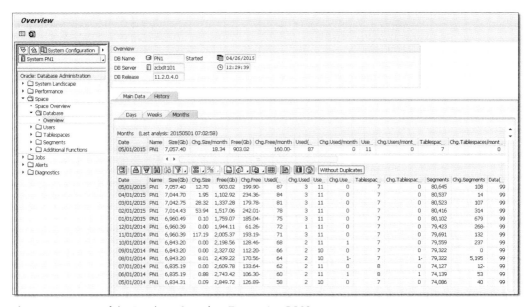

Figure 7.8 History of the Database Growth in Transaction DB02

The Overview area shown in Figure 7.8 is ideal to obtain an overview of the database growth from the past. The Months tab displays the size of the database (Size (Gb)) and the available space (Free (Gb)) sorted by month. The Chg.Free column is of particular importance. The values shown here enable you to determine the amount of space occupied or released on the database in the respective month. If space is consumed, this is indicated with a minus sign. If the database has been reorganized or if space has been added, no minus sign is displayed—that is, we have

Keeping an eye on the database growth

gained space. In our example, we had an average consumption of approximately 180 GB per month over the last six months. Because currently approximately 900 GB space is free in the database, the space will last for a maximum of 5 months. This data enables you to determine in advance when you require new storage disks at the latest or should start SAP data archiving.

[»] **Reorganizing Databases**

Note, however, that many databases, such as Oracle, do not release space immediately when the data archiving process is completed. So the database has to be reorganized at regular intervals. You can do this online for the tables affected by the data archiving process. Alternatively, you can reorganize the complete database offline. If you reorganize the database offline, the users cannot access the SAP system, so the reorganization should take place over the weekend or on public holidays and should be completed within the specified time. The space saved by SAP data archiving is released only after this reorganization. The database reorganization belongs to the area of operation, which will be discussed in detail in Section 7.3.

7.2 Communication

The communication with the persons involved in the data archiving projects, in particular after the go-live for every archiving object, should be standardized and take place at regular intervals. This way you ensure that there are no open questions and everyone can track the project's status quo.

Communication channel depends on the recipients

Here it is important to know which group of recipients you want to inform and how the communication should take place. Communication can have different forms. You should select the appropriate form on the basis of the information to be imparted. For example, it does not make sense to inform all users about a small adaptation of a selection variant for archiving object IDOC (Intermediate Document) via email. But the introduction of a new archiving object, such as FI_DOCUMNT (Financial Accounting Documents), requires at least an informative email to all users affected, if necessary with a link to training material. Let's take a closer look at the recipients of the communication in order to determine the best communication channel for these persons.

7.2.1 Recipients

For your administrator tasks, you are in contact with various persons. The following introduces the most important recipients and explains the expectations of these persons.

User

Users usually have little contact with you as the administrator. They mainly contact the IT support through the hotline or via tickets in case of problems or queries. Only after having been assigned a ticket, do you become active and directly communicate with the user if there are any open questions. You may also have direct contact with users in workshops, for example, by giving presentations or when providing support in the test phase. When you talk to users, you should avoid technical terms if possible. The technical names of the archiving objects and the *archiving object* concept as such are a matter of course for you as an administrator but can be very irritating for users. So always speak in the users' language. Talk about the archiving of financial accounting documents instead of `FI_DOCUMNT`.

Avoiding technical terms

IT Department

Your colleagues from the IT department are also very experienced in the area of SAP topics but might not be in the area of data archiving. Consequently, it is very helpful to offer a general introduction to the topic of SAP data archiving at the beginning of an archiving project. Often, other colleagues addressing archiving issues will also contact your IT colleagues. For follow-up actions, team meetings should be held at regular intervals in order to provide recent information.

Mutual training

User Department (Head of Department)

The heads of the user departments might have more contact with you as the administrator at certain occasions. They usually collect users' requests

Recent information

and queries and forward them to you. You should inform the heads of departments in due time and proactively about critical aspects, for example, about problems resulting from the delay of a scheduled data archiving process. Give them the detailed action plan and schedule and inform them about the completion of open issues. This enables them to forward the information to the users and avoids frequent queries.

External Institution (Tax, Custom, Auditor)

The data in the SAP system is audited regularly. At the beginning, the IT and tax departments have to fill out questionnaires regarding current archiving actions in the SAP system and submit them to external institutions. Auditors may also have to be introduced to how the archive can be accessed. You can offer your support in these areas.

SAP SE

Error messages to the support team

As the administrator, you are in contact with the SAP employees at home and abroad via error messages sent to SAP SE, which may lead to SAP Notes later on. Usually, the support team for the error messages is located abroad, for example, in India. This may lead to linguistic and cultural barriers that you must consider.

You can also directly contact the employees of the SAP System Landscape Optimization (SLO) consulting unit to discuss important topics that cannot be managed via the support. Please note that this external consultation is not covered by the SAP software support agreement. It is subject to charge and must be requested first.

SAP User Group (ASUG)

Exchanging experiences

In the United States, ASUG is the voice of SAP customers for SAP SE. You can take part in data archiving and SAP ILM special interest groups that deal with SAP data archiving and contribute your experiences in presentations on various events. In addition, you can also attend other special interest groups that might be interesting for you.

Virtual Contacts

With its versatile blogs and social networks, the Internet provides various options for exchanging information with colleagues who have experience in the data archiving area. For example, you can participate in the respective forums. Of course, these virtual contacts may also lead to personal meetings at a later stage. At this point, we'd like to recommend the SAP Community Network (SCN) in which you can find a separate area for SAP Information Lifecycle Management, including useful tips regarding SAP data archiving *http://scn.sap.com/community/information-lifecycle-management.*

7.2.2 Forms of Communication

The communication regarding the administration of SAP data archiving can take place either directly or indirectly. The following provides two common examples from real life for direct communication and for indirect communication.

Direct Communication

Direct communication takes place personally and synchronously between the persons involved—that is, at a specific point in time. It is ideal for topics whose recipients you know, because you want to discuss specific aspects with a specific person. Direct communication can take place in two ways: per telephone or in a meeting. Table 7.2 provides tips for a direct communication with the different possible recipients and the suitability of the various communication channels.

Personal and synchronous communication

Recipient	Telephone	Meeting
User	Only for requests and tickets requiring queries	Tests and workshops are ideal for clarifying details
IT department	Very ideal for brief queries	Very ideal for intensive discussions
User department (head of department)	Very ideal for brief queries	Very ideal for intensive discussions

Table 7.2 Tips for the Direct Communication with Various Recipients

Recipient	Telephone	Meeting
External institution	Very ideal for brief queries	Very ideal for intensive discussions
SAP SE	Very ideal for brief queries	Not common in real life, except for sales meetings
SAP user groups (ASUG)	Not ideal except if you have personal contacts there	Workshops and meetings
Virtual contacts	Not ideal except if the virtual contact becomes a personal contact	Not ideal except if the virtual contact becomes a personal contact

Table 7.2 Tips for the Direct Communication with Various Recipients (Cont.)

Indirect

Asynchronous communication

Indirect communication is asynchronous; that is, there is a delay in the exchange of questions and answers. Of course, recipients who you can reach via direct communication can also be contacted indirectly. Table 7.3 provides an overview with recommendations.

Linguistic barriers

More and more frequently, administrators also have contact with colleagues at home and abroad who don't speak English fluently. You should therefore always take your time to optimally prepare the information you want to share in order to successfully communicate with all recipients.

[◉]

Communicating Successfully

Today, the options in the area of communication are versatile. It doesn't matter which way you choose (direct or indirect communication), communication is always successful if the sender and recipient can decrypt the message properly. So ensure that the recipient of your message understands you correctly.

In reality, you will have more or less contact with the various recipients. The language of SAP data archiving is not clear to everyone, and you will probably often use too many technical terms without always being aware of it. Note that the recipient of your message may not always be able to follow your thoughts.

Recipient	Email	Intranet/Internet
User	▸ Very ideal for information exchange	Creation of an information page on the Intranet via SAP data archiving
IT department		
User department (head of department)	▸ Emails can be saved for documentation purposes	
External institution		Not ideal
SAP SE		▸ Contributions in forums on the Internet ▸ Recording of error messages
SAP user groups (ASUG)		Contributions in forums on the Internet
Virtual contacts		Contributions in forums on the Internet

Table 7.3 Tips for Indirect Communication with the Respective Recipients

7.3 Operation

In reality, the internal SAP Basis team or an external IT service provider usually ensures the operation of the SAP system. Data archiving can also be managed either internally or externally. To define the tasks for the internal employees or external service providers, you have to know which regular tasks or actions are required for data archiving. With regard to the archiving system, we discuss this topic with a focus on two areas: the tasks in the SAP system and the tasks in the storage area.

7.3.1 Scheduling the Archiving Run in the SAP System

Your most important task as an administrator is certainly the execution of the archiving runs in the SAP system as described in Chapter 6. You can either start the archiving runs immediately or specify a start time for them. But ensure that you select an appropriate time window as described in Chapter 4, Section 4.2.2. An archiving run is only complete if the information structures have also been established (if required).

Updating
documentation After having successfully completed an archiving run, don't forget to update the tickets with the information on the results for documentation and to contact the recipients involved via the appropriate communication channels.

7.3.2 Managing Space in the SAP System

Space provision The space of an SAP system is represented by the database. To ensure that sufficient space is available for the operation in the SAP system, you usually have three options in real life:

▶ **Installing new space**
Adding new space to the database is certainly the fastest way. However, this cannot be done any number of times, because in addition to the costs incurred for additional space, you must also take into account the technical possibilities.

▶ **Archiving data**
You have learned that data archiving not only enables you to control the system's performance but also releases space. Consequently, data archiving plays a central role for the operation of SAP systems. When the data archiving process is completed, however, the space is not released immediately. So a third reorganization of the database is mandatory to fully exploit the benefits of data archiving.

▶ **Reorganizing tables or databases after data archiving**
After the successful data archiving process, the reorganization of the tables or the database is a very important step. Imagine the database is a bookshelf from which you can take individual books you no longer need to make space for new books. Because you want to place the new books next to each other in a row, you have to push together or sort the old books first to create a gap with sufficient space for the new books.

The reorganization of the database works similarly. After creating sufficient space at various places on the storage media of the database via data archiving, you gain exactly the space required for using new data records by reorganizing the data. The reorganization not only leads to more space but also indirectly increases performance, because the data is located in areas that are ideal for access.

7.3.3 Managing Space for Storage

In this chapter, we assume that you use an archive system as the storage option. To be able to store the archive files in the archive system, you first need—as mentioned earlier in the book—content repositories with appropriate runtimes according to the lifecycle of the archive files. The typical tasks that you have to perform as an administrator include the following:

Managing archive systems

- ▶ **Setting up new content repositories if required**
  In this context, it is important that the content repositories are set up in the SAP system and in the archive system. Chapter 2, Section 2.1.1 describes how to do this.

- ▶ **Expanding the space for the archive system**
  You expand the space for the archive system as described by the manufacturer. In general, do not calculate the space requirements too tight, because the time gap between the order of additional storage capacities and their installation can be rather large. During this period, you will have to continue storing archive files. Do not avoid archiving data due to missing space.

- ▶ **Deleting archive files from content repositories**
  After the specified runtime of the content repository, the archive files are available for deletion. Here deletion means the irrevocable destruction of archive files at the end of the lifecycle. Each archive system provides its own functions for this purpose in which you have to select the archive files in the overview released for deletion and confirm them. Before starting the deletion process, ensure that the data is subject to a manual deletion block, because the user department requires this data.

  You can also delete certain archive files, for example, for archiving object IDOC, without further inquiry. This information is provided in the concepts for the individual archiving objects or the integrated LDAEP.

This was a summary of the typical tasks that have to be performed during the operation of an archiving system.

7.4 Monitoring

Monitoring is a task that you can perform manually or in a partly auto-mated way. It is also possible to outsource this task to external service providers, for example, abroad. In the SAP system environment, various areas are regularly monitored. This section focuses on the following four areas that play a special role within the context of SAP data archiving:

- Monitoring the jobs of an archiving run
- Regular search for relevant SAP Notes
- Checking the effects of new support packages to SAP data archiving
- Tools and functions from SAP Solution Manager

We will take a closer look at these four areas in the following sections using examples.

7.4.1 Monitoring the Archiving Run

During the archiving run for an archiving object, the system generates several jobs. Depending on the volume of the data to be archived, these jobs may have a runtime of several hours. During this time, you cannot update or monitor the status every minute, so you should adhere to two approaches when monitoring the archiving run:

- You should regularly look for terminated and long running jobs in Transaction SM37 (Simple Job Selection) to take the appropriate mea-sures. This transaction is usually part of the monitoring lists of admin-istrators. A monitoring list is a checklist with various tasks and trans-actions that have to be performed or checked daily.

- You can monitor the jobs that belong to an archiving object directly in Transaction SARA.

This enables you to keep an eye on all jobs in general and on the jobs that belong to an archiving run in the SAP system.

The important task is not only to monitor the job but also to take spe-cific actions when a certain status is reached. What do you have to do if the job runs too long or terminates? Who has to be informed about this? Which steps have to be performed when the job is completed successfully? There can be various reasons for a termination or a long runtime of a job. Consequently, depending on the reason, different measures have to be taken to solve the problem. Table 7.4 lists various common scenarios that can occur during archiving runs and describes possible reasons and actions that have to be triggered.

Scenario	Reason or Reasons	Actions
Job terminates	Missing authorization	Adjust the authorization
	Incorrect Customizing (file name or path)	Adjust the Customizing
	Inadequate selection criteria	New implementation with new selection criteria
	Not sufficient space	Extend the space or reschedule the job
Job runs too long	Inadequate selection criteria	▶ Cancel ▶ Interrupt ▶ New implementation with new selection criteria
Job is completed	Successful completion	▶ Users may have to be informed ▶ Information structures may have to be added in Transaction SARI ▶ Other tasks, such as documentation, etc.

Table 7.4 Job Monitoring Scenarios

We recommend creating an action plan for the administrators in your enterprise and documenting in detail all actions required for any scenario in an instruction manual.

Creating an instruction manual

7.4.2 Finding SAP Notes

The SAP Support Portal allows you to manually search for SAP Notes and save your search query as a template for futures searches. Within the scope of SAP data archiving, you should also search the note database for relevant SAP Notes before and after going live with an archiving object to avoid possible errors in advance.

Checking for updates on a regular basis

The data archiving objects provided by SAP are not always free of errors. Customers sometimes notice these errors rather late, because the archive is accessed only randomly. To avoid encountering unnecessary problems in SAP data archiving, you should search the SAP Support Portal for SAP Notes for your SAP release and for the archiving objects that are active and scheduled for your system.

Notes on archiving objects

Using archiving object FI_DOCUMNT (Financial Accounting Documents) as an example, the following describes how you find the relevant SAP Notes for an archiving object:

1. Call the website of the SAP Service Marketplace via the URL *https://service.sap.com*.

2. Go to the SAP SUPPORT PORTAL area and log on with your user name and password. Alternatively, you can search for SAP Notes directly via *https://service.sap.com/support*.

3. Go to the SEARCH FOR SAP NOTES area as shown in Figure 7.9.

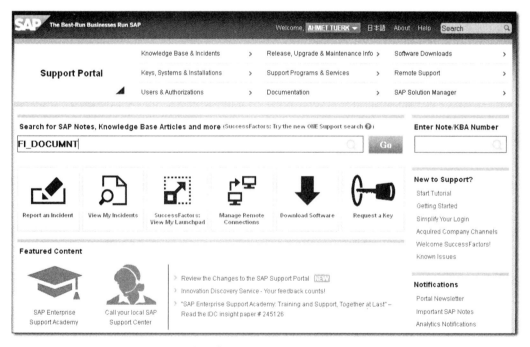

Figure 7.9 Searching for SAP Notes in the SAP Support Portal

4. In the SEARCH FOR field, enter FI_DOCUMNT and click on the GO button to confirm your entry. You can also use advanced search options with additional terms (e.g., tables, reports, and transactions). The search for the technical name of the archiving object, however, usually provides very good results.

5. A result list displays the SAP Notes found (see Figure 7.10). You should sort them by descending release date to have the system list the most recent SAP Notes at the top.

Figure 7.10 SAP Notes Sorted by Descending Release Date

6. In Figure 7.10 you can see, for example, that the most recent SAP Note with number 204426 (Reading Archived Data) was released for archiving object FI_DOCUMNT at 08.04.2015 and is available in English only. You can open SAP Note 204426 by clicking on the heading of the note.

7. The SAP Note states that archived data can no longer be reloaded to the SAP system using archiving object `FI_DOCUMNT`. Because this is a critical action, you should contact SAP Consulting.

8. In the detail view of the SAP Note, always check the valid version of the note and compare it with the support package version of your SAP system to determine if the SAP Note affects your system. SAP Notes have different versions and are correspondingly updated if necessary. In our example, this SAP Note is valid for our release and does not differentiate between support package versions. However, if an SAP Note is applicable to specific support package versions only, check to see if your SAP system is affected by the note as described in Section 7.4.3.

Referring to SAP Notes

For you as the administrator, our sample note means that you have to be careful when archiving financial accounting documents using the `FI_DOCUMNT` archiving object and that you must not make typos in the selection variant, for example, enter a wrong company code. Reloading data after archiving would involve a great deal of effort and cost.

7.4.3   Evaluating Support Packages

SAP updates the SAP Business Suite components at regular intervals. This not only includes large release upgrades but also smaller support package upgrades that introduce new functions and eliminate errors in the SAP system. Both the large release upgrades and the smaller support package upgrades may contain functions that affect data archiving, which you have to evaluate. If this upgrade adapts a display transaction, such as Transaction VA03, which your users have used to access the archive, you should check to see if there is a need for action here. You may have to adapt the user manuals and inform the users in an informative email.

Release version overview

You leverage various components in an SAP system that may have different release and support package versions. Table 7.5 provides a sample overview of the latest releases and support package levels in an SAP system. Of course, your SAP system can deviate from this overview and have a different version.

Component	Release	SP Level	Support Package	Short Description of the Component
SAP_BASIS	740	0004	SAPKB74004	SAP Basis component
SAP_APPL	617	0002	SAPKH61702	Logistics and accounting
SAP_FIN	617	0002	SAPK-61702INSAP-FIN	Enhanced financial functions for accounting
SAP_HR	600	0097	SAPKE60097	Human resources

Table 7.5 Extraction of the System Overview from an SAP System

To view the release and support package level of your SAP system, per-form the following steps:

Viewing the component version

1. In the SAP menu, click on SYSTEM and then on STATUS....

2. In the SAP SYSTEM DATA, you can see the COMPONENT VERSION field.

3. Then click on the DETAIL button 🔍 (component information).

Alternatively, you can also use Transaction SPAM (Support Package Manager). In the STATUS area, click on the PACKAGE LEVEL button to nav-igate to the respective overview.

After having gained an overview of the latest versions of the compo-nents in your SAP system, it is also important to know when and to which release or support package level you will upgrade your SAP sys-tem. This enables you to always be informed about upcoming functions and changes, in particular with regard to SAP data archiving. You can take a look at new functions in the SAP data archiving area in the SAP Help Portal (see Figure 7.11), for example. The following path navigates to information on the business function in SAP NetWeaver in the SAP Help Portal: *help.sap.com* • SAP BUSINESS SUITE • SAP ERP • SAP ERP 6.0 EHP 7 • BUSINESS FUNCTIONS IN SAP NETWEAVER

Being prepared

This website provides information on the various business functions in SAP NetWeaver, for example, for data archiving, and on standardized archiving objects. The write programs of several data archiving with SAP objects have been changed. The AVAILABLE AS OF column indicates that

Analyzing effects

these standardized archiving objects can be used as of SAP enhancement package 2 (EHP 2) for SAP NetWeaver 7.0 after the activation of the respective business functions. If you already use the affected data archiving with SAP objects in your SAP system, you should check their smooth operation after the upgrade to ensure that the data archiving process runs as planned.

Figure 7.11 New Enterprise Business Function Introduced with an Upgrade of the SAP System in the SAP Help Portal

In our example, the SAP Help Portal provides further information for data archiving via SAP NetWeaver. In the navigation bar on the left-hand side in Figure 7.11, you can see the DATA AGING and INFORMATION LIFECYCLE MANAGEMENT topics, for example. These two topics are discussed in detail in Chapter 8 and Chapter 9.

7.4.4 SAP Solution Manager

You can use SAP Solution Manager for versatile scenarios in your enterprise. It is the ideal SAP solution for monitoring and documentation purposes. Within the scope of data archiving, we recommend the two SAP Solution Manager components described in the following sections. Before you can receive the valuable information automatically, you have to implement the following components.

Monitoring and documentation

SAP EarlyWatch Alert

SAP EarlyWatch Alert (EWA) is a function from SAP Solution Manager that monitors your SAP system landscape with regard to performance and available space. Various chapters of the report contain information on performance and space that also include recommendations for data archiving. If a certain table growths very fast, the recommendation would be to implement appropriate archiving objects for that table. If you use SAP EarlyWatch Alert in your enterprise regularly, it is an ideal tool for you as the administrator to automatically obtain status reports on the system at regular intervals. If required, you can include these reports in your documentation concept for the administration and, for example, store it in a portal that your colleagues can access.

SAP Data Volume Management (DVM)

You can also leverage SAP Solution Manager to manage the data volume. For this purpose, the *SAP Data Volume Management* (DVM) component is available. Among other things, SAP DVM provides comprehensive queries and reports that contain information on the growth of the database and individual tables and determines the trend and saving potentials. For the efficient use of SAP DVM, an SAP BW system is mandatory.

In reality, SAP DVM is not widely spread. We recommend it to enterprises that have problems obtaining an overview of their data volume due to their high number of SAP systems and thus require a tool for this purpose. If you use only one or a few SAP systems, SAP DVM is not really necessary in our opinion.

7.5   Documentation

The creation of good administration documentation—in addition to SAP data archiving concepts—mainly requires a lot of time. However, this investment always pays off at a later stage, because SAP data archiving is a long-term topic. This inevitably makes it necessary to document your knowledge well and make it accessible to other persons—that is, work with efficient *knowledge management*. This way you provide an essential basis for the work of your substitutes or new colleagues who have to acquaint themselves with the corresponding tasks and can then rely on your documentation.

While you perform your daily administration tasks, you gain valuable experience that should not only be stored in your head. Comprehensive documentation enables you to assist other colleagues in avoiding known mistakes and problems.

This section discusses two questions:

▸ How and what should you as the administrator document within the scope of SAP data archiving?

▸ Where should this documentation be stored and for which persons should it be accessible?

7.5.1   Topics of Documentation

As part of the administration, you will create several documents. When creating these documents, you should use templates to ensure a standardized procedure. This way you provide for a smooth administration workflow for SAP data archiving and optimize your processes. The following sections discuss different documents that typically address the administrator and/or are generated within the scope of operational archiving.

Request

Requesting the administrator to perform a certain task can have several reasons. Perhaps an archiving object, for example, archiving object FI_ DOCUMNT (Financial Accounting Documents), should start only upon request. You may also receive frequent requests to prepare a test archiving process for a new archiving object in the test system.

Depending on the organization, this request can be expressed orally or in writing. However, we recommend working with written requests for better documentation. Ideally, requests should be made via email. In case of critical requests, however, you should create a ticket. The request must not permit misinterpretations. You should clearly define the selection variant and the time to ensure correct archiving.

Written request

Defining a Request Clearly   **[Ex]**

The request to archive the material documents in the test system, for example, is not specified clearly enough. In this case, you have to contact the user and request detailed information on the individual company codes, plants, fiscal years, document types, and so on. The emails sent enable you to trace new information and add it to the ticket as an attachment.

Ticket

A ticket contains an instruction for the administrator or a problem that—depending on its priority—needs to be solved within a predefined period of time. Consequently, a ticket is a request with an official character, because several persons can view and process the ticket. So you should always use tickets for important requests to be able to trace the processing status. Depending on its urgency, the ticket can be assigned a very high (1) or low priority (4). This priority also defines the latest time that the administrator must accept and resolve the ticket. Therefore, you should assign the tickets that you create for documentation purposes a rather low priority in order to avoid violating the *Service Level Agreements* (SLA) because you could not meet the response times. If a user creates a ticket and addresses it to you, but the priority of the ticket is too high in your opinion, you should directly contact the user and then redefine the priority.

Considering priorities

Selection Variants

To schedule a new archiving run, you require a selection variant for the write process. The selection variant documents according to the criteria data read from the tables and written to the archive files. It is stored in the SAP system in table ADMI_VARIA (Contents of the Variant for the Write Program) and contains the entry values that are used for each archiving run. If you want to analyze the previous archiving runs for an archiving object in detail with regard to which and how data has been archived, table ADMI_VARIA provides an ideal entry point.

Variants in Transaction SARA

Because Transaction SARA enables you to change existing selection variants for an archiving object and use them for new archiving runs, you can only find the original variant for an archiving run in table ADMI_VARIA.

Over time, new selection jobs for the write process of an archiving object may be added so that the obsolete variants can no longer be displayed in Transaction SARA as usual. You should therefore always use table ADMI_VARIA if you want to view the content of an obsolete selection variant. Figure 7.13 provides an example that is explained in the context of an archiving run.

Archiving Run

The archiving run documents critical information on the write process for an archiving object in table ADMI_RUN (Archive Runs Header Data). In particular, it assigns a unique identification to each archiving run (DOCUMENT field name; see Figure 7.12). It also contains information on the corresponding spool request (SPOOLID field name) and on the selection variant used (VARIANTWRI field name).

Displaying the values of the selection variant

This information on archiving run 001676 enables you, for example, to view the individual values of the selection variant in table ADMI_VARIA (see Figure 7.13).

Table ADMI_RUN Display

Check Table...

DOCUMENT	1676
OBJECT	RL_TA
CREAT DATE	06/25/2014
CREAT TIME	03:07:00
USER NAME	LMARCH
STATUS	⬤⬤⬤ Complete
COMMENTS	All Transfer Orders - Residence Time 200 Days
CLIENT	400
DELETE FLG	
OLD DOCUMN	0
NOTGUILTY	
SPOOLID	1,851,748
SYSID	
TOBE INTER	
INTERRUPTD	
VARIANTWRI	PROD_200D
WRITING	
TOBE CONT	
ORIGINAL CLIENT	
FOR DESTRUCTION	
PARTIAL DESTR	
ORIG DOCUMENT	0
ILM CONV REPL	
ILM DELTA RUN	
ILM SORTED RUN	

Figure 7.12 Fields from Table ADMI_RUN

Data Browser: Table ADMI_VARIA Select Entries   12

Table: ADMI_VARIA
Displayed Fields: 8 of   8   Fixed Columns: ⌈2⌉   List Width 0250

DOCUMENT	SEQUENCE	SELNAME	KIND	SIGN	OPTI	LOW	HIGH
001676	0001	LAUFZEIT	P			200	
001676	0002	P_AR_ILM	P			X	
001676	0003	P_COMENT	P			All Transfer Orders - Residence Time 200 Days	
001676	0004	P_DELTST	P				
001676	0005	P_DEST	P				
001676	0006	P_PROT	P				
001676	0007	P_PROT_O	P				
001676	0008	P_SNAP	P				
001676	0009	P_WRIPRD	P			X	
001676	0010	P_WRITST	P				
001676	0011	RT_LGNUM	S				
001676	0012	RT_TANUM	S				

Figure 7.13 Selection Fields for an Archiving Run in Table ADMI_VARIA

In the `SELNAME` column, you can see the `LAUFZEIT` field. Here in the `LOW` column, the corresponding value, `200`, was entered for a residence time of two hundred days. So these tables allow you to check how an archiving object was archived in the system in the past. In particular, when you take over the archiving activities for a system, you should obtain an overview on the basis of these tables.

Spool Files

A spool file (or spool request) contains critical information on the processing results of a program, in particular, for the write process of an archiving object. You can print this information as a print list or store it in the archive. In this file, the system logs the number of archived data records and the involved tables, for example. The file always includes further details on the documents that were archived or not if a comprehensive log was requested during the write process. In Figure 7.14 you can see an example spool file.

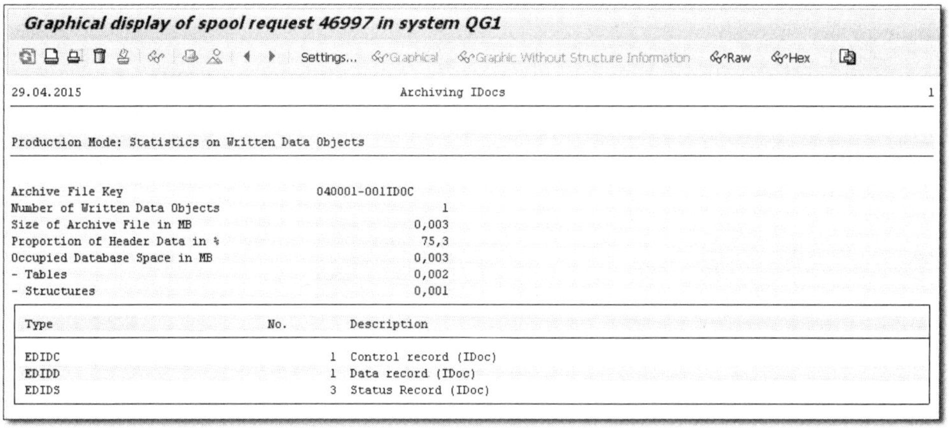

Figure 7.14 Sample Spool File

You store important spool files, for example, for archiving object `FI_DOCUMNT` (Financial Accounting Documents), in the archive using ArchiveLink. If required, you can view the spool files via Transaction SP01. You can determine the corresponding spool ID for a write process in table `ADMI_RUN` in the `SPOOLID` field (see Figure 7.12).

Releases

A release only differs slightly from a request. As the administrator, you act on your initiative if you require a release for performing a specific task.

Written confirmation

> **Release for Space Extension**
>
> A common example of this kind of situation is when you run out of space on the database or in the storage system and need to extend it. These storage media are assigned a specific cost center in the enterprise, which bears the costs for space extensions and consequently must have the respective budget. You therefore should contact the head of the cost center who then checks if the extension is within the budget.

We recommend that you document the release in writing; for example, request that the head of the cost center submit the release via email or as a ticket so that you are always able to provide the release in case of queries regarding the space extension.

Emails

For you as the administrator, emails play a major role in the context of documentation. An email exchange between the persons involved contains a lot of critical project information that cannot always be easily identified. We therefore recommend the usage of email templates or correspondingly structured subject lines to be able to easily obtain an overview of a topic in your mailbox or email folders. Emails that were answered or forwarded several times can have very long subject lines from which you can no longer determine the actual content of the individual emails.

Using templates

7.5.2 Storage Locations for the Documentation

SAP data archiving involves not only storing the archive files but also provides a thorough and appropriate storage strategy for the documentation created during the administrations. Of course, the documentation is stored in a slightly different way. The documents are not always bundled and stored at a central location. This does not have to be a problem as long as you know where these documents can be accessed if neces-

Storage systems

sary. The following sections discuss the different IT system you can consider for storing the documentation.

SAP System

Automatic logging

The SAP system in which SAP data archiving is implemented automatically documents important information, for example, archiving run, selection variants, or spool files. This documentation is performed by default. As long as this information is not archived, modified, or deleted, you can always inform yourself about the archiving runs via these logs.

Archive System

The archive system not only stores the archive files but also allows you to store the documents from the SAP system (e.g., the spool files). The archive still displays these spool files from the SAP system after they have been deleted.

SAP Solution Manager

If your enterprise leverages SAP Solution Manager, you should use its functions in particular to document processes. Within the scope of the implementation of SAP software, the system documents the processes for each component, interface, and so on in detail and stores them in SAP Solution Manager. You can also create the corresponding directory for data archiving in the SAP Basis area in which you can store the data archiving documents.

Releases and document versions

Furthermore, you can implement a release process according to which documents respective persons must first read and release. It is also possible to store different versions of the relevant documents to be able to better trace the changes in these documents. However, this may easily lead to rather high space consumption, so you should carefully consider the pros and cons.

Knowledge database

The Support Desk that is integrated in SAP Solution Manager and in which users or you as the administrator can create tickets, which are then processed by the support team, provides a good option for documenting tickets. This ticket system is also comparable to a *knowledge database*. If the tickets are described respectively, for example, with "archiving object FI_DOCUMNT...," you can find all tickets for this archiving object and browse the content for relevant information. This requires that you specify in detail in these tickets how you have solved a specific problem.

Ticketing System

As already mentioned, tickets are created to enable the IT department or administrator to process the request of a user (support desk). There are numerous providers of professional software for this area on the market. Often, enterprises leverage a ticketing system of an external provider or use it in connection with SAP Solution Manager. SAP Solution Manager is optimally adapted to SAP systems. Enterprises basically use neutral ticketing systems for other IT systems. A ticketing system is also used by the administrator to store critical information in the respective comment areas. This information can then be found via the search.

Document Management System

You do not only edit and store documents in SAP Solution Manager but also in an enterprise-wide Document Management System (DMS) that is not only aligned to the SAP system. The DMS can store documents, enable authorized users to access these documents, and also manage documents via version or change histories. Consequently, you always know which changes were added to the new version of the document.

Tracking changes

For administration documentation purposes, this system is not ideal and not the appropriate environment but technically feasible. You usually store enterprise-wide guidelines, concepts, etc. in this kind of system and not documents from the operational administration area of the IT department. Archiving concepts, however, are documents that can and should be stored in a DMS. Many enterprises have defined strict specifications for storing only certain types of documents in the DMS to avoid it becoming a pool for less important documents. You should discuss these specifications with the corresponding contact persons to decide how you can use an existing DMS.

Portals

Enterprises use different portals, such as Microsoft SharePoint, SAP Enterprise Portal, or SAP Jam, that are supposed to make it easier for teams to collaborate. In these portals, you also store documents and release them for the respective persons. Irrespective of the portal you select or use in your enterprise, you should avoid the redundant storage of documents. Because portals focus on teamwork, we recommend that you edit or store documents that are of interest to respective groups for their daily work (e.g., work instructions or checklists).

Email System

Email address for the entire administration team

Messages in an email system (e.g., IBM Lotus Notes or Microsoft Outlook) are either set up for specific persons so that only one user can access them or for a team, in particular, in the administration area. In the latter case, there is a central email address (*pool*) which all administrators can access so that a member of the team can answer the emails.

Especially if a whole team is responsible for data archiving in your enterprise, you should implement a central email address to be able to bundle and store all emails that refer to data archiving in that mailbox. Here you can create various folders for each SAP system and archiving object to sort the incoming and outgoing emails when storing them to make it easier to find them later on. If new colleagues want to take care of SAP system P01 and archiving object IDOC (21 IDOC) (see Figure 7.15), they can search this folder for relevant emails or use the full-text search of the email system.

Figure 7.15 Sample Folder Structure in Microsoft Outlook for the Pool Mailbox

A major disadvantage of email systems is mainly the increasing number of emails that can quickly become confusing. Furthermore, team members can easily delete or store emails in the wrong folders. The team should therefore define internal rules for the best way to sort the emails.

Organizing access

7.5.3 Recommendations for Documentation

Having explained how, what, and where you can and should document within the scope of SAP data archiving, we now want to provide recommendations on the basis of the experience we have gained in our projects. Table 7.6 provides an overview of the best way to ensure sufficient documentation within the scope of your administration.

Overview

How and What?	Where?	Comment
Request	Email system/SAP Solution Manager/ticketing system	Requests made per email should be stored as attachments to tickets.
Ticket	SAP Solution Manager/ticketing system	Document tickets thoroughly so that they can be reused as a solution document.
Selection variant	SAP system	The SAP system automatically saves selection variants in table `ADMI_VARIA`.
Archiving run	SAP system	The SAP system automatically saves archiving runs in table `ADMI_RUN`.
Spool files	SAP system/ archive system	The SAP system automatically generates spool files once the write process has been completed. Because spool files are often deleted from the SAP system after just a short time (usually after a week), you should store them, if required, in the archive system in due time.

Table 7.6 Recommendations for the Storage of Documentations

How and What?	Where?	Comment
Releases	SAP Solution Manager/ticketing system	Releases submitted per email should be stored as attachments to tickets.
Emails	Email system/SAP Solution Manager/ticketing system	Sort and store emails in various folders in the email system. Important emails should be additionally stored as attachments to tickets.
EarlyWatch Alert/analysis report	SAP Solution Manager/portals/Microsoft SharePoint	Ideally, you should store detailed reports on the system performance and space in a portal so that other colleagues can also access the reports.

Table 7.6 Recommendations for the Storage of Documentations (Cont.)

The documentation in the context of administration is certainly a laborious task. However, good documentation saves you a lot of time in case of queries or searches and preserves the resources of your enterprise, because you do not have to search for the information required but immediately find it.

You can apply the recommendations from Table 7.6 to your project and enterprise. Of course, you can also adapt or enhance them. From the many options available for documentation purposes, you should select an ideal documentation strategy that is tailored to your requirements.

7.6 Summary

The SAP data archiving system consists of an SAP system including the respective data to be archived and the external archive system for storing the archive files. As the administrator, you are responsible for the smooth operation of these two areas. One of your many tasks is to keep an eye on the performance and space using system analyses and avoid critical situations. Furthermore, you ensure the smooth operation of data archiving by scheduling periodic archiving runs in the SAP system and managing the space, in particular, for storage processes.

Regular reorganizations of the individual tables (online) or of the entire database (offline) at the appropriate times make the success of data archiving on the database even more visible. Proactive monitoring in the SAP Support Portal, especially of SAP Notes and new functions in release upgrades, enables you to benefit from adapting the affected archiving objects in your SAP system in due time if action is required.

This chapter also introduced the versatile communication and documentation options in the data archiving context. At this point, we want to encourage you to select and use the options that are best suited to the requirements of your enterprise. Every enterprise is unique and has its own culture with regard to communication and documentation.

SAP Information Lifecycle Management has heralded a new era for SAP data archiving. SAP ILM provides much more than rule-based data archiving. Particularly for system shutdowns, this is the only solution provided by SAP.

8 SAP Information Lifecycle Management

Historically grown, complex IT landscapes as well as continuously increasing data volumes and new compliance requirements pose major challenges for chief information officers (CIO) and their organizations — and not only due to the tight IT budgets after the global financial crisis.

According to studies from the company Advanced Market Research (AMR), many CIOs are primarily occupied with reducing the complexity and versatility of integrated systems of their application landscape and therefore commit their enterprise to a small group of providers. Although some IT leads regret this because this limitation may affect the innovative strength of an enterprise, they realize the benefits in terms of stability, reliability of system landscapes, and lower costs for IT operation and business processes.

Priorities of CIOs

An efficient management of the information lifecycle therefore takes the rocky path of infrastructure consolidation. Saving potentials that arise after the consolidation takes place strongly depend on how you handle legacy systems that result from the consolidation process and are only operated for informational purposes or meeting legal retention requirements.

Consolidation

Various scenarios exist of how an enterprise can handle information that is contained in legacy systems. Selecting the scenario (with optimized costs and minimum risk) depends on the legal context of the saved information, budgets for retaining legacy data, and availability of alternative technologies that can provide cost benefits. The goal of a system shut-

Scenarios for system shutdown

down is to meet the requirements on information provision using "risk-intelligent" ILM technologies as cost-efficiently as possible.

SAP Information Lifecycle Management (SAP ILM, formerly SAP NetWeaver ILM), provides a new option for archiving your data. However, it goes beyond data archiving and also pursues the goal of shutting down legacy SAP systems in conformance with the law. Consequently, this solution meets challenges, which CIOs are facing today, to a greater degree than classic SAP data archiving. This chapter discusses SAP ILM from two perspectives:

- Data archiving using SAP ILM
- System shutdown using SAP ILM

The following questions arise here:

- How can you make SAP ILM available in an SAP system?
- What is the difference between data archiving in the SAP standard and using SAP ILM?
- What is Retention Management?
- What is a Retention Warehouse Management?
- How do you deploy SAP ILM ideally?

8.1 Setting Up SAP Information Lifecycle Management

We answer the first question right away. To be able to use SAP ILM at all, the following preparatory activities are necessary:

- Basic configuration (storage and interfaces)
- Activate SAP ILM (licenses and costs)
- Authorizations for SAP ILM (roles and transactions)
- Prepare Retention Management
- Prepare Retention Warehouse Management

Using SAP ILM for data archiving requires an ILM-enabled storage. The storage options, which were presented in Chapter 2, are thus extended by the deployment of SAP ILM. This is usually done via an archive system that is provided with a WebDAV interface (see Chapter 2, Section 2.2).

We'll discuss the basic configuration based on Figure 8.1 which shows the technical environment of SAP ILM.

Basic configuration

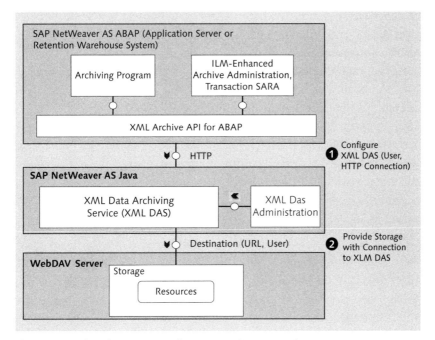

Figure 8.1 Technical Environment for SAP ILM (Source: SAP)

This environment is subdivided into three blocks:

System environment

▸ **SAP NetWeaver Application Server AS ABAP**
This server stands for the ABAP application system (central SAP system) or retention warehouse system (an additional SAP system for system shutdown in which you retain data from legacy systems and from which you can display the data).

▸ **SAP NetWeaver AS Java**
This server stands for the SAP NetWeaver component SAP ILM, which is provided via a web interface using the Java programming language.

▸ **WebDAV server**
This server allows for ILM-enabled storage of archived data.

In the upper area, the AS ABAP represents the SAP system for which Information Lifecycle Management is supposed to be implemented. Here a distinction is made as to whether it involves the central application system or an additional Retention Warehouse Management system for system shutdowns. The archiving programs and SAP ILM-enhanced Transaction SARA run in these systems as you'll learn in Section 8.3. The ABAP systems communicate with the AS Java via an HTTP connection. SAP ILM is an SAP NetWeaver service that uses the Java programming language and a web interface. So you will use both the SAP front-end system (user interface) and a web browser, for example, Microsoft Internet Explorer, when you deploy SAP ILM. AS Java, in turn, communicates with the WebDAV server—that is, the SAP ILM-enabled storage system via the XML Data Archiving service (XML DAS). In this process, the storage of resources (archive files) takes place using a Uniform Resource Identifier (URI). You must set up the interfaces between the SAP system, XML DAS, and the WebDAV server as specified by the manufacturer before you can utilize the storage.

Activating SAP ILM   In contrast to the functions of classic SAP data archiving, the new SAP ILM functions are not included in the standard SAP scope. SAP ILM is a fee-based premium solution and requires a license before you can use it in production. As soon as you've acquired this license, you can activate SAP ILM in your SAP system. For this purpose, you must first enable the SAP ILM function using Transaction SFW5 (Switch Framework Customizing):

1. Call Transaction SFW5 and scroll to the SAP ILM business functions in the business functions list (see Figure 8.2).

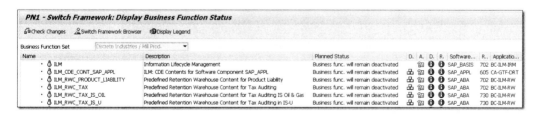

Figure 8.2 Business Functions in the SAP System

2. The text BUSINESS FUNCTION WILL REMAIN DEACTIVATED is displayed in the PLANNED STATUS column, which means that SAP ILM must still be activated in this system. You must enable some of the business functions listed here in the application system or in the retention warehouse system. The business functions for the retention warehouse system are particularly required if you want to shut down SAP systems.

3. Click on the SWITCH FRAMEWORK BROWSER button to navigate to the view of Figure 8.3.

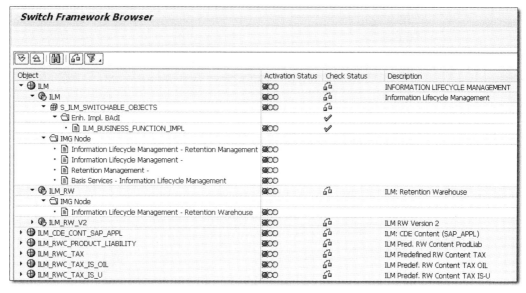

Figure 8.3 Switch Framework Browser

4. Open the individual subfolders of the OBJECT column. In the ACTIVATION STATUS column you can see that the functions have not been activated (red traffic light icon).

5. To activate the SAP ILM business function, select the SAP ILM entry and click on SYSTEM SETTINGS • ACTIVATE in the menu.

You can check very quickly if SAP ILM has already been activated in your SAP system. Even if you don't have an SAP ILM license and can't reproduce the examples in this chapter in your SAP system, the descriptions in this chapter can provide you with an initial overview and introduce you to working with SAP ILM. It is important to us that you become more familiar with the options available in SAP ILM and compare them with classic SAP data archiving. Based on this comparison, it is your enterprise-specific decision if you can determine added value for your enterprise and implement this solution.

Authorizations for SAP ILM

Before you can use SAP ILM, you must assign the appropriate authorizations for these new transactions. Transaction SARA, which we've used for performing data archiving so far, is still used in SAP ILM. However, lots of new transactions are added in SAP ILM, which Table 8.1 describes briefly. The users who are supposed to work with these new transactions should be trained in advance.

Transaction	Description	Role
ILM	Creates the menu for Context Data Extractor	None; authorization only required for the transactions in the menu
ILM_C_RAOB ILM_C_RAOB_TAB ILM_C_SOEX ILM_C_OBJECTS ILM_C_CON ILM_C_C_CON ILM_C_STRC ILM_C_APPL ILM_C_RELA	Transactions in the menu generated by Transaction ILM	None; authorizations for the authorization object S_TABU_DIS or S_TABU_NAM
ILMAPT	Processing of audit package templates	SAP_ILM_WP_ADMIN
ILMARA	Processing of audit areas	SAP_BC_ILM_AUDIT_AREA SAP_ILM_WP_ADMIN
ILMCHECK	Define and execute check sums	SAP_BC_ILM_CHECKSUM
ILM_DESTRUCTION	Data destruction	SAP_BC_ILM_DESTROY
ILM_LH_AL	Propagate legal holds for ArchiveLink	SAP_BC_ILM_ARCHIVELINK

Table 8.1 Important Transactions and Roles for SAP ILM

Transaction	Description	Role
IRM_CUST IRM_CUST_BS	Information Retention Manager Customizing	SAP_BC_ILM_IRM
IRMPOL	Information Retention Management	SAP_BC_ILM_IRM
SARA	Archive Administration	SAP_BC_CCM_DATA_ARCHIVING
SCASE	Legal Case Management	SAP_BC_LHM_USER SAP_BC_CM_ADMINISTRATOR SAP_BC_CM_ADMINISTRA-TOR_TR SAP_BC_CM_USER SAP_BC_RM_ADMINISTRATOR SAP_BC_RM_USER

Table 8.1 Important Transactions and Roles for SAP ILM (Cont.)

Transactions IRM_CUST (see Figure 8.14) or IRM_CUST_BS (see Figure 8.16) for direct access to SAP ILM objects enable you to perform Customizing for the *Information Retention Manager* (IRM). The IRM manages all rules with regard to the retention and storage of data that has been stored in Transaction IRMPOL (see Figure 8.19). To learn more, refer to Section 8.4. This Customizing is a mandatory requirement for *Retention Management*. Using Transaction SCASE, you can create a *legal case* within the scope of Retention Management. By means of a legal case, you can map law cases and protect the associated data and documents on the database and in the archive from destruction using Transaction ILM_DESTRUCTION. Table 8.1 is just an excerpt of the most critical transactions and roles in the SAP ILM environment, which you must definitely integrate into your role concept when you implement SAP ILM.

Adapting the role concept in your enterprise

To be able to deploy SAP ILM at all, you require the functions of Retention Management. Retention Management is subdivided into two tools:

Preparing Retention Management

▸ The *Information Retention Manager* is responsible for managing retention rules.

▸ *Legal Case Management* (LCM) is based on the functions of *SAP Records Management* and *SAP Case Management* and allows you to set legal case-related locks. By means of an *electronic discovery (e-discovery) report* (see Section 8.4), you can determine dependent documents for an original document in the archive. These documents are managed in a record on a *case*.

[»] | **SAP Records Management and SAP Case Management**

SAP Records Management is a standard solution for electronic records management in an SAP system. Here the focus is on a *record* in which you can collect and store information, for example, about an applicant, in various folders.

In SAP Case Management, the focus is on a *case* and not on the record. For example, if you received a customer complaint on a product, you can create a case and enrich it with information in a record until the case is solved—that is, until the customer is satisfied. From this perspective, SAP Case Management is based on the technological possibilities of SAP Records Management (record) and supplements it with options for processing a case.

Preparing retention warehouse

You can store data from legacy SAP systems, which you must retain for legal or internal reasons for a specific period of time, in a retention warehouse system. Before you transfer the relevant data from the systems to be shut down to the retention warehouse system, you must make preparations both in the legacy system and in the retention warehouse system. In particular, you must maintain the retention rule in the retention warehouse system so that the archive files to be transferred from the legacy system can be supplemented with appropriate information on the lifecycle.

[◉] | **Preparing the Usage of SAP ILM**

Before you can use SAP ILM, you must first require a valid license. You can then activate the corresponding business functions. You connect the SAP system with the WebDAV server within the scope of basic configuration. Additionally, you assign the transactions and roles for SAP ILM to the appropriate users. In this context, it is important to instruct and train the users so that they can run the transactions correctly.

Retention Management manages the retention rules. You must always maintain Customizing for this purpose. If you want to shut down legacy systems, you must also perform the customizing for the retention warehouse system.

8.2   Tasks of SAP Information Lifecycle Management

This section provides an overview of the columns of SAP ILM. The individual functions of each of these columns are discussed in the subsequent sections of this chapter using examples.

So far, this book has informed you on how to archive the data in your SAP system using classic SAP data archiving and thus preserve the performance of your system. We use the phrase *classic SAP data archiving* because these methods are established, standard methods for archiving data. Over the course of years, classic SAP data archiving has evolved by continuously supplementing the individual archiving objects with new functions and improvements with regard to archive access.

Classic SAP data archiving

In case of SAP ILM, however, we can consider it as a revolution of the data archiving approach. For a long time, the focus of data archiving was on data volume management and preservation of performance. The priority was not to manage the lifecycle of this data. Instead, it was important to answer the questions as to when and how you could remove this data from the SAP system. The demand for a holistic solution that goes beyond data volume management and performance optimization, manages the data's lifecycle, and is even capable of shutting down an SAP system at the end of its lifecycle (thus conforming to the law) resulted in the solution SAP ILM. SAP ILM enables you to securely and efficiently control your data throughout its lifecycle—from data creation and usage, to archiving and final destruction. This chapter shows you how to control the lifecycle of data in the SAP system using SAP ILM and the role data archiving plays in this context.

In the SAP ILM context, we use the term *ILM-enhanced data archiving*. To illustrate the difference from classic data archiving, you must first get to know SAP ILM and the individual functions.

ILM-enhanced data archiving

> **Goal of SAP Information Lifecycle Management (ILM)**   [«]
>
> SAP ILM is a holistic approach whose goal can be described as follows: the processes, policies, procedures, and tools of SAP ILM help enterprises to leverage the business value of its information without exceptions and cost-efficiently thanks to an appropriate IT infrastructure. SAP ILM already applies when data is created and accompanies the lifecycle of information until the final destruction of data. SAP ILM is SAP SE's solution to implement these requirements.

Columns and foundation

If you illustrate the tasks of SAP ILM graphically, you obtain an illustration with two columns (Retention Management and system shutdown) under the roof of SAP ILM and a common foundation (data archiving; see Figure 8.4). You can consider data archiving as the core of SAP ILM.

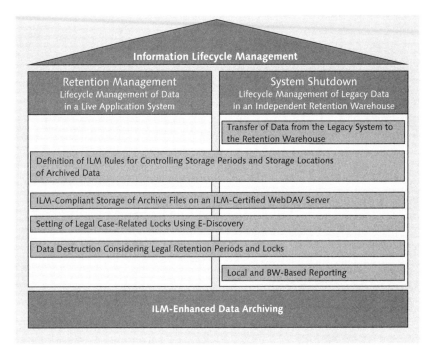

Figure 8.4 Structure of the SAP Information Lifecycle Management Solution (Source: SAP)

Data archiving

SAP ILM is based on conventional data archiving functions and extends them with new functions. The write jobs of archiving programs have been enhanced in such a way that they not only allow for data archiving but also for data destruction and creation of *snapshots*. Section 8.3 provides a corresponding example. Particularly for system shutdowns, snapshots allow you to also archive data whose status would not permit archiving because archivability criteria are not met. SAP ILM therefore provides options for archiving that go beyond the functions of classic data archiving.

The first column of SAP ILM, Retention Management, manages the life-cycle of data in a live SAP system. The Retention Management functions are also required in the retention warehouse system.

Retention Management

Retention Management and SAP ILM-enhanced data archiving are therefore an inseparable couple. You can't deploy SAP ILM without defining rules with regard to retention and storage in the Information Retention Manager. An important function of Retention Management is to destroy data after the maximum retention period has been reached. This can be prevented with another function if this data is required for legal processes and is thus locked.

System shutdown is the second column of SAP ILM. Even after legacy systems have been shut down, data is still available in a retention warehouse system. Using an additional SAP BW, you can extend the retention warehouse system to include a centralized inspection and reporting system. Here the local evaluation options of the SAP ILM system are available at any time. Although they are restricted compared to the data evaluation options in a live SAP system, you can download the archived data to a local drive or display it in a table browser.

System shutdown

You can use SAP ILM for two scenarios:

Two SAP ILM scenarios

▶ In a live application system

▶ In a retention warehouse system within the scope of system shutdown

Figure 8.5 illustrates the essential characteristics of these two scenarios. If you deploy SAP ILM in a live application system, you use it to manage data in your existing SAP ERP system, for example. Instead of using the classic data archiving functions, you now utilize the ILM-enhanced data archiving; in other words, you may, for example, create snapshots and stipulate the destruction of data at the end of the lifecycle. The retention rules are maintained centrally for all ILM-enabled archiving objects in the IRM. The storage locations are also maintained in the IRM and can then be determined automatically before you store the archive files. The data that is relevant for legal cases can also be determined and locked against deletion. Overall, you can use this scenario to specifically control and manage the lifecycle of data and information in your SAP system. The SAP ILM reporting options also allow you to create archived data in

Live application system

the form of view files in the SAP audit format for tax auditors even without creating DART extracts.

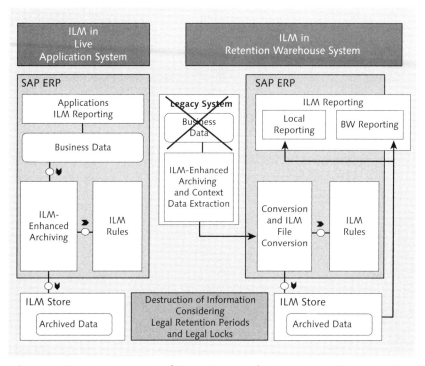

Figure 8.5 System Components of SAP ILM per Application Scenario (Source: SAP)

System shutdown   In the second scenario, a retention warehouse system is introduced within the scope of a system shutdown. This involves a new SAP system to which you transfer all data and information from legacy systems that must be preserved for legal reasons. For this purpose, you not only deploy ILM-enabled archiving objects but also extract context data, for example, Customizing of the legacy system, so that this information is not missing in the retention warehouse system. The functions of Retention Management are also required here so that you can manage the lifecycle of the transferred archive files. SAP ILM reporting can be run either locally in the SAP ILM system or via the SAP BW system. We recommend using the BW system for large amounts of data.

We can summarize that SAP ILM cannot work without data archiving. The ILM-enhanced data archiving forms the foundation both for the Retention Management and for the retention warehouse system. As soon as you activate the SAP ILM component in your SAP system, the archiving objects change. These *ILM-enabled archiving objects* require information from the IRM to be aware of their lifecycle and storage location. Here too, these archiving objects provide two new functions—snapshots and destruction of data. Section 8.3 will discuss these functions in detail. Because you can use SAP ILM even if you don't plan any system shutdown of an old SAP system (scenario 1), a changeover from classic SAP data archiving to ILM-enabled data archiving is possible quickly.

ILM-enabled archiving objects

8.3   Archiving Data

Now that you've obtained an initial overview of SAP ILM in the previous section, let's go into detail. We start with the ILM-enhanced data archiving, which forms the foundation of SAP ILM. Data archiving using SAP ILM only changed in some points compared with the data archiving that we have presented to you in this book so far. The differences already become apparent in the names: *ILM-enabled archiving objects* or *ILM-enhanced data archiving*.

This section answers the questions that arise when you change over from classic SAP data archiving to SAP ILM:

Changeover from classic archiving

▶ How do I handle already existing archive files in my SAP system?

▶ What do the new write programs look like for ILM-enhanced archiving objects?

▶ What are snapshots, and how do you create them?

▶ How do I destroy data?

Data archiving remains an essential part of the information lifecycle and a critical task of system administration also in SAP ILM. Your tasks and functions are merely adapted to the new options and requirements of SAP ILM.

8.3.1 Converting Existing Archive Files

An important question you might ask yourself is what happens to already existing archive files if you decide to change over from classic data archiving to SAP ILM. This is definitely a fair question, because the archive data that is not created in SAP ILM doesn't include any information about its lifecycle (in contrast to the archive files that are created in SAP ILM).

File conversion For this reason, you must supplement these archive files with retention rules and specify storage locations as required by Retention Management. This update is referred to as *file conversion* in the SAP ILM environment. Report RSARCH_CONVERT_TO_ILM, whose initial screen is displayed in Figure 8.6, is available for this purpose.

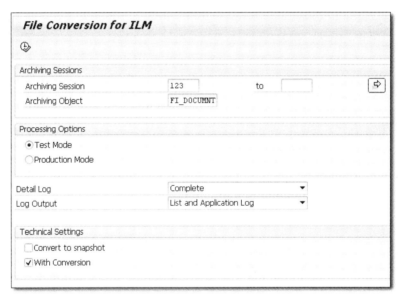

Figure 8.6 Converting Existing Archive Files into the SAP ILM Structure Using Report RSARCH_CONVERT_TO_ILM

Selection of the archiving session In the Archiving Sessions area, you can find the selection criteria Archiving Session and Archiving Object. You'll recall that for each archiving session, a sequential number is assigned for identification and managed in table ADMI_RUN. Based on this identification number, you can determine uniquely for which archiving session you want to perform file conversion. Specifying the archiving object also ensures that you don't convert another archiving session accidentally. The combination of Archiving Session and Archiving Object specified in this selection screen must be available in this form in table ADMI_RUN.

You can run the RSARCH_CONVERT_TO_ILM report either in Test Mode or in Production Mode as illustrated in the Processing Options area. It is always recommended to schedule a job in the background in the test mode and evaluate its logs in the job overview in Transaction SM37 before you start the report in production mode. *Processing options*

We advise you to record a complete Detail Log as a List and Application Log of the report so that you can easily comprehend the results of the file conversion. *Detail log*

In the Technical Settings area, you can start report RSARCH_CONVERT_ TO_ILM in two variants: *Two variants*

▶ Convert to snapshot
You should only activate the first variant if you want to shut down legacy systems and transfer archiving objects that are master data-like and for which you can't define any rules with distinctive values for the minimum retention period. Don't select this option if you use SAP ILM in the Retention Management scenario only.

▶ With conversion
This setting is preselected. If you keep this selection, the archive files are adapted with regard to their current structures of table fields, which improve the SAP system's response times. For this reason, we recommend keeping this setting.

But what exactly happens when you run this report? The file conversion process can be subdivided into the following phases: *File conversion process*

1. Create new archive files.

2. Destroy original archive files.

3. Destroy and set up archive infostructures.

4. Store new archive files.

New archive file is created
:   Each single data record from the archive file is compared with the rules from IRM and copied to a new, sorted archive file. The existing archive files are thus replaced by new archive files. In archive management, these archive files are listed under REPLACED ARCHIVE SESSIONS.

Destroying the original archive file
:   Because the archive files now exist redundantly in the system, you can destroy the original archive files. This is accomplished either automatically if the AUTOMATIC DESTRUCTION OF REPLACED ARCHIVE FILES flag is set under FILE CONVERSION FOR ILM in archiving object-specific Customizing or manually in the archive management in Transaction SARA.

Infostructures
:   Archive infostructures for the respective archiving session are destroyed and set up automatically after the conversion of the archive files.

Storing archive files
:   The new archive files are stored either manually or automatically if the START AUTOMATICALLY option was selected in Customizing under FILE STORAGE TO STORAGE SYSTEM. After you've stored the new archive files, you have formatted all archive files that exist outside the ILM context in such a way that they can be used in SAP ILM.

8.3.2 New Write Programs for SAP ILM

Due to the implementation of SAP ILM, the existing write programs of data archiving with SAP objects had to be modified. Only archiving objects with these new write programs are ILM-enabled archiving objects. SAP Note 1180653 (Application-Specific Content for SAP ILM) provides a list of ILM-enabled archiving objects that are currently available.

ILM-enabled objects
:   ILM-enabled archiving objects are not provided with SAP ILM but are already part of the SAP standard and are available as of SAP ERP 6.0 EHP 6. If you use an older release or require archiving objects in ILM that have not been ILM-enabled so far, you should contact SAP Consulting for System Landscape Optimization (SAP SLO).

Example FI_DOCUMNT
:   Figure 8.7 shows an example of how the write program was extended for the archiving object FI_DOCUMNT (FI Documents).

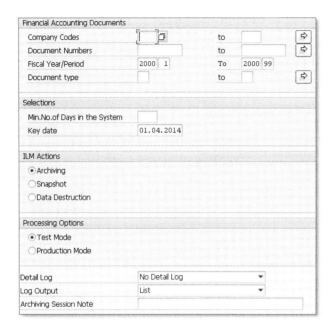

Figure 8.7 New SAP ILM Actions in Write Programs

The ILM ACTIONS area is new. You can't use these actions until you've activated SAP ILM. The following SAP ILM actions are available in the write program:

ILM actions

▶ ARCHIVING
The ARCHIVING option is preset. Data archiving is executed if you choose this option. Section 8.3.3 details this option.

▶ SNAPSHOT
If you select the SNAPSHOT option, the system creates snapshots of the dataset when the write job is started (see Section 8.3.4).

▶ DATA DESTRUCTION
When you select the DATA DESTRUCTION option, you can destroy data automatically (see Section 8.3.5).

To enable the write job at this point to derive retention periods and storage locations, you must maintain the corresponding rules in the Information Retention Manager's Customizing in advance.

8.3.3   Implementing Archiving

There's only one major difference between the data archiving ILM action and classic SAP data archiving. Although you use the FI_DOCUMNT_WRI report for the write job of the (ILM-enabled) archiving object FI_DOCUMNT in both cases, the SAP system no longer checks the settings for the archive routing or the application-specific Customizing in which you maintained the account and document type runtimes in the case of the ILM action.

Tight integration with Retention Management

Instead, the write job is based on retention rules that have been maintained in the Retention Management of the Information Retention Manager component. The new write program was designed in such a way that it either can be used as usual for archiving without SAP ILM actions or accesses Retention Management if you activated the SAP ILM component. All other steps that you learned in Chapter 6 for implementing archiving, for example, creation of selection variants and scheduling of jobs, remain the same.

8.3.4   Creating Snapshots

If you select the second SAP ILM action in the selection mask of the write job, you can create a snapshot. Snapshots are copies of transaction data originating from open business processes and of master data and context data (Customizing, metadata, etc.). So they comprise data that usually cannot be archived in classic data archiving.

Creation methods

There are two methods to create snapshots:

▸ **Via the ILM-enabled archiving object**
If you create snapshots using the write job of an archiving object, you extract the data that could not be considered within the scope of archiving. Snapshots ignore the archivability criteria, for example, if the document already has the *complete* status. Snapshots also write open documents that relate to incomplete business transactions into the archive files. You thus ensure that all data for a document is archived.

▸ **Using the Context Data Extractor (CDE)**
The SAP ILM objects of the CDE extract the data that could not be considered by archiving objects, for example, Customizing settings or master

data. Special SAP ILM objects, for example, `SN_FI` (CDE: snapshots FI) or `SN_META` (CDE: snapshots META), are available for this purpose. The archiving of these SAP ILM objects is also implemented in Transaction SARA.

Snapshots are used particularly within the scope of system shutdowns. A legacy system comprises large amounts of data that can't be archived and are required for the retention warehouse system to be complete. The snapshots bypass the archivability criteria, and the maximum scope of data is extracted.

Necessary for system shutdowns

Setting the Residence Time to Zero for System Shutdowns [+]

Within the scope of system shutdowns, it is recommended to set the residence time to 0 for the various archiving objects to be able to archive the maximum scope of data. In the best case, you then need to create hardly any or only very few snapshots for application data.

The snapshot technology is strongly based on the Data Retention Tool (DART). In both cases, you can extract data independent of its status.

Similarity to DART

8.3.5 Destroying Data

The third SAP ILM action allows you to destroy data. Here you must distinguish whether you want to destroy data directly from the tables in the database or already existing archive files from the SAP ILM store.

Data is destroyed directly by the database if you select the DATA DESTRUCTION ILM action in the write job of an ILM-enabled archiving object. Initially, an archive file is created for this purpose. Then the data records from the archive file are deleted from the corresponding database tables. In contrast to a normal deletion run, this process doesn't create the archive infostructure, and storage jobs and postprocessing runs are not started automatically either. For this reason, this option is ideal for ensuring system hygienics—that is, for removing data at the end of its lifecycle (see Chapter 4, Section 4.1.2).

Destroying data from the database

An active policy with corresponding rules is a prerequisite for destroying data in the database. After you've completed the deletion run, the temporary archive file with the corresponding administration data is deleted too.

Destroying data from the ILM store

The second option enables you to destroy already existing archive files from the ILM store. You call this option using Transaction ILM_ DESTRUCTION (Data Destruction), whose structure is shown in Figure 8.8. Here you can create a DESTRUCTION WORKLIST for *expired resources*, for example, archive files, attachments, or print lists. You can then release these resources for deletion; because the minimum (can be destroyed) or maximum (must be destroyed) retention period has been reached. Schedule a job for this purpose.

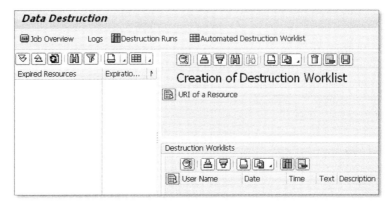

Figure 8.8 Data Destruction from the ILM Store

Creating destruction worklist

This transaction is divided into three areas:

▶ EXPIRED RESOURCES
The left area of the transaction screen lists the expired resources, for instance, archive files. A resource can be locked against deletion by a *legal hold* if the data is still required for legal reasons. Such a locked resource is indicated with a lock icon 🔒 in the list. If the destruction of a resource is overdue, that is, if it must be deleted, this resource is flagged with a red icon 🗲. A trash icon 🗑 indicates that the resource may be deleted.

▶ URI OF A RESOURCE
The resources that you dragged and dropped to the area on the right and thus selected for deletion are displayed on the right side of the transaction screen under CREATION OF A DESTRUCTION WORKLIST • URI OF A RESOURCE. Once you've transferred all relevant resources to this area, you must save your destruction worklist using the SAVE button 💾.

▶ DESTRUCTION WORKLISTS
The saved destruction worklist is then displayed in the overview of destruction worklists at the bottom right.

After you've created a destruction worklist, you can schedule the destruction of resources directly in the transaction using a job.

ILM-Enabled Archiving Objects	
You are now familiar with the three SAP ILM-specific actions of archiving objects for archiving, creation of snapshots, and data destruction. For an ILM-enabled archiving object, you must define information on its lifecycle to be able to run these SAP ILM actions. The following section informs you of how to maintain this information in SAP ILM.	

8.4 Using Retention Management

Recall the presentation of SAP ILM in Figure 8.4. We discussed the foundation of ILM, the ILM-enhanced data archiving, in the previous section. Retention Management is the first column, which is based on this foundation. The administration of the information lifecycle using SAP ILM is not feasible without the functions of Retention Management, because the Retention Management assumes the central control function and comprises all rules for retaining and storing data. Retention Management defines what data must be archived, locked, or destroyed at which point in time, and where this data may reside for and how long.

This section discusses the individual Retention Management functions in detail and illustrates the context between ILM-enhanced data archiving and system shutdown using examples.

Retention Management is subdivided into two components that provide you with the following functions:

Components and functions

▶ Information Retention Manager (IRM)

▷ Definition of SAP ILM rules for controlling retention periods and storage locations of archived data

▷ SAP ILM-compliant storage of archive files on an SAP ILM-certified WebDAV server

▷ Data destruction considering legal retention periods and locks

► Legal Case Management (LCM):

  ► Setting legal holds using ediscovery

These four functions enable you to efficiently manage the information lifecycle illustrated in Figure 8.9.

The transfer of data from the legacy systems to the retention warehouse system and to local and SAP BW-based reporting, which you can view in Figure 8.4 in addition to the four functions listed here, are only relevant for system shutdown, which is discussed in Section 8.5.

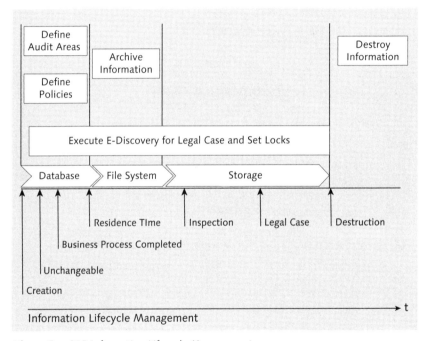

Figure 8.9 SAP Information Lifecycle Management

Figure 8.9 illustrates the management of the information lifecycle in the context of SAP ILM. You can describe SAP Information Lifecycle Management based on three characteristics:

► **Location of data**
  Data can be stored at three different locations:

- ▷ Database
- ▷ File system
- ▷ Storage

During its lifecycle, data is always created in the database first and remains there until the residence time (retention period) has passed. Only after the residence time has elapsed, can you start with the archiving of information and store the archive files temporarily in the file system. In the ideal case, the archive files are then stored in a suitable location until they can be destroyed. When you use SAP ILM, the storage involves an ILM-compliant storage in the form of a WebDAV server.

- ▶ **Activities**

  Different tasks arise within the scope of data archiving and Retention Management. These activities include, for example, the definition of audit areas and policies. Time-wise, you must complete these tasks prior to archiving of data, which is why they are positioned before the "Archive Information" activity in the timeline of Figure 8.9.

  Section 8.4.2 details the functions of the audit area and policies. The activities within the scope of SAP ILM also include the execution of e-discovery functions in legal cases and setting of locks. For these activities, no distinction is made regarding if the data is located in the database, file system, or storage. This allows you to execute e-discovery across all locations where data may exist. Locks can be set both for data in the database and for archive files.

E-Discovery [«]

The process of *e-discovery* (electronic discovery), which you can use in particular for investigating information that is stored electronically in an enterprise and compiling it for a legal case, originates from the United States and is used for taking evidence or establishing facts in court proceedings. Here the parties have the right to request comprehensive information that can be used as evidence in a legal case. This information can be available in digital and nondigital format, and it is mutually exchanged prior to the hearing. Consequently, the number of exchanged documents and data can be very high.

E-discovery is not new and has been a major topic in the United States since the end of 2006. Every enterprise should still be able to detect and provide critical data and documents within the IT systems at short notice prior to and during court proceedings. It is fatal if a party or involved enterprise is not able to detect and provide such information or has deleted it already. In such cases, the enterprise could face severe penalties and suffer a defeat in court.

For this reason, SAP ILM provides an option to meet these requirements to a large extent. Retention Management provides two functions in the Legal Case Management subcomponent for this purpose:

▶ **Search for information**
You can search for information using various e-discovery reports.

▶ **Lock the information**
The detected information can be locked against destruction—also beyond the retention period—until a legal case is closed; in other words, you can set a *legal hold*.

Besides SAP, there are many more third-party providers that offer software and services for this subject, which can be used in addition to the functions of SAP ILM if required.

▶ **Lifecycle**
The third characteristic of lifecycle management is the lifecycle of data itself divided into various phases:

▷ Creation

▷ Immutability

▷ Closed business process

▷ Residence time

▷ Check

▷ Legal case

▷ Destruction

The data in an SAP system passes through these different phases within its lifecycle. In practice, the music plays between the creation and destruction of data; that is, the data is actively used in the business processes.

Particularly, a data check or a legal case for which the data must be accessed can enhance the meaning of data again even after archiving. For this reason, adequate archive access must be available during these two phases of the information lifecycle. If required, you should also use the functions of e-discovery to restrict the destruction of data until a legal case has been closed.

Retention of Data Due to a Legal Case   [Ex]

Based on an example, we'll detail the interaction of the individual storage locations, activities, and lifecycle phases in the context of Retention Management: The leading automobile manufacturer Road Cruiser Inc. sold an exclusive vehicle to a very famous Hollywood star. Various data records are created in Road Cruiser Inc.'s SAP system during order entry and configuration of the vehicle's equipment. A sales document and a production order are created; the invoice is issued later on. The business process is completed after the invoice has been paid and the vehicle is delivered.

Due to the different residence times, it is possible that specific data, for example, FI documents, have already been archived during the course of the ongoing archiving activities while other data, for example, SD documents, are still located in the database. Road Cruiser Inc. now learns from the media that the famous Hollywood star had an accident with the said vehicle and broke his arm in the course of it. Because he can't continue with the shooting of his new blockbuster due to the plastered arm, he attributes the accident primarily to a manufacturing defect. He decides to take legal action against Road Cruiser Inc. and files a suit (product liability).

As a result, the enterprise's legal department requests the IT department to detect and provide all relevant data and documents for the vehicle in the SAP system. Due to the media impact and imminent loss of image, it is a special matter of urgency and requires full provision of information. Because data has already been archived, the enterprise requires a solution that can search for data not only in the database but also in the file system and in the storage. Particularly for such legal cases, Retention Management provides the option to detect data using an e-discovery report and lock it against destruction.

You can still archive data in the database that is locked from destruction. In this case, the archive file inherits the information that a locked data object is included and thus cannot be destroyed either. The following section describes how such a legal case is set up technically in SAP ILM and how to use an e-discovery report.

8.4.1   Securing Archiving Objects

Legal Case Management

With the SAP ILM component LCM, you can protect archive data against scheduled destruction. The component enables you to create legal cases in SAP ILM. LCM is based on Records and Case Management, which you probably use in your enterprise within the scope of records management. In this area too, SAP ILM builds on a known solution and adapts it but only to a minimum extent.

Creating a legal case

To use Legal Case Management, you must first create a legal case in Transaction SCASE (see Figure 8.10). You can insert all relevant data in this record. In our Hollywood star example, you could assign all relevant archived or nonarchived evidence and documents to the legal case.

Figure 8.10 Initial Screen of Transaction SCASE

E-discovery reports

To populate the legal case with information, you must run a research. Different e-discovery reports (programs) are available for various data types to determine the relevant data including:

- `REDIS_FI11` (Posting Documents)
- `REDIS_SD11` (Sales Documents)
- `REDIS_SD12` (Deliveries)
- `REDIS_MM12` (Purchase Orders)

Similarity to DRB

These programs are built on the Document Relationship Browser, which was presented in Chapter 3, Section 3.4 in the context of Transaction ALO1. It is also a known solution that is used within the scope of SAP ILM. To be able to utilize the e-discovery reports for research in the archive, you require archive infostructures that already exist for using Transaction ALO1.

Figure 8.11 shows the initial screen of report `REDIS_SD11` for searching sales documents.   E-discovery report

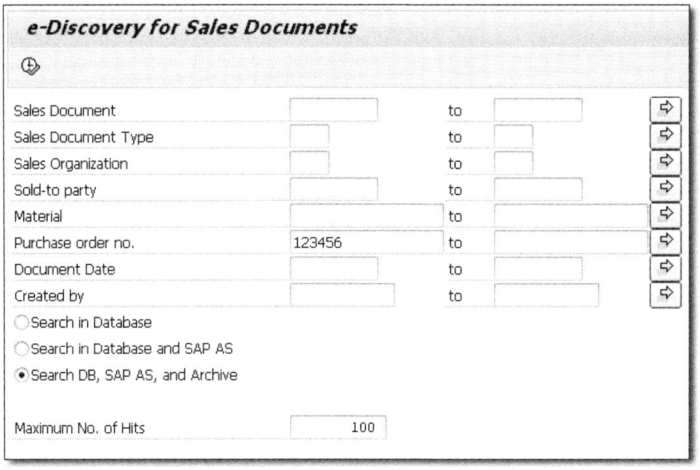

Figure 8.11 E-Discovery for Sales Documents Using Report REDIS_SD11

Here you can also enter a purchase order number, for example, to search for the sales documents relating to the Hollywood star's purchase order. In other words, in an e-discovery report, you utilize a document, in this case a sales document or purchase order number, to determine all other associated documents (document flow), which you can copy to the legal case you previously created and lock it against deletion.

The system automatically sets the necessary locks for all data added to the legal case. These locks are also referred to as *legal holds* and are managed in table `LHM_LEGAL_HOLDS`. The lock only prevents the destruction of archive files. The data in the database can still be archived despite this lock. The archive file inherits the lock from the data object.   Setting legal holds

After the close of a legal case, you should undo the locks again. You have three options to delete legal holds: Deleting legal holds

▸ You delete the reference to the object in the legal case.

▸ You delete the entire legal case.

▸ You set the legal case's status to PROCESSING COMPLETED.

All three options have the result that the corresponding locks are removed.

[◉]   **Management of Legal Cases in SAP ILM**

SAP ILM provides a simple, yet effective and IT-based aid to manage legal cases. On the one hand, you can determine the document flow for a document using an e-discovery report, which is very similar to Transaction ALO1. On the other hand, you lock the archive files that belong to the data objects against destruction as soon as the data object of an archive file is included in a legal case in Transaction SCASE.

Alternative approach for classic archiving

Classic SAP data archiving cannot provide an adequate IT-based solution for this task. Section 8.3.5 describes an alternative approach for how you can determine data records and archive files without SAP ILM using Transactions ALO1 and AS_AFB and protect them against destruction.

Figure 8.12 shows how you can search for existing legal cases in Transaction SCASE. Double-click on LEGAL HOLD: CASE SEARCH on the left-hand side. This opens the CASE SEARCH mask on the right side of the screen. Here you can restrict your search by various criteria, for example, PROCESSOR. When you click the SEARCH button, the system will display the corresponding cases at the bottom right of the window.

Figure 8.12 Search for Legal Cases in SAP Case Management

8.4.2 Defining Retention and Residence Rules

We'll now discuss the most critical area of Retention Management; that is, the definition of retention and residence rules which SAP ILM utilizes to manage the information lifecycle. The IRM is the *brain* for managing residence rules. Here you specify in detail how data is supposed to be managed. SAP ILM can't work without the definition of such retention and residence rules, because all critical actions, for example, archiving and management of data, follow these rules. For example, if you want to archive data, the ILM-enhanced archiving object refers to the rules to check how long the data must reside in the database (residence time), where it is stored, and how long it must be retained in the SAP ILM store. For this reason, you require at least two rules:

- One rule for the residence period
- One rule for the retention period

The IRM is also often referred to as *rule engine* to emphasize that the various rules are processed automatically. In this section, you will learn how to define and check retention and residence rules (simulation). But first, let's discuss some terms that are important in this context.

Rule engine

Figure 8.13 illustrates the relations between the various aspects of the policy in the IRM.

Objects in IRM

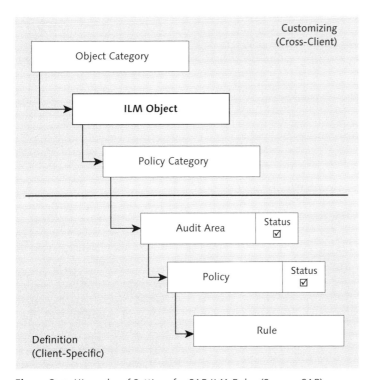

Figure 8.13 Hierarchy of Settings for SAP ILM Rules (Source: SAP)

Rule management is subdivided into two areas:

► Cross-client Customizing

► Client-specific definition of SAP ILM rules

The Customizing activities that apply to all clients in an SAP system are shown in the upper area of Figure 8.13. These settings are predefined in the SAP standard and are only enhanced for special requirements. In the following sections, we'll walk through the hierarchy of settings step by step and take a detailed look at the individual rules.

Object Category

Grouping of objects The object category is at the top of the hierarchy and is predefined by the SAP system. Each ILM object is already assigned to an object category in Customizing. The system groups the ILM objects by their application area and assigns them to an object category based on the values that are predefined in this field. The following object categories are available in SAP ILM (see Figure 8.14):

► **SAP Business Suite (OT_FOR_BS)**
This object category is intended for storing data objects in an SAP system.

► **Paper Documents (OT_FOR_PD)**
This object category is intended for nonelectronic documents—that is, physical paper documents outside the SAP system. Because the paper documents don't exist in the SAP system, you only manage the storage period but not the retention period.

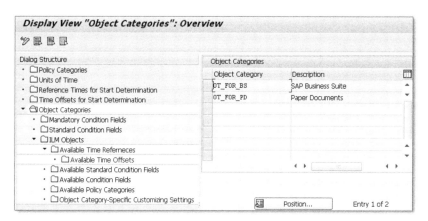

Figure 8.14 Object Categories in SAP ILM in Transaction IRM_CUST

Besides the ILM objects that have already been assigned in the SAP standard, you can also assign additional ILM objects to these two object categories that cannot be changed. The next section outlines what type of ILM objects you can assign here and what the term *ILM object* actually means.

ILM Object

The term *ILM object* exists in addition to the term *ILM-enabled archiving objects*. The term ILM object is superordinate to the term ILM-enabled archiving object; that is, an ILM object usually is also an archiving object. Each ILM-enabled archiving object must be assigned to at least one ILM object in Transaction IRM_CUST_BS. This assignment has already been done for existing ILM objects so that you only need to take action for new ILM objects.

SAP ILM also provides other types of ILM objects in addition to ILM-enabled archiving objects: **Types of ILM objects**

- Data destruction objects, for example, BC_SFLIGHT_DESTRUCTION (sample object for data destruction)
- Snapshots, for example, SN_META
- Paper document objects, for example, PAPER_DOCS

Using the various object types, you can distinguish whether an ILM object is an archiving object or another object.

> **Assignment to an ILM Object** [«]
>
> The following requirements must be met when you assign ILM-enabled archiving objects and data destruction objects to an ILM object:
> - An ILM-enabled archiving object must be assigned to exactly one ILM object. However, several ILM-enabled archiving objects can be assigned to one ILM object (1: n relationship).
> - A data destruction object must be assigned to exactly one ILM object. However, only one data destruction object can be assigned to an ILM object (1:1 relationship).
>
> Make sure to observe these relationship rules during assignment.

Customizing You can adapt ILM objects to your individual requirements in Customizing. Customizing of ILM objects can be performed in the following two areas of Transaction IRM_CUST_BS:

- General settings
- Specific settings

General settings The general settings are independent of the object categories. That is, these settings only apply to the object category SAP Business Suite (OT_FOR_BS) or only to paper documents (OT_FOR_PD), for example. The following general settings are possible:

- **Inheriting possible**
  An ILM object can inherit the rules of another ILM object if you enable inheriting. For example, an invoice can inherit the storage rule of the associated delivery data. This has the advantage that the rule is maintained at one point only. This simplifies the customizing and definition of rules for ILM objects.

- **Available time references (implicit and explicit start date determination)**
  Depending on your Customizing settings, you can use the time reference to determine which date is suitable as the *start date* for applying the SAP ILM rules. Two different methods are available for this purpose:

  - Implicit start date determination
  - Explicit start date determination

[»] **Start Date Determination**

Figure 8.15 illustrates the two methods for determining the start date. Besides creating a *time reference* using the creation date of data (CREATION_DATE), you also have the option to define a *time offset* for this creation date, for example, to time the start of rule application at the end of the year in which the data was created (END_OF_YEAR).

Determine start date explicitly
In the first step, you determine the reference date (in this case, the creation date 06/20/2014) either directly from the data record or indirectly via a function module (BADI_IRM_OT_STT). If you don't define a time offset for the creation date, the reference date and the start date are identical (06/20/2014). With the time offset END_OF_YEAR, the start date is deferred to the end of the year (12/31/2014).

Determine start date implicitly

There is no time offset for implicit start date determination. Here the time reference is used as the basis to decide whether the start date is determined directly in the data record (CREATION_DATE) or indirectly in the function module BADI_IRM_STT (END_OF_YEAR).

It depends on the ILM objects' Customizing whether the start date is determined implicitly or explicitly/directly or indirectly. It is critical to maintain the SAP ILM rules and Customizing in such a way that legal and enterprise-specific requirements are met.

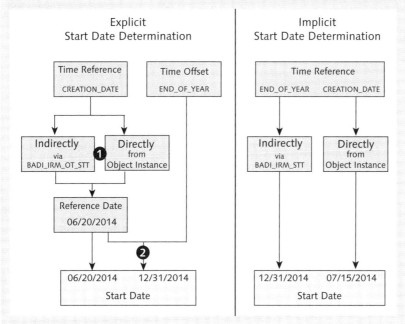

Figure 8.15 Start Date Determination (Source: SAP)

▶ **Available time offsets**

As described previously, you can specify time offsets for explicit start date determination. Among others, the following time offsets are provided in the SAP system:

▷ END_OF_MONTH

▷ END_OF_QUARTER

▷ END_OF_YEAR

With these time offsets, you can defer the start date for applying the ILM rule to the end of the month, quarter, or year. To define your own time offsets, you can use the function module BADI_IRM_TO.

[+] **Coordination with Legal Periods**

Particularly the time offset at the end of the year is a very useful setting option, because the retention period for data starts at the end of the year pursuant to most international laws. If you created a data record for an invoice on January 21, 2014, for example, in most countries, the retention period starts at the end of the year on 12/31/2014 and not directly after creation of the data record.

► **Available standard condition fields**
The standard condition fields CLIENT and SYSTEM ID are available. The information provided in these two fields is mandatory for defining SAP ILM rules so that SAP ILM can differentiate to which clients and SAP systems they apply.

► **Available condition fields**
Additional condition fields could be, for example, the company code as an organizational unit and the country assigned to this company code. You can thus refine the SAP ILM rules and create them separated by countries, for example. The appropriate condition field is called BS_COUNTRY_OF_BUKRS.

► **Available policy categories**
You must specify for each ILM object for which of the available policy categories users may define SAP ILM rules. Two policy categories are available in SAP ILM (*retention rules* and *residence rules*), which are discussed in detail in the following section.

Specific settings   The specific Customizing settings for ILM objects differ considerably from the general settings. You can call them in Transaction IRM_CUST_BS (IRM Customizing (Business Suite)), which is shown in Figure 8.16.

Under DIALOG STRUCTURE on the left-hand side, you can view various folders and setting options for an ILM OBJECT. The list of ILM objects is available on the right. There you can see the ILM-enabled archiving objects, for instance, BC_SBAL (Application Log), as well as the data destruction object BC_SFLIGHT_DESTRUCTION, among others.

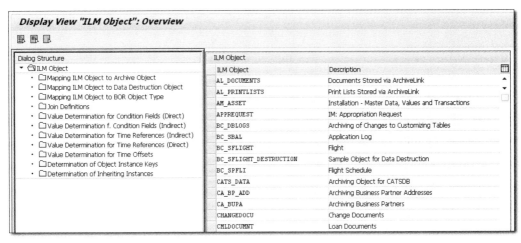

Figure 8.16 Transaction IRM_CUST_BS

Select, for example, the ILM-enabled archiving object RL_TA on the right and double-click on the VALUE DETERMINATION FOR TIME REFERENCES (INDIRECT) folder on the left. This takes you to the detail screen of this setting. In the IRM CONSTANT column, you can see that the start date is determined implicitly and indirectly because the time reference END_OF_ YEAR is entered (see Figure 8.17).

Transaction
IRM_CUST_BS

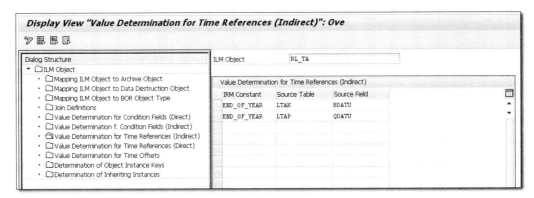

Figure 8.17 Value Determination for Time References (Indirectly)

Policy Categories

After you've received an overview of general and specific setting options in the ILM objects' Customizing, let's continue with the description of

Two policies

the individual levels of the hierarchy for SAP ILM rules—the policy categories. SAP ILM distinguishes two policy categories:

▸ Retention rules (technical key RTP)

▸ Residence rules (technical key RST)

These two policy categories control the lifecycle of data in an SAP system. The policy categories specify which type of rules can be defined for an ILM object.

Retention rules

Retention rules particularly control the lifecycle of archive files in the SAP ILM store. In contrast to the content repository whose lifecycle is controlled on the archive side, every archive file in SAP ILM is assigned with an individual minimum and maximum retention period, which is managed directly via the SAP system.

Residence rules

You can compare residence rules with the residence time of data in classic data archiving. By means of the residence rules, you specify for how long the data must remain in the database before it may be archived. The subsequent section provides examples of retention and residence rules.

Audit Area

Client-specific definition

In the lower area of Figure 8.13 you can see the hierarchy levels of the ILM rules that are defined client-specifically. In other words, all settings that you make here apply to only one client of an SAP system.

You group the ILM objects in audit areas. The grouping is based on business criteria. For example, you can define one group for tax inspections or another one for product liabilities, because inspections in these two areas are usually based on different ILM objects.

Audit areas as template

The following audit areas already exist in SAP ILM for testing purposes and as templates:

▸ TAX (tax inspection)

▸ PRODLIABIL (warranty and product liability)

▸ DEMO (for demonstration or test purposes, without SAP BW queries)

▸ GENERAL (all objects that are not assigned to a specific audit area)

In addition to objects from the central SAP ERP application, these audit areas include objects from the industry solutions, for example, SAP for Utilities (IS-U), which was described as an example in Chapter 5, Section 5.1.3.

You can view and process the audit areas using Transaction ILMARA (Process Audit Areas). To be able to create rules for ILM objects in an audit area at all, the audit area must have the *active* status.

Processing/ activating audit areas

Policies

Within audit areas, you group individual rules for an ILM object in *policies* (see Figure 8.18). It is possible to create several policies for an ILM object distinguished by countries. For ILM object FI_DOCUMNT, for example, you can create a policy for USA and a policy for Canada.

Rule collections

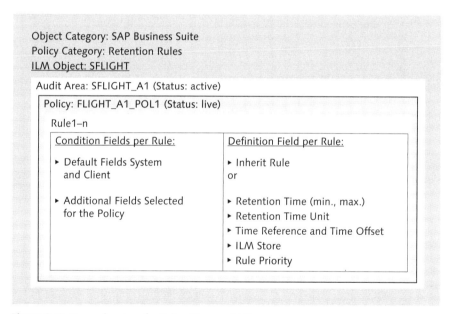

Figure 8.18 Dependencies of a Policy (Source: SAP)

A policy must have the *live* status so that it can be used in production. Only then can the individual rules be created.

Setting the policy to live

Rules

We've now reached the lowest and also most critical level of SAP IRM. With SAP ILM rules, you specify what data is archived and destroyed at which point in time. You also define where the archive files are stored. At the beginning, we identified IRM as the "brain" of SAP ILM. Analogous to this metaphor, the SAP ILM rules represent the brain cells that are required to decide as to how ILM objects are to be handled.

Defining rules

There are different approaches to define rules, because the information you require for retention rules differs from the information required for residence rules.

Defining retention rules

Let's first take a detailed look at retention rules. Retention rules ensure that data is retained in the SAP system and the SAP ILM store according to the specified period of time. For this purpose, the SAP system determines the minimum and maximum retention period for the ILM object. To define a retention rule for a policy in Transaction IRMPOL (ILM Policies), you must provide the information from Table 8.2:

Information	Description
Policy	Policy name for which you define the SAP ILM rules.
Value of condition fields	System, client, etc.
Inherit rule	If rules are to be inherited pursuant to the ILM object's Customizing, an existing rule can be inherited. No further information is required in this case.
Minimum retention time	The minimum retention time is calculated based on the start date determined.
Maximum retention time	The maximum retention time is calculated based on the start date determined. It also specifies the mandatory destruction date.
Retention time unit	The retention time unit can be specified in days, months, or years.
Time reference	The time reference is used to determine the start date based on the reference date, and it can be postponed using a time offset.

Table 8.2 Information for a Retention Rule

Information	Description
Time offset	If a time offset is set in Customizing, the reference date is postponed accordingly.
ILM store	Name of the SAP ILM store.
Content repository and logical file name	Hidden by default, can be displayed as required. The archive files are supplemented with retention information during the storage process. This is only possible for the ILM store.
Rule number	The rule number is assigned internally by the SAP system and identifies the rule.
Rule priority	This column can be shown as specified in SAP Note 1617105. In case of overlapping conditions, the SAP system selects the rule with the highest priority.

Table 8.2 Information for a Retention Rule (Cont.)

Transaction IRMPOL displays this information for a retention rule in tabular form as illustrated in Figure 8.19. Here you can see a rule in the TEST policy (POLICY NAME column). Among other things, you can identify the condition fields for the SAP SYSTEM and the CLIENT, the minimum (2) and maximum retention time (10), as well as the time unit (YEAR).

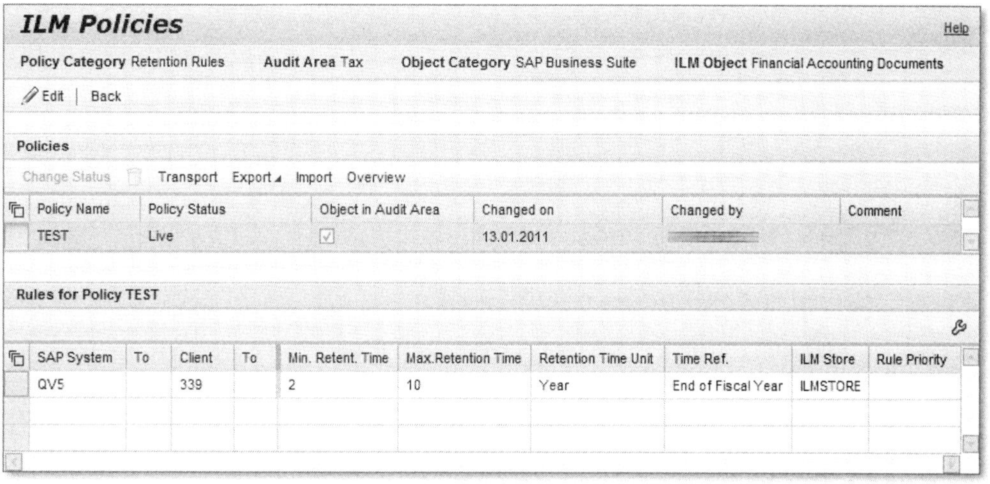

Tabular presentation

Figure 8.19 Defining Retention Rules in Transaction IRMPOL

Defining residence rules   Residence rules are defined similarly in Transaction IRMPOL. Here, however, you must provide other information, which is listed in Table 8.3.

Information	Description
Policy	Policy name for which you define the SAP ILM rules.
Value of condition fields	System, client, etc.
Inherit rule	If rules are to be inherited pursuant to the ILM object's Customizing, an existing rule can be inherited. No further information is required in this case.
Retention time	The retention time is calculated based on the start date specified.
Residence time unit	The residence time unit can be specified in days, months, or years.
Time reference	The time reference is used to determine the start date based on the reference date, and it can be postponed using a time offset.
Time offset	If a time offset is set in Customizing, the reference date is postponed accordingly.
Rule number	The rule number is assigned internally by the SAP system and identifies the rule.
Rule priority	This column can be shown as specified in SAP Note 1617105. In case of overlapping conditions, the SAP system selects the rule with the highest priority.

Table 8.3 Information for a Residence Rule

Changing the rules   You can change retention and residence rules as long as the associated policy has not been set live yet. The changes don't apply until new archiving sessions are run.

[»]   **Personal Liability**

Please be aware that you define SAP ILM rules independently and therefore assume responsibility/liability for them. Rules that have been created incorrectly can lead to undesirable results, for example, premature archiving or destruction of data. An SAP ILM rule simulation exists to prevent further complication of your work in SAP ILM due to such risks.

You can leverage Transaction ILMSIM (ILM Rule Simulation) to simulate the implementation of SAP ILM rules. Here you must select the POLICY CATEGORY and the ILM OBJECT before you run the simulation.

SAP ILM rule simulation

The following options are available for selecting the policy category when you start the SAP ILM rule simulation:

Selecting the policy category

▶ RTP (Retention Rules)

▶ RST (Residence Rules)

In the example of Figure 8.20 and Figure 8.21, we picked ILM object RL_TA for simulating the utilization of residence rules (RST) and ILM object IDOC for simulating the utilization of retention rules (RTP).

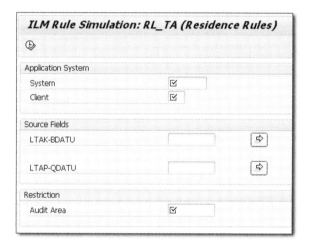

Figure 8.20 ILM Rule Simulation for RL_TA Residence Rules

The SAP ILM rule simulation for ILM object RL_TA in the area of residence rules requires you to provide information in the SYSTEM and CLIENT fields (see Figure 8.20). Additionally, you require a RESTRICTION for the AUDIT AREA. You must specify the AUDIT AREA to be able to derive the policies that qualify for this ILM object. In the SOURCE FIELDS area, you can find the fields LTAK-BDATU (creation date) and LTAP-QDATU (date of acknowledgment), which you can use for a targeted simulation based on a specific date. For this purpose, you can simply enter the desired date in the corresponding empty field.

Simulation for RL_TA

Simulation for IDOC The SAP ILM rule simulation for ILM object `IDOC` in the area of residence rules also requires you to provide information in the SYSTEM and CLIENT fields. Because you can also maintain rules for other systems and clients in IRM, this helps you to delimit the application of rules. Additionally, you require a RESTRICTION for the AUDIT AREA. In the SOURCE FIELDS area, you can find the fields `EDIDC-DOCNUM` (IDoc number) and `EDIDC-CREDAT` (creation date), which you can use for a targeted simulation based on a specific IDoc and date. In the OPTIONS area, you can select the DETERMINE DESTRUCTIBILITY setting. If you select this option, you receive information as to when this ILM object may be destroyed. If you click the corresponding button ⊕ (see Figure 8.21) to simulate the rule for the `IDOC` object, the result of the simulation is displayed in a log. Use this log to check if the rule simulation meets your expectations (see Figure 8.22).

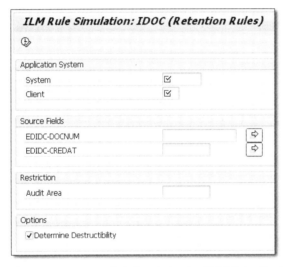

Figure 8.21 SAP ILM Rule Simulation for IDOC Retention Rules

[◉] **Summary: Meaning of ILM Rules**

SAP ILM and Retention Management are based on valid and active SAP ILM rules. Only by means of these rules can you manage the lifecycle. Because SAP ILM rules must be maintained very carefully and because you assume responsibility and liability for their correct handling, the SAP ILM rule simulator provides the option to check newly created SAP ILM rules and then continue with the archiving or destruction of objects.

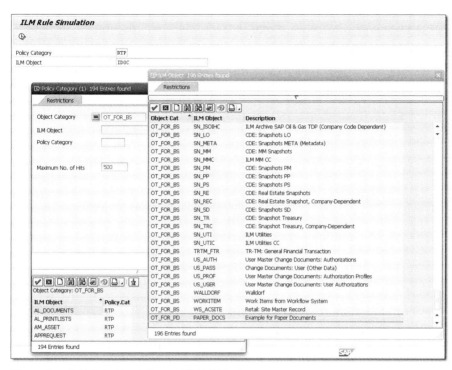

Figure 8.22 ILM Rule Simulation and ILM Objects

8.4.3 Storing Data

In the following section, you'll learn how to store data when you use SAP ILM. The storage differs from classic SAP data archiving in several points as was already described in Chapter 2, Section 2.2. Archive files are not stored in a content repository of the archive system, but via the ILM-enhanced WebDAV interface and—usually—on a WebDAV server (ILM store) according to a uniform structure. Documents and print lists, however, are still stored in a content repository via the ArchiveLink interface when you deploy SAP ILM.

Specific features

Also, the names of archive files differ considerably from those you've gotten to know in the context of Transaction FILE in Chapter 1, Section 1.4.5. The archive files are stored under their name as Unique Resource Identifiers (URI) on the WebDAV server and can be called directly via a link.

File names in SAP ILM

447

[◉] **Storage for SAP ILM**

You must consider the following points in the context of storage when you use SAP ILM:

▸ You can store archive files either on the SAP IQ database (ILM database store) or on a WebDAV server (ILM store) using the ILM-enhanced Web-DAV interface.

▸ You cannot store documents and print lists on the SAP IQ database. You still require an archive system for this purpose.

▸ Upon storage, the archive files (resources) are addressed with a URI.

▸ You can view all resources stored in the SAP ILM store via the ILM Store Browser.

The storage of archive files using SAP ILM differs from the storage in classic data archiving; the complexity, however, is negligible.

8.5   Implementing System Shutdowns

System shutdown as a challenge

Enterprises install and implement new SAP systems on a constant basis. Every new SAP system can have a predecessor system in real life, which is referred to as a *legacy system*. The legacy system can be either an SAP system or a non-SAP system. Regardless of this, the question arises as to how you should handle this legacy system in case of a system shutdown. Due to legal retention periods, enterprises are forced to keep the data of these legacy systems available for a specified period of time. After all, it could be possible that the auditor sends another request after an audit is conducted or that data must remain available for other legal obligations, for example, manufacturer's liability.

Many enterprises find it difficult to answer the question as to how they should proceed with legacy systems. Ongoing operating costs for these legacy systems are one aspect here. Also, support for aging technology no longer offered by software and hardware manufacturers or only provided at high costs is another critical topic for enterprises.

Options for system shutdown

The following options for handling legacy systems are currently available for enterprises:

- Continue the operation of the legacy system (also on virtual servers)
- Shut down the legacy system with non-SAP solutions
- Shut down the legacy system with the SAP ILM solution

In this section, we'll take a detailed look at the last option available, the system shutdown using SAP ILM. For this purpose, we'd first like to outline the procedure based on Figure 8.23 before we continue with detailed descriptions.

System shutdown using SAP ILM

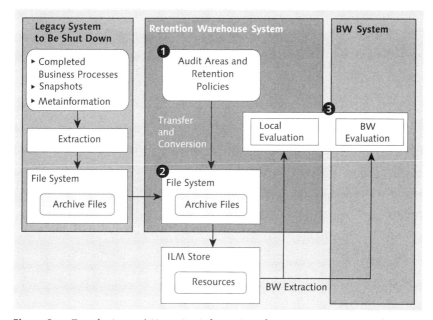

Figure 8.23 Transferring and Managing Information of a Legacy System to Be Shut Down in Retention Warehouse (Source: SAP)

In the center you can see the retention warehouse system. In case of a system shutdown, you require a new SAP system for inspection and evaluation purposes that contains the SAP ILM component. This ILM system can be supplemented with an SAP BW system so that certain evaluations in SAP BW can be made faster.

BW system is recommended

On the left-hand side of Figure 8.23, you can find a legacy system to be shut down whose data must first be transferred to the retention ware-

449

house system. The system shutdown is subdivided into the following three steps:

❶ In the retention warehouse system, you must create the audit areas and retention policies using the Information Retention Manager. You must make this step implicitly prior to transferring the archive files so that the archive files can be supplemented with this information. Only then can SAP ILM manage these archive files using rules.

❷ All relevant data is extracted or archived from the legacy system. This particularly includes data on completed business processes, snapshots (open business processes), and metainformation. Subsequently, this data is transferred to the retention warehouse system in the form of archive files. The rules are converted and stored as a resource in the corresponding directory structures of the SAP ILM store. All data that must be preserved for legal reasons is now transferred securely and completely from the legacy system.

❸ The last step is to evaluate these resources (archive files). You can do this in the retention warehouse system, which ultimately is a regular SAP system, and in an optional SAP BW system. If you use an SAP BW system, the data is extracted to this system and can be deleted again after evaluation.

In practical use, these three steps involve several individual activities. We'll detail these activities in the following sections.

8.5.1 Preparing a System Shutdown

Requirements Before you can start with the system shutdown, you must consider and prepare several points:

▸ The legacy system must be prepared for the shutdown.

▸ The retention warehouse system must be prepared for the transfer of archive files from the legacy system.

The corresponding ILM objects for all data to be transferred must be available and utilizable in the legacy system. This is not possible offhand in case of older releases. Here you must first clarify if a system shutdown of your legacy system is supported. If required, you must provide the corresponding ILM objects in cooperation with SAP SLO.

You require the IRM, a component of Retention Management, to transfer archive files from the legacy system. The IRM also plays a significant role within the scope of system shutdown so that the transferred archive files can be supplemented with lifecycle information upon storage. Section 8.4.2 described how to set the IRM.

8.5.2 Transferring Data from the Legacy System to the Retention Warehouse System

Perhaps the most critical task within the scope of a system shutdown is to transfer the relevant data from the legacy system to the retention warehouse system. Here you must clarify which data is still required, that is, whether you have to transfer all data or only specific parts thereof. On the basis of Figure 8.24, you learn which data and information is transferred from the legacy system to the retention warehouse system using SAP ILM.

In Transaction ILM_TRANS_ADMIN, these transfer steps are included in various tabs (transfer archived data from the legacy system), which you must process step by step:

Data to be transferred

1. **Transfer archive files and snapshots**

   All data from the legacy system to be shut down is transferred to the file system of the retention warehouse system in the form of archive files and snapshots. For this purpose, however, you must initially call each individual relevant archive object, for example, FI_DOCUMNT, in Transaction SARA and first run the SAP ILM action ARCHIVING.

   You then create snapshots for all data records or master data that cannot be archived using the SAP ILM action SNAPSHOT. You thus ensure that you transfer both completed and open business cases from the legacy system.

   A legitimate question is, which archiving objects do you actually require to transfer the data from the legacy system completely? This depends, on the one hand, on the SAP components deployed and, on the other hand, on the audit areas and the ILM objects contained therein (archiving objects). Only a detailed system analysis can provide a statement about the archiving objects that are relevant for your enterprise.

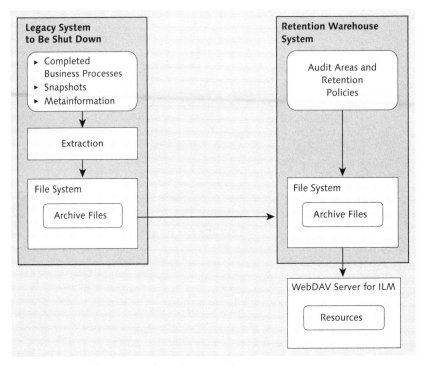

Figure 8.24 Transferring Data from the Legacy System

2. **Convert and store metainformation**
   Before you convert and store archive files and snapshots, you must first convert and store the metainformation (SN_META). This contains important information on the administration of archive files.

3. **Transfer metainformation to the repository of the retention warehouse system**
   By means of the RIWP_LOAD_REPOS report, you transfer the SN_META archive file, which has already been stored to the retention warehouse system's repository. You thus have information about the legacy system's metadata available in the retention warehouse system and can process the transferred data correctly.

4. **Optional: Define and execute checksums**
   Before you convert and store the transferred archive files and snapshots, you also have the option to calculate a checksum. This step is no longer available after the conversion for the SAP ILM store (WebDAV

server). With this checksum you can determine if all data has been converted and stored correctly and completely.

For this purpose, create an analysis variant using the fields of an ILM object's table in Transaction ILMCHECK (Define and Execute Checksums). This forms the calculation basis for comparing the archive files and snapshots before and after conversion. You can now convert and store the snapshots (step 5) and archive files (step 6) to then re-execute the checksums and compare them with the result (step 7).

5. **Convert and store snapshots**
There is a concrete sequence of how data is transferred from the legacy system to the retention warehouse system. First, we converted and stored the metadata (SN_META) in step 2. Only then can we convert and store the snapshots (SN_*) and finally the transaction data in the form of archive files (file extension *.adk*).

6. **Convert and store transaction data**
As we already described in step 5, the conversion and storage of transaction data (archive files) does not take place until you've converted and stored the snapshots.

7. **Optional: Execute snapshots**
You run the checksum analysis after file conversion using Transaction ILMCHECK again. Select the analysis variant you've created in step 4, and click the STORAGE button to run a comparison with the archive files from the ILM store. The results are divided into two areas:

- Prior to file conversion
- After file conversion

It provides you with the number of entries or sums of fields from the analysis variant. If all values are identical, you can assume successful conversion and continue with the subsequent steps.

8. **Transfer link information for ArchiveLink documents**
You not only transfer the archive files from the legacy system but also the link information (TOAx tables) for ArchiveLink documents and Customizing to the retention warehouse system. During transfer, you only create empty references to the documents that are stored in a content repository in the ILM store hierarchy. Report ARLNK_MOVE_META_REMOTE is available for this purpose. You create this report in the legacy system and execute it there.

9. **Apply retention rules for ArchiveLink documents**

In the retention warehouse system, the only thing that's left to do is to apply the retention rules to the empty references in the WebDAV hierarchy. In this context, this is referred to as *propagating*. A report is contained in the menu of the SAP_BC_ILM_ARCHIVELINK role for this purpose.

Processing these nine steps ensures that all relevant information is transferred from the legacy system to the retention warehouse system. You can now evaluate this data.

8.5.3 Evaluating Data

A very important step after a system shutdown is to evaluate the data from the legacy system. The option to evaluate is absolutely necessary to be able to shut down the legacy systems. For this reason, the requirements are particularly high at this point. Not only users but also auditors must be satisfied with the evaluation options that are provided by SAP ILM. As you've seen in Figure 8.23, the evaluation can be made either locally in the retention warehouse system or even in a BW system. This section describes both options in more detail.

View files for tax auditors

Of particular importance is the provision of tax-relevant data within the scope of electronic tax inspections that you create with DART in the case of classic data archiving. Although you can still create DART extracts in SAP ILM and also provide view files for tax auditors, you would not fully exploit the evaluation options in the retention warehouse system. There's another approach that still leads to the desired result, as you will see in the following section.

Evaluation in the Retention Warehouse System

No evaluation with standard transactions

The retention warehouse system is an SAP ILM system that you require in the case of a system shutdown. Although this SAP system includes all standard transactions, for example, FB03 (Display FI Document), you can't leverage their evaluation functions for the archive files from the legacy systems. The difference in the legacy system is that the retention warehouse system provides this data for reporting as audit packages in tabular form in Transaction IWP01. The following section presents Transaction IWP01 for SAP BW reporting, which can also be used for local reporting in a similar fashion.

Evaluation in SAP BW (Optional)

A new and more interesting option is to evaluate the data using a supplementing SAP BW. The SAP BW system enables you to analyze data from the legacy system using a different approach.

New evaluation options

First you create an audit package in the retention warehouse system in which you specify the data that is required for evaluation.

Creating an audit package

1. For this purpose, call Transaction IWP01 (Audit Package Handling; see Figure 8.25).

Figure 8.25 Creating Audit Packages

2. You can create a new audit package using the CREATE BY COPYING button 🗋. A new browser window opens that provides a wizard to guide you through the creation steps.

3. Here you are prompted step by step to specify the audit area, to select the archive files and parameters, and to enter a name and a description for the audit package.

4. In Transaction SE16, you can check in table IWP_WP (Audit Packages) if your audit package has been created successfully.

After you've created the audit package, it must be generated; in other words, it must be populated with data.

Generating an audit package

1. For this purpose, call Transaction IWP_WP_GENERATE (see Figure 8.26).

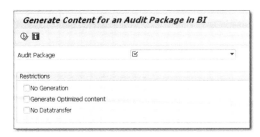

Figure 8.26 Generating an Audit Package in Transaction IWP_WP_GENERATE

2. Select your newly created audit package, and click the Execute button
⊕.

3. Subsequently, a new job is created, and the audit package is populated
with the data you've selected.

Executing the report You have different options to display data from the audit package. The
following selection buttons are available in Transaction IWP01 (see Figure 8.25):

▶ BW Reporting

▶ Local Reporting

If you select the BW Reporting option, the following options are provided for selection:

▶ Extract Audit Package to BW

▶ Display Information

▶ Display BW Table

▶ Call Audit Trail

▶ Delete Audit Package in BW

So you can first extract the data of an existing audit package to the BW
system and display it there. Subsequently, you can delete the audit package in the BW system to free up memory space.

Additionally, you can also use the SAP Business Explorer Analyzer (BEx
Analyzer) for displaying data. We'll describe this process using an example.

Execution in the To execute a report in the BEx Analyzer, you must call it. This opens
BEx Analyzer Microsoft Excel.

1. Click the OPEN REPORTS button, and enter the system ID and the client of the retention warehouse system.

2. The predefined reports are now displayed (see Figure 8.27).

3. There are various subdirectories, for example, TAX AUDIT, in the INFORMATION LIFECYCLE MANAGEMENT directory. You can find tax-relevant FI tables marked in Figure 8.27.

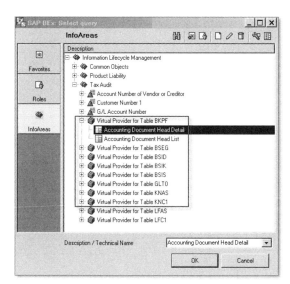

Figure 8.27 Executing Predefined Reports

4. In these tables, for example, in table BKPF, you can filter and display data records (see Figure 8.28).

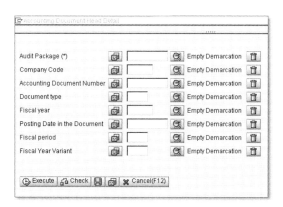

Figure 8.28 Filtering and Displaying Data Records for Table BKPF

5. The data records are displayed in Microsoft Excel after a few seconds, as illustrated in Figure 8.29.

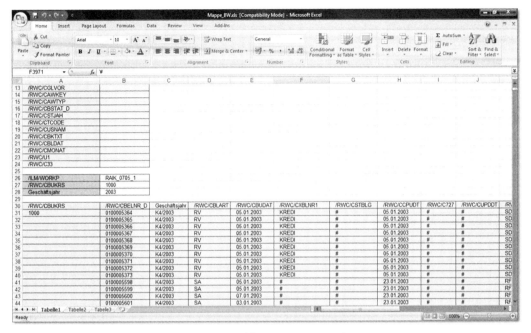

Figure 8.29 Output in Excel from Business Warehouse

6. To display attachments to a data record from table BKPF, select the corresponding row, right-click to open the context menu, and click on VIEW ATTACHMENTS. The attachments are displayed as shown in Figure 8.30.

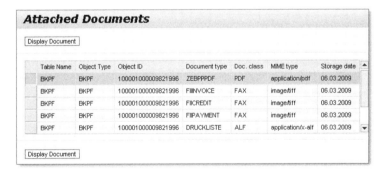

Figure 8.30 Attachment of a Data Record from Table BKPF

7. When you double-click an attachment, you can view the associated original document.

8. To compare the data records in the SAP BW system or in the retention warehouse system with the data of the legacy system, you can also call the corresponding FI document in the legacy system using Transaction FB03 (Display Document). There you will find the same values and attachments of this data record.

As soon as you've completed the evaluations for the audit package, you can delete it in Transaction IWP01 by clicking the trash button 🗑.   *Deleting a report*

View Files for Tax Auditors

You must also meet the legal requirements that arise within the scope of electronic tax inspections in various countries for shutdown legacy systems. In the United States, you usually create data extracts using DART and use them to generate the corresponding view files for tax auditors. When you use SAP ILM, you can provide view files for tax auditors from the retention warehouse system. SAP ILM has adopted this technology from DART and adapted it to the framework conditions of SAP ILM.

The menu for providing view files for tax auditors is structured as shown in Figure 8.31. This menu is contained in the SAP_ILM_WP_ADMIN role (administrator role for ILM audit package administration).   *Creating audit files*

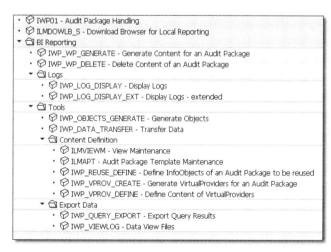

- 🞐 IWP01 - Audit Package Handling
- 🞐 ILMDOWLB_S - Download Browser for Local Reporting
- ▾ 🗀 BI Reporting
  - 🞐 IWP_WP_GENERATE - Generate Content for an Audit Package
  - 🞐 IWP_WP_DELETE - Delete Content of an Audit Package
  - ▾ 🗀 Logs
    - 🞐 IWP_LOG_DISPLAY - Display Logs
    - 🞐 IWP_LOG_DISPLAY_EXT - Display Logs - extended
  - ▾ 🗀 Tools
    - 🞐 IWP_OBJECTS_GENERATE - Generate Objects
    - 🞐 IWP_DATA_TRANSFER - Transfer Data
    - ▾ 🗀 Content Definition
      - 🞐 ILMVIEWM - View Maintenance
      - 🞐 ILMAPT - Audit Package Template Maintenance
      - 🞐 IWP_REUSE_DEFINE - Define InfoObjects of an Audit Package to be reused
      - 🞐 IWP_VPROV_CREATE - Generate VirtualProviders for an Audit Package
      - 🞐 IWP_VPROV_DEFINE - Define Content of VirtualProviders
  - ▾ 🗀 Export Data
    - 🞐 IWP_QUERY_EXPORT - Export Query Results
    - 🞐 IWP_VIEWLOG - Data View Files

Figure 8.31 Creating View Files in the Retention Warehouse System

1. Call Transaction IWP_QUERY_EXPORT or double-click the EXPORT QUERY RESULTS entry.

2. A dialog window opens in which you can enter your report from the SAP BW system in the BW QUERY field as well as the created AUDIT PACKAGE (see Figure 8.32). The dialog window also contains an OPTIONS FOR EXPORT IN FILE area, which comprises fields that are similar to those of the DART interface; you can select the SAP audit format, for example. Select the SAP AUDIT FORMAT for the view file, and click on EXECUTE ⊕.

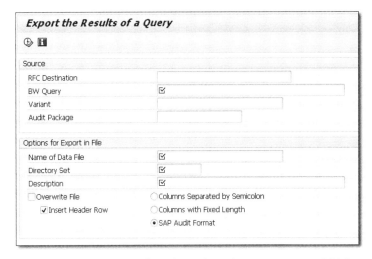

Figure 8.32 Exporting Data from the Audit Package Pursuant to a BW Query

3. After you've created the view file, you can display it by double-clicking DATA VIEW FILES in the menu.

4. The system shows an overview of all existing view files. If you select your view file and click on the DISPLAY DATA VIEWS (ALV) button 🖼 (see Figure 8.33), you can display the content.

Figure 8.33 Display of Available View Files in Transaction IWP_VIEWLOG

The SAP ILM functions ensure that there will be no redundant DART extracts created and stored within the scope of system shutdowns. The SAP ILM functions thus provide added value, because you can include archive files in an audit package and create the corresponding view files from the audit package's data. Thanks to this integration, SAP ILM remedies a major weak point of DART; namely, the creation of view files after they've been archived.

Creating view files from archive files

8.5.4 Destroying Data

In the retention warehouse system, too, you must destroy the transferred data from the legacy systems at the end of the lifecycle. Because the retention rules have already been applied during transfer, the Information Retention Manager can decide when to permanently destroy these archive files.

For this purpose, you use Transaction ILM_DESTRUCTION in the retention warehouse system, which we discussed in Section 8.3.5. In the system shutdown scenario, the archive files are also located in the storage and can be destroyed in the same way after the retention period has expired if no legal hold has been set.

8.6 Summary

You have now gotten to know new options of SAP ILM and may now decide on this basis whether you want to archive your data using SAP ILM in future or still want to use classic SAP data archiving. If you have legacy systems in your enterprise and want to shut them down, SAP ILM is the only solution provided by SAP for this purpose.

The ILM-enhanced archiving objects in combination with the Information Retention Manager enable you to efficiently control the lifecycle of data. Classic SAP data archiving doesn't provide any IT-based support for this purpose. You can only utilize the residence time to control which data may be archived from the database. Therefore, the focus of classic data archiving is to reduce the amount of data through continuous archiving activities. From this perspective, the Information Retention Manager offers real added value.

Added value thanks to Retention Management

Added value for
system shutdowns

SAP ILM is beneficial particularly for system shutdowns. In reality, system shutdowns are challenging projects for enterprises. Legacy systems not only annoy those departments that ultimately have to bear the costs for continued operation, but IT departments also face the major challenge of operating legacy systems because the hardware no longer meets the technical requirements and the software is no longer supported by the manufacturer.

Question of costs

A system shutdown is also a question of return on investment (ROI). The costs for the system shutdown should ideally amortize within a reasonable period of time; in other words, the savings you achieve through system shutdown should not exceed the costs for continued operation during the remaining retention time of legacy systems. It doesn't make sense to shut down a legacy system whose data has a remaining retention time of only two years. You should *phase out* such legacy systems. But if you're focus is on several legacy systems after you've consolidated the SAP systems in your enterprise, it is definitely a completely different business case to intensively concern yourself with SAP ILM, because the payback period of your investment decreases with the increasing number of legacy systems that you shut down. According to SAP SE, approximately ten legacy systems are the ideal prerequisite for implementing SAP ILM for system shutdowns.

Individual decision

Nevertheless, an individual cost calculation is required for every single enterprise to determine if SAP ILM qualifies for the Retention Management scenario and/or system shutdown scenario. But if you decide in favor of SAP ILM, this chapter provided you with an initial introduction to this solution, and you can leverage this knowledge in real life.

Will there still be traditional SAP data archiving in the future? How will SAP ILM establish itself in enterprises? Does SAP HANA affect data archiving? In this chapter, we provide our personal assessment with regard to these questions.

9   Future of SAP Data Archiving

A saying, credited to Heraclitus (approx. 500 BC), goes:

Nothing endures but change.

SAP data archiving has changed and developed over the last several years. And it needs to continue to do this, because the technological environment of SAP system has also changed. In this book, you learned how to successfully implement your archiving projects with traditional SAP data archiving. Furthermore, you gained an insight into the world of SAP ILM and were introduced to the new options that this solution provides.

In addition to SAP ILM, SAP HANA and cloud computing are two other developments that have been increasingly promoted by SAP. These technologies will also affect traditional data archiving to a large extent. For SAP HANA, for example, the *data aging* function is available, which enables you to move so-called *data aging objects*, e.g., FI_DOCUMENT (Financial Accounting Documents), within the database. In SAP HANA, critical data is kept in the fast memory *(hot area)* and obsolete data is transferred to the *cold area* (database). So the *data temperature* defines when data is transferred from one area to other areas.

SAP HANA and cloud computing

There is a reason why the FI_DOCUMENT data aging object has nearly the same name as SAP data archiving object FI_DOCUMNT (Financial Accounting Documents). SAP wants to build on already known terminology for the data management in SAP HANA. Section 9.3.2 describes the similarities and differences between data aging objects and SAP data archiving objects.

Outlook It is never easy to predict the future. But taking a look at the developments and trends of the past and of today is a solid basis to outline trends for the future. In the following sections, we provide our personal assessment of how SAP data archiving has developed over the last years, at which stage of development it is currently in, and which status it will have in the next ten years.

9.1 Development of Traditional SAP Data Archiving

The core of this book illustrates how you can implement your archiving project successfully with traditional SAP data archiving. The various real-life examples from our projects provided insight into versatile archiving projects at enterprises from different industries and of different sizes. We described in detail the options SAP data archiving provides.

But what were the reasons for developing data archiving, what is its status today, and where will it be in the future? Based on our experience of nearly ten years of project work in the data archiving area, the following sections describe our expectations for traditional SAP data archiving in the future. We want to try to predict the next ten years.

9.1.1 Past

Long history The beginning of traditional SAP data archiving dates back to the late 1980s and early 1990s, so SAP data archiving has a very long history. Initially, data archiving was supposed to ensure the performance of SAP systems. At that time, traditional SAP data archiving was the only method to archive data from SAP ERP systems, and it was defined as a standard by SAP. Since our first contact with SAP data archiving, it has been continuously developed and optimized.

The challenge of the archive access In particular, the archive access from standard transactions has improved considerably. Because the archive access was not always a satisfactory process for enterprises and their users, a lot of external add-on providers jumped on the bandwagon and offered their own solutions for optimized archive access.

The unsatisfactory archive access also made it harder to implement SAP data archiving projects, because archiving was not really accepted by the users due to the premature archive access. In addition to improving the archive access, the already broad selection of SAP data archiving objects has been expanded successively and the management of the archiving objects has been standardized.

9.1.2   Today

Today, SAP data archiving is still the only method to ensure the performance of an SAP system in the long run and to initiate the end of the data lifecycle. This has also not changed with the introduction of SAP ILM, because SAP data archiving also forms the basis in SAP ILM. This reassures many enterprises, because they do not have to change to SAP ILM for the already functioning data archiving processes in the SAP systems. Enterprises can continue to archive data using traditional SAP data archiving in the already implemented SAP systems, introduce new data archiving objects successively if required, and take the respective actions for traditional SAP data archiving in new SAP systems, for example, within the scope of rollouts. From this perspective, the end of traditional data archiving is not in sight, and there is no reason why enterprises should not use the established data archiving processes.

Essential part of the information lifecycle

9.1.3   Future

Today, traditional SAP data archiving is used in nearly all SAP ERP installations and will therefore also be used in this form in future. Enterprises that do not want to use SAP ILM and migrate their systems to the new SAP HANA technology will still be on the right track with traditional SAP data archiving in the future with regard to controlling the performance of the SAP system in the long term.

SAP SE, however, will implement only mandatory adaptations for traditional SAP data archiving, for example, by responding to error messages within the scope of standard support measures. Major changes cannot be expected here, because traditional data archiving has been established and proved for many years.

Necessary optimizations

In case of optimizations, we mainly expect them to be implemented in the archive access area to successively improve the quality of display transactions from which traditional data archiving and SAP ILM benefit. As described in Chapter 3, there is still considerable potential for various SAP data archiving objects and their display transactions. To motivate SAP to implement optimizations, enterprises have to submit their requests to SAP and encourage the implementation of the developments supported by groups, such as the ASUG and customer messages or development requests.

New archiving objects are possible

Furthermore, the corresponding new SAP data archiving objects could be added for SAP tables that are included in new releases and functions.

9.2 Development of Archiving Using SAP ILM

While traditional SAP data archiving primarily served to ensure performance and use resources in an optimal way, SAP ILM ushered in a new era for information management in SAP systems. Data archiving forms the basis for retention management and system shutdowns, which play a major role in SAP ILM. The following sections take a closer look at the beginning of SAP ILM, illustrate SAP ILM's status today, and provide an outlook of its future.

9.2.1 Past

From 2004 on, Information Lifecycle Management has been mentioned by SAP as a theoretical approach and has been discussed in various IT magazines. The SAP ILM solution did not exist yet, and the focus was on the approach of how the lifecycle of information could be controlled. Finally, SAP ILM was published with SAP NetWeaver 7.1 as SAP ILM 7.01 in 2007.

Further developments

SAP ILM has been continuously developed over the last years and will also improve in the future. Since June 2014, version 7.03, which includes many new functions, has been available to SAP customers.

It is important to know that SAP ILM is based on traditional SAP data archiving. Therefore, the familiar SAP data archiving objects are also used in SAP ILM. Although they are equipped with new functions, as they are ILM-enabled SAP data archiving objects, the assignment of technical names to the individual objects has not changed.

SAP ILM does not compete with traditional SAP data archiving but supports it with an additional function, the retention warehouse system, in particular in the case of system shutdowns. Before SAP ILM was introduced, there was an urgent need for action, because enterprises had difficulties managing legacy systems. Unfortunately, enterprises still have the same difficulties today, because the budget for these projects is tight and other projects usually have a higher priority.

Focus on system shutdowns

9.2.2 Today

At this time, we only know of one large enterprise that introduced SAP ILM as a pilot customer and consequently was also considerably involved in its further development. Although SAP ILM was the subject of many discussions at enterprises, the new solution has not established itself in enterprises yet. There are various reasons for this:

Not established yet

▶ On the one hand, SAP ILM is a solution that is subject to charge and requires a separate license. Furthermore, system shutdowns lead to additional costs that can be determined from the archived data volume or the number of systems an enterprise needs to shut down. Consequently, SAP calculates the costs for your enterprise individually.

▶ On the other hand, the theoretical approach behind SAP ILM and the options provided by the solution for managing data from its creation to its deletion have not found their place in most of the enterprises yet.

▶ In addition, the first versions of SAP ILM were not as sophisticated as the product is today, and they were sometimes prone to errors due to the dynamic environment with continuous developments. A lot of enterprises look at these developments from the outside at first before migrating to the new product.

9.2.3 Future

Thanks to the developments and improvements of SAP ILM over the last years, we are positive about its future. We assume that many enterprises

Prerequisites for increasing prevalence

467

will implement the new solution. To benefit from its usage, various areas need to be supported:

▸ There are not enough SAP consultants who have a good knowledge of SAP ILM. To change this, there is a new SAP SE training: BIT665 (SAP NetWeaver Information Lifecycle Management). However, the trained consultants also need projects in which they can test and deepen their theoretical knowledge in real life.

▸ Furthermore, enterprises need to be convinced of the benefit of the new options provided by SAP ILM. The migration from traditional SAP data archiving to SAP ILM can only be successful if the business case makes sense. This is the case if the investment costs for SAP ILM will be amortized in the foreseeable future, e.g., in the form of system shutdowns (as promised by SAP SE in their sales presentations).

▸ It would certainly be beneficial if SAP SE would accommodate the enterprises by reducing the license costs in order to increase their willingness to make the investment.

In collaboration with experienced SAP ILM consultants, enterprises with multiple legacy SAP systems and sufficient budgets can benefit from the implementation of SAP ILM.

9.3 Technological Trends

The continuous and fast development in the technology area creates new trends for the future. Not every development is accepted to the extent hoped for. Some are quickly beaten by even better developments and then secretly withdrawn from the market.

New trends ensure dynamics
There are also trends for SAP systems and ILM that have created a real stir on the market for several years. The following sections take a quick look at the world of SAP HANA, data aging, cloud computing, and big data. These concepts currently dominate the media when talking about SAP technologies and IT in general. The focus of the following sections is mainly on the effects that these technologies can have on SAP data archiving, so data archiving is the key topic as illustrated in Figure 9.1.

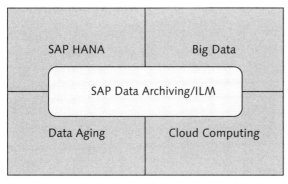

Figure 9.1 New Trends Regarding SAP Data Archiving/ILM

9.3.1 SAP HANA

SAP HANA was developed by the Hasso Plattner Institute in Potsdam (Germany) and introduced by SAP in 2010. The difference between SAP HANA and relational databases is that SAP HANA keeps the data in the fast memory (*in-memory computing*) and the data does not have to be read from the database in a time-consuming process. This allows real-time processing of data.

Access to memory

> **SAP HANA Redefines Real Time** [«]
>
> Figure 9.2 shows that the concept of *real time* has a very long tradition at SAP and has been with us for a long time already: the letter R in SAP software names stands for *real time*, for example, R/2 or R/3. As at the time of the introduction of R, the concept gains a new importance today; so history kind of repeats itself.

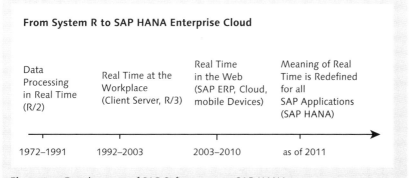

Figure 9.2 Development of SAP Software up to SAP HANA

Column-based
data storage

In SAP HANA, data is no longer stored on the basis of columns but on the basis of rows. This new technology allows for faster data access and also requires less space due to the optimized data structure.

There are versatile approaches and scenarios of how SAP HANA can be used today. The most interesting scenario for us is to provide SAP Business Suite completely on an SAP HANA platform—in the cloud or in your own data center.

Closely integrated
with other trends

As a technological trend, SAP HANA is closely integrated with other trends. Data aging, which will be further discussed in the following section, is an SAP HANA function, for example. Trends such as cloud computing and big data are also of particular importance for SAP HANA. Real-time analyses in SAP HANA—that is, the evaluation of large data volumes—enable you to actually use big data effectively. At the same time, SAP HANA is also available in the cloud and can be leveraged by enterprises that don't want to or cannot operate their own SAP HANA database.

SAP BW reporting
with SAP HANA for
SAP ILM

A possible scenario of SAP HANA is to use the in-memory database with SAP BW. If you also work with SAP ILM for system shutdowns, you can analyze large sets of data very quickly in the retention warehouse system.

Data archiving

The goal of data archiving changes with SAP HANA. If SAP HANA is used with an SAP ERP system, the performance will also be very good in the case of large data volumes, but data archiving or data aging won't become obsolete. Memory for SAP HANA is an expensive storage media that should only be used for data that is used in production.

Message of SAP
HANA

We wish to highlight that—from a strategic view—SAP HANA should form the basis for all SAP applications. This indicates the role SAP HANA plays at SAP. In the future, perhaps SAP HANA will be used exclusively as a platform for all SAP solutions in enterprises.

9.3.2   Data Aging

Data aging aims at transferring data from one storage area to another after a defined period of time. The older a data record is, the earlier it will be removed from the original storage area.

Data temperature

Aging is also often described using the temperature image (*data temperature*). Obsolete data is referred to as *cold* data and new data as *hot* data. The data aging concept is not only supported by SAP but also by various other database providers. It can also be applied to SAP HANA.

SAP data archiving also transfers the data from the database to the storage system after the specified residence time but uses archive files for this purpose. This is the main difference between data archiving and data aging. Data is always transferred from one area to another, but in the case of data archiving, it is not stored as archive files in a compressed way. It is only moved from the original table to other tables (partitioning).

Data aging aims at transferring data from the fast memory (*hot area*) to the slow space of the database (*cold area*). The following sections take a closer look at data aging in SAP systems.

Hot and cold area

To be able to use data aging in SAP systems at all, the following requirements must be met:

Requirements

- ▶ A database that supports data aging is mandatory.
- ▶ In the SAP system, the data aging business function (DAAG_DATA_ AGING) needs to be activated.
- ▶ You require data aging objects that are provided by SAP HANA only.
- ▶ You require authorizations for the data aging and partitioning objects.
- ▶ You require the abap/data_aging profile parameter in your profile.
- ▶ And, of course, you need to know how to use these objects in your SAP system.

Table 9.1 describes the authorization objects that must be integrated into your user roles for the usage of data aging.

Authorization objects

Authorization Object	Description
S_DAAG	Authorization check for data aging objects You can specify the following values for this activity: ▶ Execute—16 ▶ Activate—63 You can also limit the authorization to specific modules and data aging objects.
S_DAGPTM	Authorization check for partitioning objects You can specify the following values for this activity: ▶ Execute—16 ▶ Display—03 You can also limit the authorization to specific partitioning types and identifications (ID).

Table 9.1 Authorization Objects for Data Aging

Table 9.2 specifies the two single roles that you can use for data aging.

Single Role	Description
SAP_DAAG_ADMIN	The single role for the data aging administrator enables you to perform the following tasks: ▶ Activating data aging objects ▶ Performing data aging runs ▶ Creating partitioning objects ▶ Assigning partitioning objects to tables ▶ Creating partitioning intervals for partitioning objects
SAP_DAAG_EXPERT	The single role for the data aging expert enables you to activate data aging objects and schedule data aging runs.

Table 9.2 Single Roles for Data Aging

This was a brief description of the most important requirements for data aging. The following section outlines the data aging process to emphasize the similarities and differences between data aging and SAP data archiving.

Data aging process Chapter 5 and Chapter 6 divided the implementation of SAP data archiving into two areas. The data aging process also includes two stages:

▶ Planning stage

▶ Execution stage

The following summarizes the actions of these two stages.

Planning Data Aging

Selecting tables As in SAP data archiving, the first requirement at the planning stage is an overview of the large tables. These large tables are partitioned within the scope of data aging. That means that the system generates at least one additional table from a table such as table BKPF (Accounting Document Header). The data is then transferred to this new table after the defined period of time. As a table (e.g., table COEP (CO Object: Line Items)) can be archived by various data archiving objects in SAP data archiving, a table can be assigned to multiple data aging objects here.

So the data aging object contains tables whose data, during the data aging run, are transferred to additional tables according to the object's data temperature. You can extend the data aging object by adding more tables. This is particularly useful if customer-specific tables are supposed to be managed like standard SAP tables during the data aging run.

Data aging object

In addition to data aging objects, you also require a *partitioning object*. The partitioning object includes several tables that are partitioned according to the same scheme. You assign tables to partitioning objects in accordance with the SAP standard. Please note that a table can always be assigned to one partitioning object only.

Partitioning object

Optionally, you can create your own *partitioning groups* if the available partitioning objects do not meet your requirements. These partitioning groups are nothing else than customer-specific partitioning objects. This enables you to override partitioning objects without modifications and assign tables to the partitioning groups.

Partitioning groups

> **Activities at the Planning Stage** [◉]
>
> The following activities must be performed at the planning stage:
> ▸ Determining large and critical tables for data aging
> ▸ Selecting the corresponding data aging object
> ▸ Selecting the appropriate partitioning object
> ▸ Creating a customer-specific partitioning group if desired

Implementing Data Aging

While you should consider how to partition the tables at the planning stage, the execution stage focuses on actually partitioning the tables. Before starting the actual process, you first require at least two *partitions*—that is, two storage areas in the form of tables:

Creating partitions

▸ One for the hot area

▸ One for the cold area

Without these partitions, the data aging run cannot be processed successfully.

Activating the data aging object

After having created the partitions, you can activate the data aging object. After the activation, the SAP system performs various consistency checks, for example, with regard to the availability of the partitions. If you want to implement changes to the data aging object, you can deactivate it temporarily to do so.

Scheduling the data aging run

To perform the last step, that is, start the data aging run, you need a *data aging group*. This group contains a lot of data aging objects. After having assigned the objects to the group, you can schedule a data aging run for these data aging groups. As is the case for SAP data archiving, for this purpose you start a job that can be stopped anytime if required.

Transactions

For data aging, there are some new and—compared with the transactions of SAP data archiving—differently designed transactions. Table 9.3 lists the transactions that are available for data aging.

Transaction Code	Name
DAGOBJ	Data Aging Objects
DAGPTC	Customizing for Partitioning
DAGPTM	Manage Partitioning
DAGRUN	Overview of Data Aging Runs
DAGADM	Managing Data Aging Objects
DAGLOG	Data Aging Logs

Table 9.3 Data Aging Transactions

The names indicate the similarities with the areas in SAP data archiving, which also provide specific transactions for the areas of administration and definition of objects. Transaction AOBJ for archiving objects roughly corresponds to Transaction DAGOBJ for data aging objects.

Data aging object

The equivalent for SAP data archiving objects are the new data aging objects. Their names are nearly identical to the names of SAP data archiving objects. These similar names indicate that SAP wants to make use of the proven structure of SAP data archiving for the data aging area. If SAP HANA establishes itself as the standard for SAP landscapes, the focus might shift from SAP data archiving to data aging.

Currently, only a few data objects are available; however, we guess this will change quickly in the foreseeable future. Table 9.4 lists the data aging objects that were available when this book went to press.

Only a few data aging objects available

Data Aging Object	Description	Notes
BC_SBAL	Application logs	See also SAP Note 1909418
BC_IDOC	Intermediate Documents/ Integration Technology ALE	Equivalent to archiving object IDOC
FI_DOCUMENT	General Ledger Accounting/ Financial Accounting Documents	Equivalent to archiving object FI_DOCUMNT

Table 9.4 Overview of the Available Data Aging Objects

The equivalents of these three data aging objects are used as SAP data archiving objects in nearly all SAP systems, because the corresponding tables usually contain a lot of data. So the focus of SAP seems to be to introduce new data objects by determining their priority according to their volume of documents.

Data Aging

Data aging still is a rather new function. The technology of transferring data from the tables of the memory of SAP HANA is still in the early stages. However, if you take a look at already existing objects, you recognize that this concept has been designed with a similar structure as SAP data archiving. The question whether and how SAP ILM or SAP data archiving will interact with data aging in the future is quite fascinating.

Theoretically, data aging enables you to create, for example, ten partitions according to the legal retention period of ten years. This allows for keeping the data from the last three years in the SAP HANA memory (hot area) and transferring all data that is older than four years to the respective partitions in the cold area. If data is transferred to the tenth partition, it can be permanently deleted in the following year. This way, you can map an information lifecycle with the data aging functions. But data aging cannot shut down legacy systems. In this case, SAP ILM is the only solution in the SAP portfolio.

9.3.3 Cloud Computing

Cloud computing is perhaps the most significant IT key word of the last years. Here you first might think of the *cloud*, which is used as a symbol for this topic in numerous IT magazines. Cloud solutions are operated outside the enterprise-specific IT infrastructure.

Cloud computing already belongs to our daily work

Cloud computing is not only available for enterprise solutions. You as a private user also consciously or unconsciously use IT services from the cloud. Common examples include Google Maps and Microsoft Office apps, which you can only use with an Internet browser; that is, you do not have to install software on your computer or import updates; you can use this software in the cloud on demand.

So cloud computing provides you with IT resources (e.g., computing capacity, data storage, or software) cost-efficiently and on demand via the Internet. Another key usage area of cloud computing is the storage of data on hard disks of the external provider. There are already numerous providers on the market offering space at relatively low prices.

Virtualized systems

But is cloud computing really that new? This question can be answered with both yes and no. Cloud computing has already been around for many years even though with a different name. A lot of SAP customers do not have their own data centers and use the services of IT service providers. So cloud computing is only a modern name. The already developed new solution approaches, in particular in the software area, brought cloud computing back into the focus of IT.

Focus on software

The trend is to not only purchase or sell software but also to run the software in the IT infrastructure of the software provider or another cloud-computing provider.

In this respect, the question of which effects or developments are made possible by cloud computing and are to be expected in the context of SAP data archiving is interesting for us. In our opinion, there are two possible scenarios, which we outline in the following sections.

Usage of Space (Storage Systems) in the Cloud

Using space in the cloud is an alternative to storing archive files in an archive system. Chapter 2, however, did not describe the option of using the cloud as a storage location. Instead, we assumed that an archive system is installed and used at the enterprise.

If you use the cloud, you do not have your own archive system. Instead, you store your archive files on external servers. In this case, you must clarify in which countries the external servers are located and if the usage of these server locations is feasible according to legal requirements. In real life, these servers are often not located in the United States but abroad in countries where the operating costs are usually considerably lower and different data privacy laws apply.

Storing data on external servers

A lot of enterprises do not rely on the security of the data when they store their sensitive information on external servers. These aspects also play a major role in the context of SAP data archiving.

Data security

Benefits of cloud usage, on the contrary, are cost savings and high flexibility. Being specialized in this service, cloud-computing providers can charge considerably lower prices for space due to the size of their data centers. Enterprises that use this offer can correspondingly focus on their core competencies.

Using SAP Software (Business Suite) in the Cloud

The second scenario is to use SAP software on external servers only. This solution has been on the market for some years now: SAP Business ByDesign. Even though the press occasionally reported that SAP Business ByDesign would be stopped due to the low number of installations, SAP SE denied these reports and confirmed the continuation of the cloud strategy in this segment.

SAP Business ByDesign

In 2014, SAP set the next trend and provided SAP Business Suite with SAP HANA in the cloud. This solution is promoted as *SAP HANA Enterprise Cloud*. Figure 9.3 shows its graphical structure. The method of hosting SAP Business Suite on external servers is not new, but the combination with SAP HANA opens a new door. Enterprises can now use the entire infrastructure of SAP or other IT enterprises based on a rental model. To meet the legal (storage location of the data) and technical requirements, in particular with regard to access time, SAP has established several *data centers* across various continents.

SAP HANA Enterprise Cloud

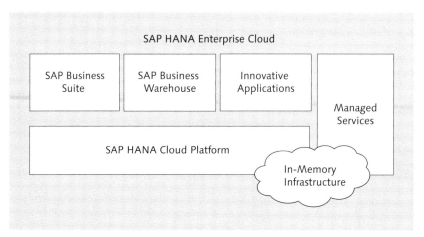

Figure 9.3 SAP HANA Enterprise Cloud

Managed services

Based on a specific calculation, every enterprise has to decide on its own if it is interested in SAP HANA Enterprise Cloud. From an SAP data archiving view, the *managed services* area (on the right-hand side in Figure 9.3) is of particular interest. With this key phrase, SAP provides services such as the monitoring of table and database growth.

Archiving as a cloud service in the foreseeable future?

In the future, it might be possible that new services will be provided in this context to keep the data growth under control. We do not want to rule out the possibility that managed services will be offered for data archiving or data aging in the future.

9.3.4 Big Data

Analysis of mass data

Everybody is currently talking about big data. Even though it seems to have little to do with SAP data archiving at first sight, we want to mention it here. Big data aims at collecting as much data as possible from versatile areas (social networks, enterprise website, etc.), evaluating the data, and making better decisions based on these results. Most of the time, the data is customer data, for example, data about consumer behavior. With regard to SAP data archiving, the question is whether or not the data in an SAP ERP system is relevant for big data. If this data enables you to gain critical insights from which your enterprise can benefit, this must be considered in SAP data archiving. If the collected data has a very short utilization period, the data should not be stored longer than actually required.

The industry in which the enterprise operates certainly plays a major role when the importance of big data is to be analyzed. Every industry does not generate or require large data volumes for analysis. Let's take the gaming industry on the Internet as an example. Several thousands of users access these games at the same time. The industry records, analyzes, and evaluates the actions of the players in real time. Every second, millions of data records are generated. The enterprise that operates a game can therefore draw conclusions in real time and, for example, offer the players virtual goods (e.g., vehicles, shirts, or weapons that may be required by the virtually involved person during the game) for sale. This data has a very short utilization period of a few seconds or minutes, for example, in which it is processed in real time and triggers a response that is equally fast.

Industry is crucial

In SAP data archiving, data archiving objects are mainly used to archive business objects, such as SD orders, deliveries, or financial accounting documents. Data that is collected in the context of big data deviates from business data because it is generated in large volumes and is supposed to be analyzed and utilized within a short period of time.

Deviating approach

> ### Data Evaluation and Forecasts at an Automobile Manufacturer [Ex]
>
> Whether or not data is supposed to be analyzed in connection with business objects in the SAP ERP system is an individual decision and depends on the goals of the enterprise. It is possible, for example, that an automobile manufacturer collects data from the configurator on the Internet in which vehicles can be assembled by trying different options (e.g., color and motor) and compares the data with the data from the actual orders in the SAP system. This enables the enterprise to draw conclusions of whether or not the actual orders confirm the results of the customer behavior analyses on the Internet. If the answer to this question is positive, the automobile manufacturer can derive possible orders, for example, for spare parts, from the configuration data on the Internet and take the appropriate actions in the future.

For big data, an appropriate technological platform is mandatory, for example, SAP HANA or SAP IQ. These databases enable you to analyze large sets of data within a short period of time and use them to make critical decisions.

Technological requirements

9.4   Summary

It is almost impossible to correctly predict the future. Although a lot of friends often say that we're quite skilled at coffee fortune telling from the coffee grounds in small Turkish cups, the future of SAP data archiving is still linked to the general conditions of fast-paced information technology and consequently not completely clear to us. Nevertheless, we try to predict the future. Back in the 1990s when the first affordable cell phones were on the market, who thought that nearly all children in school would have smartphones today and even develop their own apps? Internet surf speed on smartphones has developed faster than predicted; so not all users currently pay the respective rate today, which will probably be a standard rate in cell phone plans soon.

Acceptance of SAP HANA is possible

The trends of SAP HANA and cloud computing may also develop faster than expected. Today, most of the SAP systems still run on relational databases such as Oracle or DB2 and are hosted in the respective data centers of the enterprise. But what will change if SAP systems run on an SAP HANA platform exclusively? Or will the new offer of SAP (providing everything from a single source, that is, not only SAP Business Suite but the entire application on SAP HANA and on the servers of SAP via cloud computing) be accepted on a large scale? The corresponding product is already available: SAP HANA Enterprise Cloud. Things that seem to be debatable today may be reality tomorrow. As is the case in our smartphone example, it is always important that the new solution remains profitable. Which enterprise would select the slower technology if the rates were the same?

Misjudgments of CEOs

The following examples illustrate the misjudgments of some CEOs of technology enterprises about the future:

I think there is a world market for maybe five computers.
—*Thomas Watson, CEO of IBM (1943)*

People will soon get tired of staring at a plywood box every night.
—*Darryl F. Zanuck from 20th Century Fox about television (1946)*

Who would ever need such a silver disk?
—*Jan Timmer, President of Philips, about the Compact Disc (1982)*

The fact that the CEOs of important enterprises were so seriously mistaken suggests incompetence to us. But what is the use of a computer without operating systems and software—technologies that were not widely used before the 1980s. What is the use of television without interesting program? What is the use of a CD if you cannot listen to it on the appropriate players?

The future is unpredictable

So excuse us if our assessment of the future of SAP data archiving doesn't become true in the next 10 years as described in this book. The technology providers show us the way ahead and prepare the ground. But only if the customers also take this direction will transformation take place in the future. Consequently, enterprises need to recognize the new options offered by the technological trends and learn the benefits they provide.

Our vision of the future of SAP data archiving in the next 10 years is as follows: We expect that traditional SAP data archiving and SAP ILM will still work side by side, supplemented by the data aging concept on SAP HANA. As long as the change to SAP HANA is not final, enterprises will still have to decide between traditional SAP data archiving and SAP ILM. Here a decisive factor is if the enterprise wants to invest into the SAP ILM solution, which is subject to charge, and if it can also fully exploit its options.

Our vision of the future

If SAP HANA prevails as indicated by the latest trends, data aging may lead traditional SAP data archiving and maybe also SAP ILM into insignificance. SAP has already announced developments in the archiving and data aging area for SAP HANA. However, no one can tell what they will include and how they will interact with SAP data archiving or SAP ILM.

Data aging has potential

We therefore recommend all SAP data archiving experts to become acquainted with the new options provided by SAP HANA, data aging, cloud computing, and big data and gain specialist knowledge at an early stage. Due to the relatively similar structures of data aging and SAP data archiving, trainings will be available soon.

Training is critical

These new developments are finally bringing dynamics back to the topic of SAP data archiving. In our opinion, the new trends allow SAP data archiving and SAP ILM to start afresh. So we look forward to an exciting future of SAP data archiving.

Appendices

A Transactions

The tables in this appendix provide an overview of the most critical transactions relating to data archiving—from system analysis to SAP Information Lifecycle Management (ILM).

A.1 Transactions for Analysis

Transaction	Description
DB02	Tables and Indexes Monitor
DB15	Data Archiving: DB Tables
TAANA	Table Analysis
TAANA_AV	Table Analysis: Analysis Variants
TAANA_VF	Table Analysis: Virtual Fields

A.2 Transactions for Customizing

Transaction	Description
SE91	Message Maintenance
COISN	Customizing Order Information System
AOBJ	Definition of Archiving Objects
SARI	Archive Information System
SARJ	Archive Retrieval Configurator
OIOA	Plant Maintenance Order Types

A.3 Transactions for Data Extraction using DART

Transaction	Description
FTW0	Tax Data Retention and Reporting
FTW1A	Extract Data
FTWF	Data Extract Browser
FTWH	Data View Queries
FTWL	Display Extract Log
FTWN	View Query Log
FTWP	Settings for Data Extraction
FTWSCC	DART: Settings for Company Codes

A.4 Transactions for Storage

Transaction	Description
AL11	Display SAP Directories
FILE	File Names/Paths Client-Independent
OAC0	CMS Customizing Content Repositories
OAC2	SAP ArchiveLink Document Types Global
OAC3	SAP ArchiveLink Links
SF01	File Names Client-Dependent

A.5 Transactions for Administration

Transaction	Description
SARA	Archive Administration
COHVPI	Mass Processing Process Orders

A.6   Transactions for Display

Transaction	Description
ALO1	Determine ASH/DOREX Links
AS_AFB	Archive File Browser
OADR	SAP ArchiveLink Print List Search
SARE	Archive Explorer
VA03	Display Sales Order
VL03N	Display Outbound Delivery
VL33N	Display Inbound Delivery
FAGLB03	G/L Account Balance Display
FAGLL03	Line Items GL Accounts (New)
FB03	Display Document
FBL1N	Vendor Line Items
FK10N	G/L Account Balance Display Vendors
COR3	Display Process Order
KOB1	Orders Actual Line Items
LT21	Display Transport Request
SCU3	Table History
SLG1	Application Log: Display Logs
WE09	Search iDocs via Content
SWW_ARCHIV	Display Workflows from Archive
MIGO	Goods Movement
MB51	Material Document List
MB03	Display Material Document
VF07	Display Billing Document from Archive
ME53N	Display Purchase Requisition
ME23N	Display Purchase Order
IW63	Display Historical PM Order
VELOARDI	Display Archived Vehicles

A.7 Transactions for Display in SAP IS-U

Transaction	Description
EA22	Display Settlement Document
EA40	Display Print Document
EA63	Display Budget Billing Plan
FPL3	Display Document
FPL9	Display Account Balance

A.8 Transactions as Part of Data Aging

Transaction	Description
DAGOBJ	Data Aging Objects
DAGPTC	Customizing of Partitioning
DAGPTM	Manage Partitions
DAGRUN	Overview Data Aging Runs
DAGADM	Data Aging Object Management
DAGLOG	Data Aging Logs

A.9   Transactions for SAP ILM

Transaction	Description
ILM	Creates Menu for Context Data Extractor
ILM_C_RAOB ILM_C_RAOB_TAB ILM_C_SOEX ILM_C_OBJECTS ILM_C_CON ILM_C_C_CON ILM_C_STRC ILM_C_APPL ILM_C_RELA	Transactions in the menu created by Transaction ILM
ILMAPT	Processing Audit Package Templates
ILMARA	Processing Audit Areas
ILMCHECK	Define and Execute Checksums
ILM_DESTRUCTION	Data Destruction
ILM_LH_AL	Propagate Legal Holds for ArchiveLink
IRM_CUST IRM_CUST_BS	Information Retention Manager Customizing
IRMPOL	Information Retention Management
SARA	Archive Administration
SCASE	Legal Case Management
ILMSIM	ILM Rule Simulation
ILM_TRANS_ADMIN	Transfer of Archive Administration
IWP01	Handling Audit Packages
SFW5	Switch Framework Customizing

B   Archiving Objects—
Compact Overviews

This appendix provides you with compact overviews of the most important archiving objects described in this book.

B.1   Archiving Object BC_DBLOGS (Archiving of Changes to Customizing Tables)

You can use the BC_DBLOGS archiving object to archive data records, including changes to Customizing tables. This data is not relevant for tax inspections and is not extracted using the DART. However, this data is required on a regular basis for additional checks, for example, within the scope of internal revision. For this reason, it is recommended to retain this data on a long-term basis and define the retention period.

BC_DBLOGS

Characteristic	Description/Recommendation
Preceding archiving object	None
Leading table(s) for table analysis	DBTABLOG (Log Records for Table Changes)
Optimal residence time	▸ 12 months ▸ Possibly even less
Archive access and archive infostructure	▸ Standard Transaction SCU3 (View Table History) ▸ Archive infostructure: SAP_BC_DBLOGS
Important SAP Notes	2037593 (Audit Trail: Ignore Data from the Archive in case of Background Processing of Transaction S_AUT10)
Relevance for DART	No
Archiving interval	Weekly, monthly, or quarterly
Practical tips	You should introduce this archiving object soon, because it generates large amounts of data.

B.2 Archiving Object BC_SBAL (Archiving Object for Application Log)

BC_SBAL You can use the BC_SBAL archiving object to archive data records relating to logs from different applications. This data is not relevant for tax inspections and is not extracted using the DART. However, this data is requested on a regular basis for additional checks, for example, within the scope of internal revision. For this reason, it is recommended to retain this data on a long-term basis and define the retention period.

Characteristic	Description/Recommendation
Preceding archiving object	None
Leading table(s) for table analysis	▸ BALHDR (Application Log: Log Header) ▸ BALDAT (Application Log: Log Data) ▸ BAL_INDX (Application Log: INDX Table)
Optimal residence time	▸ 12 months ▸ Possibly even less

Archive access and archive infostructures	▸ Standard Transaction SLG1 (Application Log: Display Logs)
	▸ Archive infostructures:
	  ▸ SAP_BC_SBAL
	  ▸ SAP_BC_SBAL01
	  ▸ SAP_BC_SBAL02

Important SAP Notes	195157 (Application Log: Delete Logs)
Relevance for DART	No
Archiving interval	Weekly, monthly, or quarterly
Practical tips	You should introduce this archiving object soon, because it generates large amounts of data.

B.3 Archiving Object IDOC—Intermediate Document

IDOC By means of IDocs, you can send information from one SAP system to another SAP or a third-party system or receive information from other systems. For example, purchase orders can be sent as IDocs and generate corresponding table entries in the recipient's EKKO table (purchasing document header). These IDocs were processed successfully then acted as *envelopes* that transferred a message. Nevertheless, it is recommended that you retain in the archive IDocs for data that must be preserved for legal reasons, which also contains the original document.

Characteristic	Description/Recommendation
Preceding archiving object	None
Leading table(s) for table analysis	▶ EDI30C (Intermediate Document Cluster (data records) as of 3.0C) ▶ EDI40 (IDoc Data records for 4.0) ▶ EDIDC (Control Record (IDoc)) ▶ EDIDS (Status Record (IDoc))
Optimal residence time	▶ 12 months ▶ Possibly even less

Archive access and archive infostructures	▶ Standard Transaction WE09 (IDoc Search for Business Content)
	 ▶ Archive infostructures:
	  ▶ SAP_DRB_IDOC001
	  ▶ SAP_IDOC_001

Important SAP Notes	1999215 (IDoc: Archiving—Selection Result Other Than Expected)
Relevance for DART	No
Archiving interval	Weekly, monthly, or quarterly
Practical tips	▶ You should map archive access via Transaction WE09 using the archive information system. ▶ You can also delete specific IDoc types directly instead of archiving them.

B.4 Archiving Object WORKITEM (Work Items from the Workflow System)

Work items from the workflow system represent tasks that the SAP sys- WORKITEM
tem automatically sends to the users so that they execute them. This

way, you can optimize processes and procedures in your enterprise. There are different workflows, for instance, the workflow for approving invoices. You decide for each workflow whether you want to delete or archive the work items.

Characteristic	Description/Recommendation
Preceding archiving object	None
Leading table(s) for table analysis	▶ SWP_HEADER (Workflow Instances: Header Data of a Workflow Execution) ▶ SWW_CONTOB (Workflow Runtime: Work Item Data Container (objects only))
Optimal residence time	▶ 12 months ▶ Possibly even less

Archive access and archive infostructures	▶ Standard Transaction SWW_ARCHIV (Display Workflows from Archive)
	▶ Archive infostructures:
	  ▷ SAP_BO_2_WI_001
	  ▷ SAP_O_2_WI_001
	  ▷ SAP_WF_TEST02
	  ▷ SAP_WORKITEM001

Important SAP Notes	▶ 2049016 (Handling Attachments within the Scope of Workflow Archiving) ▶ 2083172 (Work Item Archiving: Runtime Error OBJECTS_OBJREF_NOT_ASSIGNED)
Relevance for DART	No
Archiving interval	Weekly, monthly, or quarterly
Practical tips	▶ You can delete specific work items instead of archiving them. ▶ You should check workflow tables for old and incomplete work items. This way, you can improve the quality of data in a targeted approach by contacting the corresponding user to obtain approval for archiving or deletion of the work items.

B.5 Archiving Object CHANGEDOCU (Change Documents)

In the SAP system, changes for a document are recorded as change documents. The benefit of this approach is that you can reproduce at any time which user has made which change to a specific document. When archiving change documents, however, you must observe that the recommended method is to archive a change document together with the application document. This way, the change document and the application document are included in one archive file. In certain cases where many change documents exist and you don't want to archive the associated application documents, you can run the archiving using the CHANGEDOCU archiving object.

CHANGEDOCU

Characteristic	Description/Recommendation
Preceding archiving object	None
Leading table(s) for table analysis	CDHDR (Change Document Header)
Optimal residence time	▸ 12 months ▸ Possibly even less
Archive access and archive info-structures	▸ According to SAP Note 1050935, you can access the information using known standard transactions if appropriate adaptations were made. ▸ Archive infostructures: 　▹ SAP_CDO_1_RW 　▹ SAP_CHANGEDOCU1 　▹ SAP_CHANGEDOCU2
Important SAP Notes	▸ 1050935 (CD: Reading Archived Change Documents from the Application) ▸ 1257133 (CD: Archiving Options for CDCLS)
Relevance for DART	Partial. Example: Change document objects such as BELEG for the FI document are relevant for DART.

Characteristic	Description/Recommendation
Archiving interval	Weekly, monthly, or quarterly
Practical tips	► SAP Note 1050935 describes how to automatically display archived change documents directly in the application.
	► You should only archive those change document objects that are not archived directly with the application document and are not relevant for DART either.

B.6 Archiving Object MM_ACCTIT (MM Subsequent Posting Data for Accounting Interface)

MM_ACCTIT   The subsequent posting data from SAP Materials Management (MM) raises major questions in practical usage. On the one hand, it involves very large tables and amounts of data. On the other hand, only a few persons know how to use these tables. Based on two very good notes that SAP SE provides for this purpose, it is highly recommended to decide whether you want to deactivate this archiving object.

Characteristic	Description/Recommendation
Preceding archiving object	None
Leading table(s) for table analysis	► ACCTIT (Compressed Data from RW Document)
	► ACCTHD (Compressed Data from RW Document—Header)
	► ACCTCR (Compressed Data from RW Document—Currencies)
Optimal residence time	► 3 months
	► Possibly even less
	► Consider deactivation if data is not required

Characteristic	Description/Recommendation
Archive access and archive info-structure	▸ Archive access is not necessary in practical use and only possible via Transaction SARE. ▸ Archive infostructure: SAP_MM_ACCTIT02
Important SAP Notes	▸ 48009 (ACCTHD, ACCTIT, ACCTCR tables: Questions and Answers) ▸ 1281616 (Enhancement "AC_DOCUMENT" BAdI)
Relevance for DART	No, but can be integrated with DART extraction
Archiving interval	▸ Weekly, monthly, or quarterly ▸ Not required in case of deactivation
Practical tips	▸ The ACCT* tables comprise large amounts of data that often remains unused in real life. For this reason, you should check the SAP notes and consider deactivation. ▸ Residence time should be kept very short if no deactivation is planned.

B.7 Archiving Object RL_TA (MM-WM Warehouse Management: Transport Requests)

In reality, transport requests often cause performance problems in Retention Warehouse Management. For this reason, you should archive them promptly. Particularly worth noting are the interfaces that have caused performance problems. So the optimal residence time depends on how long users and possibly interfaces access the information contained in the LTAK and LTAP tables.

RL_TA

Characteristic	Description/Recommendation
Preceding archiving object	None

Characteristic	Description/Recommendation
Leading table(s) for table analysis	▸ LTAK (WMS—Transport Request Header) ▸ LTAP (Transport Request Item)
Optimal residence time	▸ 2 to 6 months ▸ Consider interfaces!
Archive access and archive info-structure	▸ Standard Transaction LT21 (Display Transport Request) ▸ Archive access using Transaction SARE with advanced selection criteria is possible and recommended. ▸ Archive infostructure: SAP_DRB_RL_TA
Important SAP Notes	▸ 815542 (Read Program for Reading Archive Files) ▸ 1435956 (Incorrect Information in Job Log During Archiving)
Relevance for DART	No
Archiving interval	Weekly, monthly, or quarterly
Practical tips	▸ The LTAK and LTAP tables not only attract attention due to their size, but they also cause performance issues. ▸ You should thoroughly examine interfaces to external systems, for instance, a printer or barcode scanner with table access with regard to their impact on archiving. ▸ You can customize the SAP_DRB_RL_TA archive infostructure so that users have better selection options.

B.8   Archiving Object FI_DOCUMNT (FI Documents)

FI_DOCUMNT   From the tax inspection's perspective, the FI documents probably represent the most critical data in an SAP system. An optimal archive access is available for data archiving because the tax inspectors can also access this data after many years.

Characteristic	Description/Recommendation
Preceding archiving object	None
Leading table(s) for table analysis	▸ BKPF (Document Header for Accounting) ▸ FAGLFLEXA (General Ledger: Actual Line Item) ▸ BSIS (Accounting: Secondary Index for GL Accounts)
Optimal residence time	▸ 13 to 36 months ▸ Depending on data volume and performance

Archive access and archive infostructures	▸ Standard Transaction FB03 (Display Document)
	▸ All FI transactions can access the archive. For this purpose, however, several SAP Notes must be taken into account.
	▸ Archive infostructures:
	  ▸ SAP_FI_DOC_002
	  ▸ SAP_FI_DOC_DRB1

Important SAP Notes	▸ 2086202 (FI_DOCUMNT: Standard Field Catalogs Must Be Used) ▸ 1852923 (Can't access archived FI_DOCUMNT via FAGLL03) ▸ 204426 (RFUMSV00: Read Archive Data) ▸ 2029436 (System does not check archiving for duplicates when posting a document) ▸ 596865 (Archive Connection FI Line Item Lists)
Relevance for DART	Yes

Characteristic	Description/Recommendation
Archiving interval	Monthly, quarterly, or annually
Practical tips	▸ Archive access is almost optimal and can be set up as described in various SAP Notes. ▸ Define a longer residence time for secondary indexes to preserve the performance of individual document display. Otherwise, you would access the archive too often. ▸ If the archive access becomes slower over time, you should partition the infostructure and create an index.

B.9 Archiving Object MM_MATBEL (Material Documents)

MM_MATBEL Like FI documents, material documents are critical data in an SAP system. Here as well, an optimal archive access is available for data archiving because the tax inspectors can also access this data after many years.

Characteristic	Description/Recommendation
Preceding archiving object	PP_BKFLUSH (Document Log)
Leading table(s) for table analysis	▸ MKPF (Document Header Material Document) ▸ MSEG (Document Segment Material)
Optimal residence time	▸ 6 to 36 months ▸ Depending on data volume and performance

Characteristic	Description/Recommendation

Archive access and archive infostructures	▶ Standard Transaction MIGO (Goods Movements: Display Material Document)
	
	▶ Standard Transaction MB51 (Material Document List)
	
	▶ Transaction MB03 can also be modified for archive usage
	
	▶ Archive infostructures:
	  ▶ `SAP_DRB_MATBEL1`
	  ▶ `SAP_MATBEL_MARI`

Important SAP Notes	▶ 2069231 (ALO1: Archived Material Documents Are Not Displayed as Linked Documents for the Delivery) ▶ 2002210 (Archiving `MM_MATBEL`: Standardization) ▶ 431689 (MB03: Display of Archived Documents)
Relevance for DART	Yes
Archiving interval	Monthly, quarterly, or annually
Practical tips	▶ If required, you can make Display Transaction MM03 archive-ready as specified in SAP Note 431689. ▶ You can archive material documents directly after the DART extraction if no additional interfaces require longer residence times.

B.10 Archiving Object LE_HU (Handling Units)

Handling Units cause a large data volume and should be archived in a very timely manner. Because there are dependencies in preceding archiving objects, you should develop a quick implementation strategy.

LE_HU

Characteristic	Description/Recommendation
Preceding archiving object	▸ PP_BKFLUSH (Document Log) ▸ MM_MATBEL (Material Documents) ▸ SD_VFKK (Freight Costs) ▸ SD_VTTK (SD Transports) ▸ RV_LIKP (Deliveries)
Leading table(s) for table analysis	▸ VEKP (Handling Unit Header Table) ▸ VEPO (Packing: Handling Unit Item (content))
Optimal residence time	24 to 36 months
Archive access and archive infostructure	▸ Archive access using Transaction SARE with advanced selection criteria is possible and recommended ▸ Archive infostructure: SAP_DRB_LE_HU
Important SAP Notes	▸ 2000210 (HUs Involved in Several Deliveries Can Be Archived Without Condition) ▸ 1697039 (Archiving Object LE_HU: Analysis of Archived Data) ▸ 1694788 (HU Archiving—Frequently Asked Questions) ▸ 1623283 (SARI: Packaging Name Is Not Displayed)
Relevance for DART	No
Archiving interval	Monthly, quarterly, or annually
Practical tips	▸ Quickly archive handling units that are not dependent on another document or archiving object. ▸ If you have high growth rates in the VEKP and VEPO tables, quickly implement the MM_MATBEL and RV_LIKP archiving objects. ▸ Archive access is usually not required for users, which means that you can save memory for the infostructure

B.11   Archiving Object RV_LIKP (Deliveries)

You can archive inbound and outbound deliveries rather easily. For out-   RV_LIKP
bound deliveries, however, you should archive the material documents
and possibly transports first. Inbound deliveries can depend on a purchase order, which you should archive beforehand.

Characteristic	Description/Recommendation
Preceding archiving object	▸ PP_BKFLUSH (Document Log) ▸ MM_MATBEL (Material Documents) ▸ SD_VFKK (Freight Costs) ▸ SD_VTTK (SD Transports)
Leading table(s) for table analysis	▸ LIKP (Delivery Header Data) ▸ LIPS (Delivery Item Data)
Optimal residence time	24 to 36 months

Archive access and archive info-structures	▸ Standard Transaction VL03N (Display Outbound Delivery)
	▸ Standard Transaction VL33N (Display Inbound Delivery)
	▸ Archive infostructures:
	  ▸ SAP_CHVW_LIKP
	  ▸ SAP_DRB_RV_LIKP
	  ▸ SAP_LIKP_ERDAT

Important SAP Notes	▸ 2015801 (VL03N: Display Archived Delivery: Some Address Data for Communication is Missing in Partner Details) ▸ 1958501 (Incorrect Display of Archived Data in VL03N)
Relevance for DART	Yes
Archiving interval	Monthly, quarterly, or annually
Practical tips	After you've archived deliveries, you have a very good display quality using standard Transactions VL03N and VL33N. For this reason, you should keep the residence time short and directly start with archiving after the DART extraction if this is not prevented by enterprise-specific interfaces or reports.

B.12   Archiving Object SD_VBRK (Billing Documents)

SD_VBRK   You can archive billing documents after the deliveries. Transaction VF07 is available for displaying them from the archive.

Characteristic	Description/Recommendation
Preceding archiving object	▶ PP_BKFLUSH (Document Log) ▶ MM_MATBEL (Material Documents) ▶ SD_VFKK (Freight Costs) ▶ SD_VTTK (SD Transports) ▶ RV_LIKP (Deliveries)
Leading table(s) for table analysis	▶ VBRK (Billing Document Header Data) ▶ VBRP (Billing Document Item Data)
Optimal residence time	▶ 24 to 36 months

Archive access and archive infostructures	▶ Standard Transaction VF07 (Display Billing Document from Archive)
	▶ Archive infostructures:
	  ▶ SAP_CHVW_VBRK
	  ▶ SAP_SD_VBRK_001
	  ▶ SAP_SD_VBRK_01
	  ▶ SAP_SD_VBRK_02
	  ▶ SAP_VBRK_ERDAT

Important SAP Notes	▶ 1483876 (Archiving Billing Documents Subject to Volume-Based Rebate) ▶ 440033 (Information on Billing Document Display from Archive (VF07))
Relevance for DART	Yes
Archiving interval	Monthly, quarterly, or annually
Practical tips	▶ Transaction VF07 is almost identical to Transaction VF03 and enables you to display archived billing documents with minor limitations. Add this transaction to the corresponding roles. ▶ Prior to archiving billing documents, run the SDBONARCH report to initially exclude billing documents that are relevant for rebate from archiving.

B.13   Archiving Object SD_VBAK (Sales Documents)

Sales documents have a lot of preceding archiving objects. You should   SD_VBAK
particularly implement material documents, deliveries, and billing documents to be able to archive a large quantity of sales documents.

Characteristic	Description/Recommendation
Preceding archiving object	▶ PP_BKFLUSH (Document Log) ▶ MM_MATBEL (Material Documents) ▶ SD_VFKK (Freight Costs) ▶ SD_VTTK (SD Transports) ▶ RV_LIKP (Deliveries) ▶ SD_VBRK (Billing Documents) ▶ MM_EKKO (Purchasing Documents) ▶ MM_EBAN (Purchase Requisitions)
Leading table(s) for table analysis	▶ VBAK (Sales Document Header Data) ▶ VBAP (Sales Document Item Data)
Optimal residence time	24 to 36 months

Archive access and archive infostructures	▶ Standard Transaction VA03 (Display Sales Order)
	▶ Archive infostructures:
	    ▶ SAP_AUAK_VBAK01
	    ▶ SAP_CHVW_VBAK
	    ▶ SAP_COBK_VBAK01
	    ▶ SAP_DRB_VBAK_01
	    ▶ SAP_DRB_VBAK_02
	    ▶ SAP_VBAK_ERDAT

Important SAP Notes	▶ 481577 (Criteria for Archivability of Sales Documents) ▶ 577162 (Display Archived Orders via VA03)
Relevance for DART	Yes
Archiving interval	Monthly, quarterly, or annually

Characteristic	Description/Recommendation
Practical tips	▸ You can display the document flow using Transaction ALO1.
	▸ The TEXTS tab is no longer available after archiving. Here you can use the technical view in Transaction SARE.

B.14 Archiving Object MM_EINA (Purchasing Info Records)

MM_EINA In terms of quantity, purchasing info records are rather unremarkable. For the archiving of vendor master data, however, it particularly makes sense to also archive the corresponding purchasing info records of the creditor.

Characteristic	Description/Recommendation
Preceding archiving object	None
Leading table(s) for table analysis	▸ EINA (Purchasing Info Record—General Data)
	▸ EINE (Purchasing info Record—Purchasing Organization Data)
Optimal residence time	24 to 36 months
Archive access and archive infostructure	▸ If required, the archive can be accessed via Transaction SARE after an archive infostructure has been created.
	▸ Archive infostructure: None available, must be created specifically
Important SAP Notes	▸ 456129 (FAQ: Archiving in Purchasing)
	▸ 401318 (Archiving: Additional Information)
	▸ 1575350 (MM_EINA: Infostructure Inconsistent Based on SAP_MM_EINA_AS)
Relevance for DART	Yes

Characteristic	Description/Recommendation
Archiving interval	Monthly, quarterly, or annually
Practical tips	You should only consider purchasing info records for archiving if your focus is on creditor archiving. The minor amount of purchasing info records doesn't necessarily require archiving.

B.15 Archiving Object MM_EBAN (Purchase Requisitions)

You can archive purchase requisitions relating to a purchase order using the MM_EBAN archiving object.

MM_EBAN

Characteristic	Description/Recommendation
Preceding archiving object	None
Leading table(s) for table analysis	EBAN (Purchase Requisitions)
Optimal residence time	24 to 36 months

Archive access and archive infostructures	▸ Standard Transaction ME53N (Display Purchase Requisition)
	▸ Archive infostructures:
	  ▸ SAP_DRB_MM_EBAN
	  ▸ SAP_EBAN_EBKN

Important SAP Notes	▸ 456129 (FAQ: Archiving in Purchasing) ▸ 401318 (Archiving: Additional Information)
Relevance for DART	Yes
Archiving interval	Monthly, quarterly, or annually
Practical tips	You can archive purchase requisitions together with the purchase orders. You thus clear your way for implementing further archiving objects, such as PM_ORDER.

507

B.16 Archiving Object MM_EKKO (Purchasing Documents)

MM_EKKO Purchasing documents are subdivided into purchase orders, requests, scheduling agreements, and contracts. In reality, purchase orders are affected by archiving. You can archive them using the MM_EKKO archiving object.

Characteristic	Description/Recommendation
Preceding archiving object	None
Leading table(s) for table analysis	▶ EKKO (Purchasing Document Header) ▶ EKPO (Purchasing Document Item)
Optimal residence time	24 to 36 months

Archive access and archive infostructures	▶ Standard Transaction ME23N (Display Purchase Order)
	▶ Archive infostructures:
	  ▸ SAP_DRB_EKKO_01
	  ▸ SAP_DRB_MM_EKKO
	  ▸ SAP_EKKO_BANFN
	  ▸ SAP_EKKO_EKKN

Important SAP Notes	▶ 456129 (FAQ: Archiving in Purchasing) ▶ 401318 (Archiving: Additional Information)
Relevance for DART	Yes
Archiving interval	Monthly, quarterly, or annually
Practical tips	For initial archiving, you should keep residence time 1 and residence time 2 short in the application-specific Customizing (Transaction SARA) to be able to set deletion flags and deletion indicators in good time.

B.17 Archiving Object PM_ORDER (Service and Maintenance Orders)

Service and maintenance orders usually depend on FI documents, purchasing documents, and purchase requisitions. To use PM_ORDER quickly in production, you should first implement the preceding archiving objects in a timely manner.

PM_ORDER

Characteristic	Description/Recommendation
Preceding archiving object	► FM_FUNRES (Earmarked Fund) ► MM_EKKO (Purchasing Documents) ► FI_DOCUMNT (FI Documents) ► MM_EBAN (Purchase Requisitions)
Leading table(s) for table analysis	► AUFK (Order Master Data) ► AFPO (Order Item)
Optimal residence time	24 to 36 months

Archive access and archive infostructures	► Standard Transaction IW63 (Display Historical IS Order)
	► Archive infostructures:
	  ► PM_ORDER_RG1
	  ► SAP_AUAK_PMOR01
	  ► SAP_COBK_PMOR01
	  ► SAP_PM_ORDER
	  ► SAP_PM_RUECK

Important SAP Notes	► 1896250 (Archiving Object PM_ORDER: Technical Correction) ► 1971617 (Archived Orders: Display Order from Inspection Lot) ► 1843153 (PM_ORDER: No Application-Specific Customizing Possible)
Relevance for DART	Yes

Characteristic	Description/Recommendation
Archiving interval	Monthly, quarterly, or annually
Practical tips	▸ For initial archiving, you should keep residence time 1 and residence time 2 short in the application-specific Customizing (Transaction OIOA or SARA) to be able to set deletion flags and deletion indicators in good time. ▸ During archiving, you can still store the order in the database as a historical order in a compressed format. The number of the order remains unchanged; however, the memory is reduced.

B.18 Archiving Object PR_ORDER (Process Orders)

PR_ORDER Process orders are used specifically in the chemical industry. The relevant data is archived using the PR_ORDER archiving object.

Characteristic	Description/Recommendation
Preceding archiving object	None
Leading table(s) for table analysis	▸ AUFK (Order Master Data) ▸ AFPO (Order Item)
Optimal residence time	18 to 36 months

Archive access and archive infostructures	▸ Archive access using Transaction SARE with advanced selection criteria is possible and recommended.
	▸ Archive infostructures:
	  ▹ SAP_AUAK_PROR01
	  ▹ SAP_COBK_PRORD1
	  ▹ SAP_PR_ORDER001

Important SAP Notes	▸ 673290 (Setting the Deletion Flag: Performance Problems) ▸ 540834 (FAQ: Order Archiving (PP_ORDER and PR_ORDER))
Relevance for DART	Yes

Characteristic	Description/Recommendation
Archiving interval	Monthly, quarterly, or annually
Practical tips	After archiving, you can no longer access the documents using Transaction COR3 (Display Process Order). For this purpose, you should introduce the users to Transaction SARE and adapt it to their requirements.

B.19   Archiving Object VEHICLE (Archiving of Vehicles VMS)

You can archive the vehicles from the Vehicle Management System   VEHICLE
(VMS) using the VEHICLE archiving object. You must check, however,
whether enterprise-specific tables also exist in this area that should be
archived as well.

Characteristic	Description/Recommendation
Preceding archiving object	None
Leading table(s) for table analysis	VLCVEHICLE (VELO: Vehicle)
Optimal residence time	2 to 6 months
Archive access and archive infostructure	▶ Standard Transaction VELOARDI (Display Archived Vehicles) ▶ Archive infostructure: SAP_VEHICLE
Important SAP Notes	648176 (Vehicle Manager Archiving)
Relevance for DART	No
Archiving interval	Monthly, quarterly, or annually
Practical tips	A myriad of enterprise-specific tables is created in this area in real life. You should also include these in archiving so that they are not left behind in the SAP system.

B.20   Archiving Object JITO_CALL (Just-in-Time Calls Outbound)

JITO_CALL   Outbound Just-in-Time calls (JIT calls) have become an inherent part of the automotive industry. You can control the large amounts of data that are generated with JIT calls using the JITO_CALL archiving object.

Characteristic	Description/Recommendation
Preceding archiving object	None
Leading table(s) for table analysis	JITOHD (Call Header Outbound)
Optimal residence time	2 to 6 months
Archive access and archive infostructure	▸ If required, the archive can be accessed via Transaction SARE after an archive infostructure has been created ▸ Archive infostructure: None available, must be created specifically
Important SAP Notes	None
Relevance for DART	No
Archiving interval	Monthly, quarterly, or annually
Practical tips	JIT calls can depend on transport requests (RL_TA archiving object). For this reason, you should coordinate the residence times for these two archiving objects.

C   Concept Template

In the following, you will find a structure for archiving concepts, which you can use as a template when creating your archiving concepts. Creating archiving concepts is described in more detail using examples in Chapter 4, Section 4.2.

An archiving concept comprises three levels with each pursue a different goal.

Archiving concept

Strategic Level

The strategic level deals with long-term decisions. The concept should at least contain the following items:

- Overview of the SAP landscape
- Technological trends
- Storage of archive files
- Access to data
- Roadmap for data archiving
- Team for data archiving

Operational Level

The operational level deals with the implementation and administration of SAP data archiving. You must define and document tasks and responsibilities clearly:

- Define responsibilities
- Integrated long-term data archiving and extraction plan (LDAEP)
- Long-term data archiving plan (LDAP)
- Long-term data extraction plan (LDEP)

Conceptual Level

The conceptual level is divided into the areas of country and SAP data archiving object. You must create a separate concept for each country and each SAP data archiving object.

Country

The concept for a country in an SAP system can be structured as follows:

▸ Company description

▸ Extract of laws relating to archiving

▸ Retention location

▸ Retention periods

▸ Electronic tax inspection

▸ Data Retention Tool (DART)

▸ SAP Notes

▸ Access types

▸ Inspection periods and types

▸ Dependencies of SAP data archiving objects

▸ Contacts

SAP Data Archiving Object

The concept for an SAP data archiving object in an SAP system can be structured as follows:

▸ Description of the archiving object

▸ Criteria for archivability

▸ Customizing

▸ Interdependencies

▸ Archive access

▸ SAP Notes

▸ Customer-specific extensions
  (tables, transactions, reports, interfaces, etc.)

▸ Operational execution

- ▸ Retention of archive files
- ▸ Information lifecycle
- ▸ Contacts

This structure for an archiving concept has been proven many times in practical usage. You can integrate your personal topics in this structure to build your own archiving concept.

D List of Abbreviations

Abbreviation	Long Texts
ABS	Antilocking system
ADK	Archive Development Kit
AEC	Audit Extraction Cockpit
AG	Incorporated company
AK	Working group
AO	Revenue Code
AS	Archive Information System
ASUG	American SAP User Group
BD	Blu-Ray Disc
BI	SAP NetWeaver Business Intelligence
BMF	Federal Ministry of Finance
BW	Business Warehouse, see also BI
CAD	Computer Aided Design
CD	Compact Disc
CEO	Chief Executive Officer
CFO	Chief Financial Officer
CO	Controlling
DART	Data Retention Tool
DRB	Document Relationship Browser
DSAG	German-Speaking SAP User Group
DVD	Digital Video Disc
EIM	Enterprise Information Management
FAIT	Expert Committee of Information Technology
FI	Financial Accounting
GB	Gigabyte
GDPdU	Principles for data access and verifiability of digital documents
GmbH	Company with limited liability
GoBS	Principles for IT-supported accounting systems

Abbreviation	Long Texts
HANA	(formerly) High-Performance Analytic Appliance
HGB	German Commercial Law
HTTP	Hypertext Transfer Protocol
HVD	Holographic Versatile Disc
IDW	Institute of Public Auditors in Germany
ILM	Information Lifecycle Management
KG	Kilogram
kWh	Kilowatt hour
LDAEP	Integrated long-term data archiving and extraction plan
LDAP	Long-term data archiving plan
LDEP	Long-term data extraction plan
LTO	Linear Tape-Open
MB	Megabyte
MM	Materials Management
NLS	Nearline Storage
Pkw	Passenger car
PP	Production Planning
ProdHaftG	Product Liability Law
R	Real-time
SD	Sales
SLO	System Landscape Optimization
TB	Terabyte
URI	Uniform Resource Identifier
UTC	Universal Time Coordinated
VMS	Vehicle Management System
WebDAV	Web-based Distributed Authoring and Versioning

E   The Author

 **Ahmet Türk** has worked as a freelance business consultant for AHMETTUERK/IT AND STRATEGY CONSULTING in Ludwigsburg, Germany, since 2010. He studied business administration focusing on information management at Pforzheim University. In 2006, he started his career as an SAP consultant in the areas of data archiving and extraction, as well as the modules FI/CO and Treasury. As a DSAG representative of IBM Deutschland GmbH in the area of data archiving, he gave a lecture on the global system shutdown of legacy SAP systems after system consolidation at the annual DSAG Congress 2008 in Leipzig, Germany. In 2009, he worked for the auditing company Deloitte and played a significant role in building the ILM department (Information Lifecycle Management).

Index

- ► Dive deep into your system with step-by-step instructions and screenshots

- ► Walk through critical and specialized tasks to keep your system up and running

- ► Administer databases, users, security, and more

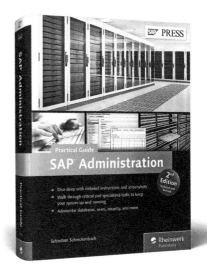

Sebastian Schreckenbach

SAP Administration—Practical Guide

Attention, administrators! Whether you're pursuing a background in SAP Basis or looking to brush up on your skills, this is the book for you! From database management to backup and disaster recovery, learn how to handle everything from the routine to the occasional hiccup. With helpful instructions and screenshots you'll master the tasks and challenges of SAP system administration in no time.

912 pages, 2nd edition, 2015, $79.95/€79.95
ISBN 978-1-4932-1024-4
www.sap-press.com/3639

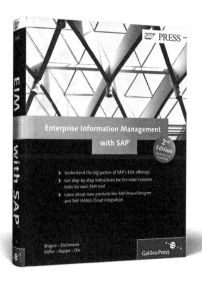

▶ Understand the big picture of SAP's EIM offerings

▶ Get step-by-step instructions for the most common tasks for each EIM tool

▶ Learn about new products like SAP PowerDesigner and SAP HANA Cloud Integration

Brague, Dichmann, Keller, Kuppe, On

Enterprise Information Management with SAP

Learn how to effectively manage your data with the tools in SAP's EIM offering. From SAP Data Services to the latest tools like SAP PowerDesigner, you'll learn what the different solutions are and how they work together. Then, get started using them for common tasks with the help of step-by-step instructions and guiding screenshots. This is the resource you need to make sure your enterprise is sitting on a solid foundation—of clean data!

605 pages, 2nd edition, 2014, $69.95/€69.95
ISBN 978-1-4932-1045-9
www.sap-press.com/3666

Interested in reading more?

Please visit our website for all new
book and e-book releases from SAP PRESS.

www.sap-press.com